PRINCIPLES OF EDITING

A Comprehensive Guide for Students and Journalists

PRINCIPLES OF EDITING

A Comprehensive Guide for Students and Journalists

DARYL L. FRAZELL
College of Journalism and Mass Communications
University of Nebraska–Lincoln

GEORGE TUCK
College of Journalism and Mass Communications
University of Nebraska–Lincoln

The McGraw-Hill Companies, Inc.

New York St. Louis San Francisco Auckland
Bogotá Caracas Lisbon London Madrid
Mexico City Milan Montreal New Delhi
San Juan Singapore Sydney Tokyo Toronto

McGraw-Hill 
A Division of The McGraw-Hill Companies

Principles of Editing:
A Comprehensive Guide for Students and Journalists

This book is printed on acid-free paper.

1 2 3 4 5 6 7 8 9 0 DOC DOC 9 0 9 8 7 6 5

ISBN 0-07-021926-5

This book was set in Century Old Style by The Clarinda Company.
The editors were Hilary Jackson, Fran Marino, and Tom Holton;
the designer was Karen K. Quigley;
the production supervisor was Richard A. Ausburn.
R. R. Donnelley & Sons Company was printer and binder.

Library of Congress Cataloging-in-Publication Data

Frazell, Daryl L.
Principles of editing : a comprehensive guide for students and journalists/Daryl L. Frazell, George Tuck.
p. cm.
Includes bibliographical references and index.
ISBN 0-07-021926-5
1. Editing—Handbooks, manuals, etc. I. Tuck, George.
II. Title.
PN162.F73 1996
070.4'1—dc20
95-25047

ABOUT THE AUTHORS

Daryl L. Frazell is an Associate Professor of Journalism at the University of Nebraska–Lincoln, where he teaches editing courses in the College of Journalism and Mass Communications. He earned bachelor's and master's degrees from Northwestern University's Medill School of Journalism and interned as a general assignment reporter at the City News Bureau of Chicago. His first newspaper job was on the copy desk of the *Minneapolis Star.* He later worked in various editing positions at the *Detroit Free Press, The New York Times* and the *St. Petersburg Times.* He is director of a Center for Editing Excellence under the Dow Jones Newspaper Fund Newspaper Editing Internship Program, which trains and places college students from around the nation in summer internships at major newspapers. He writes "The Grouch," a column of commentary on language and editing that is circulated to member newspapers by the Nebraska Press Association and a number of other state press associations.

George Tuck is a Fred and Gladys Seaton Professor of Journalism at the University of Nebraska–Lincoln, where he teaches photojournalism and graphics classes in the College of Journalism and Mass Communications. He received a B.A. in psychology from Hardin-Simmons University and joined the UNL faculty in 1970 after completing his M.A. at the University of Missouri School of Journalism. His professional work includes positions as a staff photographer and picture editor for daily newspapers and as news editor for a weekly and semiweekly. He has worked for *Newsday,* the *Houston Chronicle* and the Associated Press in New York. He received a distinguished teaching award from the university and the Robin F. Garland Award from the National Press Photographers Association for distinguished service as a photojournalism educator. He was named Nebraska Professor of the Year by the Council for Advancement and Support of Higher Education. He also served as president of the Academic Senate, the University of Nebraska's faculty governance body.

CONTENTS

PART III
DESIGN EDITING

PREFACE

EDITING AS A FIELD OF STUDY

This book is an introduction to editing as it is practiced today. Editors in the 1990s are total journalists. The idea that news writing is the start and finish of journalistic training is obsolete; today's publications conduct a constant quest for journalists capable not only of writing effectively but also of using type and illustrations to create attractive page designs. In addition, the advent of desktop publishing has made the demand for editing skills broader than ever before. This book treats editing as a field of study to be pursued *alongside* news writing.

The authors embarked on this project in the belief that no amount of change in the means of delivering news to consumers will render the editor's fundamental skills obsolete. Both authors see the future of newspapers as bright, but they are aware that others are less certain and some are downright pessimistic. Journalism educators are testing the wind and taking their programs in new directions. Out of this turmoil will come the journalism of the future, and whatever form it takes, the authors believe the bedrock will remain steady. Like their predecessors, editors of the future will need language skills, idealism and visual aptitudes.

Daryl L. Frazell entered higher education in 1990 with the goal of helping attract new talent into editing. In hiring and training copy editors for the *St. Petersburg Times,* he had found even some experienced journalists ill-prepared to revise the writing of others. Beginners, some of whom were fresh out of college, really had no concept of what to do when confronted with the task of improving manuscripts by making necessary changes. They would do too much or too little, make changes that hurt rather than helped and fail to notice problems that should have been glaringly apparent.

In teaching editing, first at the University of Kansas (1988–89) and then at the University of Nebraska-Lincoln, Frazell found students receptive to his view of the field as one full of excitement and promise. What the students wanted and needed, he thought, was not so much motivation as guidance on how to do the job well.

Frazell saw a need for a step-by-step teaching method in which the student would learn layers of skills, beginning with basic accuracy and progressing through grammar and style to creative editing, which includes coaching writers, and display editing, which includes graphic design. Believing that success in today's journalism depends more than ever on teamwork among the writer, editor and illustrator, Frazell enlisted the help of George Tuck, a master teacher of photography and typography, to help bring language arts and graphic arts together at the peak of learning. The result is *Principles of Editing.*

The teaching method at the heart of the book relies heavily on the participation and decision making of the students themselves, who are encouraged to view editing as a series of problems they can solve. They begin grappling with the monsters in style discussions.

The authors concede that the major style decisions have already been made by editors much wiser and more experienced than students in editing classes. However, the imposition of the conventional rulings as if they were engraved on stone tablets is far less effective as an educational tool than encouraging the students to reach their own conclusions and write their own rules.

The results can be startling. For example, a three-person style committee in one of the authors' classes decided that the proper way to refer to people of African descent was to coin a term, "Afrimerican." The committee was then required to explain the decision to a larger group of students, and the result was an eye-opening discussion of the responsibilities of editors in a multicultural society.

THE NEW LOOK OF COPY EDITING

The term "copy editing" is used in this book because it is still in use in newsrooms, but the authors believe it has become obsolete along with all narrow definitions of what editors do. Today's editors do *everything* in the newsroom, including most of the things once done by printers.

Editing is such a diverse responsibility that the authors have divided it into three areas:

- Line editing.
- Creative editing.
- Display editing.

Those who define editing narrowly may balk at using the term "creative." Copy editors are generally told not to get creative with the carefully crafted work of experienced reporters. The authors recognize this but assert that much of what editors do *is* creative and even artistic. Headline writing is creative. Decisions on what to publish are creative. Coaching writers is creative. Packaged presentation of news is creative. Typographical excellence is creative. Selection and display of illustrations is creative. And page design is creative. All these elements are aspects of a job that remains energetically alive in the video age and will thrive as long as excellence is valued in the use of words and pictures.

The book is designed as a step-by-step "how to do it" guide. It begins with accuracy, grammar and style and progresses to other factors, especially ethics, that influence an editor's decisions. Not only words, but also type, photographs and graphics are included in the study of the raw materials an editor uses to build the final product, the page. Examples, most of which have been taken from the nation's press, illustrate each step.

There is, of course, no "body of knowledge" in editing. Editors are generalists in an age of specialists, and they act as bridges between the experts in various fields and the generalist public. As Dave Barry has written, journalists specialize in knowing a little about a great many things.

The best a training course can do for an aspiring editor is provide a framework for lifelong continuing education. That framework consists of basic skills in language and graphic arts, a strong ethical foundation, a sense of journalistic mission and an acute critical eye. *Principles of Editing* seeks to build that framework piece by piece.

FEATURES OF THE BOOK

Principles of Editing incorporates many unique features that make the book a valuable resource for aspiring editors. Some of these features include:

- "How-to" guidelines for aspiring editors who seek to build a foundation for helpful and effective assessment and revision of news stories.
- Numerous examples of editing problems and recommended solutions.
- A teaching method that begins small and builds step by step toward the full scope of the editor's responsibilities.
- Frequent tips and advice on ways to avoid the pitfalls that await unwary editors.
- Topics designed for classroom discussion and development of ideas on ethics and style.
- Chapters that emphasize not only text but also the visual side of editing, especially photography and graphic arts.
- Checklists and "dos and don'ts" to help evaluate performance in varied tasks.
- Up-to-date discussions of desktop publishing and on-line distribution of news.

PLAN OF THE BOOK

Chapter 1, **The Big Ten Fundamental Guidelines,** is the starting point. The student is introduced one by one to the essential responsibilities of editors and is expected to comprehend each and practice it in exercises before moving on to the next. These responsibilities build on one another so that by the end of the chapter the student has been shown where to start in editing a manuscript and should have some idea where to stop.

Chapter 2, **Style: Making the Rules,** offers a new slant on a topic students generally regard as tedious. Style is presented as a dynamic set of decisions on a variety of controversial topics both linguistic and social. Students are invited to write their own style on matters as diverse as punctuation, abbreviations, race and gender issues. In the process, they learn about the prevailing style in a way that will help them remember it.

Chapter 3, **Smooth Sentences and Troublesome Words,** is a step-by-step approach to grammar, sentence structure and word choice. It begins with the parts of speech, the building blocks of good sentences, and stresses the importance of a working knowledge of the way they interrelate. This discussion is followed by an analysis of the characteristics of good sentences. The chapter concludes with a list of words that should have red flags attached because of the problems associated with their use. The emphasis is not on definitions or derivations, which can be obtained from the dictionary that is present on every editor's desk, but on what makes each word troublesome. Memory devices are offered in many cases.

Chapter 4, **A Hit List for Troubleshooters,** is about ethics and the perils of publishing. It presents libel and privacy invasion not just as legal dangers but also as moral issues. The chapter discusses fairness and its meaning to editors in their role as guardians of a publication's reputation and the publisher's pocket book. Included are declarations of ethics from professional organizations.

Chapter 5, **The Writer's Ally,** begins the study of creative editing, which goes beyond the critical and corrective to a new level where the editor becomes an advocate for constructive change. This chapter explores ways of improving a manuscript without trampling on the writer's style and promotes the view that the editor and the writer are partners working toward a common goal: good writing.

Chapter 6, **The Information Presenter,** is about the kinds of writing that are the specialty of editors: headlines, titles, briefs, breakouts and promotional items. The editor is presented as the writer's sales manager, seeking to entice readers into a text.

Chapter 7, **A Manual of Typography,** begins a section of the book that recognizes that today's editors have replaced printers on newspaper and magazine staffs and must have knowledge and appreciation of display type and its uses. This chapter is a condensed primer for editors on graphic design.

Chapter 8, **Photo Editing,** stresses not only the esthetics but also the ethics of photographic display. Today's editors must be masters not only of words and type but also of all forms of illustration, especially photographs. This chapter gives the fundamentals of photo selection and cropping and offers guidelines and principles of cutline writing.

Chapter 9, **Graphics,** takes the student inside the process of creating effective informational graphics in both black and white and color. The editor is depicted as a key participant in conceiving graphic ideas and guiding the preparation and production of successful graphics.

Chapter 10, **Page Design: Putting It All Together,** assesses the techniques and attributes of excellence in newspaper and magazine layout. The student is taken through the steps from planning to completion.

The teaching method of this book is designed to be useful in many kinds of programs, including night courses, distance learning and larger classes in which students work with home computers. Small colleges that have limited journalism programs will find that *Principles of Editing* will enable them to offer editing courses at a professional level.

The book can also be used by individuals interested in self-development in publishing.

ADVICE FOR TEACHERS

Instructors who work with this book are encouraged to use their own material as well, because prepared exercises are never as interesting or exciting as timely reporting on current issues. Possible sources for such material are:

1. Student work from news writing courses.
2. The college newspaper.
3. Any other available publication (required reading of a daily newspaper is recommended).
4. The Associated Press or other wire services where available.

The authors have attempted to make *Principles of Editing* helpful not only in the classroom but also in newsrooms where working editors want a ready reference close at hand or a source book for use in training programs.

The purpose of university courses in editing has changed in a fundamental way. In the past, editing was viewed as a skill that could be achieved only through long experience in writing. There were few "cub" editors, and they were busy learning the craft under the tutelage of the old-timers. Electronics has changed all that. Today's editors must be quick and agile, and they start young. There is strong demand for qualified editors who can go to work on "the desk" right out of school, and many managing editors worry about where the editors of the future will come from. *Principles of Editing* is designed to help meet that need.

ACKNOWLEDGMENTS

The authors wish to thank the Gilbert and Martha Hitchcock Center, which provided the grant that supported the first stages of the development of this book. We also express our appreciation to the reviewers who contributed ideas to the revisions of the manuscript: Nancy K. Bowman, University of Missouri—Columbia; Patricia Bradley, Temple University; George W. Cloud, North Carolina State University—Chapel Hill; Gary Morgan, Oxnard College; Marshal Rossow, Mankato State University; Howard L. Seeman, Humboldt State University; Carl Sessions Stepp, University of Maryland; Jane B. Singer, University of Missouri—Columbia; and Ted Stanton, University of Houston. Even editors need editors, and we are grateful to Fran Marino and Hilary Jackson of McGraw-Hill.

Daryl L. Frazell and George Tuck

PRINCIPLES OF EDITING

A Comprehensive Guide for Students and Journalists

INTRODUCTION

DON'T SHOOT THE EDITOR!

The scene was a seminar on good newspaper writing. The speaker was analyzing a prize-winning story and had just finished discussing the impact of a sentence that began with "God only knows."

"What can I do?" a participating writer asked. "My editor would never allow me to write a line like that."

"Well," the speaker responded, "you can always shoot the editor."

The remark was made in jest, of course, but the emotions were real. The questioner had run up against an unyielding editor, and the speaker, a well-known writing coach, was frustrated with yet another example of intellectual hardening of the arteries among those who occupy positions of authority in the publishing industry.

The editor in question probably had a rule against expressions of religious belief by reporters in objective news stories. This is not unusual. Many editors have rules they regard as unbendable, and they can be rigid, perhaps even tyrannical, in enforcing them.

But students of journalism are ill served by even joking advice to shoot the editor. A far more useful idea is to promote editing skills among all who may someday occupy an editor's chair. The best way to deal with editors is not to shoot them but to understand what they do.

The first step is to recognize the relationship of good editing to good writing. How sweet would piano music be without a sounding board? How could a pitcher work without a catcher? The editor is the writer's first point of contact with the reading public. Editors' reactions should be assumed to represent those of readers, and all editors, except those miscreants who are guilty of "fire-hydrant" editing (that is, like Rover, leaving their marks just to show they were there), raise questions that represent genuine problems with readability.

Editors and writers are partners, not adversaries. If their relationship too often falls short of this ideal, the fault may lie in the failure of each to perceive the needs of the other. Editors have an essential job to do: coordinating, controlling, enforcing standards. Their work is fundamental to serving readers successfully and earning their trust and respect. Good editors do not make unnecessary changes and never tinker just for the sake of tinkering. They make revisions because the readers' or the publisher's interests demand it.

The best editors leave no apparent tracks to mark their paths through writers' work, so smooth and appropriate are the revisions they make.

To those who would "shoot the editor," the authors say, "Hold your fire. You may be shooting yourself, if not in the heart, at least in the foot."

THE TWO SIDES OF JOURNALISM

Many colleges and universities offer courses in journalism, and journalism educators tend to define the subject in terms of three fields of study: communication theory, writing and reporting. Editing is often treated as an addendum to writing, not a field in itself. Editing is not recognized as an academic discipline. Instead it is seen as the dismal occupation of shortsighted gnomes who huddle in front of computer monitors and raise their heads only to argue esoteric points of grammar with others of their ilk.

This inaccurate image is belied by the fact that almost every working journalist either holds the title of editor or aspires to hold it. Every reporter works for an editor, and when reporters qualify for promotion, they become editors. So how can the negative image of editing be explained?

The answer lies in the failure to recognize that journalism consists of two cooperating sides, each equal to the other in power and significance. Neither side can survive and prosper without the other, and practitioners on one side cannot be fully qualified unless their skills and interests overlap the other (Figure 1).

On the reporting side are the information gatherers. By various means they reach out, search for and bring in facts. On the editing side are the information presenters. They decide how to use the available display space in any publication to offer facts to the public. All editors do this, whatever their place in the organizational hierarchy.

Reporters specialize in writing, but writing has no value without readers, and editors are the *first* readers of everything a writer produces. They represent all other readers in a special way: they can talk back to writers.

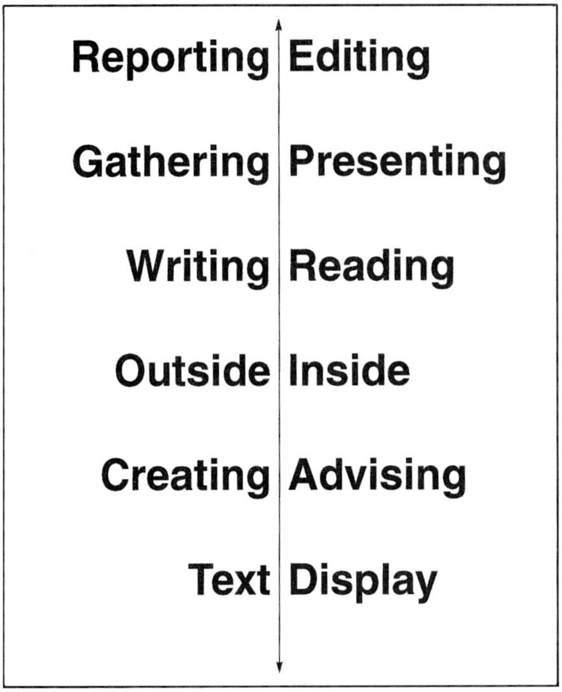

Reporting	Editing
Gathering	Presenting
Writing	Reading
Outside	Inside
Creating	Advising
Text	Display

Figure 1 The two sides of journalism.

Reporters spend much of their time outside the office, meeting the public. Editors work inside and meet the public through the printed page.

Reporters are primarily creators in the sense that every sentence they write originates in their own minds. Editors also play a creative role, but in relation to writers they are reactors: They offer feedback and sound advice and counsel.

Finally, reporters are concerned with text. Their responsibility ends when the words have been composed. Editors begin with text, which they use as raw material for building displays that reach out to readers.

Some may object to this analysis, saying no editor does all these things. Certainly, they might say, the least experienced, entry-level editors have no such all-encompassing responsibilities. It's true that all-purpose editors exist only at very small publications, but the fact remains: No reporter's efforts can reach readers without the services of an editor, even if the editor and the reporter are the same person wearing different hats.

THE TWO SIDES OF EDITING

Editing is indeed an endeavor with many facets. Recognition of it as a discipline worthy of study is long overdue. It embraces all activities in publishing short of operating the press, and in this book it is defined to include graphic design and photography. Students of editing should approach it step by step, understanding that the subject is so diverse that editing itself has two sides: creative and critical (Figure 2).

Creative editors are thinkers who strive ceaselessly for excellence in the coverage and presentation of news. Critical editors are suspicious souls who screen everything offered for publication to make sure it measures up to standards. In this book they are called "line editors."

Creative editors have a positive outlook. They believe in their reporters' ability to fulfill good assignments, and they tend to see the best aspects of a writer's work even though there may be problems in some details. Critical editors look for the problems and are fussy about the details.

Most people who edit creatively hold supervisory positions. Often they supervise both reporters and critical editors. Usually critical editors are not bosses, and their bosses expect them not to get too creative when they revise writers' work. Their job is corrective. They repair mistakes and prevent errors.

Creative editors see the big picture. Events happen in the context of other events, and creative editors work to present a coherent vision of the whole. Critical editors think small. They meticulously analyze stories word by word, seeking to forestall trouble and ensure readability.

If one were to draw a baseball analogy, the creative editor would be the pitcher, or perhaps the manager, and the critical editor would be not just the catcher, but the backstop, because anything that zips past the last barrier reaches the readers.

Creative editors plan and assign news coverage. Critical editors review the results.

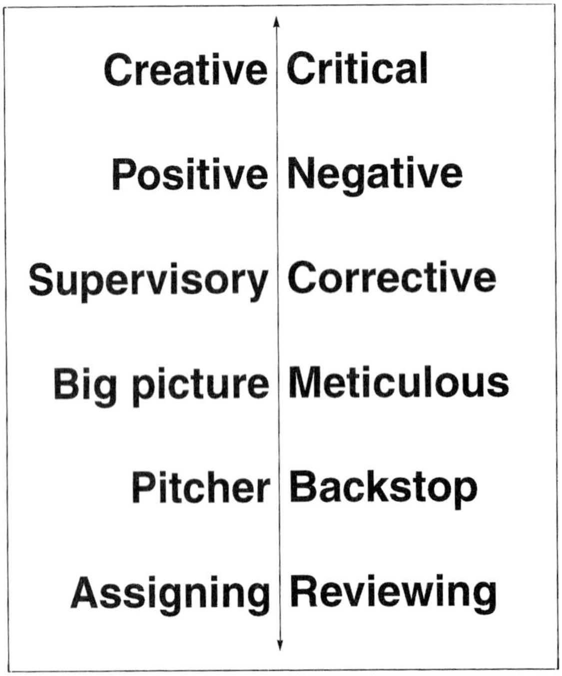

Creative	Critical
Positive	Negative
Supervisory	Corrective
Big picture	Meticulous
Pitcher	Backstop
Assigning	Reviewing

Figure 2 The two sides of editing.

In Part I of this book, the emphasis is on line editing, a vital, critical skill that all journalists should value and respect. In Parts II and III, creative editing holds sway.

HUMAN RELATIONS IN THE NEWSROOM

All journalists, wherever their duties may lie on organizational charts, have an additional responsibility beyond creating and criticizing: bridging the gaps that divide many newsrooms. Competition is natural and in some ways beneficial; but when reporters mistrust editors, and editors treat reporters with disrespect, the result diminishes everyone's performance.

All kinds of personalities find places on media staffs. Editors tend to be self-confident types who work well independently. They can conceive an idea, organize a task and carry it out without help. Reporters tend to prefer to work with others and spend much of their time outside the office meeting the public. Many other personality types find niches between these extremes, but all journalists share one trait: a love of good writing.

Their admiration of literary excellence and their desire to practice and promote it often motivate them to seek media careers in the first place. Unfortunately, excellence can be hard to find, and the definition of it is a matter of opinion. This is the source of newsroom conflicts.

Writers have a hard time seeing defects in their work; editors are relentless in finding and exposing them. Because editors are supervisors, their treatment of writers can have lasting effects, helpful or harmful. Good editors recognize this and strive to foster and encourage good technique while preserving the individual's independent flair. They act not as the writer's disciplinarian, but as a friendly coach. They make sure that any significant changes they make are explained to the writer, in advance if possible.

The result, where this is the practice, is greater newsroom harmony, which is important in a era of increasing public criticism of professional journalism.

THE MISSION OF JOURNALISM

Journalists are not very popular. On a scale of esteem they tend to rank behind less controversial professionals such as pharmacists. A mistrust of professionalism in news coverage is abroad in the land. A significant number of Americans believe that their views are excluded from the mainstream media and that the editors who control the major newspapers, newsmagazines and television news organizations do not share their values.

Michael Crichton, author of the dinosaur fantasy novel *Jurassic Park,* is among the harsh critics. He sees the journalistic "mediasaur" plunging toward extinction. "To my mind," he told the National Press Club in April 1993, "it is likely that what we now understand as the mass media will be gone within 10 years. Vanished, without a trace."

Crichton charged that news organizations were failing to serve the public:

> According to recent polls, large segments of the American population think the media is attentive to trivia and indifferent to what really matters. They also believe that the media does not report the country's problems, but instead is a part of them. Increasingly, people perceive no difference between the narcissistic, self-serving reporters asking questions, and the narcissistic, self-serving politicians who evade them.

As providers of information, their chief product, the media are superficial and unreliable, Crichton said.

> Poor product quality results, in part, from the American educational system, which graduates workers too poorly educated to generate high-quality information. In part, it is a problem of near-sighted management that encourages profits at the expense of quality. In part, it is a failure to respond to changing technology—particularly the computer-mediated technology known collectively as the Net. And in large part, it is a failure to recognize the changing needs of the audience.

Looking at their own industry, many editors are almost as harsh as Crichton. At a "Future of Journalism" symposium at San Francisco State University in 1993, Gene Roberts, managing editor of *The New York Times,* said newspapers were threatening to kill themselves.

> The big threat to journalism comes from within our profession, not from the outside. We threaten our existence with mindless rushes toward the latest journalistic trend and fad.
>
> We sabotage our newspapers by giving them a corporate look and feel, rather than letting them be as individualistic as the communities they serve. We strangle our future by not paying enough attention to our past, where there is ample evidence of how shallow, mindless formula can loosen our hold on readers.
>
> We starve our newsrooms with meager budgets that drain away the vitality we need to attract and hold readers. We undermine our ability to respond to the infinite unpredictability of news. We do it by shackling our newsrooms with rules and rote.

The challenge for the new generation of journalists moving into the profession in the 1990s will be to cope with these problems and forge a new identity for the media in both print and electronic form. The death knell for journalism has not yet sounded, and it is up to this new generation and those that will follow to make sure it never does.

The means of delivering information may change, but this does not mean the demand for good reporters and editors will diminish. On the contrary, it may increase.

Editor Roberts said, "Interactive, computerized news services have been available for quite some time, and we've learned that most subscribers don't want to search for the news. They want programed computer screens with reporters and editors at the other end, telling them what is important."

Indeed, writes John Haile, editor of the *Orlando* (Fla.) *Sentinel,* "most likely, the electronic revolution is a newspaper evolution."

George Gilder, a senior fellow at the Discovery Institute in Seattle, sees newspapers as the dominant information deliverers of the future.

> Computers will soon blow away the broadcast television industry, but they pose no such threat to newspapers. Indeed, the computer is a perfect complement to newspapers. It enables the existing news industry to deliver its product in real time. It hugely increases the quantity of information that can be made available, including archives, maps, charts and other supporting material. It opens the way to upgrading the news with full-screen photographs and videos. While hugely enhancing the richness and timeliness of the news, the computer empowers readers to use the "paper" in the same way they do today—to browse and select stories and advertisements at their own time and pace.

Despite critics like Crichton, the "mediasaur" will survive and evolve, lumbering onward into the mists of the future. Despite dissatisfaction among many consumers, the demand for news, written, edited and organized by professional journalists, will continue.

WHY PUBLISH?

News may be looked upon as a commodity, for sale to consumers like cornflakes and cars. People buy news because it, like any other product, fulfills a need or desire. Purchasers of news want one or more of three services that news provides:

- Information
- Education
- Entertainment

A sports fan, for example, will look to the sports pages for information about the latest game results, as well as entertaining articles about teams and players. The same reader might seek education about political issues from the news pages or the editorial page.

The elements that make news stories appealing to readers are called news values, and a keen knowledge of these factors and how they relate to the audience is an essential qualification for any editor. Experienced editors don't run through a checklist to evaluate an event; they know a "good story" when they see one. Yet the criteria they tacitly recognize can be summarized under these headings:

- **Significance.** The event is important in local, national or world affairs and perhaps will affect history. Well-informed people should know about it.
- **Impact.** It will affect the lives of readers, directly or indirectly, for good or ill.
- **Proximity.** It happened nearby.
- **Human interest.** It arouses some form of emotion because the reader reacts with pity, compassion, outrage or delight to the participants, human or animal, and their situation.

- **Oddity.** It stirs curiosity because it is unusual, strange or bizarre.
- **Mystery and suspense.** It is unsolved or unexplained, or it is exciting because of the action involved.
- **Celebrity.** It involves people who are famous or who lead glamorous, innovative or intriguing lives.

These same factors could be applied to any form of popular writing, including fiction, but journalists have a special mission that sets them apart. This mission was defined by the Associated Press Managing Editors Association in 1993 in a proposed Declaration of Ethics (see also Chapter 4). Although the declaration was modified before it was adopted, the mission statement remains a valid expression of the essential role of newspapers, which is to:

- Inform readers of events and facts that are important to them and to their participation in a democracy, by insuring the free flow of public information.
- Scrutinize government and other major institutions, in order to vigorously expose wrongdoing and misuse of power, whether public or private.
- Serve as a constructive critic of all segments of society.
- Provide a forum for the exchange of comment and criticism from throughout the community, particularly from those with views different from the newspaper's.
- Advocate the public interest, including needed reform and useful innovation, through the editorial page.
- Pursue the truth with unwavering vigor, in a manner consistent with these ethical standards.

Journalists who are true to these responsibilities are fulfilling the promise of a noble profession that is a pillar of free society and democratic government. Totalitarian regimes control the media above all else, and editors who are dedicated to the principles embodied in the declaration are the first to be silenced, imprisoned or killed.

To view news as merely a commodity is to see only part of the picture, yet to lose sight of the commercial side of journalism is to invite financial failure. Good editors take seriously both their social responsibilities and the need to please readers. The goals of journalism are not always understood by the public. Journalists can expect to be criticized, sometimes unjustly, for doing their jobs well. This fact is both a burden and an inspiration to those who pursue careers in editing.

BURNING ISSUES IN JOURNALISM

However satisfied editors may become with the job they are doing, they cannot afford to be complacent. Critics like Michael Crichton cannot be dismissed as cranks. Today's and tomorrow's editors face the burden of meeting these major challenges:

1. **Readership.** Older readers, who tend to be loyal to the print media, are dying out, and young people seem to prefer other forms of communication. How can the print news media increase their appeal to young people?
2. **Diversity.** Minority representation in newsrooms has improved but still falls short of reasonable goals. Moreover, many members of minority groups consider the print news media irrelevant to their lives. How can minority groups be convinced that news media are sensitive to their interests and trustworthy as sources of unbiased information?
3. **Credibility.** Many people believe the mainstream media don't respect their views and cut them out of coverage for political reasons. This partly explains the popularity of talk radio. News media critics say professional journalists don't tell the truth and instead slant everything according to an elitist bias. How can journalists stay above the political fray and maintain their position as the main force keeping watch on the government?
4. **What is news?** Sophisticated readers are questioning the value of the conventional staples of news coverage: crime and council meetings. Tom Brokaw, the NBC News anchor, described the problem this way in an article in the *Daily News* of Los Angeles in December 1994: "I think we're living through an age of real anxiety in American culture and economics, and I worry that it isn't getting much attention. If we lose sight of the fact that there is other news out there needing to be covered besides the O.J.'s and the Susan Smiths and the Heidi Fleisses, we do so at our peril."

   How can the media redefine news to strengthen and broaden their appeal?
5. **Delivery systems.** Paper costs are rising and may become a threat to the health of some publishing enterprises. How will the journalism of the future reach readers?
6. **Conformity.** Papers look more and more alike across the country, and their content relies too heavily on the judgments of wire services and syndicates. Everybody seems to want to look like *USA Today.* Can individualism ever be regained?
7. **Lack of depth.** Many readers agree with Crichton's view that newspapers are alarmingly shallow everywhere. Those who demand thorough, reliable coverage have no place to go. As Gene Roberts says, if newspapers die they will have killed themselves.
8. **Lack of motivation.** Some bright young people who would make good journalists are not attracted to the field, and some others who are attracted to it become disillusioned and turn away after short careers. Meanwhile, journalism educators are questioning their role as they seek new directions in theory and research. What can be done to stop the brain drain?
9. **Image.** The public tends to view journalists as pushy, microphone-up-your-nose types who are rude for no apparent reason. The image applies to a small minority, but everyone is tarred by it. How can journalists brush up their image?
10. **Dullness.** Despite the efforts of specialists to improve the quality of news writing, it remains for the most part drab and pedestrian. Is it time to move

away from the standard hard-news techniques and toward more interpretation of complex events for bewildered readers?

The answers to these questions will not be found in this textbook. We do not pretend to know the shape of the future as it will be designed by today's and tomorrow's journalists. We do firmly believe, however, that the fundamentals contained in this book will remain valid, perhaps with a little stretching and bending to accommodate the unforeseen.

LINE EDITING

PART ONE

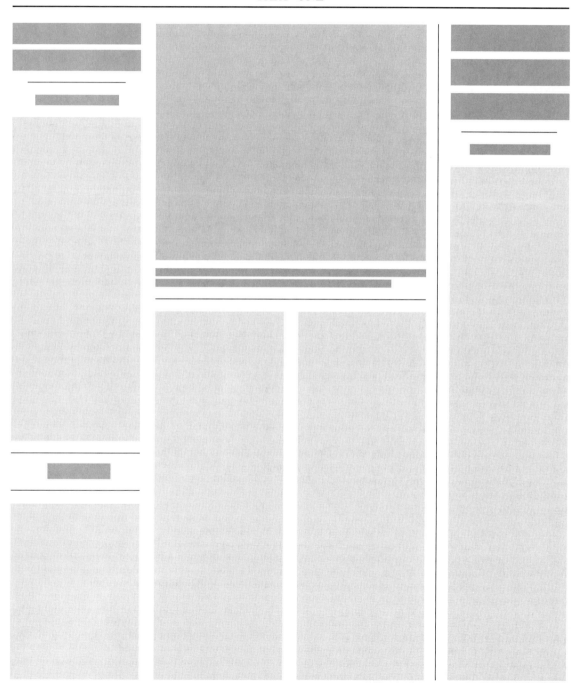

Chapter 1

THE BIG TEN FUNDAMENTAL GUIDELINES

WHAT IS EDITING?

Editor is a title with many meanings. It can be a term of leadership, denoting the person who sets policy and tone for a publication. It can refer to middle-level supervisors or to just about anybody who has responsibility for any part of the contents of a publication. Editors at all levels are decision makers. They decide what gets printed and what doesn't.

At the base of the editing pyramid are the *copy editors,* whose responsibilities are so diverse and challenging that they have been divided for purposes of this text into three parts: line editors, creative editors and display editors.

Line editors work their way line by line through news stories, checking for errors, guarding against infractions of taste and tone and enforcing the rules of language and style. *Creative editors* conceive, plan and assign stories and work with writers to revise and improve them. They also write lively headlines, photo captions and short news items, often called "briefs." *Display editors* are skilled in typography, photo editing, graphics and page design, as well as in the operation of sophisticated computerized page layout systems.

Copy editors work behind the scenes. They seldom get bylines or any other form of public recognition. Yet every publication owes its attractiveness, reputation for accuracy and unified tone to the creativity and energy of its copy-editing crew.

In the 1960s, newly hired copy editors at *The New York Times* were each given a copy of *Headlines and Deadlines,* a copy-editing handbook by Robert E. Garst and Theodore M. Bernstein. Unassailable at the time, the text would itself require some editing today, as this excerpt demonstrates:

> The copy editor is virtually the last man between his newspaper and the public. The copy may have been read several times before it reaches him, but its ultimate form, phraseology and spirit rest in his hands. Mistakes or poor writing that pass him are almost certain to reach the reader in print. . . . The function of the copy editor is critical, not creative. In no circumstances should he rewrite a story completely. If it cannot be saved except by being rewritten, that work should be done by a rewrite man or by the reporter who wrote the original story. The desk man must cope with the material that is given him and make the most of it by recasting, striking out superfluous words, substituting active or colorful words for dead ones, expressing a phrase in a word and by other similar means.

This passage demands editing because of its use of the dominant masculine to refer to both genders. Today, gender bias has been sharply reduced if not fully eliminated from the media.

Headlines and Deadlines is obsolete in other ways as well. The "rewrite man" has virtually disappeared because most of today's good reporters are also fine writers. It is no longer "almost certain" that errors missed by copy editors will reach the readers. The electronic revolution has erased all doubt by eliminating the backstops between the editors and the printing press.

Garst and Bernstein's definition is a classic expression of the duties of a copy editor, who is a critic empowered to make technical revisions in a writer's work. However, editing is no longer just a critical function. The same electronic revolution has given copy editors major creative responsibilities by merging content and display. Today's news article is only one part of a package that encompasses design, illustration and the typographical "sales talk" supplied by copy editors to draw readers into the text.

Editors are in control of their publications in ways that were impossible before the age of computers. In the old days, printers in large part determined the appearance of a publication. Today the editors do it all.

Creative, supervisory editing is the shaping of the content of a publication from conception to realization. Creative editors deal in ideas. They explore new ways of fulfilling the missions of their publications. They assign coverage and direct it and guide the presentation of it.

The focus of Part I is the kind of editing described by Garst and Bernstein. Called line editing in this book, it is still an essential skill that is perpetually in demand everywhere the presses roll.

"One prepares to be a line editor simply by mastering the world's knowledge, the specialized knowledge of one's audience and the craft of working with words," Arthur Plotnik wrote in *The Elements of Editing.*

Clearly by this standard no line editor is ever prepared for the job, but the good ones are continually striving to become so.

THE POWER OF REVISION

By definition, a line editor is a critic, not a creator. A critic's job is to form judgments about the merits of an artistic endeavor. In the arts, a critic's opinions are just that, opinions, which the artist is free to disregard; but the media place editors in a position not only to express but also to enforce their opinions by revising the work of writers. This may sound like allowing the theater critic to rewrite the play, and in a sense it is, but there is a big difference: Theater critics set their own standards, while line editors work in accordance with an informal code of revision.

In most places this code is not written down. Pieces of it may appear in a stylebook. There may also be a libel manual and statements of policy. But the most important parts of the code are intangible: the editor's experience and judgment.

Editors are supposed to know when revisions are necessary and when the rules should be bent. They are supposed to know how to make changes as smoothly and invisibly as possible and to explain their decisions reasonably and convincingly.

However, in today's newsrooms many editors lack the advantage of experience. They may be hired directly out of college and put to work beside others whose careers have also barely begun. Their primary skills and interests may lie in page design or newswriting, yet much of their time may be devoted to line editing. Their ability to make the right choices as line editors and avoid the wrong ones may go a long way toward determining their chances of advancement or even survival in the field. The result of too many mistakes may be frustration, despair and ultimately failure.

Some writers whose work they edit will welcome their contributions and tolerate their mistakes, but others will not. These writers may ask: What makes this editor's judgment superior to mine? Why must my carefully crafted story, which I believe works well, be changed to suit the whims of anybody who happens to sit in an editor's chair?

The answer is that whims have nothing to do with it. Good line editors are too busy fulfilling their responsibilities to have whims, let alone act on them. Often writers do not understand these responsibilities, and unfortunately, line editors are themselves sometimes in doubt about them. The major cause of disagreements between writers and line editors is that revisions appear to be arbitrary and are not adequately explained.

In a typical newsroom arrangement, writers turn their work over to their supervising editors, who approve it and send it on to the copy desk. At this point, in an all-too-common situation, the prose passes into a "twilight zone" where strange things happen. Commas are inserted or taken out. Words are changed. Sentences are rearranged. Sometimes whole paragraphs are rewritten, and even the entire structure of a story may be altered. Key passages may be cut, and cleverly devised endings may disappear. Often, no one explains why.

Line editors see a different picture, of course. They approach each article as a perilous minefield. Their job is to look for defects, and they frequently find them: defects in punctuation, grammar, usage, style. They may also find worse problems: errors, ambiguities, absurdities, omissions. Confronted with something they do not understand, they have only three options. They can:

- Seek clarification from the writer, who is often unavailable as the seconds tick away toward deadline.
- Compose their own clarification, often with inadequate resources, since they cannot go to the scene to obtain firsthand knowledge.
- Refrain from making any change, thus passing the confusion on to the reader.

Whatever choice they make, they know they will be held responsible for the result. It is their job to assume responsibility. Only those who can convincingly explain and defend their decisions will be successful. Everybody else is working in quicksand.

A managing editor once remarked that at his newspaper, copy editors were free to "change anything that's wrong." That sounds reasonable until one attempts to define "wrong." Does it mean only factual errors? What about passages that are simply unclear?

Box 1.1 contains "the Big Ten," a set of guidelines for everyone who toils around the quicksand bog. It is a list of fundamental problems that line editors are expected to solve. It does not cover all possibilities. There are many reasons that changes in a writer's work may be considered desirable. But these are the essentials for line editors. Anything that does not fit into these problem areas may be beyond their purview.

To raise a flag is to sound the alarm, call for help, seek advice and assistance from a supervising editor. If the line editor and the supervising editor are the same person, to raise a flag is to consult the author for clarification. In either case, the raising of the flag is a signal that the offending passage is not ready for publication until it receives further, careful consideration and perhaps undergoes revision.

THE ELECTRIC FENCE

The limit, or boundary, of line editors' freedom to make changes on their own authority is often called "the electric fence."

Every publication has an electric fence, although not all of them acknowledge or even recognize the fact. The barrier's exact coordinates are often unclear, even to supervising editors. Sometimes the only way to find the fence for sure is to be "zapped" by it.

The electric fence is the point where a line editor must get permission before making further revisions. Proposed changes beyond this point are deemed too sensitive to be left to a line editor's judgment alone.

The placement of the electric fence can vary, depending on the source of the text. Generally there is no electric fence for newspaper copy editors working with wire service stories. The standards are likely to vary for staff-written material. Line editors may have greater leeway if the writer is inexperienced. Editors may find the electric fence close to their noses for some trusted, experienced writers and relatively remote for others who are known to have problems.

The Big Ten

An editor is expected to make a change, or at least to raise a flag, if the text:

1. Contains an error of fact.
2. Offends the rules of grammar.
3. Violates style.
4. Uses the wrong word.
5. Is unfair or potentially actionable.
6. Is clumsy or unclear.
7. Is wordy or redundant.
8. Commits an absurdity.
9. Violates good taste.
10. Lacks sensitivity.

Box 1.1

The power to enforce all of the Big Ten is likely to be on the line editor's side of the fence, but even so, the editor should as a matter of courtesy discuss all substantive changes with the writer.

Going into such a discussion, the editor should be prepared to give substantial reasons for proposing revisions. "I don't like this" or "I wouldn't do it this way" don't qualify as substantial; in fact, they are not even valid. The purpose of line editing is not to transform the writer's work into something the editor might have written. Instead, the editor's goal is to help the writer's creative efforts succeed.

Recognizing and heeding that guideline is the only way for a line editor to survive on the strip of solid ground between the quicksand of uncertainty and the electric fence of vulnerability. Good line editors know where the footing is solid.

WORKING "THE DESK"

In the past, copy editors, who worked around the rim of a horseshoe-shaped desk, were chiefly line editors and headline writers. Today's copy editor is likely to have a "work station" rather than a seat on a rim, and his or her responsibilities may be much broader:

1. Creative editing involves judging the effectiveness of story composition, smoothing the flow of the writing, analyzing the structure of an article, reorganizing paragraphs, judging newsworthiness, placing a story in the context of other events that day or in the past and inserting background—perhaps even consulting sources by phone. At some publications, desk editors work closely with writers, helping to smooth and shape stories through many drafts.

2. Display editors use typography, photography and graphic arts to create exciting showcases for the writer's art. All these visual elements work together to draw readers, and they are likely to be most effective if they are shaped and organized under the control of a single creative mind. Thus, display editors must be masters of headline writing and typography. They must have an eye for photographs, graphics and other kinds of illustrations and an aptitude for design. They must be skilled writers of concise and punchy prose for briefs, teases, cutlines and readouts. They must also be expert computer operators because they are likely to have ultimate responsibility for composition (entering codes for typesetting) and perhaps for pagination (assembling type and pictures on a video display layout).

It may be unreasonable to expect every desk editor to possess all the qualities of a display editor and at the same time serve effectively as a line editor and creative editor. The newsrooms of the '90s are staffed by specialists, who work together best if their authority and responsibilities are clearly defined.

All editing skills must begin with the Big Ten. These guidelines should not be regarded as "rules." Good editors know when to be flexible. But the Big Ten is where excellence gets its start.

Abuses in every category are not hard to find in the American press. Most of the examples in this book are actual excerpts from daily newspapers, large and small. Some items have been altered to clarify or to delete names and unnecessary details, but in substance they are faithful to the originals.

THE BIG TEN

Guideline 1: Accuracy

An editor must find and correct all errors of fact.

A good editor trusts no one when it comes to facts. Checking and challenging are fundamental and could go on almost endlessly if not limited by time. Computers now offer access not only to the library files of major newspapers but also to a vast supply of information from various other sources. Many newspapers have computerized their own libraries as well.

Trusting no one means doubting oneself as well as others. The unaided memory is unreliable. An editor should never change any statement of fact because one "knows in one's heart" what is true. Check it out.

One longtime journalist learned that lesson on the second day of his first copy-editing job in 1960 when he changed all the "Ribicoffs" to "Rubicoffs" in a story about Sen. Abraham Ribicoff of Connecticut. He didn't check. He didn't need to. He knew how the man's name was spelled. The next day he was deeply embarrassed to learn that "Ribicoff" was correct, and even though no one else seemed to have noticed, the error was engraved on his memory. Always afterward, any unchecked fact was to him a Rubicoff.

There is no way any editor can be certain of the accuracy of every fact in every story. No one has the luxury of time to check it all. One can, however, ensure that two kinds of mistakes never see print:

1. Rubicoffs, which are errors introduced by the editor through sloppiness, ignorance, assumption or misunderstanding.

2. Obvious blunders, which are statements that contradict the record. Included are nonexistent addresses and historical outrages, such as the placement of the Holocaust in Occupied Germany after World War II.

Self-interest dictates development of a nose for such things. This nose should wrinkle a little at the slightest odor of inaccuracy. If, for example, a story on college courses in human sexuality quotes a student as saying she was required to have an orgasm in class, the editor should suspect a hoax or exaggeration because of the sheer improbability of the remark. The editor has no choice but to demand verification.

SOME WAYS TO PROMOTE ACCURACY

1. **Read the story more than once.** The classic pattern is three reads: once through to get the sense of the piece and look for major holes; once through again for a meticulous, word-by-word check for style and grammar errors; once through a third time, preferably after a lapse of time, to look for anything that may have been missed. The lapse is important because errors are like potholes—they tend to be invisible when one is overly familiar with the road.
2. **Read the story backward.** It may sound silly, but it can help isolate sentences from the flow of the writing and make errors more visible. Take the last sentence first, then the previous sentence, and carry on all the way to the lead. This thwarts the tendency for powerful narrative energy to carry a reader past the details.
3. **Look for inconsistencies.** Are all the names the same throughout? Do the titles and descriptions match up uniformly with the names?
4. **Make written checklists.** A mental list of things to come back to and look up is prone to error. Anyone who has tried to remember a phone number by repeating it rather than writing it down knows the problem. Another mental task is likely to intervene and wipe out the memory. Check the thing out immediately or write a note to yourself and post it where you will be sure to see it. Better yet, print out the story and circle the questionable item in red.
5. **Do the arithmetic.** Editors are likely to be strong on words and weak on numbers. Some are in journalism because they heard there would be no math. They are especially vulnerable to faulty arithmetic. When dealing with large sums of money, for example, it is important to be aware of the difference between a million and a billion. Percentages can be tricky. Make sure they add up to 100 or know why they do not (some elements may be counted more than once). Understand the difference between a percentage and a percentage point (Box 1.2).
6. **Keep the reference sources handy.** The most important ones are the dictionary, the stylebook and a current almanac. A reliable text on current history is also useful. William Manchester's *The Glory and the Dream,* for example, describes in narrative form all the major news events in the United States between 1932 and 1972.

Arithmetic Lesson

An anonymous reader offers a lesson on percentage and percentage points:

The *Philadelphia Daily News* ran a series of stories on "rape and the college athlete" some time ago and mentioned that it had run down 52 cases of sexual assaults involving athletes. All had been reported to the police. Of those, charges were dropped in 33, or 63 percent of the cases.

The story went on to point out that this rate was significantly higher than the nationwide statistic for dropped charges in sexual assault cases, which it said was 35 percent.

In *USA Today,* the series was boiled down to the usual seven paragraphs (with the mandatory three bullets), and one of the bulleted paragraphs said:

"In 33 of the 52 cases against athletes reported to police, charges were dropped. That's a 63 percent rate, almost 30 percent higher than the national statistic for sexual assault cases."

The summarizers erred. They confused percent with percentage points.

That is, perhaps, the most common mistake that newspaper reporters make today. A percentage point always refers to a portion of 100. One percentage point is one one-hundredth. Two percentage points are two one-hundredths, and so on.

A percentage point is just a unit of measurement, like a mile or a pound or a gallon or a furlong. But a percentage (or sometimes, just percent) refers to a portion of a whole, and sometimes that whole is 100, sometimes not.

An example:

Let's say there are 100 reporters at a

Guideline 2: Grammar

An editor must uphold the grammar rules, because good grammar is the hallmark of a well-edited publication.

There are many excellent manuals of grammar, and every editor should have a trusted one at hand for quick reference. None of these books is a chore to carry. All are short because the rules of grammar are not voluminous, no matter how difficult they may be to grasp.

Not all journalists regard grammar as their friend. Some abhor it as a sharp-edged tool used in butchering copy. Some regard commas as impediments to readability and write sentences that leave the reader gasping for breath. Others follow the ubiquitous and mythical "pause rule," which provides that a comma should be inserted at every natural pause in a sentence. Since no adequate definition of a natural pause has ever been devised, followers of this practice tend to use commas like grains of pepper, letting them fall where gravity takes them. Neither approach is as useful or pleasing as the standard comma rules, which allow no comma to exist without a reason.

Editors cannot live by amorphous precepts like the pause rule. They require something more solid, and thus they tend to demand strict compliance with standard grammar rules.

newspaper. Let's say that 8 understand the difference between percentage and percentage point. That's 8 of 100 (the base), so it is understood by 8 percent of the reporters.

Let's say (and this is hypothetical, of course) that as a result of this letter one more reporter understands. Now, 9 of 100 understand. So 9 percent understand. That's an increase from 8 percent to 9 percent, an increase of 1 percentage point. But it's also an increase of 12.5 percent.

To figure the percentage increase, take your base or whole (in this case 8) and the change (in this case 1) and figure out what proportion that increase (1) is of the original whole (8). So, divide 1 by 8, and you come up with .125.

As your arithmetic teacher taught you years ago, to convert a fraction to a percentage, move the decimal point two places to the right. Thus, .125 becomes 12.5 percent.

Got it?

So, in the assault cases, the increase in the rate of dropped charges was, as the *Daily News* reported, to 63 percent from 35 percent. That's an increase of almost 30 percentage points, but it's an increase of 80 percent.

Remember, the base was 35. The increase (the difference between 35 and 63) was 28. So you calculate what percentage 28 (the increase) is of 35 (the base), which means you divide the base of the fraction (35) into the gain (28) and you get, after moving your decimal point, 80 percent.

There is a difference between "almost 30 percent" and 80 percent, which is the actual increase.

—*USA Today*

Box 1.2

Yet grammar's chief value to journalists is often overlooked: Grammar helps ensure that the written word means the same thing to the reader as it does to the writer. The English language is in essence a code, which must be deciphered to be understood. One key to the code is vocabulary. Another is grammar.

Each day writers and editors wage war against a formidable enemy, ambiguity. Grammar is a powerful ally in this fight, which is more important today than ever before because of the competition the print media face. Television has two dimensions to work with, sight and sound. The print media have only one and must therefore master the art of making the printed page appeal to the eyes.

Photographs, graphics and illustrations are important contributors to reader appeal, but they cannot succeed without words. The writing must be smooth, clear and interesting; and the headlines must invite, indeed demand, readership.

Good editors should picture their readers as straphangers, weary commuters who cling to the overhead handles on buses or trains. These travelers carefully fold their newspapers or magazines into compact packages they can manipulate with one hand. While being jostled by their fellow passengers, shaken by the motion and vibration of the vehicle and assaulted by the deafening noise of their surroundings, they try to read and understand. They do not have time for confusing sentences and ambiguous paragraphs. They do not have patience with writing that forces them to stop and go back to be sure of the meaning.

Their purpose in reading is not to admire the writer's skill but to get information, and they are willing to undergo hardships to reach their goal. The job of editors is to make their quest as smooth and easy as possible, and grammar is a valuable tool to that end.

The straphanger test should be applied to all newswriting. The principle is the same for all readers. If a piece of writing is good enough to appeal to a straphanger, imagine the pleasure of someone in a quiet room in a comfortable chair with a strong light!

A GALLERY OF OFFENSES

Editors at times feel like prairie firefighters, stomping out a blaze in one patch of grass only to have it erupt somewhere else. The same grammatical problems keep popping up. The leading offenders are discussed here as well as in Chapter 3 for emphasis. They appear so often in newspapers, magazines and books that repetition of the points of grammar seems justified.

• **The dangler.** Dave Barry, the irreverent syndicated columnist, once recorded this exchange in an interview with "Mr. Language Person":

> Q. Which of the following sentences is correct?
>
> —Being a respected attorney, the dog lunged straight for Mr. Thwockett's personal region.
>
> —The dog, being a respected attorney, lunged straight for Mr. Thwockett's personal region.
>
> A. They both have their strong points.

"Being a respected attorney" is a dangler. The term is a shortened form of "dangling modifier," which refers to a phrase that is placed too far away from the word it modifies ("Mr. Thwockett") and too close to another word that it doesn't modify ("dog"). In some cases the word it modifies is not expressed at all, as in this example: "Being a kind master, my dog loves me."

Many authors have written about the dangers of such orphan phrases, which twist in the wind, having no firm noun to stand on, or attach themselves, in their loneliness, to the wrong noun (Box 1.3).

The dangler often owes its existence to the feeling that the true subject of the sentence—"I," "she," "you," or "one," for example—is understood and thus can be left unstated. In the spoken language, such sentences often seem to work, but in print they can be ludicrous (Box 1.4).

A single dangler can disrupt the tone of an entire story, especially if it comes in the lead sentence:

> Leaving town, the houses along the side of the road soon give way to wide-open fields, grazing cattle and spring-blooming trees.

(Can you picture the parade of homes leaving town?)

To repair a dangler, give it a platform to stand on and place it close by:

Classic Danglers

As a mother of five, with another on the way, my ironing board is always up. (*Since "ironing board" is the subject of the sentence, "as a mother of five" has no point of reference.*)
—William Strunk and E. B. White, *The Elements of Style.*

Swimming in the surf, her bikini fell off. (*"Bikini" is the subject, but the bikini wasn't swimming in the surf. She was.*)
—John B. Bremner, *Words on Words.*

Box 1.3

> Leaving town, one soon sees the houses along the side of the road give way to wide-open fields, grazing cattle and spring-blooming trees.

Another option:

> As one leaves town, the houses along the side of the road soon give way to wide-open fields, grazing cattle and spring-blooming trees.

The reasons for caring about danglers are not entirely aesthetic. Fairness and accuracy may also be involved:

> After pleading not guilty to the charges, County Judge Gary Graham dismissed the case.

- **Disagreement.** Two kinds of disagreement appear frequently in the media: that of noun and pronoun and that of subject and verb. Noun and pronoun disagreement is illustrated by the following paragraph from a printing company's advertising brochure:

> Every instructor has their own view on how their subject should be taught. They have their own thoughts on what is important and how ideas should be presented. And every teacher has their own favorite sources of information . . . usually a vast variety of materials that each illuminate one area of the overall picture.

A paragraph like this takes the editor beyond grammar and into politics. A usage note in the *American Heritage Dictionary* tells why:

> When referring back to a group consisting of both men and women, strict grammarians have insisted that the masculine singular "him" or "his" be used as a "neutral" form; one is thus required to say "Every one of the actors and actresses has learned his part." Since the last century, however, feminists and their allies have objected to this presumption. The writer who finds the singular "he" and "his" distasteful in these cases has the choice of flying in the face of traditional grammar and using "they" and "their" or of using the somewhat clumsier variants "his and her" (or "her and his"); attempts to introduce new pronouns like "s/he" appear unlikely

More Danglers from the Nation's Press

Original	Edited
Being naturally curious, the next move was to investigate.	Because I'm naturally curious, the next move was to investigate.
Fast and calm, all of this has shaped Rushe's philosophy of life.	All of this has shaped a philosophy of life for Rushe, who is fast and calm.
Instead of attracting 70,000 visitors a day, about 40,000 persons are passing through the fair's turnstiles.	Instead of the expected 70,000 visitors a day, about 40,000 persons are passing through the fair's turnstiles.
Written in longhand in a text of the speech Jesse Jackson's aides handed to reporters, the southern-born civil rights leader told the delegates about the people who had voted for him.	Jesse Jackson's comments about the people who voted for him were written in longhand in a text of the speech the southern-born civil rights leader's aides handed to reporters.
Looking toward the bay, the turrets on the left of the picture are part of the Detroit Hotel, still standing but encased in more modern red brick.	The turrets on the left of the picture, which looks toward the bay, are part of the Detroit Hotel, which still stands but has been encased in more modern red brick.
After being repeatedly raped, the man told her to wash the sheets.	After she was repeatedly raped, the man told her to wash the sheets.

Box 1.4

to win general acceptance. The entire matter is properly outside the scope of grammar. In the end, as Fowler put it, "everyone must decide for himself (or for himself and herself, or for themselves)."

That may be fine for grammarians and dictionary writers, but it's not so fine for editors, who must insist on consistency. There is general agreement that a well-edited publication speaks with a uniform tone in matters of grammar and style. An editor who is also a feminist (or a feminist's ally, whatever that may be) may be torn between rules and politics but will still opt for order over chaos.

Some editors will strictly enforce the preference for the "neutral" masculine pronoun, but most will seek a way to sidestep the issue. The *Associated Press Stylebook* offers a compromise:

> Do not presume maleness in constructing a sentence, but use the pronoun "his" when an indefinite antecedent may be male or female: *A reporter attempts to protect his sources.* (Not "his or her" sources, but note the use of the word "reporter" rather than "newsman.") Frequently, however, the best choice is a slight revision of the sentence: *Reporters attempt to protect their sources.*

Someday a new pronoun such as "s/he" may work its way into favor. But until such a word gains wide acceptance, editors are not likely to take the lead in allowing its use. The futility of media efforts to impose change was demonstrated by the *Chicago Tribune*'s unsuccessful attempt to simplify spelling (tho, thru). For now, "write around it" is still the best advice. The printer's brochure might be edited as follows:

> All instructors have their own views on how their subjects should be taught. They have their own thoughts on what is important and how ideas should be presented. And every teacher has favorite sources of information . . . usually a vast variety of materials that each illuminate one area of the overall picture.

Writers who wouldn't think of matching singular nouns and plural pronouns sometimes botch collectives. "Couple" is the leading culprit. It can be treated as either singular or plural, depending on the context, but there is an understandable aversion to coupling "couple" and "it." As a consequence, "couple" is sometimes mistreated as both singular and plural in the same sentence:

> Prosecutors have asked a judge to reconsider his decision to give a couple custody of their infant daughter because the couple is refusing to let state officials check on the child.

"Couple" is properly singular in this example because the couple is acting as a unit, so one way to edit the sentence would be this:

> Prosecutors have asked a judge to reconsider his decision to give a couple custody of its infant daughter because the couple is refusing to let state officials check on the child.

However, to avoid "its," many editors would do something like this:

> Prosecutors have asked a judge to reconsider his decision to give custody of an infant girl to her parents because the couple is refusing to let state officials check on the child.

Subject-verb disagreement often results from confusion over what the subject is:

> Nebraska is one of the many states that is experiencing a shortage of part-time workers.

"Nebraska" is the subject of the sentence, but the subject of the dependent clause is "that," which takes its number from its antecedent, "states." "That" is thus plural and takes a plural verb, "are." Sometimes a little logic helps: It is logical that "that" should refer to more states than just Nebraska because many states, not just one, are short of part-time workers.

In the following example, all of the criminals, not just one, have gone through the program:

Original

Haleem, who was convicted of second-degree murder in 1976 when he was 25, is one of about 3,000 to 4,000 convicted criminals who has gone through the state's Community Corrections program.

Edited

Haleem, who was convicted of second-degree murder in 1976 when he was 25, is one of about 3,000 to 4,000 convicted criminals who have gone through the state's Community Corrections program.

Box 1.5 shows further examples of agreement problems.

• **The errant apostrophe.** Actually, the apostrophe is not at fault. It is simply a bystander amid the confusion over plurals and possessives.

The first point to remember is that the apostrophe never gets involved in the formation of plural words. A singular word like "Jones" that already ends in "s" forms the plural by adding "es": "Joneses."

The second point is that when possessives of common nouns are formed, the apostrophe is usually accompanied by an "s": He borrowed his boss's car. (The exception, says the *Associated Press Stylebook,* crops up when "s" sounds collide: He borrowed his boss' skis.) Only when the plural has been formed by adding an "s" does the apostrophe stand alone.

Proper nouns that end in "s," such as "Aristophanes," take only the apostrophe (Box 1.6).

• **Objects: thrower or receiver?** Pronouns are like quarterbacks and split ends: The former throw the ball to receivers, and the latter receive it from throwers. Unlike football players, however, pronouns change their spellings when they change positions. The most frequent fumbles involve "who," the thrower, and "whom," the receiver (Box 1.7).

Original

Among the first decisions he will have to make, the governor-elect said, is who to select as chief of staff.

Edited

Among the first decisions he will have to make, the governor-elect said, is whom to select as chief of staff. ("Whom" is the receiver of "to select.")

"Who" isn't the only culprit. In the following example, "he" is the receiver of "for" and therefore should be "him":

A frustrated Senate president complained Wednesday that newspaper reports may have ruined the possibility for he and the House speaker to reach an agreement with the governor and sell it to other legislators.

• **The vague antecedent.**

The defense secretary stood by the president's side as he announced: "I have directed (him) to increase the size of U.S. forces committed to Desert Shield to ensure that the coalition has adequate offensive military option should that be necessary."

Agree or Disagree?

Choose the correct word.

1. Neither the student nor the teachers is/are going to the conference.
2. Neither the teachers nor the student is/are going to the conference.
3. Neither of the students is/are going to the conference.
4. None of the students who have/has attended the workshop is/are graduating.
5. Seven years is/are a long time for anyone to graduate from college.
6. The number of students who are graduating is/are less than last year.
7. A number of students who is/are graduating has/have found jobs.
8. The media is/are important in our society.
9. Some of the group is/are going to the performance.
10. The couple was/were living in separate apartments and sharing custody of its/their child.

1. Neither the student nor the teachers are going to the conference.
2. Neither the teachers nor the student is going to the conference.
3. Neither of the students is going to the conference.
4. None of the students who have attended the workshop is graduating.
5. Seven years is a long time for anyone to graduate from college.
6. The number of students who are graduating is less than last year.
7. A number of students who are graduating have found jobs.
8. The media are important in our society.
9. Some of the group are going to the performance.
10. The couple were living in separate apartments and sharing custody of their child.

Box 1.5

Who is "he"? Who is directing whom here? The parenthetical "him" is no help at all. Pronouns are useful devices to avoid repeating proper names or titles, but when confusion is possible over who "he" is or what "it" refers to, the reader is ill served. The vague antecedent is one of the most common violations of the straphanger test.

The remedy may be to repeat names or titles:

> The defense secretary stood by the president's side as the president announced, "I have directed (the defense secretary) to increase the size of U.S. forces committed to Desert Shield to ensure that the coalition has adequate offensive military option should that be necessary."

Even though readers can be expected to know that the president gives orders to the secretary of defense and not the other way around, such knowledge should not be a prerequisite to understanding the sentence. Editors should be acutely conscious of the difficulty of mangled sentences like this one:

> ORLANDO (AP)—The first mate of a shrimp boat told a federal court jury Monday that two crew members beat the captain to death and then tried to kill him before he jumped overboard.

Errant Apostrophes

Original	Edited
It has been almost two years since the board voted unanimously to censor Chaucer's "The Miller's Tale" and Aristophane's play, "Lysistrata."	It has been almost two years since the board voted unanimously to censor Chaucer's "The Miller's Tale" and Aristophanes' play "Lysistrata."
Advising, which begins today and runs through Nov. 4, has long been the Achille's heel of the College of Arts and Sciences.	Advising, which begins today and runs through Nov. 4, has long been the Achilles' heel of the College of Arts and Sciences.

Box 1.6

Huh?

This gallery of offenses is only an introduction to the discipline of grammar. More on the topic will be found in Chapter 3, "Smooth Sentences and Troublesome Words."

Guideline 3: Style

An editor strives to preserve the writer's style while enforcing the conventions of the publication's style.

WHAT STYLE ISN'T

Like "editor," "style" is a word with many meanings. All writers strive to develop a style that sets their work apart from others'. Good editors have no wish to trample on these efforts. In fact, they try to encourage the development of each writer's independent personality—the mannerisms, the turns of phrase, the structural idiosyncrasies, the word selections that stamp one's work as unique.

Rhythm and flow are stylistic pathways that writers sweat to create, and editors must step carefully as they enforce another kind of style: a set of conventions governing procedures such as abbreviating proper nouns and capitalizing titles. This kind of style may seem trivial, but it is essential to the tone of a well-edited publication. It should not be viewed by anyone, especially editors, as a set of commandments designed to promote a particular pattern of writing.

The *Associated Press Stylebook* has become the standard for print journalists, but it is not a mold into which all journalistic writing must fit. Such a view of style reminds one of the old comedy routine in which an actor says to a fellow clown, "Walk this way," and then ambles away with a peculiar gait, which the second performer imitates in an exaggerated manner. Writers can look to the stylebook for guidance on fine points, but their gaits are up to them.

Who versus Whom

Original	Edited
The next year his brother, whom she thought would have no problems in school, also was held back.	The next year his brother, who she thought would have no problems in school, also was held back.
Johnston said he was out of breath and couldn't catch Perkins, whom he thought had a weapon.	Johnston said he was out of breath and couldn't catch Perkins, who he thought had a weapon.
Sunday evening, police had not found the dogs' owner, whom Smith said is Dave Doe, 2219 Mary St.	Sunday evening, police had not found the dogs' owner, who Smith said was Dave Doe, 2219 Mary St.

Box 1.7

There are many individualists active in journalism today. Three of the most easily recognizable are Jimmy Breslin, Mike Royko and George Will. Few would confuse their styles (Box 1.8).

Breslin is breezy, terse, emotional. He doesn't much care if his sentences are complete or his modifiers precisely placed. Royko writes conversational, street-corner prose. Will is precise, cool, intellectual, crafting each sentence like a sculpture. Some might quibble with their grammar or punctuation, but no experienced editor would trifle with their writing styles. A stylist is entitled to the integrity of proprietary prose. A news clerk at *The New York Times* once shocked a group of editors by proposing to rewrite a lead by another accomplished stylist, Russell Baker. The clerk was informed that the idea was unthinkable.

The Associated Press is in itself a stylist. It practices generic journalism, designed to be acceptable to all tastes. Amid the smorgasbord of styles, if Will is fine wine, Royko is Coca-Cola Classic and Breslin is dark beer, AP is skim milk.

WHAT STYLE IS

Copy editors are not concerned with converting any writer's work to conform to any model. They enforce style because they want their publication to speak with a single voice on matters of form. Style rules simply represent decisions on how to proceed in the many cases where the flexible English language allows more than one choice.

For example, abbreviations: The U.S. Postal Service recognizes MI as the abbreviation for Michigan, but MI could just as easily stand for Minnesota or Mississippi. The convention among newspapers is to use the unmistakable "Mich."

Three Stylists

Jimmy Breslin: On the car radio, Ronald Reagan said so earnestly that he had pressed Gorbachev about religious freedom in Russia, which Reagan said was so vital to his life. Let God in. Reagan hasn't gone to church in years, so his religion, like the rest of his values, is fraudulent.

Mike Royko: When the news becomes too grim and depressing, as it is now, and public voices are quivering with gloom and doom, I look for a haven of harmless nuttiness. I do this by asking someone who isn't easily embarrassed to go to a supermarket and get me the latest copy of the tabloid *Weekly World News,* one of my favorite newspapers.

George Will: The Japanese are an old people but a novice nation. They have an ancient culture but are new to, and not at ease with, the essentials of modernity—individualism, pluralism, heterogeneity. Much of the messiness of American life is not mere inefficiency, it is yeastiness. It is creative fermentation, part of the fecundity of freedom. For 216 years that has made America what it remains—the rising sun.

Box 1.8

Until the 1970s there was little national uniformity in style. A reporter or editor who moved from one publication to another might have to learn a whole new set of style rules. Wire service stories were typed out in all capital letters by clattering Teletype machines, requiring extensive marking up by copy editors just to differentiate between capitals and lowercase letters. When computers arrived in newspaper offices, allowing the wire services to provide stories ready for publication with minimal editing, it became economically useful to standardize style. The Associated Press published a comprehensive manual of style in 1977, and it has gone through many printings since. Reporters and editors who change jobs today will find AP style in general use, although most publications have their own exceptions.

No book on editing can be complete without a discussion of AP style, because most editors, including students in the classroom and journalists on the job, use the *AP Stylebook,* or parts of it, or something else like it. As the chief enforcers of style, copy editors must be familiar with the book and know when, if ever, to deviate from it.

Some editors are critical of the *AP Stylebook.* They say it is larger than necessary, tries to do too many things and is difficult for the uninitiated to use because of its dictionary-style format, which places general entries under specific alphabetized headings that must be guessed at. (For example, to find out if "police officer" is capitalized or abbreviated before a name, one must look under "police titles," which refers one to "military titles" or "titles," both long entries that do not specifically answer the question.)

The best defense of the dictionary format is that nothing better has been devised. Stylebooks of the past, such as the 1950 edition of the *Style Book of The New York Times,* were organized by categories. The *Times* book had sections on abbreviations and figures, capitalization, compound words, punctuation, prefixes and suffixes, spelling and typography.

The dictionary format was adopted by the *Times* as a reform, to make things easier to find. The alphabetized *New York Times Style Book for Writers and Editors* appeared in 1962 and was supplanted in 1976 by the fat *New York Times Manual of Style and Usage,* which set the pattern for the *AP Stylebook.*

The dictionary format is remarkably congenial to users who want to check something they know is there. It is far less pleasing for those who have no idea what they may find.

The major reason for this is that so many disparate items have been lumped together. The *Stylebook* has come to resemble a hungry diner's plate at a buffet restaurant: Mashed potatoes, broccoli, Roquefort-dressed lettuce salad, Jell-O and brownies have been layered into a pile next to a mound of liver, fried fish, baked chicken and spaghetti with meatballs.

The items in the AP book fit into at least 23 categories: abbreviations, capitalization, business names, definitions, geographic terms, grammar, information, legal terms, measurements, military terms, names, numbers, organizations, policy statements, prefixes and suffixes, punctuation, religious terms, spelling, sports terms, titles, trademarks, usage and words often confused.

A simplified stylebook might, like the stylebooks of old, consist of only five of these: abbreviations, capitalization, numbers, punctuation and titles. That would make a manageable meal, but where would all the side dishes go?

Gradually the AP has moved toward dividing up the menu. In recent editions of the *Stylebook,* special sections have been set aside for "sports terms," "punctuation" and "business guidelines and style."

The AP book is wide-ranging for at least three reasons:

1. It is a ready reference, a shortcut that saves time. It lists items that are often used by journalists and thus saves them trips to the dictionary, encyclopedia, almanac or other sources.
2. It serves editors who worry about certain abuses that just won't go away, such as misuse of "lie" and "lay" and confusion over "who" and "whom."
3. It is the major vehicle for pronouncements of policy on a diversity of issues, including feminism, politics, profanity, race and sexual preferences.

Endorsement of the policy decisions is far from universal. They represent the mainstream of cautious conservatism in newspaper publishing, and local newsroom exceptions are common. The *St. Petersburg Times,* for example, has produced its own stylebook by combining selected AP items, some surgically altered, with local entries.

At the *Times,* as at many other newspapers, style rules that differ from the AP standard are written by a standing style committee, which consists of members from several departments and meets periodically to argue style issues and consider questions and requests from members of the staff.

For students of editing, participating in style debates is a good way to understand that style rules do not represent the last word but result from compromise on a variety of potential choices. An introduction to the writing of style rules appears in Chapter 2, "Style: Making the Rules," along with a simplified compendium of newspaper style.

Guideline 4: The right word

The editor helps make sure that the writer's words mean what the writer intends them to mean.

The importance of precision in the use of words was perhaps best expressed by Mark Twain, who wrote, "The difference between the right word and the almost right word is the difference between lightning and the lightning bug." A good editor must be attuned to nuances in the language.

Jack Cappon, general news editor of the Associated Press, wrote in 1988:

> People who have a high stake in the language, who want to see words used precisely, haven't had much to cheer about in recent years. They have watched helplessly while hordes of writers who can't be bothered about nuances kept trashing useful distinctions among words, shrinking the vocabulary. And they have seen damp, all-purpose words spread monotonously to every sort of context where they have no real business.

That is an effective description of the battle editors continually fight, defending the language against sloppy thinking that can dilute its beauty and power.

Often the wrong word appears because it is very close in sound and spelling to the right word:

- Although political analysts predicted strong support for the governor in western counties, her opponent faired (fared) better than expected, especially in the traditionally Republican 3rd District.
- Officials from both parties agreed that the election results could be contributed (attributed) to the way the two campaigns were run.
- Evangelist Oral Roberts, who said God told him he would die if he did not raise $8-million by the end of March, exalted (exulted) Wednesday: "It's April and I'm alive."
- The surgeon general's strategy for handling the AIDS education campaign put to rest any lingering doubts that he would heed any council (counsel) but his own.
- The sisters reluctantly agreed, fearing any extravagance would violate the tenants (tenets) of the vicar's teachings.
- It is with supreme optimism that Beach Park residents are banning (banding) together once more to accomplish great things for their neighborhood.
- His desk is rather barren (bare)—no pictures of the family, no nameplate. The walls are naked. The office has the look of eminent (imminent) departure.

Sometimes the definition of a word is confused with that of another:

- The jury is expected to resume deliberations this morning on whether the U.S. government should forfeit (seize) Norman's Cay because it was used as part of criminal activity.
- A 3-year-old mountain lion was stretched out on the cement (concrete), eyeballing everyone who came within its parameter (perimeter or, more likely, vicinity).
- I'm beginning to detect a subtle shift southward in the way things hang on my body. It is not a pretty thing. Suddenly I am no fan of metaphysics (physics or gravity).

In direct quotations, the problem may be the reporter's poor spelling.

- "Quite frankly, I think we're entitled to a very substantial increase in our budget," the head of the teachers' union said. "I think just to bring us up to parody (parity), we need an injection of about $2 million."
- "In talking with physicians that call in, hospital administrators that call in, what they seem to have in mind is something like marshal (martial) law," the special council (counsel) said. "We don't have that power."

Editors find similar beastly errors every day—and keep them out of print.

USING THE RIGHT WORD

1. When in doubt, even slight doubt, look it up.
2. Master the lists of words often abused and words often confused in Chapter 3.

Guideline 5: Fairness

The editor has a responsibility to ensure fairness to all sides and to avoid the unintentional publication of any statement that may be actionable in court.

All editors should have some training in media law. They should know about the textbook libel cases, such as *New York Times v. Sullivan,* and be able to apply the principles of libel law responsibly enough to prevent obvious transgressions. But editors need not attempt to be lawyers, and a good lawyer may not always make a good editor.

A lawyer's training fosters caution and a tendency to withhold from publication any statement that is potentially actionable, which means it invites a lawsuit. An editor's tendency is to disclose everything that is verifiable and newsworthy, even though it might be dangerous.

Editors do not go looking for lawsuits. They keep a libel manual handy at their desks, and they call lawyers for advice on questionable material. But their main protection is an ethical principle, which guides or at least influences every decision they make. It can be simply stated: "Play fair with everybody named in the news."

This means taking pains to cover all significant sides of every case. All journalists come equipped with a pronounced sense of right and wrong, and many see their mission as a crusade against evildoers. When the air is foul, they tend to hold their noses and go after the source of the odor.

Unfortunately, the stench is not always obvious or even detectable to everyone, especially where politics is involved. Usually a segment of the public is quicker to scent misbehavior by the media than by the alleged wrongdoer.

Ironically, journalists, who see themselves as defenders of the weak, are instead often regarded by the public as exploiters, hungry to sell newspapers by trampling on the defenseless. In part this dark image has been fostered by traditional methods of covering crime news.

Reporters are assigned to cover police, not crime, and their stories tend to reflect the police version of events. Officers tend to be portrayed as heroic; seldom does the offender's viewpoint see print. Typical stories invite readers to witness a night in the life of a beat cop or a raid on the home of a suspected drug dealer. Typical photographs show officers with their carefully arranged displays of seized narcotics or firearms.

The source of a police story is frequently the written report of an arresting officer. The writer takes the drab official prose and turns it into a tale that can be exciting, suspenseful or amusing, like this:

> She outmaneuvered three semitrucks trying to box her in on the highway.
>
> She lay down on her seat and kept driving when troopers aimed a spotlight into her car.
>
> And she drove off the Turnpike on an entrance ramp and came back on using the exit ramp.
>
> A 27-year-old licensed practical nurse with a history of "behavioral problems" led police on a three-hour, 235-mile chase up and down the Turnpike late Tuesday night, the highway patrol said.

The driver's misbehavior is assumed. She is painted as an irresponsible and erratic malefactor who deserves to be banned from the road or possibly locked away forever in a padded cell. The image may be accurate. The odds are that it is, but the reader can't be sure because the report is one-sided.

A startling reversal of this pattern occurred in 1991 when a bystander videotaped a brutal Los Angeles police beating of motorist Rodney King. The resulting nationwide explosion of public outrage demonstrated the potential power of a balanced approach to crime coverage, which means showing both sides.

Ensuring balanced coverage is both a duty and a burden for editors, who may find themselves standing in the path of somebody's vivid writing as they insist on fairness to the accused. Attribution and qualifiers can impede the flow of a good story, but fairness may demand them. Box 1.9 shows original and edited versions of the openings of stories, to illustrate the principle of fairness.

Serving as watchdogs of fairness may not endear editors to their enthusiastic colleagues seeking to attract readers with lively storytelling, but it will help

Fair Is Fair

Original	Edited
A man is facing up to 15 years in prison because he slugged an 82-year-old driver who he says tailgated him and almost forced him off the road.	A man is facing up to 15 years in prison because he is accused of slugging an 82-year-old driver who he says tailgated him and almost forced him off the road.
A captive audience resulted early Wednesday after a police detective reprised his role as a hired killer. When the curtain came down, the captive was Vera Manley, 37, of 1111 S. Ninth St. She was arrested for hiring the undercover cop to kill her estranged husband, police officials said.	A police detective played the role of a hired killer, and when the curtain came down, Vera Manley, 37, of 1111 S. Ninth St., was arrested on a charge of hiring the undercover cop to kill her estranged husband, police officials said.
A grand jury decided Thursday that four state caseworkers who had contact with a child-abuse victim before the child died made more than mistakes. They committed crimes.	A grand jury decided Thursday to bring criminal charges against four state caseworkers who had contact with a child-abuse victim before the child died. (Grand juries never decide guilt. They merely bring charges after conducting one-sided, prosecutorial hearings.)
After she was pulled over for careless driving Monday afternoon, a woman listened to the officer for a few minutes and then apparently decided she had had an earful. She put her 1972 Oldsmobile in reverse and hit the gas pedal. But it was a getaway gone awry.	After she was pulled over Monday afternoon, a woman listened to an officer accuse her of careless driving and then apparently decided she had had an earful. She put her 1972 Oldsmobile into reverse and hit the gas pedal, the officer said, but it was a getaway gone awry.

Box 1.9

improve the public image of the media and earn the gratitude of publishers worried about lawsuits.

In *The Elements of Editing,* Arthur Plotnik describes the troubleshooting skills of line editors as "the million-dollar talent" because so much is at stake for publishers. The responsibility can be awesome, but it is also manageable for every editor who tests each story in terms of one question: "Is this person being treated as fairly as I would demand to be treated if I were in his or her position?"

SOME WAYS TO PROMOTE FAIRNESS

1. **Make sure the story reflects bona fide efforts to tell all sides.** Every accusation should be balanced with a response or an opportunity to respond. This means efforts to reach and inform the accused must be made, and if all measures fail, the extent of the efforts should be reported. Instead of

simply repeating the usual "could not be reached for comment," give details. How many calls were made? To how many numbers? At what times of the day?

2. **Honor the presumption of innocence.** Guilt is decided by the courts, not the police or the media. The police account of a crime is always colored by the police point of view. The "perpetrator" is always guilty in the eyes of law enforcement, and the accent is on obtaining enough evidence to convict. In the media, the accent should be on providing a balanced report.
3. **In civil suits, temper the tendency to overstate.** Damages sought are often much larger than damages awarded, and the figure set by the jury may be reduced or overturned on appeal. Treat damage claims as what they are, claims, not criminal charges, and make it clear that there are two sides in every case.

Guideline 6: Clarity

Editors must never publish anything they do not understand. They must strive to clarify the clumsy and the obscure.

"I can't understand this" is a hard admission for an editor to make. The tendency is to assume that the fault is one's own. When confronted with a passage that appears to be grammatically correct but empty of meaning, one may be besieged by thoughts like these:

> "I've had a hard day, my brain is tired, and I was never all that bright anyway."
>
> "Other people will find this perfectly understandable. I'm just too stupid to grasp it."
>
> "Certainly, anybody who is interested in this subject will know what the writer means, so it makes no difference if I don't."

It is no fault to have such thoughts, but it is unacceptable to give in to them. Editors are representatives of readers. If the editor doesn't understand, the public won't either. The difference is that the public won't try very hard in most cases but instead will move on to something else. If readers were ever tolerant of dense, impenetrable writing, they certainly are not today. The competition from other media for their time is too intense.

Clarity is not the same as simplicity. Very little that goes on in the world is simple, and readers can't expect to be spoon-fed, but they can expect the media to be easily accessible to them in ways complex technical texts are not. They can expect what they read in the media to be understandable without specialized knowledge. They can expect journalists to be able to explain science to non-scientists, international relations to non-diplomats, politics to ordinary voters.

The most effective means of fulfilling these expectations is to write as recommended by the time-honored handbook of good writing, *The Elements of Style,* by William Strunk and E. B. White.

"Use definite, concrete, specific language," the authors counsel. Use terms that describe reality as readers encounter it every day. Avoid the excessive use of abstractions, redundancies, bombast, trite expressions, slang and clichés. Prefer the specific to the general, the frank to the vague. Above all, use the language gracefully.

Today's newspapers are filled with non-communication, produced by journalists who take readers for granted. This fact is not new, but it is increasingly worrisome to editors who are watching their readership steadily decline. Most newspaper stories are just plain dull, because too few writers understand the difference between talking at their readers and talking to them. Awareness is growing that some of the old ways of writing will no longer do.

The following example, involving a sentence taken from a story about the failure of a space telescope, is typical of the problems editors face:

> "I'm not sure whether to smile ear to ear or cry," said William Blair of Johns Hopkins University, revealing data of a supernova remnant that the school's telescope made before being shut down.

The copy editor did not understand "supernova remnant" and suspected that many readers would be similarly puzzled. The editor found that the dictionary defined "supernova" as an extremely bright nova and further defined "nova" as a star that suddenly grew very bright and then faded.

The placement of the clause beginning with "that" was confusing. It seemed to apply to "supernova remnant," but that was impossible, so it must modify "data."

But how had the telescope "made" data? Data are normally collected or recorded, not made. A telescope is merely an extension of the eye: it sees. How can it manufacture?

Mending an ambiguity can be hard work. It can also be risky. A wrong move can easily turn a minor puzzlement into a blatant mistake.

The editor considered revising the sentence this way:

> "I'm not sure whether to smile ear to ear or cry," said William Blair of Johns Hopkins University, revealing data on a supernova remnant that the school's telescope detected before being shut down.

That choice was rejected because of the assumption that the telescope "detected" the supernova remnant. It may merely have studied something that had already been detected by some other instrument.

A different revision was considered:

> "I'm not sure whether to smile ear to ear or cry," said William Blair of Johns Hopkins University, revealing data on a supernova remnant. The school's telescope gathered the information before being shut down.

Unfortunately, this removed some of the impact of Blair's combined elation and regret. The editor wanted a more informative paragraph, something like this:

> "I'm not sure whether to smile ear to ear or cry," said William Blair of Johns Hopkins University, revealing some scientifically important data that the school's telescope recorded before being shut down. The data were on a supernova remnant, which is the remains of a star that suddenly brightens and then fades.

However, the idea that the data were scientifically important was the editor's and could not be confirmed. Editors who plunge ahead and make such changes without checking the facts are a major cause of errors, and nobody wants to be the source of a correction that begins, "Because of an editing error. . . ."

In the end, the copy editor decided on a revision that seemed safe from error and helpful to readers:

> "I'm not sure whether to smile ear to ear or cry," said William Blair of Johns Hopkins University, revealing data that the school's telescope recorded from a supernova remnant before the instrument was shut down. A supernova is a star that suddenly brightens and then fades.

Similar work goes into every paragraph that crosses the desk of a careful editor. The potential consequences of making an incorrect change are likely to outweigh the rewards of making a good one. It's small wonder that some editors, when pressed for time, elect to make no change at all.

SOME WAYS TO PROMOTE CLARITY

1. **Eliminate abstractions or convert them to the concrete.** Abstractions relate to the mind. They describe ideas, not solid things. Without abstractions, civilization would be impossible. We would be unable to deal with complexity and could communicate only in terms of things we could see: "spear," "rock," "horse," "tree." We would never have left the caves. Yet overuse of words like "process," "issue," "situation," "question," "condition," "facilities," "activities," "experience," "factor," "proposition" and "character" can cloud understanding. In newswriting, abstractions often merely fill space, like packing in a crate. When the meaning is unpacked, they can be discarded (Box 1.10).
2. **Eliminate or translate jargon.** Every profession, every business, every organization, every discipline has its argot, which serves chiefly to smooth the way for the insiders and keep the outsiders at bay. In covering each field, journalists become insiders. They understand this specialized language and use it in dealing with news sources. When they allow it to creep into their writing, communication fails. This is especially a problem in covering government (Box 1.11).
3. **Tone down the bombast.** Some writers attempt to banish dullness by overwriting. They overinflate the significance of events by using gross exaggerations or inventing catchy but empty phrases. Such pompous language is bombast, or "hype," an effort to inject pizzazz, not with cleverness and originality but with a blunt needle of banality. "Booted, helmeted and club-swinging riot police" battle "bloodthirsty, rock-and-bottle-throwing mobs." Storms

Avoid Unnecessary Abstractions

Original	Edited
the process of writing	writing
the spending issue	spending
the critical situation	crisis
the abortion question	abortion
weather conditions	weather
medical facilities	hospitals, clinics
leisure-time activities	sports, games
the classroom experience	going to class
the factor of excellence	excellence
a practical proposition	practical
a matter of a different character	a different matter

Box 1.10

are "killer winds" that cut "paths of death and destruction" and leave in their "wakes" debris for "grim-faced rescue workers" to "search with a fine-tooth comb." Fires "sweep," "rage" or "gut." Scandals "rock" institutions. The United States was seen to "flex its military muscle" in the Middle East in 1991, and hardworking U.S. astronauts were described as "star-gazing."

4. **Discard trite, empty phrases.** One product of bombast is the instant cliché. One writer's burst of excess is picked up and repeated by others until it gains acceptance far beyond any validity it may have begun with. Examples:
   - The meaningless "Governor Moonbeam" label applied to former California Gov. Jerry Brown when he ran for president in 1991. Even after it was disavowed by its creator, columnist Mike Royko, the phony title was taken seriously by some political writers.
   - The ubiquitous false title "kidnapped newspaper heiress," acquired by Patty Hearst in the early 1970s, though she had inherited no newspapers. When, in a strange turnabout, she joined the kidnap gang and was charged with bank robbery, she became "fugitive newspaper heiress Patty Hearst."
5. **Make sure phrases are in the proper order to promote understanding.** Clumsiness is often attributable to tortured syntax. A sentence may seem grammatically sound but still be ambiguous because its phrases don't mesh properly (Box 1.12).
6. **Stamp out acronymomania.** This is the passion for abbreviations that form non-words and serve chiefly to annoy readers. Some editors call this sort of writing "alphabet soup" (Box 1.13).
7. **When in doubt, check it out.** One can never be too careful in attempting to clarify someone else's prose. If a copy editor is in doubt about whether a change in the language will also cause even a slight change in the meaning, no change should be made until the doubts are cleared up.

Eliminate Jargon

Original	Edited
The governor has a $52.9-billion backlog in services and no way to begin paying on it.	The governor has promised to build $52.9 billion worth of roads, schools and other projects but lacks the money to pay for them.
He responded that while the department must mitigate negative impacts of road-building, such as by replacing wetlands, additional four-lane roads are needed both for safety and to boost the rural economy.	He responded that more four-lane highways must be built to provide safe avenues for travel and business and that any damage to the surroundings, such as destruction of wildlife habitats, must be repaired.
The facility has not been used to pool wheat since the cooperative bought it in 1985. But there has been a slowdown in shipments of grain sorghum for export, and slowdowns in wheat movement from elevators to ports also have a negative price effect here.	The building has not been used to store wheat from combined sources since the cooperative bought it in 1985. Grain prices have slumped as shipments of grain sorghum for export have slowed down along with transportation of wheat from elevators to ports.
The restraining order prevents the Department of Corrections from opening bids and awarding the 33 separate contracts for the construction project, an 80-bed maximum-security housing unit at the penitentiary. Bidding on the multimillion-dollar unit was scheduled to begin today.	The court's order prevents the Department of Corrections from awarding 33 contracts for construction of a structure to house 80 of the most dangerous convicts at the penitentiary. Bidding on the multimillion-dollar project was to have begun today.
The thrust of the new department will be to join forces with mechanical departments in establishing or refining standards, disciplines and processes. They will work with the interdepartmental quality control committee to establish priorities and direction for the new department.	The new department will work with mechanical departments and with the interdepartmental quality control committee to improve the way jobs are done.

Box 1.11

Guideline 7: Wordiness

Editors must be stingy with space, using it wisely and to good purpose, and they therefore abhor unnecessary words, redundancies and all other forms of waste.

Eliminating wordiness is the most valuable of an editor's skills. Unnecessary words eat up space; eliminating them cuts costs. Reducing the word count also cuts reading time, a service for consumers who complain that they don't have time to read newspapers. What they mean is that they are unwilling to make

Tortured Syntax

Original	Edited
The chairman said the Board of Regents would decide what action to take at its meeting Tuesday.	The chairman said the Board of Regents would decide at its meeting Tuesday what action to take.
House Speaker Jim Wright, testifying under oath, gave a lengthy defense Wednesday of his actions in a closed-door session before the House ethics committee.	House Speaker Jim Wright, testifying under oath Wednesday in a closed-door session before the House ethics committee, gave a lengthy defense of his actions.
His troubles began when a wall collapsed while fighting a fire last June.	His troubles began when a wall collapsed on him while he fought a fire last June.
Police removed paroled rapist Lawrence Singleton from an apartment in a bulletproof vest Monday.	Police removed paroled rapist Lawrence Singleton, wearing a bulletproof vest, from an apartment Monday.
After talking with scores of people, they found a young woman who remembered seeing Jean Crouch the same night she died at a party in a mobile home near Green Key Beach.	After talking with scores of people, they found a young woman who remembered seeing Jean Crouch at a party in a mobile home near Green Key Beach the night Crouch died.
The victim may have struggled with the man who strangled her for three or four minutes before passing out and dying, a medical examiner testified Wednesday.	The victim may have struggled for three or four minutes with the man who strangled her, a medical examiner testified Wednesday.

Box 1.12

time to read because newspapers are too dense and tedious to displace something else from their tight schedules. Editors can no longer afford to tolerate excessive density and tedium.

Newspapers of the past were forbiddingly gray and full of long stories composed of long paragraphs, but today's trends favor short bites of information surrounded by colorful illustrations. Long stories still have their place, but new ways of writing and editing them have made them more appealing to readers.

Wordiness, which has become a luxury that the print media cannot afford, takes two forms:

1. Wasted words, which contribute no information. (Wasted words are in bold type in the examples.)
2. Redundancies, which are inadvertent repetitions of information. (Redundancies are underlined in the examples.)

Shun Acronymomania

Original

The former executive director of the Eastgate Development and Transportation Agency ripped state authorities yesterday, saying they had falsely accused EDATA officials of conspiring with the suspended NOACA executive director to steal public funds.

Edited

Charges of conspiracy to steal public funds brought an angry denial yesterday from the Eastgate Development and Transportation Agency's former executive director.

Box 1.13

Wordy, Wordy

Original
Deputies are investigating a sexual **battery that occurred** Thursday **against** a 19-year-old **female guest** at Exclusive Resort, according to a Sheriff's Office report. **The victim was asleep** in her room about 5 a.m. **when she was awakened by the assault, the report said. When the victim sat up in bed,** the male suspect shined a light in her face and attacked her. The suspect **then left through the patio door.** The victim was **participating** in a tennis camp at the resort, the report said. She suffered **only** minor injuries and is still at the resort. A sheriff's spokesman said the investigators had a suspect, **but no arrests had been made.**

Edited
A 19-year-old woman was sexually assaulted in her bed Thursday by an intruder at Exclusive Resort, according to a Sheriff's Office report. The victim, a participant in a tennis camp, said the man attacked her at about 5 a.m., shined a light in her face and fled through a patio door. She was not seriously injured.

Original
A man **who thought** his roommate was sleeping on the couch for two days **didn't realize** the 60-year-old was dead. The man **decided** to call police Tuesday after noticing that his roommate had been lying on the apartment couch since Sunday without moving. **Police were waiting to notify relatives before releasing the man's name.** The roommate's name also was not released. A police report stated the man had left his roommate lying on the couch at their apartment about 2 p.m. Sunday. The man called police at 11:50 a.m. Tuesday and his roommate's body was turned over to the County Medical Examiner's Office for an autopsy.

Edited
A man called police Tuesday to report that his 60-year-old roommate had been sleeping on the couch for two days without moving. Police found the roommate dead and turned the body over to the County Medical Examiner's Office for an autopsy. Neither man's name was released.

Original
A woman was walking **in her neighborhood** early Monday **when she** was attacked and raped by three men, police said. The woman was walking between 12:30 and 1:30 a.m. in an area **police described as** bounded by 50th and 70th avenues and First and 20th streets. Three men wearing hoods grabbed her and threw her to the ground, police said. Two held her down while the third sexually assaulted her **with an object.** The woman was treated at Mercy Hospital.

Edited
Three hooded men attacked a woman on the street early Monday, and one raped her while the others held her down, police said. The woman was walking between 12:30 and 1:30 a.m. in an area bounded by 50th and 70th avenues and First and 20th streets. She was treated at Mercy Hospital.

Original
A police officer used a strong bark to get a burglary suspect out of a store. Officer Fred Tabor impersonated a barking dog to scare the man out of the store early Tuesday, said Lt. Jerry Miller. Tabor **and three other officers** went to the store **after** a burglar alarm **sounded.** They found a broken window and a man trying to hide behind the counter. Tabor called for the canine unit and told the man they would be sending in a dog to get him out of the store. **There was no immediate response. At that point, the report says Officer Tabor barked vigorously, said Sgt. Ken Ruppert.** That brought the man out and he was arrested.

Edited
A police officer used a strong bark to get a burglary suspect out of a store. Officer Fred Tabor responded to a burglar alarm early Tuesday and found a broken window and a man trying to hide behind a counter, Lt. Jerry Miller said. Tabor called for the canine unit and told the man he would be sending in a dog. Then Tabor "barked vigorously," said Sgt. Ken Ruppert. The man ran out and was arrested.

In the examples, a total of 296 words was reduced to 186, allowing the same information to be presented in 36 percent less space. Of course, these stories were selected for their wordiness, but they are not unusual.

A common cause of wordiness is repetition. A point is made and made again and sometimes in long stories is made more than twice. When this is done deliberately, for emphasis, it is an effective technique, but usually redundancy is inadvertent.

Guideline 8: Absurdity

Editors must be alert for absurdity; it is more common in media writing than one might think.

Absurdity waits like a snake in the grass to bite unwary editors. It tends to blend into the background, invisible sometimes even to the wary.

Absurdities are contrary to reason; they fly in the face of common sense. Writers create them because of haste or carelessness. Editors overlook them for the same reasons.

It is reasonable to state, for example, that in 1941 no genius of air power had yet invented a silent bomber. Yet the following lead appeared on a story marking the fiftieth anniversary of the attack on Pearl Harbor:

> Fifty years ago on Dec. 7, just before the break of dawn, 350 Japanese planes flew silently toward their target.

The writer meant that the planes were unheard or ignored by the target population, not that they were silent.

Other absurdities from the nation's press:

> A woman was killed Saturday following a traffic accident in which she was thrown from the back seat of a car. (*How did the woman die? If she was killed after the accident, the cause must have been something other than the crash. Perhaps a tree fell on her.*)

> A woman drowned in her swimming pool Friday, after she was dragged from the water by several neighbors who tried to save her, authorities said. (*How did she manage to drown after being pulled from the water?*)

> Two adults and two juveniles were arrested and accused of raping an 18-year-old woman early Sunday after a neighbor heard screams and summoned police. (*Did the rape take place after the screams were heard? Or was it the arrest that happened after the police were summoned?*)

> Within 90 minutes Wednesday morning, residents discovered the victims of what police believe are two separate murders. (*Except in highly unusual circumstances, all murders are separate, because each involves a separate act of pulling the trigger or thrusting the knife. Evidently, the writer meant the murders were unrelated.*)

> Each day, 168 million gallons of crystal-clear water boils from the spring, which is the surfacing point of an immense underwater river. (*It makes considerably more sense to define a spring as the surfacing point of an underground river.*)

> He then used a carotid artery restraint. Known as a "sleeper hold" because it makes a person unconscious for a few seconds, the technique calls for applying pressure to one of the two main arteries of the neck to block the flow of blood to and from the heart. (*Blocking the flow of blood to the heart results in a heart attack, not a few seconds of unconsciousness. Obviously—or perhaps not so obviously to the medically untrained—the brain is meant.*)

> Games of jet-ski daring ended painfully Sunday when the driver of one jet ski drove into the leg of another driver, breaking both bones in the man's right calf. (*The calf is a muscle. It contains no bones.*)

> One of the man's legs was shorter than the other and probably walked with a limp, police said. (*How did the other leg walk?*)

> The body did not have any superficial wounds. (*How about profound ones?*)

The South African government also ordered that people in the unrest areas would not be allowed to carry a variety of weapons. (*Are they free to carry weapons that are all of the same type?*)

Nebraska's longest death row inmate should have his sentence reduced to life in prison because of a sentencing flaw, a federal judge has ruled. (*Just how long, or tall, is the inmate?*)

Fantastic Sam's, whose slogan is "The Original Family Haircutters," hires both male and female hairdressers, although the majority are overwhelmingly women. (*Presumably it's the majority that is overwhelming, not the women.*)

Education professor Gordon Greene always will remember the bicycle trip he took across the United States to commemorate the "Forgotten War." (*No one, including Greene, can possibly know what he will always remember. The reporter knows only that Greene said he would remember.*)

"Teams make their own judgment," said the NBA's director of player programs. "If a player has talent, and whether they feel the young man can overcome the drug problem. One of the things the NBA does not do is condone a player. They recognize that kids grow up and they may do things that they'll be sorry for." (*Condone a player? Condemn a player? Only the speaker knows for sure.*)

She testified that Douglas, her former boyfriend, made her and her husband perform various sexual acts at gunpoint before he killed her husband, and then forced him into additional sex acts. (*It sounds impossible.*)

Avoiding Absurdity

1. Never edit anything without adequate sleep or while under the influence of any sort of mind-numbing drug. Alertness is your chief defense.
2. Take nothing at face value. Probe for the inner meaning.
3. Trust your first impression. If the thing appears absurd at first look, it may indeed be absurd.

Guideline 9: Taste

Tastelessness may be calculated to achieve an effect, but the editor must ensure that it is never inadvertent.

Good taste, like beauty, is in the eye of the beholder. Every publication has a tone, and if it is an old periodical, it has a traditional tone. Readers expect this tone to be maintained throughout, and they base their choices of reading material on these expectations. No one expects to find good taste in a pornographic magazine, but one would be shocked not to find it in a serious publication such as *The Atlantic.*

Some publications trade on bad taste. Almost any form of pornography and obscenity is acceptable in their pages. Others draw a boundary at some point, and editors must know where that boundary is, because they are the guardians of taste. Part of their job is to protect their publications against overstepping their own standards with inadvertent frankness or grossness.

Editors tend to be cautious on this point because they know the final decision is theirs to make. Writers who are uncertain about the boundary of acceptability will often put questionable material into their stories, relying on the editors to determine what is fit to print.

The challenge for editors is to maintain a high level of reader interest without stepping too far beyond the boundary of offensiveness. Almost everything journalists say in print will offend somebody. Even garden club social notes will offend those who aren't mentioned or are mentioned in the wrong way.

Journalism could be described as calculated offensiveness. Its objective is to give offense purposefully, in order to throw light on things the public ought or wants to know about. Inoffensiveness, carried to extremes, results in blandness, dullness and irrelevance, all fatal diseases in print.

Viewed in this light, too much good taste can be as dangerous as bad taste. The embattled editors are, in the last ditch, responsible for achieving the right balance.

SOME WAYS TO PROMOTE GOOD TASTE

1. **Apply the "Cheerios test."** Picture readers eating breakfast. Anything that seems reasonably likely to cause people to choke on their Cheerios is over the line (Box 1.14). This is likely to eliminate stomach-turning violence and gore, explicit sex and obscene language.

   The trouble with the Cheerios test is that there are times when editors ought to insist that readers be invited to choke on their Cheerios. Some of the strongest images of the Vietnam War were those of Buddhist priests burning themselves alive on Saigon streets, of a naked little girl whose clothes had been burned away by napalm and of a suspected Viet Cong being executed with a handgun. They were published despite their tastelessness—indeed, because of it.
2. **Blank out obscene words.** Every publication should have a policy on what to do about words many readers consider unprintable. Blanking them out (f—) is one option. A good practice is to post a written list of censored words and the accepted combinations of letters and hyphens.

   Some ridicule such policies as absurd. Why blank out something everyone knows? The answer is that some readers don't want to see these words, no matter how familiar they may be. Nevertheless, the policy in the extreme can become ridiculous—for example, jack——.
3. **Watch for inadvertent double meanings.** There is no substitute for common sense and simple skepticism, but two principles should be kept in mind:
   - Standard words can acquire unexpected meanings. "Gay" and "queer," for example, were once commonly used to mean "lighthearted" and "odd," but those definitions are no longer the first to come to mind. In a 1990 book on slang, Paul Dickson reported, "One could make a list of more than a hundred of the coded terms used only in personal classified ads."

Does This Pass the Cheerios Test?

An 18-month-old boy briefly left alone in a car Friday with the motor running squeezed out of his car seat and shifted the car into drive, sending it into a group of campers and decapitating a 2-year-old boy, police said.

Some editors would say the harrowing detail of decapitation fails the test.

Box 1.14

- Slang is dangerous because it, too, can evolve and develop new meanings. "Scum," for example, has been used since the sixteenth century to mean "vile," but recently it has acquired a sexual meaning, "semen," because of the slang word "scumbag" (condom).

4. **Be wary but flexible.** No ban on obscene words should be absolute. When Richard Nixon, as president, released transcripts of his White House conversations, they were riddled with the parenthetical expression "(expletive deleted)." Later, given the chance to publish the expletives, most editors did so because the conversations did not seem real without them.

Obscene gestures? When the vice president of the United States gives his hecklers the finger, as Nelson Rockefeller once did, even crudity becomes newsworthy.

Nudity? In the 1970s a phenomenon called "streaking" enjoyed brief popularity. Naked interlopers would dash through settings where nudity was inappropriate, such as baseball games and even the sound stage where the nationally televised Academy Awards ceremonies were taking place. Editors could hardly ignore it.

Explicit sex? When a prominent doctor goes on trial on charges of sexually molesting his female patients, editors may have to rule on such passages as this:

> In his closing arguments, the defense attorney suggested that one woman may have mistaken the defendant's meaning when the doctor asked "Does this feel good?" during an examination of her groin.

It's tasteless, but to cut it out would be unfair to the defense. Some readers would argue that any coverage of such a trial would be tasteless, and some journalists would reply that because the world they cover is full of boorishness and strife, tastelessness is sometimes necessary.

Ultimately, the editor must be his or her own judge of tastelessness. Does the word, sentence, paragraph or story measure up to one's personal standards? Is it consistent with the tone of the publication? If the answer to either question is no, the editor's duty is to protest.

Guideline 10: Sensitivity

Editors must be sensitive to the concerns of readers and avoid unwarranted trespasses into the lives of newsworthy people.

In the 1981 movie "Absence of Malice," a newspaper is portrayed as a ruthless exploiter of the defenseless and vulnerable, an unscrupulous, heartless bully unconcerned with the truth. An editor in the film displays an uncaring attitude toward an innocent woman who will be deeply embarrassed if he prints her name. "Let the people decide who is innocent," he says, and publishes a story that drives the woman to suicide.

The arrogance portrayed in the film may have been typical of many, although certainly not all, newspapers at the time, but today it seems almost quaint. Today's editors are sensitive to a wide range of attitudes and feelings among the public. The arrogant editor has been replaced by the service-minded editor.

In April 1990, the journal of the Associated Press Managing Editors depicted this "new, improved" editor as having a hole in his head "to release old attitudes," a big ear to hear what the reader was saying and a heart of gold for performing community services. He carried a medicine bottle containing "a daily dose of cooperation to improve circulation," a book of telephone etiquette "to ensure politeness when speaking to readers" and a "tuning fork to fine tune community coverage." His feet were crammed into high-heeled "customer's shoes to walk a mile in."

The new, sensitive image is the industry's response to declining readership and the fear of becoming irrelevant to people's lives. One way to hasten the irrelevancy is to see the world only from the viewpoint of a single segment of the population (Box 1.15).

SOME WAYS TO PROMOTE SENSITIVITY

1. Be alert to racial, sexual and occupational stereotypes. There is a tendency to identify males by their occupations and females by their marital or family status. Such bias is often inadvertent, subtle and easy to overlook.
2. Delete stereotypical metaphors.
3. Protect the dignity of victims of sexual assaults. Especially, avoid making light of serious situations.
4. Watch for subtle racial assumptions.

Examples of Passages That Lack Sensitivity

Watching for Gender Bias

> The Supreme Court ruled Tuesday that federal courts have no power to resolve child custody disputes extending across state lines, rejecting the plea of a California doctor whose former wife took their son to Louisiana.

The former wife was also a doctor. Why is she identified as "former wife" while he is not described as "husband"?

> As his alimony hearing ended Tuesday, a man pulled out a gun and started a shooting spree that left a judge, a lawyer and a woman dead.

The implication is that "judge" and "lawyer" are strictly male categories.

> The well-liked mother of one was met a week ago on the sidewalk outside her work place, handcuffed and charged with trying to hire someone to kill her husband.

Would the husband have been described as "a well-liked father of one" in similar circumstances?

A Stereotypical Metaphor

> Like a pampered mistress, the resort hotel sits by the seashore, welcoming well-heeled visitors to frolic in the sun and sand. A pink-and-white bastion of luxury, she offers no hint that she ever knew hard times. Her facelifts have been so flawless, it would be hard to guess her age. Only her mighty bulk gives her away as belonging to a more sumptuous era and her beginnings 60 years ago.

This exploitation of an unflattering stereotype of middle-aged women is highly objectionable.

Rape Is No Joke

> The police report scenario combined terror and low farce. A man breaks into a woman's house, takes off his clothes and sneaks into her bedroom—but winds up fleeing with his clothes slung over his arm and the victim pointing a shotgun at his back.

Many are likely to see far more terror than farce.

> Threatened by a would-be rapist wielding a meat cleaver early Monday, a woman emerged unscathed while her attacker received the unkindest cuts of all. The 26-year-old woman tricked the man into putting away his cleaver. Then she grabbed it herself and used it on her assailant.

Who is to say she was "unscathed"?

A Subtle Assumption

> Two students have been suspended by school officials for possessing a bogus "employment application" containing racial slurs and innuendoes. The application, which contained language offensive to blacks, fell out of the male students' notebooks last Wednesday, the principal said.

Such language is offensive to everyone, regardless of color.

Box 1.15

BIBLIOGRAPHY AND ADDITIONAL READINGS

Associated Press. *The Associated Press Stylebook and Libel Manual.* 1990.

Berner, R. Thomas. *The Process of Editing.* Allyn and Bacon. 1991.

Bremner, John. *Words on Words.* Columbia University Press. 1980.

Garst, Robert, and Theodore M. Bernstein. *Headlines and Deadlines,* 3rd ed. Columbia University Press. 1961.

Harrington, Jane T. *The Editorial Eye.* St. Martin's Press. 1993.

Plotnik, Arthur. *The Elements of Editing.* Collier Books. 1982.

Strunk, William Jr., and E. B. White. *The Elements of Style,* 3rd ed. Macmillan. 1979.

READINGS IN RECENT AMERICAN HISTORY

Branch, Taylor. *Parting the Waters: America in the King Years.* Simon & Schuster. 1988.

Burrough, Brian, and John Helyar. *Barbarians at the Gate: The Fall of RJR Nabisco.* Harper & Row. 1990.

Ketcham, Richard M. *The Borrowed Years 1938–1941: America on the Way to War.* Random House. 1989.

Manchester, William. *The Glory and the Dream: A Narrative History of America 1932–1972.* Little, Brown. 1974.

Chapter 2

STYLE: MAKING THE RULES

NO DOGMA FOR EDITORS

Editors should regard style as a means of achieving consistency, no more, no less. No style declaration is right or wrong, simply dominant or unaccepted. The belief that any manual of style is "the journalist's bible" is unsupportable, if that term is taken to mean an article of unassailable faith. Journalists have no professional bible because skepticism is part of their job. Immutable rules invite challenge.

Editors enforce style because the alternative is chaos. An erratic image fosters mistrust among readers. A well-edited publication speaks with a single voice in matters of form, but the nature of that voice is determined by the publication's staff and thus changes and evolves as the staff changes and evolves.

The usual approach to learning style is memorization. The weakness of this method is that it places style in the same mental file folder with other rigid bodies of knowledge that one is forced to learn in school—a folder that may prove to be empty when opened in a time of need. The thesis of this chapter is that participation in the formation of style breeds enthusiasm for it and appreciation of the difficult decision-making that lies behind every rule. Style is far more than a canon of nits for professional pickers. It is a dynamic code of ethical decisions on a wide variety of technical and social issues.

Some issues are thorny, others merely troublesome. Debating the issues and writing the rules are the responsibilities of a style committee.

SOME STYLE CONTROVERSIES

Style decisions are not always unanimous, and it is often found advisable to limit style committee membership to three people to make the debates manageable. The three members might come from different departments, such as news, sports and lifestyle.

The following issues are examples of the kinds of disputes style committees face. There are no definitive answers to these questions, and students are urged to hold their own committee deliberations and try to write workable rules.

A committee may elect to ignore an issue as too divisive or too complicated to lend itself to a style rule. The staff will then be left to make decisions case by case, which means that questions may be answered one way one day, another way the next.

Remember: Style rules should be brief and uncomplicated, yet comprehensive enough to be easily and evenly enforced.

Abortion

Maintaining neutrality on an issue as emotional as this one is difficult, but most publications want to be perceived as willing to present both sides and eager to be fair to each. Readers are vigilant toward what they see as bias in the media. The style committee's role is to select preferred terms and decide whether some should be banned. "Pro-life" and "pro-choice" are popular but burdened by heavy ideological baggage. "Pro-life" implies that the alternative is to love death, and "pro-choice" ignores the issue of a fetal right to life. Possible alternatives are "pro-fetal rights" and "pro-reproductive rights," but those terms are clumsy and seldom used. A popular solution today is to describe abortion activists as either advocates or opponents of abortion rights.

Ages

When does a boy or girl become a man or woman? One crosses that divide at age 18, according to the prevailing style. The line may seem arbitrary, but it has to be drawn somewhere because "boy" and "girl" should not be applied to adults.

Also troublesome is the point where childhood becomes youth. Children are usually called by their first names in news stories, but adults are known by their last names. Calling a 3-year-old "Jones" seems excessively formalistic, but using "Fred" to refer to an adult implies a familiarity that is inappropriate most of the time. The years from 12 to 17 are a period of transition, in which "child" sometimes seems right but can also be out of place. When a teenager commits an adult crime, for example, referring to the offender by a first name may be objectionable.

For the older generations, "middle age," "senior citizen," "elderly" and "aged" are controversial. Physical fitness can make such terms seem inaccurate at any age, and many regard any reference to age groups as offensive. Sometimes these words are necessary to define categories, such as who is eligible

A Policy on Ages

People are infants up to 12 months, children up to 12 years. They are boys and girls or youths up to their 18th birthdays. From then on they are men and women or adults. Men and women may be called young from 19 to the mid-20s. Middle-aged, elderly and aged are terms that offend some people and should be avoided in describing specific individuals. If it is necessary to use such terms, however, middle age can be assumed to range from 40 to 64. For those 65 or older, elderly or aged is acceptable.

—*St. Petersburg Times Stylebook*

Box 2.1

for certain types of government assistance, but calling anyone under 65 elderly or anyone under 50 middle-aged is likely to invite angry letters from readers (Box 2.1).

"Kids" is in widespread use, but some editors restrict it to direct quotations, except in reference to goats.

Courtesy Titles

Once they were the rule in social interaction, but courtesy titles (Mr., Ms., Miss, Mrs.) have become increasingly rare, perhaps because of a decline in civility. When answering the phone today, one is frequently addressed by first name even though the caller is a stranger. Instant use of one's first name would have been an affront in earlier times; today it is routine. Courtesy titles have largely disappeared from the media.

A style committee has only three options:

1. Courtesy titles for nobody
2. Courtesy titles for everybody
3. Courtesy titles for certain groups but not for others

Although the first and second options are more evenhanded, the third is currently the most popular media choice, partly because of the differences between generations. Older citizens, particularly women, are more likely to have courtesy titles. An elderly woman, still accustomed to a different era's tokens of respect, might be jarred or offended to be called "Jones" rather than "Mrs. Jones" in print. She might also prefer to be referred to as "Mrs. John Jones" rather than "Mary Jones." It is respect for these women, and for the civility of the past, that prompts many editors to retain courtesy titles for women.

In practice, such a policy encounters considerable difficulty because of many women's reluctance to be known by or even to disclose their marital status. The Associated Press requires reporters to determine the preference of each woman mentioned in the news, but the question (Do you prefer to be referred to as Mrs. Jones, Ms. Jones or Jones?) is easily forgotten in the heat of action. It is also resented by many women, who justifiably ask why they should be treated differently from men. Others object to "Ms." as too radical.

A Policy on Courtesy Titles

In general refer to women on first reference by first name, middle initial if she uses it, and last name only, with the exceptions noted below. In instances in which the first name does not adequately indicate an individual's sex, try to include pronoun references like she and her.

The use of Mr., Mrs., Miss or Ms. is, of course, acceptable in quoted material.

In obituaries, the feminine titles should be used on second reference.

In society news, features and columns the use of Mrs., Miss or Ms. is acceptable, but not mandatory. In entertainment stories, and in the rest of the paper, the last-name-only rule applies—with the exceptions noted below.

A couple may be referred to on first reference by the first names of each in addition to the surname: John and Joan Smith.

If there is any possibility of their relationship being misunderstood, early reference to their marital ties should be made:

Dist. Atty. Joan Smith and her husband, John

John Smith and his wife, Joan Jones

If a husband and wife, or a man and a woman with the same last name, are referred to in a story and it is necessary to distinguish between them, it is best to repeat the first names on second reference. First names alone may be used in some features.

Exceptions to the last-name-only rule:

1. Historic women may be referred to as Miss or Mrs. if it has been customary: Mrs. Roosevelt, Mrs. Lincoln, Mme. Curie.
2. Women whose position or years are deemed to merit it or whose stature borders on the historic may likewise be referred to by courtesy titles.
3. Women who are the victims of crimes of violence or severe physical accidents should generally be referred to by courtesy titles. To do otherwise sounds callous and uncaring.

It remains incumbent on the reporter to determine which courtesy title should be used in a given instance if it is to be used at all.

—Los Angeles Times Stylebook

Box 2.2

One way to deal with the controversy is to give courtesy titles to both women and men. This has long been the policy at *The New York Times,* where every surname must be accompanied by a title of some sort, such as Mr., Ms., Dr., Judge or Senator. Sports figures are an exception because it is considered extreme to write that "Mr. Jackson slid into second base" or "Miss Evert scored an ace." At one time the *Times* deprived convicted felons of courtesy titles on the ground that they had forfeited their entitlement to respect, but during the 1960s the denial of "Mr." to some black militants led to charges of racism. The exception for felons was abolished.

The most telling objection to courtesy titles for everyone is that the policy is cumbersome and expends precious news space unnecessarily.

A popular alternative is courtesy titles for no one, but here, too, exceptions are often regarded as necessary. In obituaries, the dead are sometimes accorded the title of respect that was denied them in life. Ministers and priests frequently get courtesy titles, especially on religion pages. In some publications, a special exception to the ban on courtesy titles is provided for the president of the United States.

Another View on Courtesy Titles

In almost every instance, Mr. is to be used in second and subsequent references to an adult male who does not have a title of a kind that replaces the ordinary honorific. We do not omit the Mr. in subsequent references to a person convicted of crime or having an unsavory reputation. Should the use of Mr. in some such cases seem ludicrously out of place, judicious editing and the use of pronouns or terms like the defendant or the suspect will solve the problem.

Mr. is not needed in subsequent references to people of pre-eminence who are no longer living: Newton, Lincoln, Lenin, Churchill, Picasso, etc. . . . Mr. is not used with the names of sports figures in sports-section stories or in stories of sports contests that appear on page 1. . . . Some youths under the age of 18 should have the Mr., and some should not. There can be no precise rule, but the nature of the story should be controlling. If Mr. is omitted, call the subject Charles or Charles Manley, not the Manley boy or the Manley youth. . . .

In almost all first references to women—married or single, well known or not—given names should be used and the honorifics Mrs., Miss and Ms. should be omitted. Mrs., Miss, and Ms. (which see) should be used in subsequent references for women who do not have titles of the kind that replace the ordinary honorifics. Thus: Golda Meir, former prime minister of Israel, is taking her first real vacation in years. Mrs. Meir is spending it . . . .

Ms.—Use this title in second and subsequent references to a woman who prefers it or whose marital status is unknown to us. If we know a woman's marital status but not her choice of title, use Mrs. or Miss.

If a woman has a title, it is used just as a title is in the case of a man: Prime Minister Joan Manley, in first references; in subsequent references, Prime Minister Manley, the Prime Minister, or Mrs. or Miss Manley. . . .

—*The New York Times Manual of Style and Usage*

Box 2.3

A special problem arises when two or more people share the same last name. Confusion is avoided if first names are used, but referring to "Sam" or "Irma" in a news report is usually inappropriate because it implies an unwanted intimacy with a news source. For couples, "Mr. and Mrs." can be a good solution, but many editors prefer to use full names, such as "Sam Jones" and "Irma Jones," wherever there is a possibility of confusion (Boxes 2.2, 2.3).

Dependencies

Should alcohol, drug and tobacco dependencies be treated as habits or diseases? The distinction can be crucial in determining the choice of terms to be used in news stories.

The Associated Press requires that "those afflicted with the disease of alcoholism" be described as "recovering" rather than "reformed" (Box 2.4). No similar provision exists for those addicted to drugs. They are routinely described as "abusers." Smokers, on the other hand, simply "use" tobacco.

Habits are voluntary, but diseases are caught by their victims. Is it fair to say alcoholics are "afflicted," but not drug addicts and smokers? Are there "victims" of drug addiction and tobacco abuse?

A Policy on Alcoholism

alcoholic Use recovering, not reformed, in referring to those afflicted with the disease of alcoholism.

—*Associated Press Stylebook and Libel Manual*

Box 2.4

These questions may seem too technical for a style committee, but the answers are more social than medical. The ill effects of drugs and tobacco are well documented, and the difficulty of quitting them is undisputed. The main difference is that some dependencies are more socially acceptable than others.

Any decision by the media to use the same terminology for different dependencies would be extremely controversial. It could lead to social change.

Fairness

The style committee may want to adopt a statement on the importance of fairness and the correct method of ensuring that all sides of a story are told (Box 2.5).

Here, for guidance, is a fairness checklist compiled by the Society of Professional Journalists:

1. Is the meaning distorted by overemphasis or underemphasis?
2. Are facts and quotations in proper context?
3. Have you given this story the length and display appropriate to its importance, and have you presented it with dignity and professionalism?
4. Are the headlines and teases (promotions) warranted by the texts of the stories?
5. Have you done your best to report all sides of the story, and not just one side or, just as problematic, two artificially polarized points of view?
6. Have you been compassionate in your reporting?
7. Have all relevant people, particularly those who may be affected or harmed by the story, been given an opportunity to reply?
8. If sources are not fully identified, is there a justifiable reason?
9. When substantive errors or distortions appear in your paper or on the air, do you admit and correct them voluntarily, promptly and with a prominence comparable to that given the inaccurate statement or statements?
10. Are you fostering an open dialogue with your readers, viewers and listeners? Do others, both in the newsroom and outside it, feel the story is fair to those involved?

    Fair Play: Journalists at all times will show respect for the dignity, privacy, rights and well-being of people encountered in the course of gathering

A Policy on Fairness

Extreme care is required in dealing with criminal charges, court suits and other accusations.

Factual correctness is the first, though not the only, consideration. Newspaper clips and wire service items are not enough backup when crime or misbehavior is concerned. We have to get as close as possible to official sources. Quoting a person or publication does not excuse us for a mistake of fact or judgment, even though in some cases we can show better faith by attributing a statement than by making it on our own.

Up-to-date information is essential. It is unsafe to write without checking the possibility of appeal, new evidence or other change. Therefore we must keep contact with the situation, never work just from old material.

Both sides are important. If a person is accused in any manner or his position is attacked, every effort must be made to present his reply. If our sources have not provided any response, it is up to us to look for one.

Suitable words are a matter for careful choice and examination, to avoid any implication of guilt when guilt has not been proved in court. "Arrested for theft" is the classic error of this type. "Arrested on a charge of theft" is one right way to say it if that really is the charge—and we had best make certain it is an official charge. Other references have to be watched at least as closely. The culprits and similar phrases make trouble on two counts. First, they lump together several individuals, some of whom may suffer by association. Second, they may indicate guilt when no guilt has been proved.

Allegations of bad behavior by a public official may be subject to restriction unless they concern the administration of office. Doubt has been cast on the defense that social prominence opens the way to damaging news. And the excuse that a mistake was made without malice has been turned down by the courts.

Caption writing presents a special risk. Crowd scenes in which people can be identified are often troublesome; for instance, if a photograph illustrates a crime or disorder, our description must be tailored to avoid implicating any persons who might be innocent bystanders. A child's face in a story about classes for the retarded must be treated with the utmost caution: If he is not retarded, we of course get into serious trouble by leaving any implication that he might be; but even if he is, we might have to worry about causing pain or embarrassment.

—U.S. News & World Report Stylebook for Writers and Editors

Box 2.5

and presenting the news. The news media should not communicate unofficial charges affecting reputation or moral character without giving the accused a chance to reply.

Gender

Gender-specific job titles, such as foreman, policeman, fireman and telephone lineman, used to be common. Moreover, certain non-specific titles, such as lawyer and physician, were once assumed to imply maleness, and a woman in such a role might be referred to as a "lady lawyer" or a "lady doctor." Nurses, by contrast, were presumed to be female, and the exceptions were called "male nurses."

Today most editors strive to use gender-neutral terms, such as supervisor, police officer, firefighter and utility worker. They also avoid the masculine pronoun if the antecedent is gender neutral.

Every noun has one of four genders:

1. Masculine (man, father, nephew)
2. Feminine (woman, mother, niece)
3. Neuter (tree, streetlight)
4. Common (author, editor, journalist, gymnast)

"Much of the misguided, though well-intentioned, convolution of language to cleanse it of any taint of sexism would be dispelled if people would realize that English has a fourth gender, common to both sexes," the master teacher of editing, John Bremner, wrote in *Words on Words.*

Unfortunately, pronouns come in only three genders:

1. Masculine (he)
2. Feminine (she)
3. Neuter (it)

The lack of a common pronoun is the cause of the convolution Bremner deplored. The indefinite pronouns (one, anyone, everyone) are no help in a sentence like this: Every firefighter wore (his, her, their) hat. Because the plural form (they, their) is the same for all three genders, the tendency is to use it as the common pronoun even though the antecedent is singular (Every firefighter wore their hat). Though widely heard in spoken English, this practice is not accepted in the written language and is regarded by some authorities as an abomination.

Most editors recommend that writers avoid the issue by writing the sentence another way (The firefighters wore hats). Some find "his or her" acceptable (Every firefighter wore his or her hat). Inventing a new pronoun (Every firefighter wore hiser hat) has been suggested but has not caught on.

Many editors also avoid "gender-enders," feminized forms such as actress, comedienne, executrix, heroine, poetess and starlet. Actor, comedian, executor, hero, poet and star are preferred (Box 2.6).

Juveniles

> The sirens make a mournful sound as emergency vehicles arrive at a small house in a poor neighborhood. The woman who lives in the house has found her 9-month-old daughter dead, smothered in her crib. The baby has been sexually molested. The woman's two sons, aged 10 and 9, have been entrusted with the baby's care. After investigating, the police charge the two boys with murder.

Should the media name the boys?

Some states have laws against disclosure of the names of juveniles accused of crimes, but exceptions are sometimes made when the crimes are adult in nature. Some editors believe readers are entitled to know all the facts about serious crimes, regardless of the age of the accused. Others say offenders must have reached the age of responsibility before they are named, and that age is usually set at 16. Younger children can be rescued from hostile environments and go on to lead responsible lives, according to this view, and publicity can be permanently harmful. The opposing argument is that the media are in business to disclose, not withhold, information. Publicity can have a deterrent effect on juvenile crime, according to this view, and some juvenile criminals are just as hardened as their adult counterparts.

Minorities

In 1992 *The Oregonian* of Portland, Ore., banished Indians, Braves, Redmen and Redskins from its sports pages. "We do not expect the rest of the journalistic world to fall into line behind us, nor do we presume that our action will change any team names," the managing editor, Peter Thompson, said in a statement. "But we have concluded that we will not be a passive participant in perpetuating racial or cultural stereotypes in our community—whether by the use of nicknames or in any other way." The policy means that the Atlanta Braves, for example, must be referred to as the Atlanta team, the Atlanta players or just Atlanta in news stories.

Native Americans have long contended that sports team names relating to their culture are derisive and belittling, but the team organizations have shown no inclination to change their ways. Despite criticism, the fans in Atlanta have continued to use the "tomahawk chop," a hacking motion of the arm, in support of their team. *The Oregonian,* by declining to report the team's name, has chosen to use style as a means of censuring behavior it disapproves of. As an alternative, it might have elected to include a rebuttal paragraph, describing the minority group's objections, in every story containing an offensive team name.

The decision to eliminate such words is unusual but not unprecedented. Racial epithets have long been banned by news organizations and are often dropped or blanked out even from direct quotations. The Associated Press bans "honky" and "nigger" except in direct quotations.

Many other terms are considered offensive by different minorities, and sometimes by minorities within minorities (Box 2.7). One's reaction to a list of sensitive terms is likely to reflect one's race, gender or socioeconomic status. A style committee, striving to be neutral, should consider such terms, not as a group but one by one. Should they be avoided, banned or left to the judgment of individual editors?

Obscenity, Profanity

Most family-oriented publications, whose readership may include children, do not print obscenities, words that the editors consider offensive to normal standards of decency. Many also exclude profanity, which is language that is considered irreverent or blasphemous. Attempting to shield children from words they probably hear regularly in the corridors at school may seem absurd, but printing such words can lend them legitimacy that scrawls on bathroom walls cannot provide. In addition, many adults who may be used to hearing such words are nevertheless offended by the sight of them in print in a respectable publication.

A Policy on Gender

Men and women should be treated as people, not as members of one sex or the other. Women and men share humanity and common attributes. Neither women nor men should be stereotyped by being arbitrarily assigned primary or secondary roles; both should be dealt with on an equal basis and treated with the same respect, dignity and seriousness.

1. Assumptions. Don't assume that certain jobs or pastimes are done by one sex or another. For instance:

   Don't refer to "the consumer" or "the shopper" as "she"; make it consumers or shoppers . . . they.

   Don't refer to "the breadwinner" and "his earnings"; make it breadwinners and their earnings, or the breadwinner and his or her earnings.

   Don't assume that the secretary is "she"; make it secretaries, and refer to them as they.

   Don't assume that readers of a story are all of the same sex; write "you and your spouse" not "you and your wife"; write "when you brush your teeth in the morning" rather than "when you shave in the morning."
2. Condescension. Condescending terms are unacceptable. For instance:

   Don't call someone a "career girl" or "career woman"; name the woman's profession: Edith Smith, a lawyer.

   Don't refer to "the girls in the office"; refer to the secretaries, typists, clerks, stenographers or office staff (if the jobs are what you are referring to), or write "the women" (if you are referring to female employees).

   Don't call someone "a sweet young thing"; make it young woman, or girl (if she is under 18).
3. Description. One sex should not be described by physical attributes while the other is defined by profession or mental attributes. References to a man's or a woman's appearance or charm should be avoided when irrelevant; when relevant, such characteristics should be described in similar terms.

   Avoid: "Eleanor Britt, a striking blonde, is married to Michael Britt, a veteran broadcaster."

   Preferable: The Britts are an attractive couple. Michael is dark-haired and handsome and Eleanor is a striking blonde. Or: The Britts are respected in their fields; Eleanor is a musician and Michael is a lawyer.
4. Generic generalizations. Terms such as doctor and nurse include both men and women, and modified titles such as "woman doctor" and "male nurse" should not be

As discussed in Chapter 1, standards of taste are relative to the tone the publication projects. The style committee's job here is to assess the readership, discuss tone and set a policy on the use of obscenity and profanity both within and outside direct quotations (Box 2.8).

Polls and Surveys

The style committee should consider establishing a policy on news coverage of public opinion polls. The amount of weight an editor assigns to a poll can influence readers' interpretation of the results. The American public is so frequently canvassed by so many different organizations that the reliability and significance of any particular poll may be hard for readers to judge. Editors should consider the standards set by the National Council on Public Polls:

used. Words also should not be stereotyped, as in "a man-sized job" or "women's work." A gee-whiz attitude toward competent women is unacceptable, but breakthroughs in formerly all-male areas are legitimate news.

5. Generic pronouns. Avoid the use of he and she as generic pronouns, as in "The average American drinks his coffee black." Rather than change it to "his or her," it's preferable to rephrase to a plural construction: "Americans generally drink their coffee black." Even better, "Americans generally drink coffee black."
6. Inclusive and exclusive. When possible, use a term that includes both sexes to avoid unnecessary references to gender. The English language, however, should not be corrupted, nor should traditional repositories of the language, such as the Bible or Shakespeare, be rewritten.

   Specifically, mankind, not humankind, is the word used to define the human race, although humanity is also acceptable. Middleman is a term with a specific meaning in the language, although agent, processor, distributor or packager is acceptable.

   The generic, preferable term is police officer but, for individual males or females, policeman or policewoman is acceptable. This also applies to other occupational terms, such as member of Congress or congresswoman or congressman.

   Where the term tends to stereotype by sex, through either inclusion or exclusion, it should be avoided. Examples:

   Don't refer to "a five-man staff"; make it a "five-member staff" or "a staff of five."

   Don't refer to "men in the field" when you mean the representatives or agents, staff or personnel in the field.

   Don't refer to "the best man for the job"; make it the best person or candidate for the job.

   Don't refer to a "coed" when referring to a female college student. Make it female student.
7. Marital status. Irrelevant references to or unnecessary emphasis on a person's marital status is unacceptable. The number of children a person has should not be mentioned unless it is relevant to the story.
8. Parallel language. Comparable words should be used for men and women. Examples:

   Don't refer to "man and wife"; make it husband and wife or man and woman.

   Don't refer to "Madame Curie and Alexander Graham Bell"; make it Marie Curie and Alexander Graham Bell.

—*Newsday Stylebook*

Box 2.6

1. Who paid for the poll? Do the backers advocate a point of view relevant to the poll?
2. How recently was the poll conducted? Opinion swings can be volatile and quick.
3. How did the poll takers reach the respondents? If the poll was conducted by telephone, how did the poll takers compensate for the growing number of people who resist telephone solicitation, either by refusing to answer or by screening calls with answering machines?
4. How were the questions worded? Were they loaded to favor a particular outcome?
5. How were the respondents selected? Were voter registration lists used? Census data? Telephone books, from which unlisted numbers are excluded? Was care taken to ensure that the selection was random?

Words That Some May Find Offensive

Words, like people, can carry baggage. News writers and editors can hardly afford to ignore that fact regardless of their opinions about political correctness. Carelessly used, words can wound, and it is easy to give offense without intending to.

Sensitivity means seeking to understand and respect the perceptions of others. Full understanding is difficult, perhaps impossible, to achieve because one cannot shed one's background and don somebody else's like a new cloak. However, one can try.

Here are some terms worth thinking about:

African. No one is likely to be hurt when this term is applied to the people, languages or cultures of the continent. However, applying it to an individual simply because of skin color may be objectionable.

African-American. When it is necessary to mention race, many, but by no means all, prefer this term. Some favor "black."

Amazon. Stick to geography when using this term, which can characterize women as predators or as large.

American Indian. Many find this offensive because it is a European name for Native Americans. Others have trouble with "Native American" because it could technically be applied to anyone born in the United States. Besides, "American" is itself a European term stemming from the name of a Portuguese explorer. The best advice may be to use the proper tribal name if it is known. In no case, however, should one carelessly use such as words as "wampum," "warpath," "powwow," "tepee," "brave" or "squaw."

articulate. Describing someone as "articulate" may be intended as a compliment but can backfire if it is interpreted as a reference to the ability of a minority group to handle the English language.

banana. It may be interpreted as a slur upon Asian-Americans.

barracuda. When it does not refer to a species of fish, this can be a negative generalization implying lack of morality, often directed at forceful women.

beautiful. Bias is difficult to avoid when describing people as beautiful. It may be best to reserve this term for scenery and sunsets.

black. It is accepted by many as an adjective (*He is black*) but found objectionable as a noun (*There's a black*). Some prefer "African-American."

blue-haired. Older people may get steamed up over this one.

boy. When applied to an adult, this can be a fighting word.

burly. Some see a reference to ignorance in this term for a large, muscular man.

buxom. It may be regarded as a demeaning sexual reference.

Chicano. This term for Mexican-American was popular in the 1960s and 1970s but may offend some older people.

chief. The Kansas City Chiefs mean no disrespect, but the use of "chief" with a Native American motif strikes some as derisive and trivializing.

coconut. It may be interpreted as a slur upon Mexican-Americans.

community. When used in connection with a racial minority, it can imply a monolithic culture in which people act, think and vote in the same way. Obviously, there is no such thing.

credit to his/her race. This is unfortunate in any context.

deaf and dumb. The deaf are not dumb. Many prefer "speech impaired."

dear. Some may find it objectionable in sentences such as "He is a dear man" or "She is a dear."

female. Police reports tend to use gender as a noun, as in "Two females were apprehended," but when the media use similar language it seems insultingly impersonal, as if "women" would be inappropriate for some reason. As an adjective in phrases such as "female firefighter," the term can be insulting too, as a way of saying, "Here is a woman in what is normally a man's job."

feminine. Some women object to this term because it implies traits that might disqualify them from some jobs.

fried chicken. In some circumstances this can be a stereotypical allusion to the cuisine of black people.

fragile. When applied to a woman, this can be a stereotypical term associated with femininity.

full-figured. Only women are described this way, and many resent it.

geezer. Doddering, over-the-hill men like the authors see little humor in this term used only by immature youths.

gender-enders. Feminized forms such as "actress," "aviatrix," "comedienne," "executrix," "heroine," "poetess" and "starlet" were once common but now are seldom seen. Today's preferred terms are "actor," "aviator," "comedian," "executor," "hero," "poet" and "star." However, "actress" survives at Academy Award time. "Waitress" has been abandoned in favor of "server."

golden years. Ask somebody in the later years of life how idyllic it all is, and you're likely to get a blunt answer.

handicapped. A handicap is a disadvantage that stands in the way of achievement. A disability is a condition that makes some tasks difficult or impossible. "Disabled" is generally preferred over "handicapped" to refer to people who use wheelchairs or other devices to help them move around, but most of those people would prefer not to be characterized by a term that emphasizes what they can't do. They are likely to be insulted by "crippled" or "invalid."

Hispanic. It's widely used to refer to people whose ancestry is in countries where Spanish is the dominant language, but not all such people accept the term. Some prefer "Latino" or "Mexican-American."

homosexual. This is the correct term for both sexes. "Gay" refers only to men; "lesbian" refers only to women. There was a time when editors fought to preserve "gay" as a synonym for "lighthearted," but most have given up. In fact, the word is now unlikely to be read that way.

honey. Like "dear" and "sweetie," it has been used so often by men as a demeaning way to address women that is likely to be misinterpreted even when its purpose is endearment.

housewife. Although many women proudly use this term to describe themselves, others object to the gender reference. They prefer "homemaker," which can apply to either sex.

illegal alien. This is especially sensitive these days. "Undocumented" is less likely to raise hackles than "illegal," and "worker" or "resident" is worth considering in preference to "alien," which has been taken over as a UFO or sci-fi term.

inscrutable. People of European descent once considered all Asians inscrutable, which means hard to figure out. The term is now considered a slur by many Asian-Americans.

Box 2.7

Jap. It was used routinely and derisively to refer to the enemy in World War II. Today it is a racial slur.

Jew. When used as a verb, it's offensive.

jock. Even women athletes are sometimes characterized by this term, which implies powerful muscles and weak brain power.

leader. When combined with the name of a minority, it implies followers, who may not exist. People are not sheep. A "leader" speaks for himself or herself and probably some others, but no one can speak for an entire group. A better option might be "politician" or "activist."

man. It has long been used to refer to both men and women in situations where no better term is available. "Man's best friend," for example, wouldn't have the same impact if it became "people's best friend" or "an individual's best friend." However, the anger and resentment inspired by "the best man for the job" are understandable to everybody.

Mongoloid. It once was used to describe mentally impaired children and is now a word to be avoided in any context.

Negro. It is not only out of fashion but also a slur to many.

old maid. Beware of using this term for unpopped kernels at the bottom of a bowl of popcorn. It is stereotypical and archaic because it stems from an objectionable reference to an unmarried woman.

Oreo. Like "banana" and "coconut," this is a food term that has acquired a nasty taste in relation to race.

Oriental. Many find this an objectionable racial term and prefer Asian or Asian-American.

project. This has become a racial term, stemming from "public housing project." Instead of "he lives in a project," it might be less controversial to say he lives "in a development" or "in subsidized housing."

qualified minorities. This has been recognized as a catchword in affirmative action stories, implying that minorities are usually unqualified.

refugee. It is appropriate to refer to people who have fled oppression or persecution and are not yet settled as "refugees." Once they have become "residents," "refugees" is no longer correct.

retarded. This adjective, which means slow or backward in mental or emotional development, has lost support among those who work with mentally or emotionally impaired people because of its emphasis on what they cannot do instead of what they can do. "Challenged" is the most common substitute. As a noun, "retard" is offensive.

savages. It may be found in stories about American or African history. The peoples to whom it was applied may have seemed "savage" to European eyes but actually represented ancient cultures and in some cases advanced civilizations.

senile. What used to be called senility is now recognized as Alzheimer's disease, a disorder that strikes late in life but is not simply a symptom of old age. The disclosure that former president Ronald Reagan suffers from Alzheimer's and has difficulty recognizing old friends has drawn sobering attention to the problem. "Senile" should be avoided.

senior citizens. At what age does one enter this exclusive club? It's a touchy question, because some who may be so labeled because of their silver hair or other physical attributes will resist the honor. Surely no one under 65 should be called a senior citizen. Also touchy are "aged" and "elderly," which may be associated with uselessness and dependency. They are mild,

Box 2.7 (cont.)

however, when compared with "oldster," "matronly," "well-preserved," "codger," "coot," "geezer," "silver fox," "old-timer," "Pop" or "buzzard."

some of my best friends. People accused of racial bias have been known to respond with "Some of my best friends are (fill in the blank)." As a result, "some of my best friends" has become both a cliché and a "buzz" phrase signaling insincerity.

spec eds. It's short for "children in special education classes" and has become a sneer aimed at kids with disabilities.

swarthy. This reference to skin color is found in bad novels but should be shunned along with "yellow," "paleface," "redskin," "lily-white" and others too offensive to mention.

token. It means more than just "minority jobholder." A token is hired solely because of race, ethnicity or gender and is not qualified for the job.

vegetable. Beware of using it to describe someone incapable of caring for himself or herself.

wannabe. It's slang that cuts deeper than just "aspires to become." It can also mean outsider or mimic.

wheelchair. People who use wheelchairs are normally not lashed or handcuffed to them. Many drive cars and can walk with crutches, braces or other kinds of assistance. Franklin D. Roosevelt used a wheelchair but did not allow himself to be photographed in it, and when he appeared erect in public he was supported by braces and the arm of his son. He did not want to seem infirm. "Wheelchair-bound," "bound to a wheelchair" or "confined to a wheelchair" are inaccurate and demeaning.

without rhythm. A stereotype about whites.

woman. Lots of terms that once were routinely applied to women are no longer acceptable (if they ever were). Probably the worst example is "girl," which once meant any female, especially in old movies. Now it is appropriate only for those 17 and under. Others that won't fly include "sweet young thing," "gal," "dame," "lady," "little woman," "matronly," "pert," "petite," "foxy," "buxom," "fragile," "feminine," "stunning," "gorgeous," "statuesque" and "full-figured."

you (or those) people. Ross Perot ran into trouble with this one during his presidential campaign in 1992. Objections to it stem from the view that it turns minorities into outsiders who don't belong in the "in" group.

6. How large was the sample? What is the margin of error in projecting the results to a larger group?

The style committee may want to require that some or all of these questions be answered for readers whenever poll results are published.

Race

When is it appropriate to mention race in a news story? The traditional answer has been "when it is relevant," but the relevance of race is not always clear (Box 2.9).

Is it relevant when a member of a minority achieves some high office or award that is unusual, or a first, for his or her race?

A Policy on Obscenity

Our policy on the use of profanity, obscenity and blasphemy is based on the premise that *The Inquirer* should appeal to the widest possible audience. Unlike movies, whose rating system warns potential viewers of the kind of language they will be exposed to, newspapers should offer a G-rated product every day. It is true, of course, that society's attitudes are changing and that we now freely use some language that a few years ago was thought to be too frank. Still, there is a danger of being more tolerant than our audience as a whole; we should carefully monitor the use of profanity, obscenity and blasphemy and restrict it to extraordinary circumstances.

Central to any decision is this question: Is an important journalistic purpose served by the use of the questionable language? The harsher the language, the more important and serious our purpose must be. This means that we have to refrain from publishing some quotations that we ourselves would find funny; in the interest of simply entertaining our readers, we should not resort to language that might offend many of them. This is an area in which only the broadest sort of guidelines can apply. A word or phrase that may be used in one context may be entirely objectionable in another. When in doubt about whether any language is appropriate, ask for guidance. The practice of referring those decisions helps maintain uniform standards throughout the paper. The following guidelines are intended to help editors make decisions in this area.

The use of any questionable language is almost exclusively limited to quoted material. It should be rare indeed that our own writers employ it. Generally, if a news subject utters profanity, obscenity or blasphemy when no one is present but one or two reporters, we will not use it. The decision becomes more difficult when the number of listeners is larger and the personage of the speaker more important. When President Carter said in public of a potential campaign opponent, "I'll whip his ass," that was deemed to be a situation in which the verbatim quotation was justified.

Sometimes language that is not in itself profane, obscene or blasphemous might be objectionable on the ground of taste. On the other hand, we should not hesitate to write in clinical terms on matters pertaining to human anatomy, sex and excretory functions when relevant to the news. In most cases, when language is deleted from a quotation, an ellipsis will be inserted to indicate that something is missing.

Occasionally—and on approval of a ranking editor—it is permissible to suggest the word or phrase by using the first letter of the word followed by an em dash. The use of "bleep" and "bleeping" as substitutes for profanity is restricted to the sports pages. Most decisions concerning the use of questionable language should be resolved by departmental editors and copy chiefs. These line editors may determine when circumstances warrant the use of expletives such as "hell" and "damn." Line editors may also authorize the use of such terms as "goddamn," "son of a bitch" and "bastard" when the speaker is a reasonably important person, the audience is a fairly substantial one, or the quotation is in a long, serious piece in a section of the paper such as Review and Opinion or Inquirer Magazine. When the circumstances are not clear-cut, or if stronger language or a question of taste is involved, the executive editor or managing editor must be consulted. In the absence of these editors, the editor in charge must be consulted. Hard-core obscenities such as "s—t," "f—k," "p—s," "c————r," "mother———" and their variations may be used only by express approval of the executive editor or the managing editor.

—*The Philadelphia Inquirer*

Box 2.8

A Policy on Race

The race of a person in the news won't be reported unless it is clearly relevant to the story or is part of a detailed physical description. If a strong case cannot be made for mentioning race, it should be omitted. Racially and ethnically derogatory terms are to be treated as obscenities; such a term should be spelled as an initial followed by hyphens, and be used only in quoted material, when it is essential to a story, and with approval of a managing editor. Photos or art work that foster racial stereotypes are to be avoided unless there is justifiable news value. In such cases, a supervising editor should be consulted. . . .

—*Detroit Free Press*

Box 2.9

Is it relevant when social unrest, or a riot, has occurred in an area inhabited primarily by people of one race?

Is it relevant when it may provide the reader with insights into the political or cultural issue that is the topic of the story—for example, public housing, welfare, public or private schools?

Is it relevant when the outcome of an election may be influenced by unorganized but clear racial groupings?

Is it relevant in a crime story even though mention of it may tend to perpetuate stereotypes about the criminal tendencies of a racial group?

Is it relevant in a crime story if the suspect is still at large and considered dangerous, even though little or nothing is known about the suspect except his or her race?

A COMPENDIUM OF STYLE

Stylebooks of the past were relatively simple. They contained rules on abbreviations, capitalization, numbers, punctuation, prefixes and suffixes and spelling. Policy guidelines were largely left unwritten.

The following compendium of style is designed to resemble the stylebooks of old. Associated Press variations from standard usage are noted. Punctuation guidelines will be found in Chapter 3.

ABBREVIATIONS

1. **Addresses.** Abbreviate street, avenue, boulevard in specific addresses (remember STAB). *1701 A St., 205 N. Second St., 3301 S. 29th Ave., 6602 Martin Luther King Blvd.* If no specific address is given, do not use abbreviations. *Ninth Street, Martin Luther King Boulevard.* Do not capitalize "streets" when identifying intersections. *13th and O streets.*
2. **Avoid "alphabet soup."** This is a type of writing in which a key term, such as the name of an organization, is mentioned once and thereafter is referred

to by a set of initials. Example: *The Southeast Compact Import Policy Committee (SCIPC) voted 3-0 to recommend that the Central Interstate Low-Level Radioactive Waste Compact (CILRWC) be allowed access to a low-level radioactive waste disposal site at Barnwell, S.C.*

Abbreviations are a convenient way of saving space, but they should not be allowed to impede reader understanding. The names of most organizations, companies and government agencies should be spelled out on first mention and shortened after that but never abbreviated. *The American Legion, the legion; the Chamber of Commerce, the chamber; the Department of Agriculture, the department.* Some abbreviations are widely recognized. *ABC, AIDS, AWOL, AT&T, MIA, POW, CIA, FBI.* They may be used without full identification.

3. **Companies.** Abbreviate "company" and "corporation" when either word appears at the end of the name of a company or corporation. *Ford Motor Co., General Motors Corp.* Do not abbreviate if the word appears someplace other than the end of the name. *Aluminum Corporation of America, the Corporation for Public Broadcasting.*
4. **Dates.** Abbreviate Jan., Feb., Aug., Sept., Oct., Nov., Dec. when used with a specific date. *Pearl Harbor was attacked on Dec. 7, 1941.* When no specific date is given, do not abbreviate. *The United States entered World War II in December 1941.* Never abbreviate March, April, May, June, July.
5. **Names.** Abbreviate Jr. and Sr. when they are part of a name. *The singer was Hank Williams Jr.*
6. **Nations.** Do not abbreviate the names of nations with the single exception of the United States, which is abbreviated as U.S. when used as an adjective. *U.S. government.*

   U.S.S.R. may be used for the former Union of Socialist Soviet Republics.

   United Nations is abbreviated as U.N. when used as an adjective.
7. **States.** The U.S. Postal Service adopted a set of abbreviations that represent each state by a pair of initials without periods (AK for Alaska, for example). In the media the standard abbreviations are preferred because they are more familiar and easier to decipher than the artificial two-letter versions (MI could be Michigan, Minnesota, Missouri or Mississippi).

   Abbreviate state names when they follow city names. *Madison, Wis.; Albany, N.Y.*

Standard abbreviations are:

Ala.	Kan.	Nev.	R.I.
Ariz.	Ky.	N.H.	S.C.
Ark.	La.	N.J.	S.D.
Calif.	Md.	N.M.	Tenn.
Colo.	Mass.	N.Y.	Vt.
Conn.	Mich.	N.C.	Va.
Del.	Minn.	N.D.	Wash.
Fla.	Miss.	Okla.	W.Va.
Ga.	Mo.	Ore.	Wis.
Ill.	Mont.	Pa.	Wyo.
Ind.	Neb.		

8. Titles. Abbreviate the following titles before a name:

Title	Abbreviation
Admiral	Adm.
Brigadier General	Brig. Gen.
Captain	Capt.
Colonel	Col.
Commander	Comdr.
Corporal	Cpl.
Doctor	Dr.
General	Gen.
Governor	Gov.
Lieutenant	Lt.
Lieutenant junior grade (U.S. Navy)	Lt.j.g.
Major	Maj.
Private first class	Pfc.
Private	Pvt.
Representative	Rep.
the Reverend	the Rev.
Senator	Sen.
Sergeant	Sgt.
Specialist (U.S. Army)	Spec. 4 (5, 6, 7)

All other titles are spelled out in full in every use.

CAPITALIZATION

Follow a "down style," in which only proper nouns, certain titles preceding names, full names of institutions and organizations and composition titles (names of literary, artistic and musical works) are "up" (capitalized). The preference is for avoiding capitals unless there is a specific style rule calling for an exception.

1. **Composition titles.** Capitalize the principal words in the titles of academic courses, artworks, books, films, lectures, newspapers, magazines, operas and other musical works, plays, poems, radio and television programs and speeches. Always capitalize the first word in the title, including the articles "a," "an" and "the." All other words in the title are capitalized except prepositions of fewer than four letters and the articles. *History of Journalism; The Thinker; Gone With the Wind; The Good, the Bad and the Ugly; Ostrich or Eagle: Comments on U.S. Foreign Policy; The New York Times; Time magazine* ("magazine" is not part of the name); *Beethoven's Fifth Symphony; Death of a Salesman; The Midnight Ride of Paul Revere; I'll Fly Away; the State of the Union Address.*
2. **Governmental units.** Capitalize their full names. *Congress, the Senate, the House of Representatives, the House Ways and Means Committee, the St. Petersburg City Council, the Virginia House of Delegates, the Lancaster County Commission.* Capitalize City Council, School Board, County Board and similar terms when they refer to specific governmental units. Lowercase generic

terms that refer to governmental units. *the council, the board, the committee, the commission.*

3. **Institutions and organizations.** Capitalize their formal names. *the American Automobile Association, the Ford Motor Co., General Motors Corp., the University of Pennsylvania, the University of Nebraska College of Dentistry, Kiwanis, the Society of Friends, the Presbyterian Church (U.S.A.).* Lowercase generic terms referring to the formal titles. *the association, the company, the corporation, the university, the college, the club, the society, the church.*
4. **Proper nouns.** Capitalize the specific names of people, places and things. *Albert Einstein, the United States of America, Ford Mustang, the Republican Party, the Mississippi River, Pike's Peak, Main Street, South Dakota.* Lowercase generic terms referring to proper nouns. *the scientist, the nation, the automobile, the party, the river, the mountain, the street, the state.*
5. **Titles.** Capitalize formal titles when they precede the name. *President Clinton, former President Richard Nixon, Sen. Edward M. Kennedy, former Sen. Barry Goldwater, Attorney General Robert F. Kennedy.* Lowercase all titles when they stand alone or follow the name. *the president, the former president, the senator, the attorney general, the university chancellor.*
6. **Trademarks.** Registered trademarks are zealously guarded by their owners, who protect their interests by insisting on capitalization. Trademark holders whose trade names become generic terms, such as "heroin" and "thermos," lose their rights. Xerox protected its name through strenuous efforts, and Frisbee, a trademark for a brand of flying disk, has resisted erosion to the point where an errant newspaper once received a carton of disks, all labeled "st. petersburg times." Even professional titles, such as Realtor, can be registered trademarks.

   Trademarks are capitalized and should be used only to refer to the appropriate brand-name articles. *Adrenalin, Aqua Lung, Bakelite, Band-Aid, Benzedrine, Bromo Seltzer, Chemical Mace, Dumpster.*

NUMBERS

In general, spell out one through nine and use figures for 10 and above. The exceptions to this rule are numerous:

1. **Acts and scenes.** *Act 1, Scene 3.*
2. **Addresses.** *She lived at 301 Ninth St., Apartment 8.*
3. **Ages.** *The girl was 5 years old. The girl, 5, was starting school.*
4. **Aircraft designations.** *The jet was an F4 Phantom. The DC-6 took off.* But *The president's plane is Air Force One.*
5. **Betting odds.** *The horse won the race despite 3–2 odds.*
6. **Channels.** *The show was on Channel 5.*
7. **Chapters.** *The fundamentals of editing are discussed in Chapter 1.*
8. **Courses.** *He was taking History 1 and English 2.*
9. **Court decisions.** *The Supreme Court ruled 5–4.*
10. **Court names.** *2nd District Court, the 8th U.S. Circuit Court of Appeals.*
11. **Dates.** *His birth date was Oct. 5, 1972.*
12. **Decimals.** *The house was 1.2 miles from the main road.*

13. **Dimensions.** *He was 5 feet 10 inches tall. The 6-foot-5 left tackle weighed 295 pounds. The doorway was less than 3 feet wide. The storm left 2 inches of snow. The rug was 9 by 12. The board was a 2 by 4.*
14. **Districts.** *He represented the 5th Congressional District.*
15. **Highways.** *He followed U.S. 1 to Mount Vernon.*
16. **Large numbers** (more than 1 million). *China has a population of more than 1 billion. About 2.4 million people live in the metropolitan area.*
17. **Money.** *She owed him 5 cents. The item was priced at $3. The City Council budgeted $3 million for road repairs.*
18. **Military units.** *He was assigned to the 1st Infantry Division.*
19. **No.** *He picked No. 5 on the betting card.*
20. **Pages.** *The* Times *put the story on page 1.*
21. **Percentages.** *The consumer price index increased 0.2 percent. The unemployment rate is about 7 percent.*
22. **Proportions.** *To make my breakfast, mix 2 parts water with 1 part oatmeal.*
23. **Scores.** *The Jets beat the Dolphins 7–0.*
24. **Sizes.** *His shoes were size 9.*
25. **Speeds.** *He cruised through the parking lot at 5 miles per hour.*
26. **Temperatures.** *The temperature was 9 degrees Fahrenheit, and the wind chill was minus 4.*
27. **Votes.** *The council voted 5–4 to buy three new police cruisers.*

PREFIXES AND SUFFIXES

all- Usually hyphenated: *all-American, all-around, all-out, all-over, all-clear, all-star.* But *all right.*

anti- Usually solid: *antiaircraft, antibias, antibiotic, antibody, antibusing, antichrist, anticlimax, antidepressant, antidote, anti-dumping, antifreeze, antihistamine, anti-inflation, anti-intellectual, anti-Jewish, antilabor, antisemitic, antislavery, antisocial, antitank, antitrust, antivenin, antiwar.* The Associated Press has adopted a style that varies from this standard. In AP style, anti- is usually hyphenated: *anti-aircraft, anti-bias, anti-labor, anti-slavery, anti-social, anti-war.*

bi- Usually solid: *biannual* (twice a year), *biennial* (every two years), *bifocal, bilateral, bilingual, bimonthly, bipartisan.*

by- Usually solid: *bygone, bylaw, byline, bypass, byproduct, bystreet, byway, byword.* But *by-election.*

co- Usually solid: *coauthor, co-chairman, codefendant, coequal, coexist, cooperate, coordinate, cosigner, costar, co-worker* (keep out "cow"). The Associated Press hyphenates words that "indicate occupation or status," including: *co-author, co-defendant, co-signer, co-star.*

de- Solid in standard formations: *debar, debrief.* Hyphenated in unusual formations: *de-gum, de-hair.*

-fold Solid after a non-hyphenated number: *thirtyfold, hundredfold.* Hyphenated after a hyphenated number: *seventy-five-fold.*

-goer Usually solid: *churchgoer, partygoer.*

-holder Usually solid: *officeholder, penholder.*

in- Usually solid: *indeterminate, inroad.* Hyphenated in *in-depth, in-law.*

-in Hyphenated: *break-in, cave-in, sit-in, stand-in, walk-in, write-in.*

-long Solid: *daylong, lifelong, monthlong, yearlong.*

mid- Solid unless it precedes a proper noun: *midair, mid-Atlantic, midday, Mideast, midland, midlife, midocean, mid-Pacific, midterm, Midwest, midwinter.*

mini- Solid: *miniskirt, minivan.*

non- Hyphenated: non-aligned, non-restrictive.

off- Usually solid: *offbeat, offhand, offset, offshore, offside, offstage.* But *off-Broadway, off-center, off-color, off-key, off-limits, off-line, off-white.*

-off Solid: *blastoff, cutoff, layoff, payoff, playoff, standoff, takeoff.*

on- Usually solid: *oncoming, ongoing, onshore, onside, onstage.* But *on-line, on-site.*

-on Hyphenated: *come-on, pull-on.*

out- Solid: *outdate, outfield, outfox, output.*

-out Nouns are usually solid: *fallout, flameout, pullout, walkout, washout.* But *cop-out, fade-out, hide-out.* Verbs are two words: *cop out, fade out, fall out, flame out, hide out, pull out, walk out, wash out.*

over- Solid: *overconfident, overdo, overestimate, overextend, overfly, overrate, override, overrule, overthrow.*

post- Usually solid in "after" sense: *postdate, postgraduate, postmeridian, postoperative, postwar.* But *post-mortem.* Solid in postal sense: *postcard, post-paid.*

pre- Solid in regular formations: *prerecord, preregistration, preschool.* Hyphenated in coined or unusual formations: *pre-convention, pre-dawn, pre-holiday.* Hyphenated before words beginning with "e" or a capital letter: *pre-eminent, pre-Civil War.*

pro- Hyphenated: *pro-choice, pro-labor, pro-life, pro-war.*

re- Hyphenated before "e": *re-emerge, re-enroll.* Hyphenated before other vowels if combination is confusing: *re-own, re-urge.* But *rearm, readmit.* Hyphenated if necessary to avoid confusion with another word: *re-count, recount, re-cover, recover, re-creation, recreation, re-lease, release.*

semi- Solid: *semicolon, semitrailer, semiweekly.*

trans- Solid: *transatlantic, transcontinental, transoceanic, transpacific.* The Associated Press prefers *trans-Atlantic, trans-Pacific.*

un- Solid: *unjustified, unnoticed.* But *un-American.*

under- Solid: *underestimate, undervalue.*

up- Solid: *upbeat, upbraid, upcoming, update, updraft, upfront, uphold, upkeep, upright, upstage.*

-up Usually solid: *buildup, checkup, cleanup, coverup, crackup, holdup, lineup, makeup, setup, windup.* But *call-up, close-up, grown-up, mix-up, mock-up, push-up, runner-up, shake-up, tie-up.*

wide- Hyphenated: *wide-angle, wide-awake, wide-eyed, wide-open, wide-screen.* But *widespread.*

-wide Solid: *citywide, statewide, nationwide, continentwide, worldwide.*

-wise Solid: *clockwise, otherwise.*

SPELLING

The following are the preferred spellings of some commonly misspelled words.

A

able-bodied
aboveboard
absent-minded
ad-lib
admissible
ad nauseam
adviser
advisory
aesthetic
air-condition
airmail
airtight
air traffic controller
à la carte
à la king
à la mode
align
allotted
all right
also-ran
amok
ashcan
ashtray
ax

B

ball carrier
ballclub
ball player
ball-point pen
barbecue
barbiturate
barrel-chested
bellwether
best-seller
bigwig
broccoli

C

cactuses
Caesarean section
canceled
changeable
chauffeur
cigarette
citywide
claptrap
cleanup
clear-cut
coattails
colorblind
combated
commitment
compact disc
cover-up
cure-all
curtain raiser

D

defendant
dietitian
disc jockey
disk

E

embarrass
en route
exaggerate
executor
exercise (work out)
exorcise (banish)
expelled
extolled
eyestrain
eyewitness

F

facade
fact-finding
fallout
far-flung
far-off
far-ranging
farsighted
Ferris wheel
ferryboat
fiord
flack
flak
flare-up
flimflammed
flip-flop
floodwaters
fluorescent
flutist
folk singer
forbade
forgo
forsook
fortuneteller
forward
frame-up
free-for-all
free-lance
freewheeling
freeze-dried
french fries
front-runner
fulfilled
full-time
furlough
fuselage
fusillade

G

gauge
gaiety
game plan
gamy
getaway
get-together
ghettos
girlfriend
glamour
gobbledygook
go-between
go-go
goodbye
groundskeeper
groundswell
grown-up
G-string
gubernatorial
guerrilla
gung-ho
guru
gypsy moth

H

hallelujah
halos
handmade
handpicked
hangover
hanky-panky
harass
harebrained
headlong
head-on
health care
hearsay
heaven
heliport
helter-skelter
hemorrhage
hemorrhoid
hideaway
hi-fi
high-tech
hocus-pocus
hodgepodge
ho-hum
holdup
homemade
horsepower
hurly-burly
hush-hush

I

impelled
implausible
indexes
indiscriminately
innocuous
innuendo

impostor
inasmuch as
incurred
indispensable
in-law
inoculate
insofar as

J

judgment
jukebox

K

ketchup
knickknack
kidnapped
know-how
kowtow

L

lager
lamebrain
lame duck
lawsuit
left-handed
legerdemain
letup
liaison
life-size
lifestyle
lifetime
lift-off
lightning
likable
limousine
livable
long-term
longtime
lowercase

M

makeup
malarkey
manageable
marketbasket
marketplace
meager
medieval
melee
mementos
memos
memorandums
menswear
merry-go-round
middleman
minuscule
mix-up
mock-up
moneymaker
monthlong
moped
mop-up
mosquitoes
mothers-in-law

N

naive
narrow-minded
nationwide
negligee
newsstand
nightclub
nighttime
nit-picking
nitty-gritty
no-man's-land
nowadays

O

oases
occurred
oceangoing
oddsmaker
officeholder
OK'd
old-time
one-sided
overall

P

paddy wagon
pantsuit
peddler
pell-mell
potatoes
pothole

pantyhose
paralleled
pari-mutuel
parishioner
part-time
passers-by
pasteurize
patrolled
payload
peacekeeping
peacemaker
peace offering
peacetime
permissible
phenomena
pianos
picnicked
pigeon
pileup
pipeline
pleaded
plow
policymaker
politicking
pooh-pooh
predominantly
privilege
propeller
prophecy
prostate gland
provisos
pullback
pullout
push-button
push-up
putout
pygmy

Q

questionnaire
quick-witted

R

raccoon
reconnaissance
recurred
redhead
red-handed
red-hot
re-elect
referable
referendums
rescission
resistible
restaurateur
riffraff
rip-off
rock 'n' roll
roll call
roly-poly
roundup
runners-up
running mate
rush hour

S

saboteur
sacrilegious
salable
salvos
sandbag
sandwich
sanitariums
scurrilous
second-guess
second-rate
seesaw
sellout
send-off
serviceable
setup
shake-up
shape-up
shirt-sleeves
shoeshine
shut-in
shutoff
shutout
sightseeing
single-handedly
sisters-in-law
sit-down
sit-in
sizable
skillful
sledgehammer
sleight of hand
slowdown
slumlord
slush fund
small-arms fire
small-business person
smashup
smolder
springtime
stadiums
stand-in
standoff
standout
states' rights
statewide
station wagon
steppingstone
stifling
stool pigeon
stopgap
storyteller
straitjacket
strikebreaker
strong-arm
strong-willed
subpoenaed
successor

shopworn
shortchange
short-lived
showcase
showoff
shutdown
soft-spoken
soliloquy
spaceship
speechmaker
speedup
spilled
sunbathe
supersede
swastika
sweatshirt
syllabuses

T

tablecloth
tailspin
tailwind
take-home pay
takeoff
takeout
takeover
takeup
tattletale
teammate
teenager
telecast
telltale
tenderhearted
tenfold
threesome
throwaway
tidbit
tying
tie-in
tie-up
tiptop
titleholder
tobaccos
toward
trade-in
trade-off
trafficking
transferred
traveled
travelogue
trigger-happy
tryout
T-shirt
tuneup

U

ukulele
under way
upside down
U-turn

V

vacuum
vendor
vice versa
videotape
vied
V-neck
volleys
voodoo
vote-getter

W

walk-up
warhead
warlike
warlord
wartime
washed-up
wastebasket
weak-kneed
weather vane
weekend
weeklong
weirdo
well-being
well-to-do
well-wishers
wheelchair
wheeler-dealer
whereabouts
wherever
white-collar
whitewash
wholehearted
whole-wheat
wigwag
wildlife
wind-swept
windup
wingspan
word-of-mouth
word processing
workday
work force
working class
workout
workweek
worldwide
worn-out
worshiped
worthwhile
wrongdoing

X-ray
year-end
yearlong
yesterday
yuletide
zeros
zigzag

BIBLIOGRAPHY AND ADDITIONAL READINGS

Bremner, John. *Words on Words.* Columbia University Press. 1980.

Copperud, Roy. *American Usage and Style: The Consensus.* Van Nostrand Reinhold. 1980.

Stylebooks of The Associated Press. *The Los Angeles Times, the Miami Herald, Newsday, The New York Times, the St. Petersburg Times, U.S. News & World Report.*

Wilhoit, G. Cleveland, and David H. Weaver. *Newsroom Guide to Polls and Surveys.* Indiana University Press. 1990.

Chapter 3

SMOOTH SENTENCES AND TROUBLESOME WORDS

BUTCHERED SYNTAX

"Throw Momma from the Train" was the title of a 1987 movie comedy that no doubt drew inspiration from a popular song:

Throw Momma from the train a kiss, a kiss . . .

This line of butchered syntax was an ethnic joke ridiculing a manner of speech in which German patterns are imposed on English sentences. The result of such linguistic mingling is always awkward and sometimes ludicrous. Each language has its own rhythms and sequences, which are programed at birth or learned in the cradle by native speakers. Even for native speakers, however, the ability to write smooth English sentences does not come easily. It takes hard work and practice. Experienced journalists can be guilty of crafting an occasional "throw Momma from the train" sort of sentence, like this one taken from the front page of a major newspaper:

> Officers went to the man's house by tracing a license plate number on the car in which the man who shot at Bell allegedly sped away. Bell later identified the man's car as the one in which the shooter was in.

The editor's job is to tighten it up and smooth it out without changing the meaning:

> Officers went to the man's house after tracing the license number of the alleged gunman's escape car. Bell later identified the man's car as the same vehicle.

In the next example, it is unclear whether the president or Congress will avoid confronting the Democrats:

> WASHINGTON—In his State of the Union address, the president is expected to challenge Congress to act on the economy without criticizing or directly confronting the Democrats.

A revision is necessary to make the sentence clearer and more easily understood:

> WASHINGTON—In his State of the Union address, the president is expected to avoid criticizing or directly confronting the Democrats as he challenges Congress to act on the economy.

THE PARTS OF SPEECH

Building a sentence is like building anything else: the parts must be put together in the proper order. The parts have names, and while it is possible to do the job without learning the names, the names are necessary to any discussion of method.

Every word has one of nine labels:

1. Noun
2. Verb
3. Pronoun
4. Adjective
5. Adverb
6. Preposition
7. Conjunction
8. Article
9. Interjection

In English a word may have more than one definition and thus more than one label, but only one label is correct each time the word is used. The label defines the role the word plays in the sentence, and each word can play only one role at a time.

THE NOUN

A noun is the name of a person, place or thing. "Thing" is broadly defined to include abstractions such as "thought" and "idea."

A common noun is a general term, such as *man* or *dog,* and is not capitalized.

A proper noun is a specific name, such as *Albert Einstein* or *Xerox Corp.,* and is capitalized.

Nouns

Police and others talked to a 13-year-old **boy** after he was held hostage briefly by **a gunman** who later shot his **mother** in their **home.**

THE VERB

A verb takes action: *says, sews, shoots.*

A transitive verb acts on something, which is its object. (*Acts on* is the verb. *Something* is the object.)

An intransitive verb acts independently. (*Acts* is the verb. There is no object.)

A linking, or copulative, verb expresses identity between words. *John is a bus driver.* (*John* is a proper noun, and *bus driver* is a noun identifying him by his occupation. *Is* links them.) *He is tired.* (*He* is a pronoun, and *tired* is an adjective describing *he. Is* links them.) Besides the forms of to be, some common linking verbs are become, seem, smell, look, grow, feel, get, sound, appear, taste.

Verbs

Police and others **talked** to a 13-year-old boy after he **was held** hostage briefly by a gunman who later **shot** his mother in their home.

THE PRONOUN

A pronoun substitutes for (*pro*) a noun, which is called the antecedent. *John drives* ***his*** *car.* (*John* is the antecedent of *his.*)

A personal pronoun takes the place of the name of a person. ***I*** *drive* **my** *car.* ***You*** *drive* ***your*** *car.* ***She*** *drives* ***her*** *car.*

A relative pronoun (who, whom, which, that) introduces extra or identifying information about a noun. *The woman* **who** *wrote that book is dead. The lawn mower,* **which** *is in the garage, is broken. The plane* **that** *dropped the bomb was a B-52.*

An interrogative pronoun (who, which, what) introduces a question. ***What*** *are we having for lunch?* (The antecedent of *what* is the answer to the question.)

A demonstrative pronoun (this, that, these, those) points something out. ***This*** *is the book you are assigned to read.*

An indefinite pronoun (each, all, everyone, either, neither, one, somebody, whoever) has no definite antecedent. Indefinite pronouns are sometimes the antecedents of other pronouns. ***Each*** *of the students brought his or her book to class.*

A reflexive pronoun (formed by adding self) refers action back to its antecedent. *The road curved sharply, twisting back upon* ***itself.***

A type of reflexive pronoun, the intensive pronoun, adds emphasis. *I'll do it* ***myself.***

Pronouns

Police and **others** talked to a 13-year-old boy after **he** was held hostage briefly by a gunman **who** later shot **his** mother in **their** home.

THE ADJECTIVE

An adjective modifies a noun or pronoun. A modifier changes a word by describing or limiting it. *He drives an* ***ugly, battered*** *car. I broke* ***three*** *eggs.*

Adjectives

Police and others talked to a **13-year-old** boy after he was held **hostage** briefly by a gunman who later shot his mother in their home.

THE ADVERB

An adverb modifies a verb or an adjective, but never a noun or pronoun. *He drives a* ***badly*** *battered car. I sing* ***poorly.*** *She sings* ***well.***

Adverbs

Police and others talked to a 13-year-old boy **after** he was held hostage **briefly** by a gunman who **later** shot his mother in their home.

THE PREPOSITION

A preposition combines with a noun or pronoun, which is its object, to form a phrase. ***about*** *the subject,* ***after*** *the game,* ***against*** *all odds,* ***among*** *the spectators,* ***around*** *the mountain,* ***at*** *the lectern,* ***before*** *nightfall,* ***behind*** *the eight ball,* ***below*** *par,* ***beside*** *herself,* ***between*** *the goalposts,* ***beyond*** *the horizon,* ***by*** *morning,* ***down*** *the slide,* ***for*** *the people,* ***from*** *the summit,* ***in*** *the street,* ***inside*** *the house,* ***into*** *the forest,* ***like*** *wildfire,* ***of*** *the people,* ***on*** *the table,* ***outside*** *the house,* ***over*** *the hurdle,* ***to*** *the goal line,* ***toward*** *the summit,* ***under*** *fire,* ***up*** *the slope,* ***upon*** *the roof,* ***within*** *the airliner.*

Prepositions

Police and others talked **to** a 13-year-old boy after he was held hostage briefly **by** a gunman who later shot his mother **in** their home.

THE CONJUNCTION

A conjunction (and, but, for, nor, or, so, whereas, yet) connects or joins words and other elements of a sentence.

Conjunction

Police **and** others talked to a 13-year-old boy after he was held hostage briefly by a gunman who later shot his mother in their home.

THE ARTICLE

Articles (a, an, the) are short adjectives used to make a noun definite (the) or indefinite (a, an).

Articles

Police and others talked to **a** 13-year-old boy after he was held hostage briefly by **a** gunman who later shot his mother in their home.

THE INTERJECTION

An interjection is an exclamation, often expressing astonishment, that stands apart from the structure of a sentence. ***Ouch!*** *That hurts.* ***Yes,*** *I'm ready.* ***Oh,*** *I see.*

THE ELEMENTS OF SENTENCE STRUCTURE

A sentence is a statement that contains a subject and a verb and ends in a period, question mark or exclamation point. A good sentence is a smooth, clear, coherent statement that makes sense. Editors are frequently called on to convert the former into the latter.

THE SUBJECT

The noun or pronoun that initiates or directs the action of the verb is the subject. *The* ***window*** *broke. The* ***street*** *is made of asphalt. My* ***heart*** *is beating rapidly.*

Subjects

Police and others talked to a 13-year-old boy after **he** was held hostage briefly by a gunman **who** later shot his mother in their home.

THE OBJECT

The noun or pronoun that receives or absorbs the action of the verb is the object. *The football broke the* ***window.*** *His knee struck the* ***pavement.*** *You are breaking my* ***heart.***

Objects

Police and others talked to **a 13-year-old boy** after he was held hostage briefly by **a gunman** who later shot **his mother** in their home.

THE PHRASE

A group of words that does not contain a subject-verb combination is a phrase. *in the room, driving down the street, has been gone for three years.*

Phrases

Police and others talked **to a 13-year-old boy** after he was held hostage briefly **by a gunman** who later shot his mother **in their home.**

THE CLAUSE

A group of words that does contain a subject-verb combination is a clause. *who works at the grain elevator*

A clause that makes a complete statement is an independent clause. *My brother lives on Main Street.*

A clause that makes an incomplete statement is a dependent clause. *who is younger than I.*

Independent Clause

Police and others talked to a 13-year-old boy after he was held hostage briefly by a gunman who later shot his mother in their home.

Dependent Clauses

Police and others talked to a 13-year-old boy (1) **after he was held hostage briefly by a gunman** (2) **who later shot his mother in their home.**

THE SENTENCE

A group of words that contains at least one independent clause is a sentence. *My brother, who lives on Main Street, works at the grain elevator.*

A group of words that does not contain at least one independent clause is a sentence fragment. *My brother, who lives on Main Street.*

Complex Sentence

Police and others talked to a 13-year-old boy after he was held hostage briefly by a gunman who later shot his mother in their home.

TYPES OF SENTENCES

A simple sentence contains one independent clause. *The locomotive smashed into the truck at the crossing.*

A compound sentence contains two or more independent clauses. *The locomotive smashed into the truck, and 14 freight cars were derailed.*

A complex sentence contains one independent clause and at least one dependent clause. *The locomotive, whose engineer had fallen asleep, smashed into the truck at the crossing.*

A compound-complex sentence contains two or more independent clauses and at least one dependent clause. *The locomotive, whose engineer had fallen asleep, smashed into the truck at the crossing; and 14 freight cars were derailed.*

The type of sentence that is most effective in media writing is the subject-verb-object (SVO) combination. Verbs in active voice are preferred. *The locomotive demolished the truck at the crossing, and 14 freight cars tumbled from the tracks.*

PRINCIPLES OF SENTENCE STRUCTURE

1. The elements of the sentence should show a clear relationship to one another. Journalists are sometimes under pressure to clutter a sentence with too many facts because a complicated story has many facets to be covered. The following lead is from Oct. 25, 1989:

> BOSTON—Outrage grew Wednesday over the murder of a pregnant suburban lawyer and the shooting of her husband, while their baby born by Caesarean section struggled for survival.

Unless the reader knows the background of the case, the relationship of the first part of the sentence to the second part is unclear. The sentence appears to be a grab bag of facts, assembled no more carefully than this one: *Although Jack detests anchovies, he walks to work and loves to feed the birds.*

Carefully crafted sentences have cohesion and symmetry, like visual art:

I like Janet, but Alice talks too much.

The quarterback went to the left, and his blockers went to the right.

Although the food was awful, the conversation was good.

Often a cluttered sentence can be reshaped and clarified by separating the diverse elements into separate thoughts.

> BOSTON—Outrage grew Wednesday over the murder of a pregnant suburban lawyer and the shooting of her husband. Their baby, taken from the dead woman's womb by Caesarean section, struggled for survival.

Non Sequitur

Original
Although the council members were drenched with rain when they arrived, the City Council voted 10-3 to buy 15 new police cruisers at its December meeting.

Edited
The City Council members were drenched with rain when they arrived at their December meeting. They voted 10-3 to buy 15 new police cruisers.

2. The arrangement of the modifiers should leave no room for confusion or erroneous interpretations.

He wrote to the woman from Kansas City. (Was he writing from Kansas City, or was the woman from Kansas City?)

There is a woman on the bus from Kansas City. (Was the bus or the woman from Kansas City?)

The woman was identified as the one who was abducted by the officer. (Did the officer do the identifying or the abducting?)

The man was found murdered by his parents in his home. (Was he found by his parents or murdered by them?)

Muddling Modifier

Original
The Academic Senate voted yesterday to table a resolution that opposes additional budget cuts until its next meeting.

Edited
The Academic Senate voted yesterday to table until its next meeting a resolution that opposes additional budget cuts.

3. No modifier should be left to dangle. As explained in Chapter 1, every modifier must have an expressed word to modify. The modifier should be placed where its relationship to the word is clear.

Wrong: *Leaving town, the houses become fewer and farther apart.*
Right: *Leaving town, one sees the houses becoming fewer and farther apart.*

Wrong: *After scrubbing the floor, the furniture was dusted.*
Right: *After scrubbing the floor, he dusted the furniture.*

Wrong: *In order to be a good quarterback, the defense must be carefully studied.*
Right: *To be a good quarterback, one must study the defense carefully.*

Wrong: *While driving to Omaha, my car broke down.*
Right: *While I was driving to Omaha, my car broke down.*

Dangling Modifier

Original
Working with bloodhounds, the trail led police to a house at the corner of Cypress and Lincoln streets.

Edited
Working with bloodhounds, police followed the trail to a house at Cypress and Lincoln streets.

4. The relationships of modifiers in series should be unmistakable. Modifiers may act independently *(the old, battered car),* or the first may modify the second *(the dark green car),* or the first may modify the combination of the second modifier and the noun *(a thick science book),* or the modifiers may combine to form a unit, which itself becomes a modifier *(a Bible-school student).*

When the modifiers act independently, they should be joined by a comma or a conjunction.

happy but tired workers

weary, penniless men

a long and pensive look

air, sea or land transportation

When they form a unit, they should be joined by a hyphen, particularly where confusion is possible.

a high-school teacher (the school, not the teacher, is high)

a wicked-witch costume (the witch, not the costume, is wicked)

a clean-water bill (the water, not the bill, is clean)

When an adverb ending in "ly" modifies an adjective, a hyphen should never be used.

a highly motivated schoolteacher

a badly battered car

a poorly planned attack (but a *well-planned attack*)

Multiple Modifiers

A small, nearly bursting thermometer lay on the 10-inch insulated steam pipe.

5. Modifiers should not "squint." When a modifier can apply either to what precedes it or to what follows it, it "squints."

Wrong: *He asked her while she was abroad to write to him.*
Right: *He asked her to write to him while she was abroad,* or *While she was abroad, he asked her to write to him.*

Wrong: *I was advised quietly to seek counseling.*
Right: *I was advised to seek counseling quietly,* or *I was quietly advised to seek counseling.*

Wrong: *She urged me after dinner to take a walk.*
Right: *After dinner she urged me to take a walk,* or *She urged me to take a walk after dinner.*

Squinting Modifier

Original
The counselor told the student confidentially to give the information to the professor.

Edited
The counselor confidentially told the student to give the information to the professor, or, The counselor told the student to give the information confidentially to the professor.

6. Restrictive (essential or identifying) clauses should not be set off by commas. Non-restrictive (non-essential or amplifying) clauses require two commas, one at the beginning and the other at the end. "That" may not be used to introduce a non-restrictive clause.

Restrictive: *The lawn mower that is in the garage is broken.* (The broken lawn mower is being identified as the one in the garage.)
Non-restrictive: *The lawn mower, which is in the garage, is broken.* (The location of the broken lawn mower is added to the sentence as extra [amplifying] information.)

Restrictive: *The train whose whistle we heard was the Metroliner.*
Non-restrictive: *The train, whose whistle pierced the night, reached a top speed of 85 mph on its run to New York.*

Essential Clause

The Internet is a worldwide network of more than 1 million computers **that are used to distribute information and electronic mail freely to more than 12 million users every day.**

Non-essential Clause

The Internet, **which is becoming a household word,** is a worldwide network of more than 1 million computers that are used to distribute information and electronic mail freely to more than 12 million users every day.

7. The antecedents of all pronouns should be readily identifiable, and each pronoun should agree in number with its antecedent. A film released in the early 1990s contained a line of dialogue something like this: "If you love someone, and they don't return your love, your life is hell."

This is indeed the way we speak. The conflict between the singular "someone" and the plural "they" is of no consequence to us because the meaning is clear. Yet grammarians insist on consistency: a singular antecedent requires a singular pronoun. The sentence should be "If you love someone, and he or she doesn't return your love, your life is hell" or "If you love someone, and that someone doesn't return your love, your life is hell."

Neither choice is quite satisfactory for the spoken language. "He or she" sounds tentative, as if we can't make up our minds, and "that someone" sounds pretentious, as if we are trying to be poetic. The fact is that the English language doesn't offer a good alternative, so we fall back on "they" by default.

This doesn't mean "they" is acceptable in print. Writers are held to a higher standard. They must adhere to the singular form or appear uneducated. Most are skillful at avoiding the issue, by shifting, for example, to a plural subject: Not *Each student carries his or her lunch in a brown bag,* but *All of the students carry their lunches in brown bags.* There is no graceful way, however, of making this dodge work with a sentence like *If you love someone, and they don't return your love, life is hell.*

Someday, perhaps, this use of "they" will become respectable in print. The English-speaking world seems to be moving in that direction.

According to the *American Heritage Dictionary,*

> At least one major British publisher has adopted this usage for its learners' dictionaries, where one may read such sentences as *If someone says they are "winging it," they mean they are improvising their way.* But in formal style, this option is perhaps less risky for a publisher of reference books than for an individual writer, who may be misconstrued as being careless or ignorant rather than attuned to the various grammatical and political nuances of the use of the masculine pronoun as generic pronoun.

A graceful writing style thus requires attention to this detail, even though it is often ignored in speech.

Wrong: *If the student lives at home before school starts, they can earn $3,325 after taxes.*
Right: *A student who lives at home before school starts can earn $3,325 after taxes.*

Wrong: *Everybody has their favorite parts of the American dream.*
Right: *Everybody has a favorite part of the American dream.*

Wrong: *Everybody needs their tickets.*
Right: *Everybody needs a ticket.*

Wrong: *Nobody can return from a war zone and remain the same person they were.*
Right: *Nobody can return from a war zone and remain the same person as before.*

Wrong: *Rafting isn't an activity that everyone will enjoy, whether they are disabled or not.*
Right: *Rafting isn't an activity that all will enjoy, whether they are disabled or not.*

Wrong: *This is an open society in which everyone can achieve their full potential.*
Right: *This is an open society in which everyone can achieve one's full potential.*

Wrong: *The law prohibits anyone under 18 from operating a forklift as part of their job.*
Right: *The law prohibits anyone under 18 from operating a forklift as part of his or her job.*

Wrong: *Almost one in four people thinks it is all right to cheat on their car insurance.*
Right: *Almost one in four people thinks it is all right to cheat on one's car insurance.*

Wrong: *She said every homosexual should come forward, even if they needed help opening the door.*
Right: *She said every homosexual should come forward, even those who needed help opening the door.*

Questionable: *Everyone went their separate ways, taking their umbrellas.*

In the last example, the sense of "everyone" is clearly plural despite the grammatical rule that it must be singular. Logic and grammar part company here. They don't, in fact, go hand in hand in many cases, which explains why so much of grammar has to be memorized. Some authorities accept "everyone went their separate ways," but by no means all. Others will insist on: *All went their separate ways, taking their umbrellas.*

For writers and editors, what this all means is that one's ear, trained in the spoken language, may not be trustworthy in all cases for print.

Vague Antecedents

Original
Police and others talked to a 13-year-old boy after he was held hostage briefly by a gunman who later shot his mother in their home.

Edited
Police and others talked to a 13-year-old boy after he was held hostage briefly by a gunman who later shot the boy's mother in her home.

TROUBLESOME TECHNICAL TYRANNIES

Grammar is a collection of rules, some of which are more difficult to remember than others because they are so frequently violated. Good editors train themselves to be constantly alert for these:

1. Collectives may be singular or plural, but they may not be both in the same sentence. A collective noun is a singular word that stands for a group. Some common collectives are: clergy, committee, couple, company, crew, enemy, group, family, flock, public, team.

In American English the preference is to match these words with singular verbs and pronouns.

The team is on the field, wearing its game uniforms.

The crew is aboard ship, ready to take up its battle stations.

An exception is made when the members of the collective are not acting as a unit, but as individuals.

As the team warmed up, their names and hometowns were announced to the crowd.

The crew were granted liberty and went to their homes.

One of the most troublesome collectives is "couple." A common practice in speaking is to mix the singular and plural in the same sentence, usually by using a singular verb and a plural pronoun, but this is unacceptable in written English. Wrong: *In a time when material possessions seem to signify success, one couple has elected to enrich their lives with experiences, not money.*

When the couple is acting as a unit, it should be treated as singular. However, "couple has elected to enrich its lives" offends some ears because "it" seems out of place in reference to two people. The editor may prefer to convert to a plural verb: *In a time when material possessions seem to signify success, one couple have elected to enrich their lives with experiences, not money.*

Confusing Collective

Original

The couple, both 31, was arrested Feb. 28 after authorities received a hotline report that their child was being abused. The couple was accused of beating the boy in December at their home about 150 miles northwest of St. Louis.

Edited

The couple, both 31, were arrested Feb. 28 after authorities received a hotline report that their child was being abused. The couple was accused of beating the boy in December at the family's home about 150 miles northwest of St. Louis.

2. The possessive of a singular noun is formed by adding the apostrophe and "s," except when it is not. The time-honored rule on possessives was stated in 1798 by Joseph Priestley:

> The genitive case is that which denotes property or possession; and it is formed by adding (s) with an apostrophe before it to the nominative; as Solomon's wisdom, The Men's wit; Venus's beauty; or the apostrophe only in the plural number, when the nominative ends in (s) as the Stationers' arms.

Editors would have an easier time if this rule had no exceptions, but unfortunately possessive forms vary. The *AP Stylebook* states that singular common nouns that end in "s" or an "s" sound form the possessive with "'s" unless the next word begins with "s."

my boss's necktie

my boss' shirt

Proper nouns ending in "s" take only the apostrophe in AP style, no matter how the next word begins.

Venus' beauty

Jones' statement

However, the *Oxford Companion to the English Language,* published in 1992, says the choice can go either way. *Mr. Harris's job* or *in Jesus's name* is just as correct as *Mr. Harris' job* or *in Jesus' name.*

Arguing right or wrong in the matter is pointless. Editors are best advised to go with the traditional preference at the publication where they work, or if lacking a preference, to establish one.

Something that is acceptable nowhere is to form the possessive by inserting the apostrophe into a singular noun that ends in "s." Typical is *John Jone's house.* Make it *John Jones' house* or *John Jones's house.* In the plural, it is *the Joneses' house.*

Apostrophe Atrocities

Original
The Karpisek's make all of their sausage and luncheon meats by hand. The Karpisek's attention to the basics is evident in their Wilber Wieners.

Edited
The Karpiseks make all of their sausage and luncheon meats by hand. The Karpiseks' attention to the basics is evident in their Wilber Wieners.

3. The relative pronoun "who" applies only to people; "that" applies to people or things; "which" applies only to things. "Who" is preferred over "that" for people.

Acceptable: *The man that wore the white hat was the hero.*

Preferred: *The man who wore the white hat was the hero.*

The possessive form "whose" is acceptable for inanimate objects. *The house, whose front door was red, stood next to a country lane.* This avoids such awkward constructions as *the front door of which was red* or *of which the front door was red.*

Robot Technicians

Original
Only one of the six technicians that work in the lab is a physician.

Edited
Only one of the six technicians who work in the lab is a physician.

4. Reflexive pronouns (myself, yourself, himself, herself, itself, ourselves, yourselves, themselves) cannot be used alone. They must be accompanied by an antecedent. Misuse of reflexive pronouns is common in the spoken language. In writing, the reflexive should be used only to refer action back to the subject.

Wrong: *John, May and myself were on the committee.*
Right: *John gave the award to himself.*

Reflexive Rubbish

Original
The gift was presented to both his brother and himself.

Edited
The gift was presented to both him and his brother.

5. Gerunds require the possessive. A verbal is a form of a verb used as another part of speech. The three verbals are the infinitive, the participle and the gerund.

Participles substitute for adjectives.

Swimming in the surf, he suffered a cramp.

Defeated, he gave up.

Having been surrounded, the fugitive surrendered.

Infinitives (to swim) and gerunds (swimming) substitute for nouns.

To swim in the surf is enjoyable.

Swimming in the surf requires skill.

Nouns and pronouns that accompany gerunds must take the possessive form.

Wrong: *I hated my brother dying so young.*
Right: *I hated my brother's dying so young.*

Wrong: *I liked John winning the award, but I disliked him giving it to himself.*
Right: *I liked John's winning the award, but I disliked his giving it to himself.*

Parallel Construction

Original
After retiring, he plans on traveling to see his daughters, research and to keep playing the piano.

Edited
After retiring, he plans to travel and see his daughters, to conduct research and to keep playing the piano.

or

After retiring, he plans on traveling to see his daughters, conducting research and continuing to play the piano.

or

After retiring, he plans on travel to see his daughter, research and a continuation of his piano playing.

6. "Whom" cannot be ignored. "Whom" is seldom used anymore in the spoken language, and when it is, it is likely to be misused. Even when it is used correctly, it tends to sound stuffy and pompous. Yet "whom" survives in this commonly used phrase: *To whom it may concern.*

Certain questions demand the use of "whom": *For whom was the gift intended?*

Editors who cannot make the correct choice between "who" and "whom" are asking for trouble. At some point they will inevitably make an embarrassing mistake. The most important thing to remember is that "whom" must be the object of a verb or preposition. It can never be a subject. It is always the receiver of the action, and never the sender. The following sentences can be edited to avoid the issue:

You never know whom you might run into at Yosemite National Park. "Whom" is the object of "might run into." Better: *You never know who might cross your path at Yosemite National Park.*

She had a younger sister, Elizabeth, whom she quickly overshadowed. Elizabeth was the object of the overshadowing, so "whom" is correct. Better: *She quickly overshadowed her younger sister, Elizabeth.*

Marlene Dietrich remained married all her life to her first husband, Rudolf Sieber, whom she married in 1923. If in doubt, try substituting "he" for "whom." You would not write, *She married he in 1923.* "Him" is correct, both by ear and grammatical rule, and so is "whom." Better: *Marlene Dietrich married Rudolf Sieber in 1923 and remained his wife for the rest of her life.* (The sentence required editing for two other reasons: She wasn't married all her life, only after 1923, and Sieber couldn't have been her first husband unless there had been a second.)

"Whom" can often be eliminated simply because it is the wrong word. *Joe Montana, whom coach George Seifert said wouldn't need surgery, wasn't available for comment.* Montana cannot be the object of "said." You wouldn't write, *Seifert said him wouldn't need surgery.* Therefore, "who" is correct.

His brother, whom he said was suffering from depression, threw himself in front of a freight train. Treat "he said" as parenthetical: *who (he said) was suffering from depression.*

The prize will be given to whomever shows up first. The entire clause, whoever shows up first, is the object of the preposition "to," but "whoever" is the subject of "shows up."

Despite its unpopularity, "whom" is still the right word to use in some sentences that cannot be improved upon: *Sevareid told us whom to root for in wars.* Eric Sevareid, the renowned radio and television commentator, also got his "whoms" right.

Doom for "Whom"

Original
She has agreed to testify against her husband, whom she alleges masterminded the kidnapping scheme.

Edited
She has agreed to testify against her husband, who she alleges masterminded the kidnapping scheme.

THE POWER OF PUNCTUATION

Punctuation, especially the powerful comma, is a tool for clarifying the relationships of sentence elements. It provides a means of grouping words, setting some apart while forcing others together. It expresses in print the pauses and inflections imparted by a speaker to the oral language. Three marks of punctuation—the comma, the semicolon and the dash—are particularly troublesome for editors.

THE MIGHTY COMMA

The writer is entitled to some discretion in the use of commas, which can aid understanding but can also break up the flow of a sentence. Editors should insert or remove commas only with good reason. Here are some guidelines:

1. When two verbs share a common subject and are joined by "and" or "but," no comma should be used before the conjunction.

The provincial premier was in Montreal [,] but hurried back to the capital.

2. Make an exception to Rule No. 1 when the sentence is long and the comma adds clarity.

The politician disclosed Thursday that she was sexually abused by a 60-year-old neighbor when she was 5, and urged parents to be explicit in warning their children about improper behavior by adults.

The subject is "politician." The verbs are "disclosed" and "urged." Without the comma, it could appear that the politician did the urging when she was 5.

3. When a noun is preceded by adjectives in series, separate the adjectives with a comma only if they each modify the noun independently.

The voters gave the candidate a crucial, hair's breadth victory Tuesday.

4. Use no comma between adjectives in a series when one modifies the combination of the other and the noun they both modify.

The performer was still a little-known [,] regional figure. The car represented a sleek [,] new design.

5. Use a comma before "and" in a compound sentence (two independent clauses).

The truck went out of control and destroyed a car, and as a result the porch was ripped off a day-care center.

6. Make an exception to Rule No. 5 when the sentence is short.

He swung [,] and the ball soared out of the park.

7. Do not use a comma before "and" in a series.

In preparation for the race, Miller, 32, ran 80-90 miles a week, bicycled [,] and skied cross-country.

8. Make an exception to Rule No. 7 if the comma is needed to avoid confusion.

A tornado hit suburban Minneapolis-St. Paul on Thursday night, heavily damaging a shopping center, injuring at least 128 people with flying glass, and overturning cars and trucks.

9. Make an exception to Rule No. 7 if the sentence is long and the series contains diverse items.

The president's agenda included a two-hour meeting with Chinese Premier Zhao Ziyang on a range of global political and Sino-American economic issues, 90 minutes with Communist Party General Secretary Hu Yaobang, and a banquet in the Great Hall of the People.

10. Use commas to set off a non-restrictive, amplifying, non-essential clause.

Republican Gov. Terry Branstad immediately labeled the session a "disappointment," while Democrats, who control the Legislature, described it as "historic."

11. Do not use commas to set off a restrictive, identifying, essential clause.

The artist [,] who created the sculpture [,] attended the unveiling.

12. Use a comma to set off an introductory word or phrase that modifies the whole sentence and not just the subject.

In Denver, the snowfall has totaled 28 inches this winter.

Instead, America should be instituting and encouraging economic policies that would allow it to compete successfully in a global marketplace.

Throughout the night, they searched the forest for the lost boy.

Drenched with rain they searched the forest for the lost boy.

Without dissent, the high court affirmed the district court in the case.

Under the new legislation, people convicted of drunken driving a second time would undergo a substance-abuse evaluation.

Gaining the additional momentum that he badly needed, the Democratic candidate romped past his rival Tuesday night.

13. Use commas to set off attribution in a direct quotation.

The jubilant candidate declared, "The voters of this state have said they are not ready for this race to be over."

14. Use commas around phrases in apposition. An appositive is a noun or noun phrase that is placed next to another noun or noun phrase and could be deleted without changing the meaning or grammar of the sentence.

Liverpool honored its four most famous sons, the Beatles, by unveiling a statue of them Thursday.

A comma is required both before and after an appositive.

The prime minister of Britain, John Major, attended the meeting.

15. When a title precedes a name without an article, no commas are used because the title cannot stand alone without the name.

British Prime Minister John Major attended the meeting.

THE SEMICOLON

Some editors believe semicolons impede readability, and they will go to some lengths to avoid them. One way to keep away from semicolons is to write short sentences that do not contain items in series. The semicolon could be termed a "supercomma." It is used to make an emphatic division in a sentence where a comma would be ambiguous.

1. The semicolon can substitute for a conjunction between two independent clauses.

Jackson sat on the bench throughout the game; he was suffering from the flu.

A sentence in which a comma alone is used to separate independent clauses is called a "comma splice" or a "run-on sentence."

Jackson sat on the bench throughout the game, he was suffering from the flu.

To avoid this, editors who hate semicolons have three options:

- Turn one of the independent clauses into a dependent clause.

Jackson, who was suffering from the flu, sat on the bench throughout the game.

- Insert a conjunction.

Jackson was suffering from the flu, and he sat on the bench throughout the game.

- Break the sentence into more than one.

Jackson sat on the bench throughout the game. He was suffering from the flu.

2. The semicolon is used to mark breaks in a series of items containing commas.

Sitting out the game were Jackson, who was suffering from the flu; Simms, whose collarbone was broken in the game against Houston Sept. 18; and Barnes, who twisted his ankle in the Miami game.

Enumeration, which means forming a separate paragraph for each item in the series and preceding it with a number or a typographical device such as a bullet, is one method of avoiding the semicolons:

Three players sat out the game:

- *Jackson, who had the flu.*
- *Simms, whose collarbone was broken in the game against Houston Sept. 18.*
- *Barnes, who twisted his ankle in the Miami game.*

THE DASH

The dash, which is sometimes called the "long dash" to differentiate it from the hyphen, is often misused in place of the colon, comma or semicolon. The dash is best used to mark an abrupt change of thought within a sentence.

My tire blew out—who can explain it?—just after I crossed the narrow bridge.

PUNCTUATING QUOTATIONS

Direct quotations play a special role in news coverage: They enliven a story by enhancing narration and description, and they promote credibility by attaching real names to real spoken words. Special punctuation rules apply to quotations:

1. Periods and commas always go inside closing quotation marks.

"We have the potential of blending television, print and radio into a new medium," said Roger Fidler, director of the Knight-Ridder Information Design Laboratory in Boulder, Colo. "The goal is to keep newspapers as the focal point."

2. Colons and semicolons go outside closing quotation marks.

So-called videotext services have failed, he said, partly because "searching a database is work"; people don't have time to hunt down the news they want.

The electronic tablet will deliver more than just the printed word on its "pages": Video clips, sound bites and even interactive advertising will be offered.

3. Other marks of punctuation may go inside or outside quotation marks, depending on the sense of the sentence. Single quotation marks are used for quoted matter within a direct quotation. If both quotes end together, a thin space should be placed between the single and double quotation marks.

"Have you read 'Gone with the Wind'?" he asked.

"No, but I just finished 'Is Paris Burning?' " she replied.

4. Quotations of more than one paragraph should be preceded by attribution and a colon. Quotation marks go at the beginning of each paragraph and at the end of the last paragraph. The attribution is not repeated.

Columnist David Broder wrote:

"George Stephanopoulos, the president's counselor, blames it all on the availability of Nexis, the electronic information retrieval system that makes it easy for journalists to compare Clinton's actions with his campaign rhetoric.

"But it is not that simple. The problem is not Nexis but political reality.

"Clinton cannot bring himself to abandon his broad goals, nor can he muster the political firepower to achieve them—so he finds himself looking feckless as he negotiates for unattainable objectives."

5. Partial quotes are quote fragments. They are not set apart from the attribution by commas and do not begin with capital letters, unless they begin sentences. When a partial quote appears at the end of a sentence, and the quotation continues, the partial quote must be closed, and the rest of the quotation must have separate attribution.

Wrong: *Fidler said the venerable printed newspaper, "Is a very easy-to-use, random-access, non-linear medium. A large part of the pleasure is the serendipity of encountering something you're interested in that you didn't know you were interested in."*

Right: *Fidler said the venerable printed newspaper "is a very easy-to-use, random-access, non-linear medium."*

"A large part of the pleasure is the serendipity of encountering something you're interested in that you didn't know you were interested in," he said.

6. No quotation marks are used in question and answer (Q&A) formats.

Q. After a disaster occurs, what sort of information do local officials need to gather to involve the state in the response?

A. After they have an emergency of a severity that is beyond the local government's capability, they will declare a state of emergency and begin a damage assessment process.

7. Quotations from different speakers should not be placed in the same paragraph. When a transition from one speaker to another is made, the attribution should appear at the beginning of the paragraph to signal the reader that a new speaker is being quoted.

Wrong: *"It's imperative that we get this package through" lest interest rates rise and undermine economic recovery, Treasury Secretary Lloyd Bentsen said Sunday on "Meet the Press." "It's going to be very close, but we must pass it," said House Speaker Tom Foley on "Face the Nation."*

Right: *"It's imperative that we get this package through" lest interest rates rise and undermine economic recovery, Treasury Secretary Lloyd Bentsen said Sunday on "Meet the Press."*

On "Face the Nation," House Speaker Tom Foley said, "It's going to be very close, but we must pass it."

8. Readers may not make the connection between a news source mentioned in one paragraph and a direct quotation in a separate paragraph that follows. If the quotation carries no attribution, it becomes an "orphan quote."

Wrong: *Fidler said he didn't expect the printed newspaper would disappear anytime soon.*

"Newspapers were supposed to be dead when radio was invented, when television started, and when videotext came along. We're still around."

Right: *Fidler said he didn't expect the printed newspaper would disappear anytime soon.*

"Newspapers were supposed to be dead when radio was invented, when television started, and when videotext came along," he said. "We're still around."

SEQUENCE OF TENSES

This bugaboo is far less scary than it has been portrayed. It is neither a useless invention of pedants nor an icon of natural law. No editor can afford to be ignorant of it because some of the nation's largest and most prestigious news organizations, such as *The New York Times,* use it. Others, such as the Associated Press, do not.

The best argument in favor of sequence of tenses is precision, which is important to print journalists in ways broadcasters needn't consider. The life of the written word is as long as that of the paper it is printed on. The printed word does not disappear immediately into some electronic never-never land, to be recalled only by those who bother to play back a tape. It may be around for decades, perhaps even preserved under glass.

Sequence of tenses is precise because it requires that all the verbs in a sentence be compatible in time with one another. The dominant tense in journalistic writing is past. There is good reason for this. Journalists write what they know at a given moment. Subsequent information may alter their knowledge or cast new light on old facts, but nothing can change what has already been published. To assume knowledge beyond the moment is to risk error. Sequence of tenses places events in the proper context of time.

He said he was sick. (He was sick at the time he said it but may not be sick by the time his words reach readers.)

He said he is sick. (He has a chronic illness.)

He said he had been sick. (He was sick at an indefinite time in the past and was well at the time he said it.)

He said he was sick last Friday. (He was sick at a definite time in the past and was well when he said it.)

He said crime doesn't pay. (A perpetual truth.)

He said he drives a car. (He does it regularly.)

He said he drove a car. (Explaining how he got to his destination.)

He said he would drive a car. (At the time he said it, he planned to drive to his destination.)

Notice that each of these examples begins with "he said." For journalists, this type of sentence, known as reported speech, is the most frequent occasion for sequence of tenses. "He (or she or they) said (or asserted, alleged, declared,

Sequence of Tenses in Action

Senator John H. Chafee of Rhode Island **said he thought** "we can come up with not only a darn good bill but a very appealing one."

Senator John B. Breaux said, "There is much more that we have in agreement than disagreement."

But the senators declined to discuss the progress **they said they had made.** Senator Bob Kerrey, Democrat of Nebraska and a mainstream group member, **said they saw** no advantage in disclosing partial agreements that critics **might** focus on. **He said their purpose was** to "present to the Senate, at least, a proposal that is darned hard to vote no on."

He also said they were committed to passing a bill because they felt "an urgency to act, not a political urgency, a health care urgency."

Senator George J. Mitchell, the majority leader, who will have the task of selling any agreement to Democrats disappointed that universal coverage has been lost, **said,** "We believe that there is a possibility of agreement on most of the issues." **He said he and the group believed** "it is both possible and desirable to get a good bill passed this year."

—The New York Times

Box 3.1

charged, insisted, reiterated or any other verb carrying the sense of said)" is the dominant subject-verb combination in the sentence. The sequence of tenses rule says that when "he said" is followed by a "that" clause ("that" may be either expressed or implied), the verbs in the subordinate clause must conform in tense to "said."

Confusion arises because any other placement of the attribution requires no special sequence of tenses. "He said" or its equivalent becomes an attribution tag instead of the dominant clause in the sentence.

> Direct quotation: *"I plan to introduce a crime bill tomorrow," Sen. John Manley said Monday.*
>
> Paraphrase: *He plans to introduce a crime bill Tuesday, Sen. John Manley said Monday.*
>
> Reported speech: *Sen. John Manley said Monday he planned to introduce a crime bill Tuesday.*

In reported speech, the controlling verb ("said") and the subordinate verb ("planned") are in the past tense. This preserves the accuracy of the quote by capturing it in the proper time frame (Manley planned it at the time he said it).

If the action in the subordinate clause is in the future, the tense becomes conditional: *Sen. John Manley said Monday he would* (not will) *introduce a crime bill Tuesday.*

"Would" leaves open the possibility that Manley may change his mind. It makes his intentions conditional on events that may follow his conversation with the writer.

Writers and editors should use sequence of tenses where it falls naturally. They should not allow it to lard their work with perfect tenses: *He said he had*

had fish too often and had decided not to have it again soon. Whenever "had" appears in the form of a multiheaded monster, the best option is to revise the sentence and come at it another way (Box 3.1).

USING THE RIGHT WORD

Some words are more often misused than others, and some of the most frequently fractured are given here in two lists: Words Often Abused and Words Often Confused. Each item represents a red flag on the landscape for copy editors, who should memorize the lists or keep them handy.

The usage notes in Words Often Abused reflect the prevalent view. In many cases, there is disagreement. In Words Often Confused, devices are offered to aid the memory.

WORDS OFTEN ABUSED

accused (1) "Accused murderer" has almost the same force as "murderer" in implying guilt. It simply means "murderer who has been accused." Principles of fairness demand the presumption of innocence, and unless there has been a conviction, terms like "murderer" should not be used. (2) One can be "accused of" but not "accused with" a crime.

admit, admitted One of its meanings is "confess." Its use in this sense should be restricted to cases of wrongdoing or shame. For example, one should not write, "He admitted he was gay," if he was actually announcing the fact.

aggravate Its first meaning is "worsen," not "irritate" or "annoy."

alleged (1) Something that is "alleged" is asserted or represented as true, and journalists tend to use the word as a mild disclaimer of responsibility. It offers little or no lessening of the burden of a falsehood and should not be regarded as a protection against libel action. (2) "Alleged" becomes redundant when coupled with attribution, as in this sentence: "The man was allegedly armed with a knife, police said." (3) Some contend that because you can assert a thing but not a person, it is incorrect to call someone "an alleged criminal." Nevertheless, the term is often used to denote someone who has been officially accused but not convicted of an offense. (4) An "alleged crime" is an offense that has been reported to the police or other authority but has not been verified. Do not say "alleged murder" if the crime is known to have taken place. Do not say "alleged suspect" unless the person's status as a suspect is in doubt.

all right Like "all ready" ("already"), "all right" has a shorter twin, "alright." But unlike "already," "alright" is not widely accepted as standard and thus is best avoided.

allude (1) To "allude" is to mention indirectly. *He alluded to the Bill of Rights when he spoke of "our precious constitutional protections."* To mention directly is to "refer." (2) "Allude" should not be confused with "elude," which means "escape from."

altar (1) It is a table used in religious rites. Sermons are not normally delivered from the altar but rather from the pulpit. (2) "Alter," with an "e," is a verb meaning "change."

alternative The term can be applied to one of two or more choices, but "alternative" carries an imperative sense that "choice" does not: The selection of one "alternative" excludes the others.

ambivalent To be "ambivalent" is not simply to be undecided but to be torn by conflicting feelings, such as love and hate.

anticipate It means "to expect and prepare for." If there is no preparation, use "expect."

approximately A long, stuffy word for which "about" may usually be substituted.

arrested When accompanied by "for," it implies guilt. *He was arrested for strangling his wife.* To be scrupulously fair to the accused, one should use "charged" when mentioning a criminal offense. *He was arrested and charged with strangling his wife.*

assassin (1) Attempting a political murder makes one an "assassin," whether or not the attempt succeeds. (2) The act of assassination takes place at the time of the attack, even though the victim may not die until later.

attorney A lawyer often acts as an attorney, but an attorney needn't be a lawyer. An attorney is anyone empowered to represent someone else. A lawyer is an "attorney at law."

awhile It means "for a while." Say "he stayed awhile" or "he stayed for a while" but not "he stayed for awhile."

bail (1) It is not synonymous with "bond." "Bail" is a sum of money posted with a court in return for the freedom of someone accused of a crime. A "bond," or insurance guarantee, may be used to post "bail" and usually is, which explains why lawyers and judges speak of setting or denying "bond." Strictly, "he went free on bond" is correct only if a bond is used to post bail. (2) One is not kept in jail "on" or "under" bail. The court keeps custody of the person unless the money or a guarantee is deposited in substitution for the body. Thus, one is imprisoned "in lieu of bail."

based Fostered by the growth of business conglomerates with offices in many places, the use of "base" as a verb has become annoyingly commonplace, as in "the Kansas City, Mo.-based insurance corporation." Even individuals are now described as "based" ("a Lincoln, Neb.-based professor"). The practice may have some value in business writing, but elsewhere it is lazy and graceless.

basically This term has crept into the spoken language as a kind of meaningless filler word used to bridge gaps in thought. *Why did you decide to* *study editing? Well, basically, I don't know.* It may be used as a synonym for "fundamentally" but should be avoided in the sense of "in general" or "on the whole."

boost It means an upward push from below. Like "hike," it should not be casually used as a substitute for "raise" or "increase."

boycott It is derived from the name of a nineteenth-century landlord whose tenants ostracized him because of high rents. "Boycott" is best used to refer to an action by consumers against a merchant. It should not be confused with "embargo," which is a government ban on movement of goods.

burgeon "Burgeoning" means "sprouting," "budding" or "newly emerging," not "growing." Expressions like "the burgeoning suburbs" are not only hackneyed but also incorrect.

center around A center is a point. Actions can take place around it but can "center" only "on" it.

character (1) It should not be confused with "reputation." One's "character" consists of a set of intrinsic traits, and one's "reputation" is made up of others' opinions. (2) If overused, "character" can contribute to verbal clutter. Wrong: *This is a case of a different character.* Right: *This case is different.*

charged One is "charged with" or "accused of," but never "charged of" or "accused with," a crime.

claimed Theodore Bernstein wrote of a condition called "synonymomania" that afflicts many writers. A symptom is the willingness to do almost anything to avoid repeating "said." A word often used as a substitute for "said" is "claimed," but "claimed" carries an implication of doubt that "said" lacks. For example, "he claimed he was an expert on the Middle East" indicates doubt about his qualifications. Unless such doubt is intentional, "claim" should be avoided as a verb.

cohort Derived from the Latin term for a company of soldiers, "cohort" is often applied to an individual in the sense of ally. It has a negative tone and may be used in place of "confederate" or "accomplice" but not of "companion," "associate" or "colleague."

compare to, compare with Use "to" when likening something to something else. Use "with" when looking for similarities and differences. For example, any writer may find it useful to compare his or her work "with" Hemingway's, but to compare it "to" Hemingway's may be presumptuous.

comprise The whole comprises its parts. The parts compose the whole. The whole is composed, not comprised, of its parts.

concern (1) As a verb it can mean either "worry" or "involve" and thus fosters imprecision and vagueness. *The Persian Gulf war concerned every American.* (2) This "flabby" word is so overused, says Jack Cappon, "that you can come across it every three or four column inches." Look for a livelier, stronger word.

criteria Like "data," the word is plural. The singular is "criterion."

currently It is flabby and usually superfluous. Delete it without effect from "we are currently reviewing your application."

different AP insists that it takes "from" in all uses, even though the rule makes some sentences difficult to revise. Editors who do not mind making exceptions to AP style avoid using "than" unless the sentence must be rewritten to make "from" work. *Conditions were different in the twentieth century than in the nineteenth.*

dilemma It denotes a choice between two equally undesirable alternatives. Otherwise, use "problem."

disinterested It means detached, uninvolved. A judge, for example, should be disinterested yet interested in the cases he or she hears. To express lack of interest, use "uninterested."

drunk Despite frequent appearances of the term "drunk driving," the preferred use of "drunk" is after a form of "to be," as in "he was drunk." Before a noun, "drunken" is preferred, as in "he was arrested on a charge of drunken driving." Of course, "drunk driving" must be used where it appears in the names of organizations such as Mothers Against Drunk Driving.

each Standing alone, it is singular, as in "each takes a separate path." When "each" follows a plural subject, it doesn't affect the verb, as in "they each are taking separate paths."

each other, one another John Bremner explains the difference this way: "If two persons are having a conversation, each is talking to the other. They are talking to each other. If three persons are having a conversation, each is talking to one and to another one. They are talking to one another."

enthuse This is a back-formation, a verb created from a noun, "enthusiasm." Although some other back-formations have been accepted as standard, "enthuse" remains an outcast.

etc. Far too inexact to be useful to journalists, it means "and other things," which is so vague that it might be construed to encompass almost anything.

facility A "facility" is something that serves some function. It could be almost anything, and the word is widely overused where a more precise term, such as "building," would convey more meaning. Bremner calls "facility" a "flatulent word," meaning, perhaps, that it denotes nothing but hot air. "Facility" is often dispensable, as in this sentence: "The state's prison facilities need to be upgraded."

fact A "fact" is verifiable information, such as a date. It cannot properly represent matters of judgment, as in "she regretted the fact that he was a boor."

factor Like "facility," "factor" is a flatulent word that often contributes to clutter and wordiness. It can simply be deleted from sentences like "Air power will be the decisive factor in the war."

fewer Use "fewer" for items that are normally counted individually, such as "fewer students." For bulk things, such as flour, use "less."

finalize Its use should be terminated on the ground of vagueness. Exactly how does one "finalize" something?

firm It can be applied to a partnership but is not a synonym for "company" or "corporation."

fix To "fix" is to "set firmly in place." Despite the adage, "If it ain't broke, don't fix it," "repair" is the best word for setting things right.

flammable It means the same as "inflammable."

following "After" is preferred because it is shorter.

former, latter A media writer who is tempted to use "the former" and "the latter" should reconsider. These terms are denounced by Bremner as characteristic of "signpost writing" (the more cluttered the landscape, the more signposts you need).

fortuitous It means "by chance" and is not a synonym for "fortunate."

from whence This is a good example of pleonasm, the use of more words than required to express an idea. "Whence" means "from where," so "from whence" is a redundancy. Pleonasm eats precious space.

fulsome It means "offensively flattering and insincere." So "fulsome praise" is not a good thing.

got It is preferred over "gotten," a form peculiar to the American language. Eliminate "got" from expressions like "I haven't got any." Instead of "They had gotten out of the burning building," say they had escaped.

hike Along with "boost," "hike" is journalese and a poor synonym for "increase" or "raise."

hopefully Battle lines have been drawn over this word. It has come to symbolize the views of the purists, who insist it can only be used as an adverb meaning "with hope." Some say the battle has been lost and that "hopefully" can stand for "it is hoped" just as "regrettably" means "it is regretted." Bremner argues without effect for coining a new word, "hopeably." Careful editors still avoid "hopefully" in sentences like "Hopefully the soup is hot."

impact Noun-into-verb disease is an affliction that causes writers lazily to use a noun when unable to think of a good verb. "Impact" is a leading example, and most editors object to its use in sentences such as "The tax increase will impact heavily on the middle class." "Affect" is preferred.

input It is useful as a noun for computer data but unacceptable to many editors for human interactions, perhaps because it implies scientific exactitude ("I'd like your input on this").

inside of Delete "of" unless you mean "in less than." *I'll be there inside of five minutes.*

knots per hour Like "from whence," this is a pleonasm. "Knots" are nautical miles per hour, so "knots per hour" is redundant.

kudos It comes from the Greek for "glory," and although it is singular, the AP insists it takes a plural verb ("Kudos go to . . ."). Do not, however, allow anyone to award a single "kudo."

lay, lie The headline, "Israel urged to 'lay low' if war comes," which was true to the source, demonstrates that even high-level diplomats have trouble with "lie" and "lay." Israel would have to "lie low" because the verb lacks an object. Presumably another option would be to "lay its cards on the table." The word for the reclining type of action is "lie": "I will lie here for a while." "I lay here for two hours yesterday." "I have lain here for as long as eight hours." The word for placing is "lay": "I will lay the blanket on the bed." "I already laid the pillow there." "I have laid the foundation for a good night's rest."

loan, lend "Lend" is the preferred verb, although "loan" is accepted as a verb if money is involved. Right: "The bank loaned me money." Right: "My friend lent me his car." Wrong: "My friend loaned me his car."

like, as Bremner said the failure to distinguish between the two was "one of the most common blunders in written and spoken English." He suggested this test: Substitute "similar to" or "similarly to" for "like." If the sentence still works, "like" is correct. Otherwise, use "as."

literally It means "in the exact sense of the word." When confused with "figuratively," it can create a ludicrous image. For example, "he literally flew to the finish line."

local How often have you read that "the injured were rushed to a local hospital"? Or "local police arrested two suspects"? In both cases, "local" is superfluous. Readers know the injured will be taken to a nearby hospital unless there are unusual circumstances. They also know police make arrests in areas where they have jurisdiction. Avoid "local" unless it's really necessary.

located (1) "Situated" is preferred to denote a site, if any word is needed. "Located" and "situated" are both superfluous after a form of "to be," as in "the building was located on O Street." (2) Avoid "locate" as a synonym for "find."

meaningful It's often meaningless. Diplomats speak of "meaningful talks" or "fruitful negotiations" when they want to convey no information about what went on.

media It's plural. *The media were invited to interview the mayor.*

nature Like "character," it's an ally of wordiness. Example: *Crimes of a violent nature are increasing.*

nice It's too imprecise to be used in newswriting, although people frequently speak of "a nice guy" or "nice weather."

none It takes a singular verb ("none was") in most but not all cases.

off of Delete "of" from sentences like "he fell off of the chair."

ongoing It's clumsy and usually superfluous, as in "the ongoing program."

only Misplacement can alter meaning drastically. Move it around in this sentence to see the effect: *He met her in the cafeteria only on Saturday.*

outside of Delete "of" from sentences like "he stood outside of the house."

over "More than" is preferred when dealing with numbers. *The United States had more than (not over) 400,000 troops in Saudi Arabia.*

partially It's not interchangeable with "partly." Use "partly" when referring to parts of a whole. *The building was partly underground.* Use "partially" when referring to completeness. *The story was partially written.* But beware of "partially's" other meaning: "in a biased manner."

plus It's a preposition meaning "with the addition of" and is not a substitute for "and." *The sandwich plus a cup of coffee was a satisfying lunch.*

presently It is best used to mean "soon." For "now," use "now."

prior to Bremner: "If you wouldn't use 'posterior to,' why use 'prior to'?" "Before" is preferred.

reason is because "Because" means "for the reason that," so "the reason is because" is redundant. Say "the reason is that."

regretful It shouldn't be confused with "regrettable." *The newspaper apologized for its regrettable* (not regretful) *error.*

relate to Avoid it in expressing rapport, as in "they relate well to each other."

respective, respectively Rewrite to avoid these ponderous terms. Instead of "the winners of the piano and cello competitions were Jones and Smith respectively," write, "Jones won the piano competition, and Smith won the cello award."

self-confessed It's redundant. Who else can confess but oneself?

some "About 300 people" is preferred over "some 300 people."

stated Don't allow synonymomania to lead you into substituting this stuffy word for "said." "Stated" has its uses, though, as in "he stated his objections."

temperatures They get higher or lower, not warmer or cooler.

than Don't leave essential words out of sentences containing "than." "It looks more like a duck than a goose" can mean either "It looks more like a duck than like a goose" or "It looks more like a duck than a goose does."

thrust It's overused in expressions like "the thrust of the report was."

transpire Using it to mean "happen" is a form of synonymomania.

try and It should be "try to."

type Don't use it to mean "kind of," as in "a nasty type guy."

unique It means one of a kind, so a thing can't be "more unique" than another thing.

utilize "Use" is preferred.

very Very often, if not always, it should be dropped as unnecessary.

viable Resist the temptation to tack it onto words like "alternative" and "option."

while Avoid it as a substitute for "although" or "but."

-wise "The sober writer will abstain from the use of this wild additive," say Strunk and White, alluding to concoctions like "taxwise" and "pricewise."

worthwhile It's a weak, emaciated adjective, say Strunk and White, who suggest stronger words like "promising," "useful," "valuable," "exciting."

WORDS OFTEN CONFUSED

accept, except "Accept" is to INclude; "except" is to EXclude. *I accepted the gift. I excepted him from the list of guests.*

adverse, averse One is normally "averse" (opposed) to something "adverse" (unfavorable).

affect, effect To "affect" is to influence. To "effect" is to bring about or accomplish. As a noun, "effect" means "result." Do not use "affect" as a noun.

aid, aide Do not add the "e" unless you are referring to a person who is assisting someone.

allude, elude Remember that "flee" and "elude" have similar meanings and two "e's."

alternately, alternatively "Alternately" is for taking turns: *He alternately drove and rode with a neighbor.* "Alternatively" is for substitute choices: *He drove to work; alternatively, he could take the bus or ride with a neighbor.*

among, between "Among" is derived from the Old English word for "crowd." "Between" is related to "two" and "twin." Thus, one chooses "between" two items and "among" three or more.

arbitrate, mediate To "arbitrate" is to hear both sides and make a judgment. To "mediate" is to sit in the middle and try to get the two sides to agree. In labor negotiations, the difference is crucial.

bail, bale "Bail," which is spelled like "jail," is money or credit deposited in return for freedom pending trial on a charge. A "bale" is a large bundle.

baloney, bologna "Baloney" is blather; "bologna" is food. To write of a "baloney" sandwich is acceptable, but hooey should not be described as "bologna."

bazaar, bizarre A flea market is a "bazaar." Sometimes the items for sale are "bizarre" ("e" for "eccentric").

beside, besides To help decide which is correct, substitute "next to" for "beside" and "in addition to" for "besides."

biannual, biennial "Biannual" is twice a year. "Biennial," with two "i's" for "(y)ears," is every two years.

bloc, block A group of nations is a "bloc." A rectangular piece of wood is a "block," with a "k" for "knock your block off."

breach, breech A "breach," which is spelled like "break," is a failure to observe the terms of a law or contract. A "breech," with an extra "e" for "end," is the lower or back part of something, such as a gun barrel at the point where the cartridge is inserted. "Breeches" (pants) cover the human posterior.

bug, tap Both are eavesdropping devices, but a "bug" is in the walls, a "tap" is on the line.

buses, busses "Buses" are vehicles. "Busses," with the double "smooch," are kisses.

cannon, canon A "cannon" is an artillery piece; a "canon" is a rule or body of rules. The term *loose cannon,* which means an uncontrolled destructive force, stems from the days when cannons aboard ships could break loose and roll around the deck.

canvas, canvass "Canvas" is heavy cloth. The extra "s" in "canvass" emphasizes that it is a survey.

capital, capitol The "capital" city usually contains the "Capitol" building. (The "o" represents the dome.)

careen, career (v.) A car "careers" (rushes) when it is speeding but does not "careen" unless it lurches and swerves uncontrollably. Although the *American Heritage Dictionary* terms this distinction "pedantic," editors should be aware of it.

carat, caret, karat "Caret," which is a proofreader's mark, contains an "e" for "edit." Diamonds are measured in "carats," and gold is measured in "karats" ("k" for Fort Knox).

caster, castor A "caster" is a wheel. "Castor" contains an "o" for "oil."

celebrant, celebrator Both mean "one who celebrates," but "celebrant" should be reserved for religious ceremonies.

cement, concrete "Cement" is a powder that is mixed with sand, gravel and water to form "concrete." Sidewalks, foundations and other structures are constructed of concrete. To describe such things as made of cement is to join forces with "The Beverly Hillbillies," who swam in a "cement pond."

censor, censure To "censor" is to prevent or control publication. To "censure" ("re" for "reproach") is to scold or admonish.

chili, chilly There is no "chill" in chili, a hot, spicy stew.

clamor, clamber, clangor "Clamor" has the same root as "claim" and refers to the sound of voices. "Clamber" has the same root as "climb" and is similar to it in meaning. "Clangor," from the Latin *clangere* (sound), is used to describe the metallic banging of objects like bells.

climatic, climactic "Climatic" relates to "climate," "climactic" to "climax," or point of high dramatic tension.

complacent, complaisant One who is "complacent" is self-satisfied, or lax, while one who is "complaisant" is amiable, or pleasant.

complement, compliment "ComplEment" is related to complEteness. "ComplIment" describes polIte words of praise.

connote, denote A word "connotes" what it implies and "denotes" what it specifically means. Poverty denotes low income and connotes misery.

continual, continuous Something that is "continual" is closely repetitive, while something "continuoUS" is Uninterrupted and Steady.

convince, persuade To "convince" is to cause to believe. To "persuade" is to cause to act. "Convince" is properly used with "that" or "of," while "persuade" is accompanied by "to."

council, counsel, consul A "counCil" is a Commission or board. A "counSel" is an adviSer. A "consUl" is a diplomat, or consUltant abroad.

discomfiture, discomfort "Discomfiture" is more troublesome than "discomfort," which is unease. The roots of "discomfiture" are "destroy" and "defeat," and it should be used only where those meanings are appropriate.

discreet, discrete The two "e's" in "discreet" (tactful) are coupled, while the two "e's" in "discrete" (separate) are divided.

equal, equitable "Equitable" is a synonym for "fair," not "equal," which means identical.

farther, further Use "farther" for physical distance and "further" for degree.

faze, phase To "faze" is to aFFect. To "phase" (in or out) is to perform in Stages.

fervor, furor "Fervor" is passion. "Furor" is rage.

flack, flak "Flak" is antiaircraft fire or public disapproval (slang). "Flack" is pejorative slang for "press agent" and should be avoided.

flail, flay "Flay" is an oldtime headline word for "assail" or "excoriate" but is best avoided except in its first sense, "strip the skin from." To "flail" is to "beat as if with a threshing instrument."

flair, flare A "flair" is a talent. A "flare" is a bright light.

flaunt, flout The younger generation "flouts" (disregards) its elders and "flaunts" (ostentatiously displays) its independence.

flier, flyer A "flier" is both an aviator and a handbill. Use "flyer" only as a proper noun, as in "Radio Flyer."

flounder, founder An unseaworthy ship "flounders" (struggles) in a heavy storm until it "founders" (sinks).

forbear, forebear An ancestor is not a "forebearer," as some have written, but a "forebear." The "fore" in "forebear" should call to mind "before." The "for" in "forbear" (abstain despite pressure) should call to mind "forget" and "forbid."

forego, forgo To "forego" is to go before. To "forgo" is to renounce. Even though the dictionary lists "forego" as a second spelling for "forgo," a precise editor will maintain the difference.

fortunate, fortuitous Some things that are "fortuitous" (happen by chance) are also "fortunate" (lucky), but others are not.

foul, fowl An owl is a "fowl." A "foUl" ball calls for an Umpire.

gamut, gantlet, gauntlet A "gamut" is a full ranGe, such as A Meal. The menu ran the gamut from appetizer to dessert. A "gauntlet" (or "gantlet") is a glove or ordeal. The fraternity pledge was forced to run the gauntlet of members swinging paddles.

garnish, garnishee, garnishment To "garnish" is to decorate a serving of food. To "garnishee" is to seize someone's wages to pay a debt. A "garnishment" is a court order requiring an employer to pay part of one's wages to someone else. Never use EEl to garnish a platter.

gibe, jibe To "gibe" is to Goad with a derisive remark. To "jibe" is to Join amicably in agreement. ("Jibe" is also a sailing term meaning to allow the sail to shift from one side to the other while the boat is running before the wind.)

good, well A Ghost is "good" when it Writes "well." When one is in "good" health, one is "well."

gourmand, gourmet A "gourmand," or excessive eater, Always demaNds Dessert. A "gourmet," or connoisseur of fine food, Eats Truffles.

hanged, hung One who is "hanged" is Executed by Dangling. "Hung" lacks an "e" because it is never used for executions.

hangar, hanger A "hangar" is a GARage for airplanes. "Hanger" is for Every other use of the term.

healthy, healthful When you eat "healthFul" Fare, You are "healthY."

historic, historical A "historic" place is where history happened. A "historical" place, such as a book or marker, is where history is recorded, such as in A Library.

immured, inured One who is "immured" is walled off, or iMMobilized. One who is "inured" is Not susceptible.

impassable, impassible, impassive It is impossible to be "impassible" (oblivious) or "impassive" (unaffected) when confronted with an "impassable" (unyielding) object.

imply, infer A sPeaker "imPlies." A listeNer "iNfers."

incredible, incredulous Upon beholding something "incredible" (unbelievable), one is "incredulous" (unbelieving).

majority, plurality In elections, one can win by a plurality (more votes than any other candidate) but fail to attain a majority (more than 50 percent of the votes).

mantel, mantle A "mantel" overhangs a firEpLace. A "mantle" is a Long capE.

masterful, masterly A sUpervisor is "masterfUl" (domineering). Rembrandt was a "masterly" artist. NOTE: "Masterful" is acceptable for "skilled" or "expert," but "masterly" cannot be substituted for "domineering."

militate, mitigate To "miliTAte against" is to Take Action against. To "mitiGate" is to liGhten, assuaGe or lessen.

nauseous, nauseated To be "nauseous" is to cause nausea. To be "nauseated" is to be afflicted with nausea. These are the preferred uses of these terms, although "nauseous" is frequently used to mean afflicted with nausea.

naval, navel "Naval" pertains to the seA, while "navel" pertains to the bElly.

pedal, peddle To "pedAL" is to Apply Leverage. A "peDDler" goes Door to Door.

pore, pour To "poRE" is to REad. To "poUr" is to Upend a pitcher or gUsh.

practicable, practical Something "practicABLE" is capABLE of achievement. Something "practical" is in touch with reALity.

precipitate (adj.), precipitous A "precipitATe" action is AbrupT. A "precipitouS" Slope is Steep.

presumptive, presumptuous A decision based on a presumption is "presumptive." A "presumptuouS" person is cheeky and inSolent.

pretense, pretext A "pretense" is an act of pretending. A "pretext" is an act of deception.

principal, principle "PrincipLE," which means tenet or beLiEf, is a noun. "Principal" can be an adjective meaning foremost or a noun meaning administrator. The princiPAL is my PAL.

rack, wrack Wreckage is "Wrack." A framework or torture device is a "rack." *This town is going to wrack and ruin. The batter took a bat from the rack.*

regretful, regrettable You are regretful when you commit a regrettable act.

reign, rein God reigns. Horses are led with reins.

reluctant, reticent The "s" sound in "reticent" is a reminder that to be reticent is to be reluctant to speak.

rifle, riffle The double "f" in "riffle" is a reminder of the fluttering of pages as one riffles through a book. To rifle is to ransack.

robber, thief, burglar There are important legal distinctions among these words. One who steals is a thief. A thief who uses the threat of violence is a robber. One who enters a premises illegally is a burglar.

seasonal, seasonable A seasonal event, such as a summer festival, recurs with the season. Weather is seasonable if it is appropriate to the season.

sensual, sensuous If the libido is involved, the right word is "sensual." Something that pleases the senses, especially artistically, is "sensuous."

sewage, sewerage Sewage flows into the sewer. Sewerage is the pipes.

sometime, some time I'll get around to it sometime when I have some time. "Sometime" should not be used to mean "occasional" or "former."

stanch, staunch These words are synonyms both as adjectives—*He is a staunch defender of the First Amendment*—and as verbs—*He applied pressure to stanch the flow of blood.* However, "staunch" is the preferred adjective, and "stanch" is the preferred verb.

straightlaced, straitlaced A tight place is a strait. That is the preferred spelling for "straitlaced" (overly strict) and "straitjacket" (a restraining garment).

suit, suite Add the "e" for a suite (sweet) of rooms.

tortuous, torturous This job is torturous (punishing). The road is tortuous (winding).

turbid, turgid Prose can be "turbid" (murky, impenetrable) or "turgid" (swollen, overblown). Sometimes it is both.

verbal, oral A "verbal" agreement is in words, either written or spoken. An "oral" agreement is spoken but not written. Anything "oral" is related to the mouth, so be careful of double meanings. *The candidate took oral swipes at his opponent.*

BIBLIOGRAPHY AND ADDITIONAL READINGS

Bernstein, Theodore. *The Careful Writer.* Atheneum. 1965.

Bernstein, Theodore. *Miss Thistlebottom's Hobgoblins.* Simon and Schuster. 1971.

Botts, Jack. *The Language of News.* Iowa State University Press. 1994.

Brooks, Brian S., and James L. Pinson. *Working With Words.* St. Martin's Press. 1989.

Copperud, Roy. *American Usage and Style: The Consensus.* Van Nostrand Reinhold. 1980.

Gordon, Karen Elizabeth. *The Deluxe Transitive Vampire: The Ultimate Handbook of Grammar for the Innocent, the Eager, and the Doomed.* Pantheon Books. 1993.

Graves, Robert, and Alan Hodge. *The Use and Abuse of the English Language.* Paragon House. 1990.

Kessler, Lauren, and Duncan McDonald. *When Words Collide.* 2nd ed. Wadsworth. 1988.

The Merriam-Webster Dictionary of English Usage. Merriam Webster. 1989.

Morris, William, and Mary. *Harper Dictionary of Contemporary Usage.* 2nd ed. Harper and Row. 1985.

Newman, Edwin. *Strictly Speaking: Will America Be the Death of English?* Warner Books. 1974.

Roberts, Philip Davies. *Plain English: A User's Guide.* Penguin Books. 1987.

Shertzer, Margaret. *The Elements of Grammar.* Macmillan. 1986.

Venolia, Jan. *Write Right!* Revised ed. Ten Speed Press. 1988.

Chapter 4

A HIT LIST FOR TROUBLESHOOTERS

THE PERILS OF PUBLISHING

Publishing is a perilous enterprise. Publishers are regularly sued by people who are angry about what has been said about them in print. If a suit has merit, the publisher may lose in court and have to pay a large sum in compensation. Sometimes, even if the suit does not have merit, the publisher settles out of court to avoid the expense of litigation. In any case, the lawyers must be paid.

The publisher may be the owner of a publication or an officer or employee of the corporation that owns the enterprise. In return for profits, the publisher bears the responsibility for the impact of published words and pictures on individuals, groups and the society. Some publishers serve as editors. More often, editors work for publishers and share the responsibilities of publishing.

At most newspapers, those who decide what gets published work either in news or advertising. No one on those staffs is exempt from lawsuits. The reporter whose name appears on an offending story is likely to be sued along with the decision-making editors and the publisher. The publisher, however, is usually the one with the "deep pockets," which means the ability to pay large judgments, even though the impact of such a judgment on the financial health of the publication may be devastating. Editors and reporters, though they may lack deep pockets, are protecting their jobs as well as their honor when they shield publishers from lawsuits. Awareness and vigilance toward potential trouble are essential journalistic skills.

Caution may be the prudent course, but overcaution breeds dullness and insignificance, which are both fatal maladies in publishing. A good editor balances caution against the powerful forces working in favor of publication of information the public needs to know. Chief among these forces are the duty to foster the free exchange of ideas and information and the need to survive and prosper economically.

THE FIRST AMENDMENT

The principle that no one should be prevented from using a printing press (or by extension any other means of mass communication) to express ideas and spread information is embodied in the first article of the Bill of Rights, the First Amendment to the Constitution of the United States:

> Congress shall make no law respecting an establishment of religion, or prohibiting the free exercise thereof; or abridging the freedom of speech, or of the press; or the right of the people peaceably to assemble, and to petition the Government for a redress of grievances.

In no other place has so much liberty been enclosed in a single sentence. The article, by prohibiting the government from restricting freedom of religion, speech or press, frees the people to worship, speak and write as they please. All Americans, especially those who work in the media, should celebrate the First Amendment, which protects from government interference not only the publishing industry, but also anyone who possesses the means to publish.

The purpose in granting such protection was not to give newspaper owners a license to make money, although that was one of the outcomes. The purpose also was not to enable manipulators to sway public opinion for private aggrandizement, although that, too, was an outcome.

The intent was to establish a free marketplace of ideas, an arena where truth and falsehood could battle it out on equal footing. In a fair fight, according to this reasoning, truth will always win, and so will the people, who will get the information they need to make intelligent choices in governing themselves.

History has proved the wisdom of that philosophy time and again, especially in Nazi Germany, where government control of the media enabled a gang of ruthless bigots to lead a powerful nation down a bloody road to war and destruction. Such a political disaster is unlikely to happen in the United States, where the busy, if imperfect, mass media keep constant watch on everyone who holds even a small amount of political power. How well journalists are doing their job is a matter of disagreement and debate, but few would argue that the job is not being done.

Because the First Amendment forbids the government to legislate the behavior of journalists, it has been left to the news media themselves to decide what constitutes proper conduct in the gathering and publication of news. In 1975, the Associated Press Managing Editors Association adopted a Statement of Ethical Principles, intended as a non-binding set of guidelines for working journalists (Box 4.1). It was not the only ethics code in existence but was influential because it was drawn up by editors and represented their view of what was practicable.

In 1993, a committee of the APME proposed a more comprehensive declaration, longer and much more detailed than the 1975 code (Box 4.2). The proposed code was based on the "core ethical values" of trustworthiness, fairness, respect, accountability and public service and addressed new issues, such as technology, plagiarism, community involvement, diversity and the separation of news and advertising content. A year of debate and discussion followed, and the result was a slimmed-down model code (Box 4.3), adopted in October 1994 and designed as a foundation for newsroom discussions of ethics.

The comprehensive declaration was revised and shortened mainly because of opposition from editors and lawyers who feared it might provide ammunition in court for people who sue the media.

Some journalists point out that any such code of ethics merely records on paper the same standards that have long been in effect by tradition. The fact that a professional organization finds it necessary to put these principles, some of which are matters of common sense and decency, into writing is reflective of the moral malaise of the late twentieth century, these critics observe. Moreover, they say, no code will have an effect on the unethical behavior of a person who chooses to ignore it. A code cannot be enforced because any attempt to discipline a journalist under the provisions of a code of ethics would establish licensing, or qualifications for admission to the profession, similar to the rules that govern the practice of law. Such licensing of journalists would violate the spirit of the First Amendment.

So why is a written code necessary, or even desirable?

Michael Josephson, president of the Josephson Institute of Ethics, who helped draw up the proposed comprehensive declaration, says the answer is public trust.

> The press cannot carry out any of its major functions effectively unless there is a bedrock of public trust. The press must be respected and believed. Just as public officials have an ethical obligation to preserve faith in government by avoiding both actual and apparent improprieties, journalists must avoid any conduct that undermines public trust or diminishes respect for journalism.

Because journalists are always in a hurry, they may not have time to ponder ethical questions when making decisions. A written code can be helpful, especially to editors in their role as troubleshooters.

THE ELEMENTS OF TROUBLESHOOTING

An editor's responsibility is to detect potential trouble before it is too late, which means before the dangerous material is printed and in the hands of readers. After debate and consideration, the decision may be to go ahead and publish despite the danger, but the potential problem should not go unrecognized until

Associated Press Managing Editors Code of Ethics for Newspapers and Their Staffs

This code is a model against which newspaper men and women can measure their performance. It is meant to apply to news and editorial staff members and others who are involved in, or who influence, news coverage and editorial policy. It has been formulated in the belief that newspapers and the people who produce them should adhere to the highest standards of ethical and professional conduct.

Responsibility

A good newspaper is fair, accurate, honest, responsible, independent and decent. Truth is its guiding principle.

It avoids practices that would conflict with the ability to report and present news in a fair and unbiased manner.

The newspaper should serve as a constructive critic of all segments of society. It should vigorously expose wrongdoing or misuse of power, public or private. Editorially, it should advocate needed reform or innovations in the public interest. News sources should be disclosed unless there is a clear reason not to do so. When it is necessary to protect the confidentiality of a source, the reason should be explained.

The newspaper should background, with the facts, public statements that it knows to be inaccurate or misleading. It should uphold the right of free speech and freedom of the press and should respect the individual's right of privacy. The public's right to know about matters of importance is paramount, and the newspaper should fight vigorously for public access to news of government through open meetings and open records.

Accuracy

The newspaper should guard against inaccuracies, carelessness, bias or distortion through either emphasis or omission.

It should admit all substantive errors and correct them promptly and prominently.

Integrity

The newspaper should strive for impartial treatment of issues and dispassionate handling of controversial subjects. It should provide a forum for the exchange of comment and criticism, especially when such comment is opposed to its editorial positions. Editorials and other expressions of opinion by reporters and editors should be clearly labeled.

"oops!" is the only possible response. Like a pilot getting ready for takeoff, the editor should run through a mental checklist, or "hit" list, to make sure all the hatches are closed.

Although the First Amendment prevents governments from interfering with publication before the fact, a practice called censorship or prior restraint, the people are not powerless to resist transgressions by the media upon their rights. They can take their complaints to court.

Chief among their defenses is the law of libel, which simply says the media must pay a penalty if they publish lies that damage reputations. Privacy rights are another growing area of media law. The penalties are financial, not criminal. Although criminal libel laws remain on the books in some states, they are rarely enforced. Editors don't go to jail for practicing their craft in this country, unless they incur the wrath of judges and are held in contempt. They do, however, regularly face the threat of lawsuits that can be damaging and even disastrous.

The newspaper should report the news without regard for its own interests. It should not give favored news treatment to advertisers or special-interest groups. It should report matters regarding itself or its personnel with the same vigor and candor as it would other institutions or individuals.

Concern for community, business or personal interests should not cause a newspaper to distort or misrepresent the facts.

Conflicts of Interest

The newspaper and its staff should be free of obligations to news sources and special interests. Even the appearance of obligation or conflict of interest should be avoided.

Newspapers should accept nothing of value from news sources or others outside the profession. Gifts and free or reduced-rate travel, entertainment, products and lodging should not be accepted. Expenses in connection with news reporting should be paid by the newspaper. Special favors and special treatment for members of the press should be avoided. Involvement in such things as politics, community affairs, demonstrations and social causes that could cause a conflict of interest, or the appearance of such conflict, should be avoided.

Outside employment by news sources is an obvious conflict of interest, and employment by potential news sources also should be avoided.

Financial investments by staff members or other outside business interests that could conflict with the newspaper's ability to report the news or that would create the impression of such conflict should be avoided.

Stories should not be written or edited primarily for the purpose of winning awards and prizes. Blatantly commercial journalism contests, or others that reflect unfavorably on the newspaper or the profession, should be avoided.

. . .

No code of ethics can prejudge every situation. Common sense and good judgment are required in applying ethical principles to newspaper realities. Individual newspapers are encouraged to augment these APME guidelines with locally produced codes that apply more specifically to their own situations.

Adopted by the APME Board of Directors, April 15, 1975

Box 4.1

Media law is primarily case law. That is, it has evolved through a series of decisions in specific cases that have established some general principles. Every editor should know the major cases, and every student of journalism should take at least one course in communications law. However, the job of daily decision-making is not a matter of matching news events with corresponding cases. Things are not that simple. No two news events are precisely alike, and similarities may be misleading. Troubleshooting is like slogging through a minefield, uncertain when or where the next explosion may come. The mines are unmarked, of course, but editors have some clues to where they may lie.

LIBEL: THE BASICS

Libel is damage to reputation caused by the publication of a false statement of fact about an identifiable living person. The elements of libel are:

(cont. on p. 130)

Associated Press Managing Editors Declaration of Ethics (Proposed, 1993)

PURPOSE: The purpose of this Declaration of Ethical Standards is to define professional standards by which newspapers build and maintain public trust. It is intended as a beginning point for editors in codifying such standards for their individual newspapers. Because newspapers are accountable to the public they serve, APME encourages each member newspaper to:

- Adopt written ethical standards and policies.
- Make them known to the public.
- Train and motivate their staffs to respect them.

APPLICATION: The principles in which this declaration is grounded are meant to apply to all journalists—news and editorial employees, as well as free-lancers—who are involved in, or who influence, news coverage or editorial policy. Of course no statement of standards can prejudge every contingency. Common sense and good judgment are required in applying ethical principles to newspaper realities.

THE MISSION OF JOURNALISM: The essential role of newspapers is to:

- Inform readers of events and facts that are important to them and to their participation in a democracy, by insuring the free flow of public information.
- Scrutinize government and other major institutions, in order to vigorously expose wrongdoing and misuse of power, whether public or private.
- Serve as a constructive critic of all segments of society.
- Provide a forum for the exchange of comment and criticism from throughout the community, particularly from those with views different from the newspaper's.
- Advocate the public interest, including needed reform and useful innovation, through the editorial page.
- Pursue the truth with unwavering vigor, in a manner consistent with these ethical standards.

CORE ETHICAL VALUES: The following standards are derived from core ethical values:

TRUSTWORTHINESS, which assures credibility and includes

- Accuracy.
- Honesty.
- Promise-keeping.
- Independence.

FAIRNESS, which includes:

- Impartiality.
- Context.
- Completeness.

RESPECT, which includes:

- High regard for personal privacy.
- Sensitivity to community standards and taste.
- Treatment of individuals with courtesy and compassion.

ACCOUNTABILITY, which includes:

- Pursuit of journalistic excellence.
- Responsiveness to questions and complaints from the public.
- Acknowledgment and correction of error.
- Exercise of self-restraint in the public interest.

PUBLIC SERVICE, which includes:

- Publication of newsworthy information to help readers make informed decisions.
- Vigilance in acting as watchdog over government and other major institutions.
- Timeliness in getting news to readers, within the constraints of these ethical standards.

DIVERSITY, which includes:

- Commitment to coverage of all communities and groups served by the newspaper.
- Commitment to creating a staff with diverse backgrounds, to help assure coverage that is inclusive.

Standards of Ethics

I. TRUSTWORTHINESS. Newspapers earn the public's trust through accuracy, honesty, promise-keeping and independence.

A. ACCURACY. A newspaper must be passionately devoted to accuracy, the foundation of credibility and trust.

1. Facts. Newspapers must be committed to the accurate reporting of facts. They must never knowingly publish inaccurate or misleading information.

a. Newspapers should develop and use safeguards to avoid error. These should include systematic verification of facts and quotations, and corroboration of critical information.

b. Newspapers should guard against carelessness, bias and distortion—resulting from either emphasis or omission—in all stories, headlines and captions.

2. Quotations. Quotes must be precise and must fairly reflect the context of conversations.

a. Alteration. While some newspapers may impose a stricter standard, there may be little or no actual harm in altering quotes in the following limited circumstances:
- Correcting grammar that could make the statement confusing or would make the speaker appear foolish.
- Avoiding dialect that is not essential to the story.

b. Sequence. In reporting quotations in a different sequence from the one in which they were made, newspapers should be certain that the change in order does not alter meaning or create misleading or unfair impressions.

c. Omission. When not essential to a story,
- Dialect should be avoided.
- Offensive language should be avoided.

d. Ellipses. The use of ellipses is helpful to indicate the omission of confusing or extraneous material, as well as dialect or offensive language. However, they should never be used to make quotes appear to be contiguous in time when they actually were taken from different segments of a conversation.

3. Photos and graphics. Both photographs and graphics must be precise and accurate representations of reality.

a. Technical enhancements. It is permissible to use technical enhancements only when the resulting work is faithful to the reality of the scene or situation depicted.

b. Alteration or manipulation. The actual content of a photograph should not be altered or manipulated, except for illustrative purposes, in which case the image must be clearly labeled to indicate it has been altered.

c. Posed pictures and models. Where there is a possibility that readers will believe a picture portrays a spontaneous event, the use of posed situations or models should be noted in print.

B. HONESTY. Honesty requires a good faith intent to be truthful and non-deceptive in all communications. In most cases it requires candor. Honesty speaks directly to the credibility of a newspaper with both sources and readers.

Box 4.2

1. Plagiarism. Stealing someone else's wording, quotes or other work is wrong. Readers have a right to expect that what they read in the newspaper is the author's own work, unless otherwise indicated.
2. Deception. Deceptive practices such as misrepresentation, trickery, impersonation and the use of hidden tape recorders or cameras in newsgathering can seriously undermine a newspaper's credibility and trustworthiness. These practices are outside the bounds of generally accepted journalistic behavior. An editor confronted with a decision to exceed those bounds should meet the following minimum conditions:
   - **a.** Public importance. The expected news story must be of such vital public interest that its news value clearly outweighs the damage to trust and credibility that might result from the use of deception.
   - **b.** Alternatives. The story cannot reasonably be recast to avoid the need to deceive.
   - **c.** Last resort. All other means of getting the story must have been exhausted.
   - **d.** Editorial approval. The decision to use deception must be approved at the highest level of the newsroom after thorough discussion.
   - **e.** Disclosure. The deceptive practices and the reasons they were used must be disclosed in print at the time the story is published.
   - **f.** Questions. In addition to meeting these conditions, as a final caution an editor should ask these questions:
     - Was the decision to deceive discussed, as thoroughly and broadly as feasible, and do other staffers generally accept the decision?
     - Will readers and staff members tend to agree that the story justified the deception?
3. Taping. Journalists should not audio- or videotape their interviews without the knowledge of those being taped.
4. Labeling. Opinion should be clearly labeled, as distinct from news, in a way that is easily understood by the average reader.
5. Polls and surveys. Statistical data derived from polling and surveying are especially susceptible to misunderstanding, misinterpretation and misuse.
   - **a.** Differentiation. Newspapers should clearly distinguish between scientific polls and non-scientific surveys such as reader call-ins or write-ins and person-on-the-street inquiries that are reported in statistical terms. This must be done in a way that is likely to be understood by the average reader.
     - In using scientific pools, the sample size, nature of the sample and margin of error should be disclosed.
     - In using non-scientific surveys, the manner in which they were taken and their limitations should be clearly explained in print. Merely labeling a survey as "non-scientific" is not sufficient.

- Surveys that do not meet minimal scientific standards of validity and reliability should not be identified as polls, not should they be portrayed in language suitable for scientific polls.
- Great caution should be used in employing non-scientific polls to address substantial questions of public policy or to describe the popularity or approval rating of public officials or public actions.

b. Headlines and graphics. Special care should be taken with respect to headlines and graphic representations of scientific and non-scientific data, in order to avoid confusing or misleading readers.

6. Confidential sources. The use of confidential sources should be rare rather than routine. It is the obligation of newspapers to resist their use.

a. Editors and reporters should seriously consider whether the information received from confidential sources is vital to readers before deciding to print.

b. Pledges of confidentiality by reporters should be given only as a last resort.

c. Every effort should be made to get the information on the record before publishing it without attribution.

d. When a source must remain unidentified, the reason should be stated in print.

e. The responsible editor should know the identity of the source before publication.

C. PROMISE-KEEPING. Trustworthy organizations and individuals can be relied upon to keep their promises. Because broken commitments undermine credibility and threaten trusting relationships in the future, newspapers and journalists should treat them as solemn bonds.

1. Prudence in making promises. Journalists should make promises only with great care and restraint. All parties should clearly understand the nature of such commitments, and any contingencies that might affect the keeping of a promise should be understood. Journalists should not promise anything outside the scope of their authority. Promises made in such circumstances cannot be considered binding on the newspaper. Senior editors should ensure that staff members understand the limits of their authority.

2. Promises by journalists.

a. Limitations on use. Promises made to a news source regarding conditions of use or attribution (including such designations as off-the-record, on background, not-for-attribution and embargoed) or prepublication review of any sort should be kept by the newspaper, or the information should not be used.

- Journalists are responsible for assuring that agreements made with sources are clear, precise and understood by all parties.
- Journalists who have any doubt whether a source understands that all information is on the record, unless otherwise explicitly agreed, should inform the source of this fact at the earliest opportunity.

Box 4.2 (cont.)

D. INDEPENDENCE. A newspaper must maintain its independence so that it is free of obligations and impervious to pressures that would obstruct its ability to make news judgments in the public interest.

1. Conflicts of interest. Journalists should avoid actual and apparent conflicts of interest.

a. Actual conflicts are economic, personal and political relationships and activities that impede the ability to make all journalistic judgments on the merits and in the public interest.

b. Apparent conflicts are relationships and transactions that undermine the credibility of the journalist or the newspaper, by creating in the mind of a fair-minded, disinterested observer the belief that the journalist's private interests conflict with journalistic duties.

2. Community involvement. Journalists are encouraged to be involved in their communities to the extent that such activities do not create actual or apparent conflicts of interest or otherwise raise questions about the impartiality of news coverage.

a. Journalists should not be involved in the news that they cover.

b. Journalists should avoid activities that could compromise their newspaper, even in situations where they are not directly involved in coverage. For example, they should avoid:

- Signing petitions or participating in demonstrations.
- Serving outside the newspaper in a decision-making capacity or as a fundraiser in organizations that can be expected to, or actually do, generate significant news.

3. Financial interests. Journalists should be free of financial and other obligations to news sources and special interests.

a. Gifts and gratuities. Journalists should not accept favors or gifts, subsidized or free travel, accommodations, special discounts, tickets to sports or entertainment events, or other benefits from news sources or organizations that the newspaper may cover. Items of nominal value need not be returned if it would be awkward to do so.

b. Expenses. The expenses that are incurred in connection with news reporting should be paid by the newspaper.

c. Relationships with newsmakers. Journalists should avoid any financial interest that could raise questions about their impartiality, such as co-authoring a book or engaging in other business activities with newsmakers they cover.

4. Advertising/advertorial. The credibility of the newspaper, hence its business and journalistic viability, depends on the clear separation of news and advertising.

a. News decisions should not be compromised by the newspaper's business and advertising relationships.

b. News coverage should not be promised in exchange for advertising.
c. Reading matter produced outside the newsroom for advertising and promotional sections should be clearly labeled and presented in such a way as to distinguish it from news.

5. Disclosure. Some conflicts may be impossible to avoid. Any that could compromise the credibility of the newspaper should be disclosed to readers.
6. Contests. Stories, photographs and illustrations should not be published for the purpose of winning awards or prizes. Blatantly commercial journalism contests or others that reflect unfavorably on the newspaper or the craft should be avoided.

II. FAIRNESS. Fairness requires the presentation of relevant facts without bias and in context.

A. IMPARTIALITY. News decisions must be approached with open minds and without prior judgment.
B. CONTEXT. News should be presented in sufficient historical and factual context to assure that a fair and accurate picture is conveyed. Stories should be free of distortion that could be created by omission, inappropriate emphasis or the selective use of fact.
C. COMPLETENESS. Newspapers should assure that a story contains the relevant facts, and represents any substantial and relevant body of opinion, in matters of significant controversy.

1. Opposing views. An honest and vigorous effort must be made to include responsible opposing views in news stories.
2. Opportunity to reply. In reporting any statements that could injure the reputation of an individual or group, those affected must be given the earliest opportunity to reply.
3. Motives. The motives of those who press their views upon journalists must be routinely examined, and, where appropriate, revealed to the reader.
4. Developments. When stories have been prominently displayed, fairness requires that substantial subsequent developments be covered, and similarly displayed.

III. RESPECT. Newspapers should treat with respect the people they cover and the communities they serve.

A. PRIVACY. A high regard for personal privacy is essential. Journalists must recognize that ordinary citizens have a greater right to privacy than public figures.

1. Ordinary citizens. Newspapers must be especially sensitive to the legitimate privacy concerns of ordinary citizens who are thrust into the news, such as innocent bystanders, witnesses, victims, heroes, whistleblowers and minors. The value of publishing such information as names, religious beliefs, sexual orientation, ethnicity and past behavior must be weighed against the relevance to the story and compassion for the individual.
2. Public figures. Those who are in public roles also have a right to privacy. However, it is limited by the degree to which their personal conduct bears on their public roles and responsibilities, and the degree to which they voluntarily conduct their private lives in the public limelight.

Box 4.2 (cont.)

3. Journalists must recognize the danger to individual privacy and loss of credibility inherent in publishing intimate details about ordinary citizens that are obtained from electronic databases or cover surveillance.

B. COMMUNITY STANDARDS. Newspapers should embrace high standards of taste and decency, and should be sensitive to community values.

1. Offensive language, including profanity and insulting comment, should be published only when essential to a significant story.
2. Offensive and intrusive photographs must have sufficient news value to outweigh potential public objections and harm to the individuals portrayed.

C. COURTESY AND COMPASSION. Journalists and their newspapers should treat news sources and subjects with courtesy and compassion.

1. Journalists should be especially sensitive to news sources in times of grief, personal loss or extreme emotional distress.
2. Special care should be taken to treat sensitively those who are unaccustomed to dealing with the press. The danger of exploitation is particularly acute when dealing with children.

IV. ACCOUNTABILITY.

A. PURSUIT OF JOURNALISTIC EXCELLENCE. Journalists share an obligation to ensure that their work reflects the core values on which these standards are based. Implicit in this is the need to recruit a high-quality staff, provide adequate training and enforce specific journalistic standards.

B. RESPONSIVENESS. Journalists—especially newsroom leaders—have a responsibility to remain accessible to readers and to explain their newspapers' decisions and processes. They should be open to complaints. Newspapers should make known to the public their standards and policies. In stories that are likely to raise ethical questions in the minds of readers, newspapers' rationale for their decisions should be explained in print. Each newspaper should provide a forum for a wide variety of opinions and views, especially from those who disagree with its editorial positions and news practices.

C. ERROR. Newspapers have a responsibility to correct prominently and promptly all errors of fact and to clarify errors of omission and context. All assertions of error must be investigated

1. Defamation, which is an attack on someone's good name
2. Identification, which means a specific person is clearly the target of the attack although not necessarily mentioned by name
3. Publication, which means the defamatory information is passed on to someone else in written or printed form (spoken defamation is slander)

If everything printed in newspapers were true, libel would be no problem. As the fictional lawyer in "Absence of Malice," a film written by a former news-

and resolved in a timely way.

D. SELF-RESTRAINT. News judgments should be influenced by compassion for individuals, by the consequences of publication and by readers' need to know. There are occasions when the journalist's exercise of self-restraint will be in the public interest, such as when significant harm can be reasonably anticipated with no equivalent countervailing public benefit.

V. PUBLIC SERVICE. The role of the press in the nation's history, and the constitutional protection that the press enjoys, suggests a special responsibility to operate in the public interest.

A. RELEVANCE. While a newspaper performs many functions, its primary obligation is to provide the information that citizens need to make informed decisions and to participate effectively in civic life.

B. VIGILANCE. Journalists must serve as watchdogs, with respect to the major institutions of society, monitoring the conduct of the public's business, in government and in the private sector. The press itself is such an institution and must be scrutinized.

C. TIMELINESS. Readers are best served when they get the news in a timely manner. Newspapers are obliged to provide information promptly. Inevitably, the need for publishing immediately will, on occasion, come into conflict with meeting other ethical obligations. In those instances, journalists must weigh the good that will be achieved with speed against the harm that could be inflicted by compromising other values.

VI. DIVERSITY. A newspaper is obligated to serve all of the community of which it is a part.

A. SCOPE. Diversity is an issue with respect to age, gender, race, ethnicity, religion, socio-economic status, sexual orientation and disability.

B. STAFFING. Editors must make concerted, sustained efforts to recruit, retain and develop staffs that reflect the variety of the communities they serve.

C. INCLUSION. It is important to achieve diversity not only in the choice of events and issues covered, but also in the choice of sources for that coverage.

D. STEREOTYPING. Newspapers should avoid coverage that perpetuates group stereotypes or objectifies individuals.

E. PROFESSIONAL CONDUCT. Journalists should conduct themselves in a way that underscores a commitment to fair treatment for all people. Membership in discriminatory clubs and organizations undermines a journalist's credibility.

Box 4.2

paper editor, observes, "If newspapers printed nothing but truth, they would never employ attorneys, and I should be out of work, which I am not."

Unfortunately, truth is elusive. Stories are based on sets of facts that are never complete. Always there is at least one unresponsive source, one unanswered question, one avenue left unexplored because of the pressure of time, one unsuspected ingredient in the mixture of events. Years, decades and even centuries after a major event, historians still search for undisclosed facts. Journalism, it has been said, is history's first draft. Mistakes are inevitable.

Associated Press Managing Editors Statement of Ethics (Approved, 1994)

These principles are a model against which news and editorial staff members can measure their performance. They have been formulated in the belief that newspapers and the people who produce them must adhere to the highest standards of ethical and professional conduct.

The public's right to know about matters of importance is paramount. The newspaper has a special responsibility as surrogate of its readers to be a vigilant watchdog of their legitimate public interests.

No statement of principles can prescribe decisions governing every situation. Common sense and good judgment are required in applying ethical principles to newspaper realities. As new technologies evolve, these principles can help guide editors to ensure the credibility of the news and information they provide.

Individual newspapers are encouraged to augment these APME guidelines more specifically to their own situations.

Responsibility:

The good newspaper is fair, accurate, honest, responsible, independent and decent. Truth is its guiding principle.

It avoids practices that would conflict with the ability to report and present news in a fair, accurate and unbiased manner.

The newspaper should serve as a constructive critic of all segments of society. It should reasonably reflect, in staffing and coverage, its diverse constituencies. It should vigorously exppose wrongdoing, duplicity, or misuse of power, public or private.

Editorially, it should advocate needed reform and innovation in the public interest.

News sources should be disclosed unless there is a clear reason not to do so. When it is necessary to protect the confidentiality of a source, the reason should be explained.

The newspaper should uphold the right of free speech and freedom of the press and should respect the individual's right of privacy. The newspaper should fight vigorously for public access to news of government through open meetings and records.

Accuracy:

The newspaper should guard against inaccuracies, carelessness, bias, or distortion through emphasis, omission or technological manipulation.

It should acknowledge errors and correct them promptly and prominently.

Honest mistakes are excusable in many states, especially if the publisher of an offending statement apologizes. A trial occurs when the aggrieved party asserts that a statement is false, and the publisher insists it is true. A jury may be called on to decide who is right. If the jury supports the publisher, the libel suit fails because proof of truth is a solid defense. If the jury sides with the wronged party, or plaintiff, the publisher may be required to pay damages, a sum of money the court decides is appropriate. (It is incorrect to say the publisher was found guilty; terms like "guilty" are reserved for criminal trials.)

Damages come in two forms: actual (general, special) and punitive (exemplary). Actual damages compensate the plaintiff for hurt feelings, tarnished reputation and loss of business income. Punitive damages are a kind of punishment; they are supposed to teach the publisher a lesson. To make an impression, they

Integrity:
The newspaper should strive for impartial treatment of issues and dispassionate handling of controversial subjects. It should provide a forum for the exchange of comment and criticism, especially when such comment is opposed to its editorial positions.

Editorials and expressions of personal opinion by reporters and editors should be clearly labeled. Advertising should be clearly differentiated from news.

The newspaper should report the news without regard for its own interests, mindful of the need to disclose potential conflicts. It should not give favored news treatment to advertisers or special-interest groups. It should report matters regarding itself or its personnel with the same vigor and candor as it would other institutions or individuals.

Concern for community, business or personal interests should not cause the newspaper to distort or misrepresent the facts.

The newspaper should deal honestly with readers and newsmakers. It should keep its promises.

The newspaper should not plagiarize words or images.

Independence:
The newspaper and its staff should be free of obligations to news sources and newsmakers. Even the appearance of obligation or conflict of interest should be avoided.

Newspapers should accept nothing of value from news sources or others outside the profession. Gifts and free or reduced-rate travel, entertainment, products and lodging should not be accepted.

Journalists are encouraged to be involved in their communities, to the extent that such activities do not create conflicts of interest. Involvement in politics, demonstrations and social causes that could cause a conflict of interest, or the appearance of such conflict, should be avoided.

Work by staff members for the people or institutions they cover also should be avoided.

Financial investments by staff members or other outside business interests that could create the impression of a conflict of interest should be avoided.

Stories should not be written or edited primarily for the purpose of winning awards and prizes. Self-serving journalism contests and awards that reflect unfavorably on the newspaper or the profession should be avoided.

Box 4.3

have to hurt, and for that reason they tend to be much higher than actual damages. Some states have abolished punitive damages to discourage lawyers from taking cases with no fees, gambling that they will share in heavy punitive damages awarded to plaintiffs (a practice called contingency).

Predicting how a libel case will be decided in court is difficult because the rules are unclear and even a bit whimsical. It matters whether the plaintiff is a public official, a public figure or a private figure, and the difference is not sharply defined. In *New York Times v. Sullivan* (1964), the U.S. Supreme Court ruled that public officials could collect damages only if they could prove that libelous statements were published with actual malice. This means that mistakes were not honest mistakes but intentional ones, designed to hurt somebody, that false statements were printed even though the editors and reporters knew they were not true. In short, the publishers of these statements recklessly disregarded the truth.

Actual malice is hard to prove, and the Supreme Court intended this to be the case, because the court wanted reporters and editors to comment without fear on the activities of public officials, thus acting in essence as a government watchdog. The practical effect of the *Sullivan* case was to make it virtually impossible for a public official to collect damages in a libel suit. The "Absence of Malice" attorney observes, "We may say whatever we like about Mr. Gallagher, and he is powerless to do us harm. Democracy is served."

"Mr. Gallagher" could stand for anybody with potential cause to sue a publisher. If he is not a public official, which means he was not elected or appointed to a position in which the taxpayers pay his salary, he may be a public figure.

"What does it take to make him a public figure?" a reporter asks the attorney in "Absence of Malice."

"If I knew that I should be a judge," he replies. "They never tell us until it is too late."

In two cases following *New York Times v. Sullivan,* one involving a football coach and the other involving a retired general who promoted right-wing causes, the Supreme Court ruled that a public figure was someone who was associated with affairs and issues in which the public had an interest and who had reached a level of prominence where the media tended to focus attention. Such plaintiffs, the court said, would be treated as public officials and required to prove actual malice.

Later, in a case involving a lawyer who charged that a right-wing publication had called him a Communist, the court said a public figure had to be not only widely known but also an activist who had been thrust into the spotlight in regard to some major controversy. Subsequently, two classes were defined:

1. Pervasive public figures, who are famous enough to be in the public eye no matter what they do, such as movie and sports stars.
2. Limited-purpose public figures, who campaign actively for public attention in regard to topics or controversies whose outcomes they try to influence. Except in relation to those subjects, these people remain private figures.

Anyone defined as a private figure need not prove actual malice but merely negligence, which means showing that editors and reporters were careless with the facts. Being careful with the facts is elementary to ethical journalists. However, the courts recognize that in the rush to publish, mistakes happen, and they have established protections for journalists, so that publishers don't shy away from potentially hazardous topics. Sometimes the public—and by extension, jurors—don't understand why it's necessary to rush, but the law does. It protects journalists under two umbrellas: privilege and fair comment and criticism.

THE JOURNALIST'S PRIVILEGE

Absolute privilege protects members of Congress, who may speak freely on the floor without fear of legal retribution, and speakers in some other official proceedings. The journalist's privilege is not absolute. It requires a fair, accurate and balanced report of any official record or proceeding. In other words, the official news source may offend someone, but the media may report the offensive material fairly, accurately and with balance. This does not mean editors and reporters are free to print information they know is false, but the privilege protects responsible journalism.

"Fair, accurate and balanced" is really three ways of saying the same thing, because no report can be fair without being accurate and balanced. The standard requires more than just telling the other side. It means well-rounded reporting and editing that do not select out only those facts that support a premise or a point of view.

Some states have gone beyond privilege to create a shield for journalists against overzealous lawyers. "Shield laws" allow journalists to refuse to disclose confidential sources or to testify about information they may have obtained but not reported in a published story. Even in states without such laws, courts may honor a shield.

THE OPINION PRIVILEGE

Opinions are not libelous. As long as it is clear that an offending statement is merely an opinion, which no reasonable person would mistake for fact, courts will not sustain a libel action. Journalists may thus engage in fair comment and criticism, judging the quality of a performance, for example, or assessing a candidate. News sources, as well, may be quoted when they express opinions, even if someone is insulted.

However, journalists may tend to overvalue this protection. Telling the difference between a fact and an opinion is an inexact science. A sentence like "In my opinion, he's a liar," may be considered opinion in some courts and not in others, especially if the insulted person can demonstrate personal truthfulness.

THE RIGHT OF PRIVACY

News-gathering efforts may result in lawsuits charging invasion of privacy, but the danger is small in comparison with libel. Most privacy discussions among reporters and editors involve ethics rather than the law. Is it proper to name rape victims? Is it right to name juveniles accused of crimes? Is it right to publish the address where a burglary took place if the resident is elderly and lives alone and thus is vulnerable to being victimized again? These are questions for editors, not courts, to decide, because newsworthiness generally overcomes any legal right to privacy.

Privacy poses a legal danger for journalists when they dig up information from the past that may or may not be considered newsworthy in the present. If the information is factual, it is not defamatory, and no libel suit can be sustained. However, the publicity may upset somebody who had thought the past was buried, and the embarrassment may be so acute that the person may sue for invasion of privacy. A well-known case of this kind involved a former child prodigy who had been able to write and type in both English and French at the age of 1. At 39, long out of the limelight, the man was portrayed as leading a pathetic and eccentric life in a "where are they now?" profile in *The New Yorker* magazine, and he sued. The court ruled in favor of the magazine, saying that despite a long period of obscurity, the man remained newsworthy because the public was fascinated by him.

Another privacy peril involves the concept of "false light," which means using a person's name or picture in a context that may give readers an erroneous impression of the person's social, political or economic role. An example might be a biography of someone who objects to the writer's interpretation or selection of facts or accuses the writer of making something up, even though the result is not legally damaging, just inaccurate. Instead of filing a libel suit and facing the necessity of showing damage to reputation, the offended party might file a privacy invasion suit under the doctrine of false light. This is a relatively new threat to publishers and is not recognized in every state.

Pictures carry a particular false light danger if they are used in a misleading way. For example, a street scene might be used to illustrate an article on neighborhood drug pushers and create an erroneous impression that an identifiable person in the picture was a dealer or a user.

Besides the dangers of dredging up the past and placing people in a false light, journalists must be aware of two other privacy dangers: appropriation and intrusion.

Appropriation is using someone's name or picture for a commercial purpose, as in advertising, without permission. News coverage is not a commercial purpose.

Intrusion is breaking into a private area or entering uninvited or by trickery. Photographers are sometimes tempted to intrude to carry out a difficult assignment or capture an elusive subject. Trespassing is no more a legal activity for them than for anyone else.

PLAGIARISM

Stealing someone else's property is a crime, and although journalists don't go to prison for *plagiarism,* which means stealing someone else's words, they do pay penalties. They may be sued, and the offended party may collect damages. More commonly, offenders may lose their jobs.

Plagiarism is considered a firing offense at many publications. It consists of lifting phrases, sentences or paragraphs from a source other than one's own work and republishing them without alteration or attribution. The facts are usually not at issue, because the act of writing about them does not establish the writer's ownership of them. However, the writer is the owner of his or her words, phrases, sentences and paragraphs, and if another writer's subsequent work is sufficiently similar, the plagiarist may be found out. It is rather like being caught with the stolen jewels in one's pocket.

"Sufficiently similar" usually means that the stolen passages must be verbatim, or identical to the original, but it may be enough to match the character of a work. In 1988, the drama critic of the *St. Paul Pioneer Press Dispatch* resigned after a reader noticed similarities between a play review and another critic's 1982 review of the same play. The newspaper's editor, Deborah Howell, wrote in a "Notice to Readers" that the *Pioneer Press Dispatch* review duplicated the structure and thesis of the earlier work and contained some identical "key phrases."

"Plagiarism is one of the most serious of all journalistic sins and cannot be tolerated," Howell wrote.

The critic, who blew the whistle on himself after receiving a letter from the reader, said in a farewell column that his research notes had become "commingled" with notes taken during the performance. This is a danger for any writer who is careless about attribution in note taking.

Plagiarism is often discovered by chance when readers detect a familiar ring to a piece of writing. However, ominous possibilities were raised in a court case in 1993 in which two government agents looking for plagiarism in the works of a prominent historian used a computer program called the "plagiarism machine" to scan for repetitive phrases.

Editors can help guard against inadvertent plagiarism, like the drama critic's, by watching for unattributed statements that appear to need attribution. Crediting the source may be all that is required to avoid plagiarism charges. The ultimate defense, however, is the writer's own cautious vigilance.

HOAXES

Reporters do a lot of their interviewing by phone, and they don't always bother to verify the identity of the person at the other end. The voice may seem right, and the manner may be impressive, but nevertheless the news source may be a hoaxer. Regrettably, people who set out to trick the media into publicizing phony news events are likely to succeed, for several reasons:

1. They offer unusual, intriguing stories that are usually humorous or astounding—just the sort of thing that captures editors' interest.
2. Unless they have been taken in at least once by a hoax, editors tend to be receptive because they are hungry for offbeat stories.
3. Tricksters who understand newspaper deadlines can time their phony events to make it difficult for reporters to check up on them before the story is published.

Some examples of hoaxes that succeeded in fooling at least some editors:

- The body of Vladimir Lenin is offered for sale by the Russians after the collapse of the Soviet Union.
- A man who says he is broke offers to sell a lung or a kidney for $25,000.
- Members of a cult eat cockroach hormones to fight acne and menstrual cramps.
- A man says he has home movies to prove that Elvis Presley is alive.
- A group called the Fat Squad is paid by overeaters to keep them from food.
- The Society for Indecency of Naked Animals advocates clothing for pets.

The defense against being embarrassed by such trickery is skepticism. News releases with realistic, official-looking headings can be created by just about anybody with a home computer. Telephone pranksters can masquerade as someone they are not. If a story sounds too outrageous to be true, the reporter should thoroughly check it, even at the cost of missing a deadline.

FABRICATION

Journalists have their own form of hoax, the fictionalized news story, in which the writer takes liberties with the facts to create an effect, make a point or bend reality to fit a preconceived frame. Such fabrications are rare because no ethical journalist would even entertain the idea of making up a story, but editors have been keenly aware of the danger since a 1981 Pulitzer Prize feature from the *Washington Post* was revealed to have come, at least in part, from the writer's imagination.

The story by *Post* reporter Janet Cooke was about "Jimmy," an 8-year-old heroin addict who supposedly lived in the District of Columbia. When it was published, it "hit Washington like a grenade," in the words of a *Post* headline. The newspaper's switchboard was jammed with calls from outraged readers who wanted to help Jimmy. The police chief ordered a citywide search for the unfortunate boy. Janet Cooke's moving account won the Pulitzer Prize for feature writing.

Reality set in when Jimmy and his family could not be found, and Cooke admitted that they were inventions, based on a composite of information she had obtained from social workers and other sources. The coveted Pulitzer Prize was withdrawn, the newspaper was embarrassed, and Cooke resigned.

Post editor Benjamin Bradlee said: "The credibility of a newspaper is its most precious asset, and it depends almost entirely on the integrity of its reporters. When that integrity is investigated and found wanting, the wounds are grievous, and there is nothing to do but come clean with our readers, apologize to the Advisory Board of the Pulitzer Prizes, and begin immediately on the uphill task of regaining our credibility."

One aspect of coming clean with readers was the assignment of the newspaper's reader representative, or ombudsman, William Green, to investigate how the fabricated story had come to be published. Among Green's findings were these:

1. Reliance on confidential sources, whose identity is known only to the reporter, is dangerous. "If the reporter can't support the integrity of his or her story by revealing the name to his or her editor, the story shouldn't be published," Green wrote.
2. The scramble to win prestigious prizes like the Pulitzer is poisonous. It undermines the primary obligation of informing readers.

The Cooke incident caused news staffs nationwide to engage in a good deal of soul-searching. At the *St. Petersburg Times,* editor Gene Patterson, a moral force of national stature in journalism, made these remarks:

> Once confidentiality is pledged to a source, the editor must share with the reporter the burden of trust which neither can betray, even if it means going to jail together rather than breaking the confidence. Mutual trust and respect for each other's work is essential between reporter and editor. But responsibility for what's printed rests on the editor who clears it, and he or she can never duck that responsibility by blaming a reporter. It is our general rule, of course, that confidential sources should be used simply as tipsters whose information can then be verified by identifiable sources. We expect it to be a rare event when and if a story we print is attributed to a confidential source. On the contrary, our emphasis is on identifying all sources by name. . . .
>
> We work for our readers, not for prizes. If we do exceptional work for our readers, recognition will find us out. But that is the proper order of things. The Pulitzer Prize is the highest recognition in our line of work, and if we have done deserving work for our readers we should not hesitate to enter it in this competition with the nation's best. But that's the afterthought, not the motive.

The legacy of the Cooke affair for today's journalists should be a continuing appreciation of the "burden of trust" they all bear—trust between editors and reporters and trust between both of these and their readers.

COPYRIGHT INFRINGEMENT

Federal law protects authors against unauthorized reproduction of their works. Any literary work, including a newspaper and all its contents, can be registered with the Copyright Office. A publisher who reprints copyrighted material without permission may be subject to a number of penalties. The offending copies of the publication may be seized and destroyed, and an injunction against further publication may be issued. Fines may also be imposed.

Editors can run afoul of copyright law unintentionally. For example, they may use the lyrics of a popular song in a headline or in some other decorative form on a page. Or they may clip a cartoon or other illustration from a newspaper or magazine and reproduce it. Any such use of copyrighted material is an infringement.

Protecting against violation of the copyright law requires obtaining permission from the copyright holder in advance of publication. A fee may have to be paid, but it will be a minor obligation in comparison with the potential consequences of infringing copyright.

SOME GUIDELINES FOR TROUBLESHOOTERS

The array of legal perils editors must deal with in their daily work may seem bewildering, but a set of natural defenses is always in place. These defenses are simply the editor's own instincts about right and wrong. As in all human endeavors, going ahead despite reasonable doubts is risky. Editors regularly take risks, but they are calculated risks, and the odds tend to be favorable because good editors take precautions as reflected in the following guidelines:

1. The key word is fairness. It is a word worth examining in detail, and here are some definitions:

> Fairness means pursuing the truth with both vigor and compassion, and reporting information without favoritism, self-interest or prejudice.
>
> Accuracy and fairness mean challenging traditional definitions of news, ensuring coverage of societal issues and groups of people under-reported in the past.
>
> Accuracy and fairness also mean portraying individuals and issues with a basic sense of open-mindedness, avoiding biased reporting, stereotypical portrayals, and unsubstantiated allegations.
>
> —Jay Black, Bob Steele and Ralph Barney, *Doing Ethics in Journalism,* 1993

> The truth is something more than just a collection of facts. Facts have a relationship to one another and to all other facts, forming a larger whole. Yet analytic coverage of American institutions, of science and technology, of elections, and of social movements is rare.
>
> —Phillip Patterson and Lee Wilkins, *Media Ethics: Issues and Cases,* 1991

> In addition to being accurate, a truthful story should promote understanding. . . . The goal should be to provide an account that is essentially complete. A story should contain as much relevant information as is available and essential to afford the average reader or viewer at least an understanding of the facts and the context of the facts.
>
> —Louis A. Day, *Ethics in Media Communications: Cases and Controversies,* 1991

> Reporters and editors of *The Post* are committed to fairness. While arguments about objectivity are endless, the concept of fairness is something that editors and reporters can easily understand and pursue. Fairness results from a few simple practices:
>
> - No story is fair if it omits facts of major importance or significance. So fairness includes completeness.
> - No story is fair if it includes essentially irrelevant information at the expense of significant facts. So fairness includes relevance.
> - No story is fair if it consciously or unconsciously misleads or even deceives the reader. So fairness includes honesty—leveling with the reader.
> - No story is fair if reporters hide their biases or emotions behind such subtly pejorative words as "refused," "despite," "admit," and "massive." So fairness requires straightforwardness ahead of flashiness.
>
> Reporters and editors should routinely ask themselves at the end of every story: "Have I been as fair as I can be?"
>
> *—The Washington Post Deskbook on Style,* 1978

> Beyond concern with fairness in his deportment toward news sources, employers, colleagues, and the public, there is another and equally fundamental sense in which a journalist must be concerned with justice. This relates to his or her voluntarily assumed responsibility, as a practitioner under the First Amendment to the U.S. Constitution, to monitor the status of the larger contract of which the First Amendment is a part. That is, the journalist in a free society seeks to know whether and to what extent is it a free society, whether the preamble's promise to establish justice and promote the general welfare has, in fact, been fulfilled.
>
> —Edmund B. Lambeth, *Committed Journalism: An Ethic for the Profession,* 2nd ed., 1992

2. Careful editing and careful reporting minimize risk. In a libel action, lawyers may seek to show that editors and reporters were negligent, which means they were not as careful with the facts as professional fact gatherers ought to be. Here is some good advice on how to ensure that a negligence charge cannot be made to stick:

> Journalists can protect themselves by taking good notes, diligently corroborating and checking facts, and relying on official records whenever possible. Most reporters find that getting comment from a person who is the subject of a damaging report adds to the story journalistically and also lends an appearance of fairness, which helps legally. When reviewing stories for accuracy and completeness before publication, take stock of all the elements—headlines, pictures and captions included.
>
> Pay close attention to minor characters who are not the focus of a story but who are mentioned in some unflattering way. If the reporting on them is not complete, either devote the necessary time to verifying the information or consider omitting it. And be a stickler for accuracy in the area of police and court reporting, a treacherous minefield where almost any misstep may result in libel. Typical mishaps occur with a mistaken identification of a criminal—right name but wrong address, or wrong name—or a misunderstanding of legal terms.
>
> —Barbara Dill, *The Journalist's Handbook on Libel and Privacy,* 1986

3. Getting the other side of the story should be standard procedure. This means making an honest effort to reach the other side even in the face of hostility. Making one phone call, then writing that the other side could not be reached for comment, is probably not sufficient.

4. Malicious comments should be out of order in the newsroom. Informal chatter across the desk or messages sent by computer may become an issue in a court case. Even a joking comment like "Man, we are going to nail that crook this time" can have regrettable results.

BIBLIOGRAPHY AND ADDITIONAL READINGS

Adler, Renata. *Reckless Disregard.* Alfred A. Knopf. 1986.

Andorka, Frank H. *A Practical Guide to Copyrights and Trademarks.* Pharos Books. 1989.

Associated Press. *The Associated Press Stylebook and Libel Manual.* 1990.

Broder, David. *Behind the Front Page: A Candid Look at How the News Is Made.* Simon and Schuster. 1987.

Dill, Barbara. *The Journalist's Handbook on Libel and Privacy.* The Free Press. 1986.

Kurz, Howard. *Media Circus: The Trouble With America's Newspapers.* Random House. 1993.

Malcolm, Janet. *The Journalist and the Murderer.* Alfred A. Knopf. 1990.

National News Council. *After "Jimmy's World": Tightening Up in Editing.* 1981.

Phelps, Robert H., and E. Douglas Hamilton. *Libel: A Guide to Rights, Risks, Responsibilities.* Collier Books. 1969.

Powe, Lucas A., Jr. *The Fourth Estate and the Constitution: Freedom of the Press in America.* University of California Press. 1991.

Sandman, Peter M., David M. Rubin, and David B. Sachsman. *Media: An Introductory Analysis of American Mass Communications.* 3rd ed. Prentice Hall. 1982.

Shaw, David. *Press Watch: A Provocative Look at How Newspapers Report the News.* Macmillan. 1984.

Stoler, Peter. *The War Against the Press: Politics, Pressure and Intimidation in the '80s.* Dodd, Mead. 1986.

CREATIVE EDITING

PART TWO

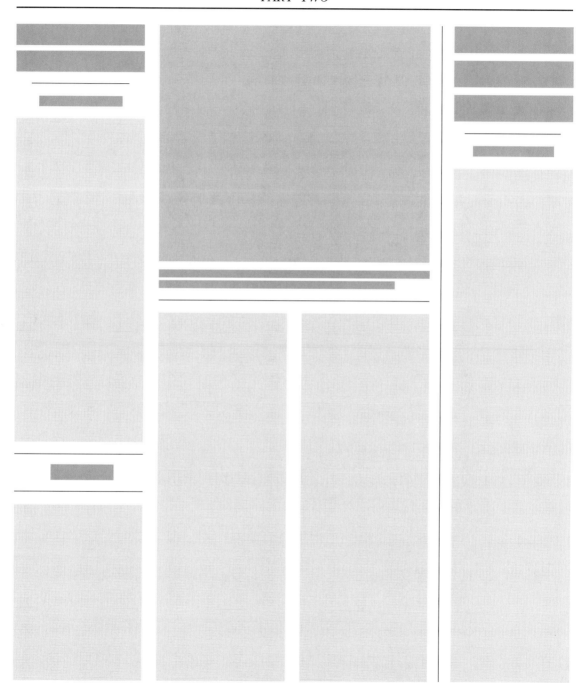

THE WRITER'S ALLY

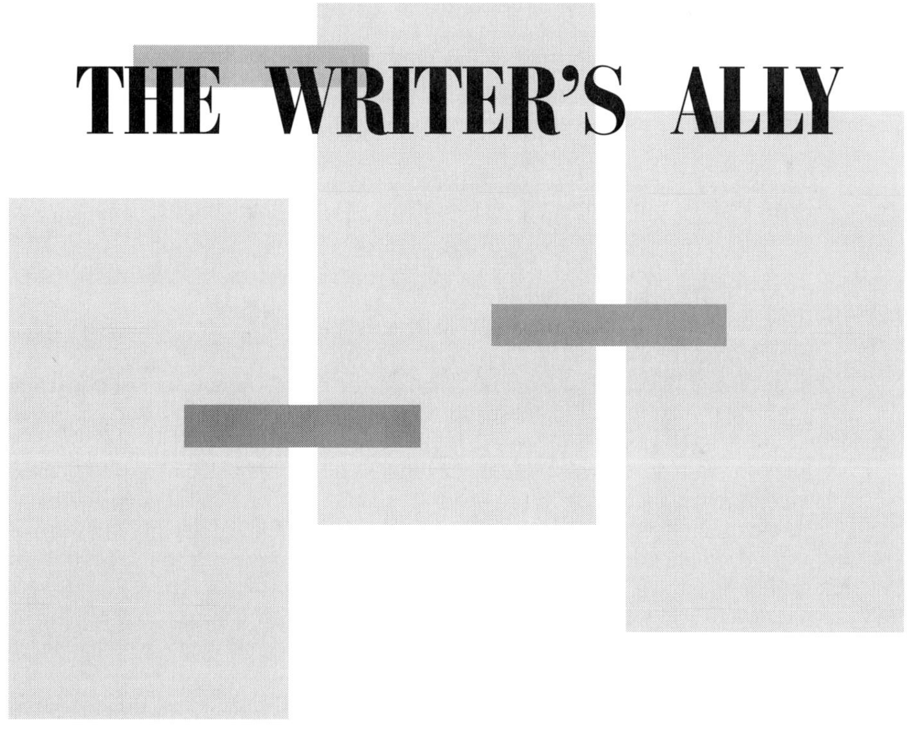

TELLING STORIES

"Little Red Riding Hood" is a bedtime story for children; and despite its frightening, violent aspects, parents often tell it by lamplight amid the gathering shadows of night. They do not emphasize the violence; instead they stress the victory of good over evil. The tale begins idyllically, with Little Red Riding Hood skipping happily along in the sunshine to visit her loving grandmother, and ends in triumph, with the child safe and ready to live happily ever after.

No parent would tell the story as it is shown here in a fanciful newspaper story:

> A 40-year-old woman was bitten to death Friday by a crazed prowler who was in turn slain by a rescuer after the woman's 9-year-old granddaughter screamed for help, police reported.
>
> In a bizarre twist, the prowler was reported to have devoured the woman and then donned her nightgown in an attempt to lure the granddaughter into his clutches. A passing hunter intervened with just moments to spare and shot the intruder with his assault rifle.
>
> The incident happened at a remote forest cabin where the victim, Mrs. M. Y. Grandma, lived alone. The attacker, identified by police as Big Bad Wolf, 4, was

homeless and unemployed. He was believed to have dwelled in a cave or dugout near the cabin.

Police theorized that the granddaughter, Little Red Riding Hood, of 707 Happy Valley Lane, was the ultimate target of the attack. Wolf reportedly attempted to abduct the girl as she strolled along Forest Trail, but she escaped. He then sprinted ahead to Mrs. Grandma's house to await Little Red's arrival, police said.

Little Red was rescued by Stalwart Woodsman, 32, who was hunting deer near the cabin. Hearing the girl's cries, he burst into the cabin and shot Wolf dead, police said.

Sgt. Reginald Copp of the Forest Police gave the following account:

Little Red set out at about 1 p.m. to deliver to her grandmother a basket she had made in school. The basket contained "some goodies," Copp said. When Wolf appeared, the girl ran fast to escape him because she had been warned by her mother and her teacher to avoid strangers.

Wolf, described as unkempt and looking demented, ran to Mrs. Grandma's cabin and pounded on the door.

Expecting a guest, Mrs. Grandma opened the door without her usual caution and was brutally assaulted. Blood-spattered walls were evidence that she struggled for her life.

After she was dead, Wolf pushed her remains under the bed and attired himself in her nightgown, apparently in the belief that Little Red wouldn't recognize him.

However, the girl wasn't fooled. She commented on his big, blood-red eyes and sharp, protruding teeth and refused to get near him. When she screamed, Woodsman came running.

"He (Wolf) will never bother another innocent girl," Woodsman told police.

Copp said Wolf had a long record of vagrancy and had been arrested three times for child molestation but never convicted.

Little Red was reunited with her mother, Mrs. Winston Riding Hood, shortly after the attack. Mrs. Riding Hood was not available for comment.

However, Little Red's third-grade teacher, Ms. Melody Kindergarten, told reporters Mrs. Riding Hood was "extremely grateful" to the little girl's rescuer.

"We were all extremely fortunate that Mr. Woodsman was nearby," Ms. Kindergarten said.

The teacher said the girl was one of the brightest in the third-grade class and was very brave.

"She wasn't afraid of the woods," she said. "She visited her grandmother often."

Copp said no charges would be filed in the case.

This is no way to tell a bedtime story. The climax is given away at the beginning, destroying all suspense. The events are not presented in sequence but are instead grouped in lumps, like badly cooked rice. The ending has no "happily ever after"; in fact, there is no ending. The story simply fades away, like a popular recording that just keeps going as the volume diminishes into silence.

Unnatural as it may seem, this form is the chief way stories are told in newspapers. The technique is called the "inverted pyramid," because the facts are presented in descending order of interest and importance, so that the story tapers from a broad, thick top to an insignificant point at the bottom. Some say a collection of facts presented in this manner is not a story at all, "story" being defined as a narrative or short work of fiction. At *The New York Times,* writers and editors do not refer in print to a news item as a "story." "Article," which means non-fiction composition, is preferred.

Nevertheless, "story" is the standard term for a newspaper account of an event, and the inverted pyramid, despite shortcomings that are widely recognized, is the dominant form. It originated in the days when reporters sent their dispatches to the home office by telegraph, not satellite. The wires were vulnerable to storms, sabotage, vandalism and other forms of failure, so the writers developed means to protect themselves against interruption.

During the Civil War, they began "compressing the most crucial facts into short, paragraph-long dispatches, often destined for the top of a column of news," Mitchell Stephens writes in *The History of News: From the Drum to the Satellite.* "From here it was not a long distance to reserving the first paragraph of their stories, the 'lead,' for the most newsworthy facts and then organizing supporting material in descending order of importance."

Interpreting these dispatches and correcting transmission errors was the work of copy readers employed to prepare the news for publication. Today, the telegraph is long gone, but the copy readers, now called copy editors, are still with us, and so is the inverted pyramid (Figure 5.1). Though it has been maligned as baggage from the past that ought to be discarded, the inverted pyramid survives for a couple of good reasons:

1. It is the best structure for wire service stories, which must serve a variety of clients with varying needs and desires. The inverted pyramid is designed to be easily trimmed to fit a limited space. The bottom can be lopped off at almost any point.
2. It serves the needs of skimmers, readers who don't have time to read long stories, because it does not demand to be read to the end.

In today's inverted pyramid, the initial paragraph, or lead (also spelled lede), is "hard," which means it contains the essential facts. Traditionally the essential

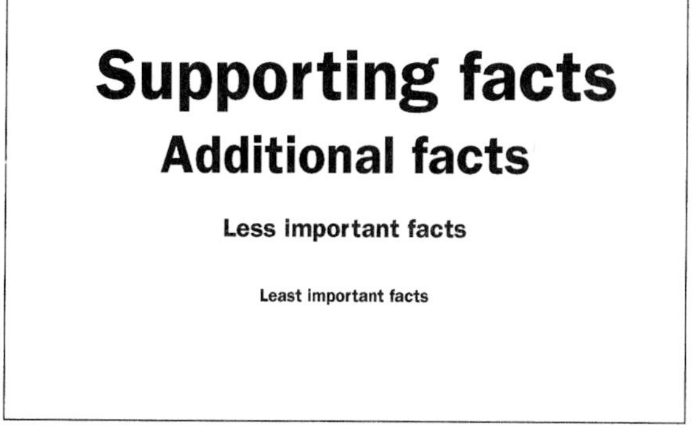

The lead

Supporting facts

Additional facts

Less important facts

Least important facts

Figure 5.1 Structure of the inverted pyramid.

facts have been defined as the "five w's and h"—who, what, when, where, why and how. The first four almost always appear in the lead. The "why" and the "how" may be left out of the lead to avoid clutter but appear high in the story.

Secondary facts, which support, explain or amplify the initial information, directly follow the lead.

A chronological account is often included, but it comes after the essential facts have been reported.

Nothing is delayed, held back or reserved for a snappy ending. The reader gets everything up front and can expect to find only extra details, description or explanation deeper in the story.

THE EDITOR'S ROLE

The editor is the writer's ally. As the saying goes, "Everybody needs an editor," and no writer should lose sight of the value of editorial assistance. Editor and writer work as a team to achieve their common goal: a news story that appeals to readers. The editor, as the first reader, evaluates the effectiveness of the piece and suggests changes if any are needed. Like master carpenters working side by side, the writer and the editor make sure the pieces of the story fit together smoothly to form a sound structure.

The line editor's job, described in Part I, is usually done independently, without the writer's consultation or cooperation, except where clarification is needed. However, there are times when the editor questions the writer's judgment about the style and form of the story or the selection and placement of facts within the story's framework. At this point, the line editor becomes a creative editor.

EVALUATING THE LEAD

The questioning begins with the lead, which is crucial to establishing and maintaining reader interest. The editor asks, does it work? If it doesn't, why not?

1. **Does the article fulfill the lead's promises?** Every lead promises to provide certain information that the reader who continues into the story can expect to find. If the article strays from the lead and never returns, the promise is betrayed.

   In the following example, the lead promises not only to tell about the fire and the family, but also to describe the house and explain how it was historic:

   > A historic three-story house, home to eight members of an extended family, was gutted by a Wednesday morning fire, and practically all the residents' possessions inside were destroyed.

2. **Does the lead try to do too much?** One should not try to cram too many thoughts into the first sentence. Simple leads, containing one or two clear thoughts, are usually best.

Cramming Too Much in the Lead

Original	Edited
Rigoberta Menchu, orphaned by civil war in her native Guatemala, was hailed as a "vivid symbol of peace and reconciliation" by the committee that awarded the 1992 Nobel Peace Prize to the Indian rights activist Friday.	A Guatemalan Indian activist won the 1992 Nobel Peace Prize Friday.
Michael A. Jones, 19, a first-year student at the University of Nebraska-Lincoln and the son of Mr. and Mrs. Sean Jones of 14532 N. 108th St. in Omaha, died about 3:30 p.m. Friday when his car swerved off the westbound lanes of Interstate 80 near Gretna and overturned.	A University of Nebraska-Lincoln student was killed Friday when his car swerved off Interstate 80 and overturned.
A report released Friday by the U.S. Department of Transportation discussed fatal accidents on interstate highways. In the report it was stated that of the approximately 2,754 fatal accidents that occurred on interstate highways last year, two-thirds involved only one vehicle and more than half of the deaths took place on Friday, Saturday or Sunday.	Two-thirds of the fatal accidents on interstate highways last year involved only one vehicle each, the government reported Friday.

Box 5.1

3. **Does the lead contain interesting and significant information?** A story need not be told chronologically, although that is sometimes the most effective structure. The lead should reveal or promise to reveal facts that are new or intriguing.
4. **Does the lead miss an opportunity to emphasize a fact that sets this story apart from others?** No two events are exactly alike. Often the unusual aspects provide the best lead.
5. **Does the lead start with a name, location or time element?** These are usually the weakest options.
6. **Does the lead miss a local angle?** The lead should include a local angle, if there is one.
7. **Is the latest information in the lead?** The lead should play up developments that readers will not have obtained already from earlier editions or television or radio news.
8. **Is the structure of the lead effective?** In general, direct quotations and questions do not make good leads.
9. **If the lead is hard, should it be soft?** A hard lead summarizes the story. Sometimes the reader is better served by a delayed (soft) lead that preserves an element of mystery.

Slow Beginnings

Original	Edited
The weekly meeting of the City Council took place at 7:30 p.m. Friday at City Hall.	The City Council voted Friday to authorize the hiring of 15 new firefighters.
The presidential candidates debated for the third time Monday night.	President Bush denounced Bill Clinton as a draft dodger Monday night in the last of three presidential campaign debates.
The need for an ombudsman to represent and assist university students was the main topic considered at Monday night's meeting of the Student Senate.	A controversial plan to hire an ombudsman was defeated Monday night by the Student Senate.

Box 5.2

10. **If the lead is soft, should it be hard?** When overworked, the soft approach can exasperate readers by failing to come to the point fast enough.

The editor who finds unsatisfactory answers to any of these questions proposes a revision. In some cases all that is needed is a suggestion to the writer. In others, the editor may elect to write a new lead and propose it to the writer. In the give-and-take that follows, the two minds working together produce something that works well for both. Of course, the writer gets the byline.

VARIATIONS ON THE THEME

Many editors are dissatisfied with the predominance of the inverted-pyramid form. In recent years journalists and scholars have experimented with other story shapes in an effort to bring about a general improvement in newspaper writing. The Poynter Institute for Media Studies in St. Petersburg, Fla., has been a pioneer in this effort. Its research indicates that the traditional newswriting style, emphasizing the five w's and h, is driving away readers. Putting all the flash in the first paragraph means the reader's interest will inevitably sag in the second paragraph and is likely to die shortly thereafter.

The traditional news story has other weaknesses as well:

1. It tends to assume that readers know what was in the paper yesterday and the day before and the day before that, so that little background information or explanation is necessary. For regular readers, the assumption is probably accurate, but what about people who aren't in the know for some reason?
2. Description is usually weak or absent, because the demand for tight writing and hard facts leaves no room for it.

Emphasizing the Unusual

Original	Edited
A youth was seriously injured Friday while operating machinery on his family's farm.	A farm youth's arms were torn off Friday by machinery he was operating, yet he managed to phone for help.

Box 5.3

3. Characterization, the main strength of fiction writing, is flat and drab if it exists at all in news stories. The reason is that it requires interpretation by the writer, who tends to be restricted by standards of objectivity.

In short, the indictment against newswriting is that it is not good storytelling. It does a poor job of entertaining readers, who are drifting away to new and exciting competitors. Creative editors are realizing that they must find new ways of presenting information and that writers must be encouraged to explore new forms.

The Poynter Institute has suggested some novel ideas, including:

1. Point of view, in which the writer adopts a viewpoint; makes it immediately clear to the reader; addresses the reader directly, perhaps by using the second person, and cements the viewpoint in the reader's mind by emphasizing it at the end of the story.
2. Radical clarity, in which the explanation comes first and is followed by or woven together with the essential new facts.

For readers who expect hard leads, the institute suggests that experimental story forms be accompanied by summary headlines (see Chapter 6) or side items in which key points of information are enumerated.

Part of the challenge for creative editors in the '90s is to help guide experimentation and shape the news stories of the future.

BEYOND THE INVERTED PYRAMID

While wire services stick to the hard-news form, other newspaper stories are taking new paths. These are the most popular structures in wide use today:

1. **The champagne glass** (Figure 5.2). The name describes the shape of the story. The top (the bowl) is a compelling summary of the event that contains most of the key details. The story then narrows into a chronological account (the stem of the glass) and ends with a kicker, or interesting fact held back from the lead (the base).

Placing the Time Element

Original	Edited
On Thursday, a jet trying to land at Tokyo Airport crashed in a field, killing 83 persons.	All 83 aboard were killed Thursday when a jet crashed as it attempted to land at Tokyo Airport.

Box 5.4

2. **The narrative box** (Figure 5.3). A more conventional way to tell a story is to describe events in order as they happened, with revelations occurring along the way. In this form the lead does not give away everything, and there is no point where the structure narrows as the interest level wanes. There is no dropoff even at the end, where a resolution is reached. The goal of this structure is to maintain interest throughout.
3. **Building blocks.** This form is useful for long stories that cover a number of topics. The material is arranged in separate sections, often under subsidiary headlines and with informative "grabbers" at the beginning of each segment.

The lead is a summary of the most important facts, told in compelling fashion.

Following the lead is a narrative that flows down from the bowl and through the stem.

The base is a kicker, or fact saved for the end.

The residents went to bed uneasy Sunday night at the Valley Vista apartment complex.

Just 24 hours earlier, a fire believed to have been the work of an arsonist did about $40,000 worth of damage to Apartment 8, on the second floor of Building 42. The apartment was vacant because its tenant had been evicted two days before.

At 12:30 a.m. Monday, the building's residents were startled from their sleep again, this time by a booming sound.

"It was like an explosion," resident Ralph White said. "Somebody was out there. I heard somebody holler, 'Get the hell out of there.'"

Fire broke out on the roof above the vacant apartment and swept quickly through the building, driving about a dozen residents into the open air in their nightclothes. No one was injured. Fire Chief Jerry King, who estimated the damage at $600,000, said he suspected arson in this fire, too.

Brian Hammer, who lived in Apartment 7, was lying on his new $1,000 black lacquer waterbed when his roommate began shouting about the fire.

"You could feel the heat through the Sheetrock, and you could feel the apartment sizzling," Hammer said. "It wasn't just a flame, it was an inferno. It was so funny how the building ignited — it was just like paper."

Hammer's belongings were destroyed, including the waterbed, and he had no insurance.

"As a matter of fact, I was going to get it this week. Life goes on, I guess," he said.

John Oldman, a resident of the building next door, was forced to evacuate.

"I turned toward the bedroom window, and all I saw was orange. I got out, and it wasn't even five minutes before the entire roof, from one end to the other, was in flames."

Carter Edwards, who moved into Apartment 3 of Building 42 just a month ago, lost most of his possessions in the fire.

"I grabbed my clothes and put them in the car. By the second trip, the smoke was so bad it was ridiculous. It wouldn't make any sense to jeopardize your life for a couple more things. Things can be replaced. I was lucky. I had $10,000 renter's insurance. A lot of others didn't."

Martha Denman, assistant to the apartment manager, said the homeless tenants would be housed at a nearby Holiday Inn temporarily, then moved into other available apartments in the complex.

As the firefighters worked, one of the bystanders kept crossing firelines despite several warnings and was arrested on a charge of obstructing firefighters. He was Phillip John Carswell, 25, who until Wednesday afternoon had been the tenant in Apartment 8, Building 42. Denman said he was evicted for non-payment of rent.

Monday he was in the county jail, held in lieu of $5,000 bail.

Figure 5.2 Structure of the champagne glass.

Playing Up the Local Angle

Original	Edited
All 83 aboard were killed Thursday when a jet crashed as it attempted to land at Tokyo Airport.	All 83 aboard, including three Seattle residents, were killed Thursday when a jet crashed as it attempted to land at Tokyo Airport.

Box 5.5

THE NUT GRAPH

To improve the quality of storytelling, newspapers have turned to the soft lead, in which the essential facts do not appear at the top and may be withheld for several paragraphs. A soft lead may be an anecdote, a chronological narrative, a bit of wordplay or a teasing device to induce further reading.

Eventually the writer comes to the point, reaching a resolution or explanation. The introduction of the essential facts comes in a paragraph or passage that becomes a form of hard lead. This part of the story is called the "nut graph," because it contains the nut, or core, of the news. If this "what" is delayed too long, however, readers may be annoyed or lose interest.

The story starts at the beginning and continues straight through, usually chronologically, without a drop in sustained interest. This propels the reader through the whole story but leaves little room for a summary lead or a nut graph. These may be provided by the headline writer.

For Trooper Bruce Ames, the murder case began Tuesday as a routine traffic stop on Interstate 80.

He received a report that a rusty black van was weaving from lane to lane and chased down Harvey Holt, 30. Ames said Holt had no license and gave a fake name.

"The officer was very cautious. Things just didn't seem right," Highway Patrol Lt. Brian Patrick said.

Without looking inside the van, Ames arrested Holt on a charge of careless driving and took him to the county jail.

For five hours, the rusted van sat undisturbed at the side of the road. Then, at 2 p.m. Tuesday, the Highway Patrol was notified that Holt was wanted for questioning. Holt's girlfriend, 25-year-old Amy Charline Smith, had not been seen since 10 p.m. Monday, when neighbors heard shouts and a gunshot from the couple's trailer.

Troopers hurried to the parked van and peered in through a scratch on the film coating the passenger window. They saw part of an arm.

"Once they got the vehicle open, they discovered a body wrapped in a blanket and covered with a jacket," Patrick said.

Smith had been shot once in the chest with a large-caliber gun.

Holt was charged with first-degree murder and held without bail in the county jail.

He and Smith were transients who had lived in the rented trailer for about two weeks, Patrick said.

Neighbors didn't immediately report the shouting and gunshot they heard Monday evening. And no one alerted authorities at 4 a.m. Tuesday when Hart was reportedly seen loading heavy objects into his van.

At 8 a.m. Tuesday, the park manager checked the trailer and discovered the couple had moved out. He found a blood-soaked mattress and a bullet hole in the west wall.

Officials said they didn't know where the suspect may have been going with the body when Ames stopped him at about 9 a.m.

"People do odd things," Patrick said. "If he was going to dispose of the body, why didn't he do it while it was dark? It's just unbelievable. If Trooper Ames hadn't stopped the man, he might have left the state."

Figure 5.3 Structure of the narrative box.

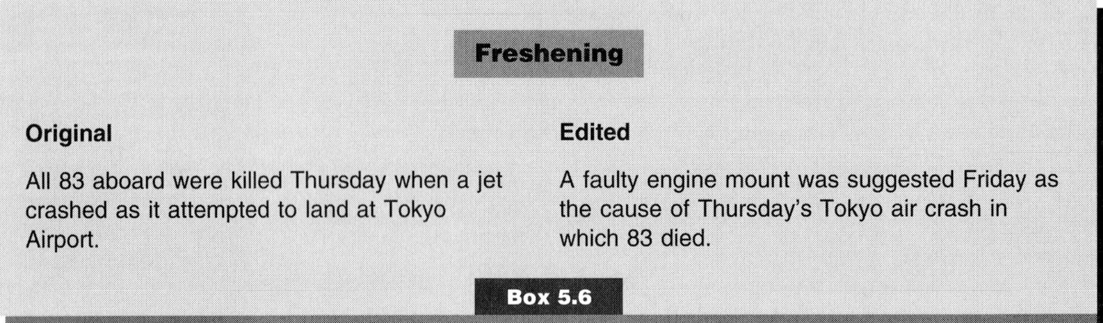

Freshening

Original	Edited
All 83 aboard were killed Thursday when a jet crashed as it attempted to land at Tokyo Airport.	A faulty engine mount was suggested Friday as the cause of Thursday's Tokyo air crash in which 83 died.

Box 5.6

The soft approach is not normally used for breaking news, such as a report of a plane crash, but it is a popular form for many other kinds of stories.

LOOKING FOR HOLES

Every news story is missing something. Part of the skill of newswriting is the ability to select out the necessary facts from those that would only add clutter. The editor's job is to raise questions that readers may wonder about and that appear answerable. Most of these questions fall under one of these headings:

1. Background
2. Explanation
3. The basics

Questions of all three types are raised by the following example.

What's Missing?

Joan Konner, dean of the Graduate School of Journalism at Columbia University in New York, said today that credibility is a journalist's most important product.

Journalists must rely on their own sense of what's right, Konner said. The profession has no authority to impose standards upon journalists even if it has a code of ethics, she said.

Organizations may set limits, but individual journalists must set their own standards, sense of taste and judgment, she said, and those who cannot do that should leave the profession.

Konner said she was worried about the "hype and the profit motive to get ratings" in TV journalism.

For example, NBC News staged a safety test of a General Motors pickup.

"NBC made a serious mistake," she said.

Konner also said that newspapers have a special challenge because people expect more from newspapers than from television news.

"Newspapers must go deeper into the community to ferret out the quiet voices," she said.

Quotation or Question?

Original	Edited
"I'm completely bewildered by what I saw in the sky last night," a student said Friday.	A pattern of colorful lights hovered over Oldfather Hall for 15 minutes Friday night, a student reported.
Are UFOs real?	The UFO debate gained new energy Saturday after a student reported a 15-minute sighting over Oldfather Hall.

Box 5.7

Background questions: When and on what program did NBC broadcast the results of their safety test? What was the "serious mistake"? Such information can be obtained from the newspaper's library files or from computerized archives.

Explanation needed: The phrase "even if it has a code of ethics" is vague. Is there such a code? The answer may be found in the library or in the unused portion of the speaker's remarks (or in Chapter 4).

The basics: Where, how and why were these comments made? If the context was a speech, what was the forum?

The story is not ready for publication until the answers have been found and added to the text. It is up to the editor to make sure this is done. Questions like these are called "holes," and the ability to find and plug them is an important skill of the creative editor.

Asking questions is not much of an accomplishment in itself. Anyone can ask questions. Children are the masters of questioning the irrelevant or the unfathomable. Editors must ask significant, necessary questions, to which the answers are attainable. In analyzing each piece of newswriting, they should address fundamental standards of good composition:

1. Is the reporting thorough? In addition to probing for missing essential facts, the editor should consider **background** and **context.** For example, when administrators at a Texas middle school announced to the students that then-President George Bush had died, a reporter wrote that the students had been studying Orson Welles' 1938 radio broadcast "The War of the Worlds," and the administrators were trying to demonstrate the impact of shocking news on people. The news story said Welles' broadcast about an invasion from Mars had caused a panic, but it did not give adequate background on the extent and seriousness of the reaction and did not mention the context of the broadcast, which used news techniques in a way that seemed real and reached an audience that was naive about media trickery and anxious about the world's drift toward war.

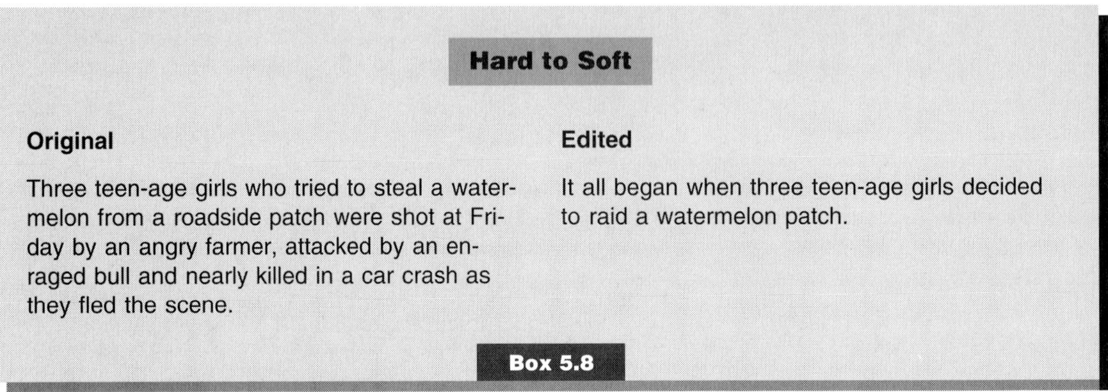
Hard to Soft

Original	Edited
Three teen-age girls who tried to steal a watermelon from a roadside patch were shot at Friday by an angry farmer, attacked by an enraged bull and nearly killed in a car crash as they fled the scene.	It all began when three teen-age girls decided to raid a watermelon patch.

Box 5.8

Modern readers, many of whom knew little about the broadcast, could not be reasonably expected to comprehend the story without these facts.

2. Is the story well-balanced? The importance of balance was discussed in Chapter 4. It means giving adequate attention to all relevant sides of an issue.

3. Are the facts consistent? Are the names spelled the same way throughout? Does the story seem to contradict itself? For example, if paragraph 2 says the fire started on the east end of the first floor and paragraph 8 says arson investigators concentrated on the west end of the basement, the apparent inconsistency must be explained.

4. Is the story reasonable and logical? Absurdity was discussed in Chapter 1, where the focus was on sentences and paragraphs that defied reason. Entire stories can have similar problems. For example, one feature story told of an interview with a woman who had lived numerous lives in different periods of history and matter-of-factly described her experiences in each of them. The editor found the tone of the story too gullible and asked for a rewrite.

5. Do the sentences flow smoothly from beginning to end? Transitions are difficult for many writers, especially when the facts are diverse and the subject is complex. Editors often can recognize problems that fall into writers' blind spots and can suggest helpful solutions.

THE COLLOQUY

The decision on whether the story is ready for publication lies ultimately with the editor, who may have serious reservations about structure or content and may insist on a delay to allow time for further fact-gathering or clarification. However, copy editors seldom make such decisions unilaterally. Instead, a colloquy (conversation) takes place among a responsible group, which includes the reporter and one or more supervising editors.

If the story is not breaking news, and there is time for discussion, the colloquy may go on for days or longer as the editor and reporter work together to

Soft to Hard

Original	Edited
Melvin Jones had just retired for the night on his brand new, black-lacquered waterbed. In the living room of the apartment he shared with Jones, Richard Gonzalez turned down the stereo so his roommate could sleep. Then they both smelled smoke.	A flash fire that started in a vacant apartment killed three residents and injured 14 others at the Richardson Arms Friday night, and authorities said they suspected arson.

Box 5.9

improve and polish the piece. Mutual respect is of course essential to such teamwork.

WIRE EDITING

Some see editing as a stifling, isolated job in which the worker withdraws into a cocoon with a computer terminal and shuns the external world. This monkish view of editing ignores the excitement and adventure involved in shaping a report of world events for readers. Editors have the world at their window and each day's most significant events at their fingertips.

Wire editing is creative editing because the wire services provide a steady flow of ever-changing news that becomes raw material for editors to turn into a final product appropriate to their readership. News stories change hour by hour and sometimes minute by minute as events unfold. The river of leads, adds, inserts and rewrites doesn't stop for any editor's deadline. The editor who assembles, revises and in many cases rewrites these fragments of news into smooth, coherent stories must have vast knowledge and superb word skills to do the job well. The greatest challenges come when major news events happen, and the editor must cope with a breaking news story.

The term *wire editing* continues to be used, although today's news is delivered to the editor's desk by satellite, not telegraph wire. The text is still called "copy," even though it is written on a computer, not a typewriter making multiple copies. Most copy editors do some wire editing; some specialize in it. Many find it rewarding because it affords substantial opportunity to shape and improve stories.

Many newspapers subscribe to multiple wire services, and millions of words pour into each publication's data system every day. Wire editing involves sorting, evaluating, assembling and selecting the relatively small number of stories that will actually be printed. The task begins with the advisory file in the computer program that sorts the massive daily flow of stories and pigeonholes them in groups, or folders.

CHECKING THE ADVISORIES

"Advisories" are messages from the wire service editors to the newspaper's wire editor. This list includes the "budgets" compiled by the wire service news editors. The budgets are digests of the top stories of the day. They do not include all stories, only those selected as most important.

The Associated Press sends two budgets each day, the "PM Digest" for afternoon newspapers and the "AM Digest" for the following morning's editions. The PM Digest is available well before dawn, and the AM Digest is delivered early in the afternoon. Wire editors base their plans for the day on these budgets.

CHECKING THE URGENTS

"Urgent" stories have been tagged by the wire service news editors as high priority and late breaking. There are three classes of urgent news:

1. Flash. This designates a big story, such as the assassination of a president.
2. Bulletin. This is for important, sudden events, such as plane crashes, and major new developments in continuing stories.
3. Urgent. The lowest category is for sudden events of lesser magnitude and any fresh development in a continuing story.

UNDERSTANDING WIRE TALK

The Associated Press identifies its stories with standard abbreviations that are part of the wire editor's vocabulary. For example, during the Persian Gulf crisis in 1991 and 1992, when Iraq captured Kuwait and the United States joined an international force to expel the invaders, the AP transmitted daily stories rounding up events in the region. The following code words were used:

1. "Gulf Rdp, Bjt-2 takes" meant the story was a "Roundup" (Rdp) of Persian Gulf news and that it appeared on the digest, or budget (Bjt), for the current cycle. It consisted of two takes, or pages.
2. "Gulf Rdp, Bjt-1st add" designated the first additional take, or second page of the story.
3. "Gulf Rdp, Bjt-1st Ld" was a new lead. Such a lead often carries a message explaining to the wire editor what is being changed and what new information is being added. The new lead will end with a pickup line something like this: "Altogether, the, 15th graf pvs." This means the new lead substitutes for the first 14 paragraphs of the previous (pvs) story and that the 15th paragraph begins with "Altogether, the . . ."
4. "Gulf Rdp, Bjt-INSERT" designated a brief insert, usually a paragraph clarifying or adding information. Inserts, too, end with pickup lines.
5. "Gulf Rdp, Bjt-WRITETHRU" denoted a rewritten version of the story that incorporated all previous takes. A writethru will usually carry a message explaining what new information, if any, has been added. Editors can expect writethrus whenever they are editing breaking stories that consist of multiple takes, leads and inserts.

6. Each story was tagged "PM," "AM" or "BC." The bulk of PM-cycle copy is supplied between midnight and noon for afternoon papers. Most AM-cycle copy is sent between noon and midnight for morning papers. BC copy is for both cycles.
7. The end of each story was marked by a line of type that said something like this: "ap-ah-01-24-92 0011cst." This is the wire service equivalent of "30." It marks the end of the take and gives the date and time it was transmitted. The time is on a 24-hour clock, so "0011cst" means 11 minutes after midnight Central Standard Time.

EDITING A MAJOR STORY

To be a wire editor is to occupy a front-row seat in the theater of history and current events. When a major story breaks, the work is intense, feverish and fascinating. One must keep up with every twist and turn the story takes while remaining mindful of the newspaper's deadline and preparing the latest possible information for publication.

A major story does not necessarily involve war or international issues. Any event that interests a national audience, affects a great number of people and contains elements of human drama may be regarded as major.

For example, on April 19, 1993, a major story with an unusual number of shocking developments occurred near Waco, Texas. For weeks the national media had been keeping watch on a compound occupied by an armed religious group, the Branch Davidians, and besieged by federal authorities trying to induce the group to surrender and give up its weapons.

That morning, a dispatch signaled that a break in the siege was about to occur.

URGENT PM-Armed Cult,0153
Media Told to 'Take Cover' Near Cult Compound
WACO, Texas (AP)—Authorities today warned people near the compound of cult leader David Koresh to "take cover" and reporters heard popping sounds.

A radio station reported that an armored vehicle knocked a hole in a wall at the compound. A door at the compound opened and a flag of some sort was draped outside.

Earlier today, a school bus headed for the compound and an ambulance raced through a checkpoint leading to the compound with its lights flashing.

There was no immediate comment from FBI agents who have the compound surrounded. The media has been kept about a mile away.

A standoff with Koresh and his followers was going into its 51st day today. The standoff began Feb. 28, when four agents of the Bureau of Alcohol, Tobacco and Firearms were killed trying to arrest Koresh and search for illegal weapons.

ap-kx-04-19-93 0717cdt

About an hour later, wire editors received a first lead disclosing that gas was being used.

BULLETIN PM-Armed Cult, 1st Ld,0144
Eds: Report of gassing.
By CHIP BROWN
Associated Press Writer

WACO, Texas (AP)—Armored vehicles today knocked at least three large holes in walls of a compound where cult leader David Koresh and his followers have been barricaded for 51 days.

A television station, citing unidentified sources, said federal agents called the compound and told cult members to give up or they would be gassed. The person inside the compound hung up, KHOU-TV reported.

A tank then broke several holes in the compound and the gassing began, according to the KHOU source.

The holes could be seen from about two miles away, where the media has been kept since a Feb. 28 gun battle that killed four federal agents. Koresh said six cult members died.

FBI agents had no immediate comment.

MORE
ap-kx-04-19-93 0816cdt

"MORE" notified the editors that this first lead consisted of more than one take. As it turned out, this first lead was actually a writethru, since none of the earlier story was retained, or "picked up." The second take, called the "first add," carried no "pickup line" at the end.

URGENT PM-Armed Cult, 1st Ld-1st Add,0203
WACO, Texas: immediate comment.

FBI spokesman Carlos Fernandez said "There's something going on" but "this whole thing has been planned out." He declined to elaborate.

A school bus headed for the compound. An ambulance raced through a checkpoint leading to the complex with its lights flashing. Two other ambulances also went past the checkpoint.

Shortly after 6 a.m., reporters were warned by a state Department of Safety officer to "take cover." Reporters heard popping sounds.

Koresh is the leader of the Branch Davidian cult. A Bureau of Alcohol, Tobacco and Firearms raid on the compound led to the gun battle. Four ATF agents were killed and 16 agents were injured when more than 100 agents tried to arrest Koresh and search for illegal weapons at the fortress east of Waco.

Koresh, who has claimed to be Jesus Christ, is holed up with 95 followers, including 17 children. Thirty-seven people, mostly children, have left the compound since the standoff began.

After ditching earlier pledges to end the siege, the doomsday preacher said he would give up after completing a manuscript that attempts to solve the Bible's Seven Seals, which hint at an end to the world.

ap-kx-04-19-93 0828cdt

At 9:19 a "2nd lead-writethru" informed editors that an FBI briefing was coming up shortly. Wire editors had to decide if their deadlines would allow them to wait for the next lead or force them to go with this one. "EDT" denotes Eastern Daylight Time, which means the briefing was set for 10:30 Central Daylight Time.

URGENT PM-Armed Cult, 2nd Ld-Writethru,0423
Eds: Later details; FBI briefing scheduled for 11:30 a.m. EDT.
By CHIP BROWN
Associated Press Writer

WACO, Texas (AP)—An armored vehicle ripped into cult leader David Koresh's compound early today, tearing down and punching large holes on the 51st day of a standoff.

A television station, citing unidentified sources, said federal agents called the compound and told cult members to give up or they would be gassed. The person inside the compound hung up, KHOU-TV reported.

A tank fitted with a battering ram then broke several holes in the compound and, according to KHOU, the gassing began. The television source did not say what type of gas was used.

The work began about 6 a.m. Two hours later, no one had emerged from the compound. The tank's boom was seen reaching into a second-floor window, tore down a wall and punched a hole in the roof. Other holes were also punched into walls.

FBI agents said they would have no comment until a briefing.

Reporters had been warned by a state Department of Safety officer to "take cover." Reporters heard popping sounds.

A school bus headed for the compound. An ambulance raced through a checkpoint leading to the complex with its lights flashing. Two other ambulances also went past the checkpoint.

The holes could be seen from about two miles away, where the media has been positioned since a Feb. 28 gun battle that killed four federal agents. Koresh has said six cult members died.

FBI spokesman Carlos Fernandez said "There's something going on" but "this whole thing has been planned out." He wouldn't elaborate.

Hillcrest Baptist Medical Center, the area's main trauma center, was put on a low-level alert, said nursing supervisor Cheryl Eady.

Koresh is the leader of the Branch Davidian cult. A Bureau of Alcohol, Tobacco and Firearms raid on the compound led to the gun battle. Four ATF agents were killed and 16 agents were injured when more than 100 agents tried to arrest Koresh and search for illegal weapons at the fortress east of Waco.

Koresh, who has claimed to be Jesus Christ, is holed up with 95 followers, including 17 children. Thirty-seven people, mostly children, have left the compound since the standoff began.

After ditching earlier pledges to end the siege, the doomsday preacher said he would give up after completing a manuscript that attempts to solve the Bible's Seven Seals, which hint at an end to the world.

ap-kx-04-19-93 0919cdt

Unexpectedly, the FBI made some comments in Washington that formed the basis of a third lead. Notice the "pickup line" at the end, which notified editors that the last three paragraphs of the previous story should be preserved.

URGENT PM-Armed Cult, 3rd Ld,0516
Eds: Assault resumes, FBI comment from Washington, president informed, other details; FBI briefing scheduled for 11:30 a.m. EDT.

By CHIP BROWN
Associated Press Writer

WACO, Texas (AP)—An armored vehicle ripped and punched gaping holes in the walls of a religious compound today, and the FBI said it pumped tear gas inside the buildings where David Koresh and 95 followers have been holed up for 51 days.

The ramming began shortly after 6 a.m. and stopped for a time. Then, shortly after 9 a.m., a combat engineering vehicle—a modified tank equipped with a boom—appeared to bash down the front door of the compound.

Although a school bus and several ambulances were rushed to the site, there was no indication that any cult members had been injured by the ramming or had surrendered.

The assault was by far the most aggressive action taken by the federal government since a gun battle on Feb. 28 that began the siege. Four federal agents died in the shootout, and cult leaders have said six of their members were killed.

In Washington, FBI spokesman Charles Mandigo said "a generic tear gas of some kind" had been sprayed into the compound, which consists of several interlocking buildings and is believed to include underground rooms and passageways.

He said the holes knocked into the buildings provided a way out for the cultists, and also allowed some of the tear gas to escape.

"This is a way of sending a message that this is not going to go on forever, that the time has come to bring this to a conclusion," Mandigo said. "It was carefully crafted to prevent injury but to give some incentive for them to leave."

The FBI had previously said it was reluctant to use tear gas because of the danger it might pose to children.

There are believed to be 17 children among the 95 followers holed up with Koresh, who has claimed to be Jesus Christ. Thirty-seven people, mostly children, have left the compound since the standoff began.

President Clinton said in Washington that he had advance notice of the assault, and that Attorney General Janet Reno made the decision to begin the operation.

A television station, citing unidentified sources, said federal agents had called the compound early and informed cult members to give up or they would be gassed. The person inside the compound hung up, KHOU-TV reported.

Although the news media have been kept at least two miles away from the site, telescopic camera lenses captured the dawn assault in which an armored combat engineering vehicle, with a battering ram attached, reached into a second-story window, tore down a portion of the outside wall and punched a hole in the roof.

Reporters had been warned by a state Department of Safety officer to "take cover." Reporters heard popping sounds.

At mid-morning, cultists hung a banner from one of the second-floor windows saying: "We want our phones fixed."

Koresh is the leader, 11th graf
ap-kx-04-19-93 1039cdt

Thirty-six minutes after the FBI briefing began, a fourth lead was transmitted, reflecting fast work by AP reporters and editors.

BULLETIN PM-Armed Cult, 4th Ld,0160
Eds: FBI briefing.
By CHIP BROWN
Associated Press Writer

WACO, Texas (AP)—FBI agents used an armored vehicle to rip gaping holes in the walls of a religious compound today, and then pumped tear gas into the buildings where David Koresh and 95 followers have been holed up for 51 days.

"At this point we're not negotiating," FBI spokesman Bob Ricks said. "We're saying come out. Come out with your hands up. This matter is over."

Heavily-armed members of the Branch Davidian cult fired as many as 200 rounds of gunfire as FBI agents rumbled into the compound in a modified tank equipped with a boom, Ricks said. There were no reports of injuries.

Ricks said tear gas probably would be pumped into the buildings all day. "We will continue to gas them and make their lives as uncomfortable as possible until they do exit the compound," he said.

MORE

ap-kx-04-19-93 1106cdt

The second take of the fourth lead carried a faulty guideline ("51 days" should be "he said"). The error was understandable in light of the fast-changing situation and the haste of the AP editors. Wire editors easily corrected it.

BULLETIN PM-Armed Cult, 4th Ld-1st

Add,0209

WACO, Texas:51 days.

The operation began shortly after 6 a.m. when a combat engineering vehicle flying an American flag began bashing and tearing holes in one building of the compound. The ramming stopped for a time. Then, shortly after 9 a.m., the armored vehicle returned and bashed down the front door of the compound.

Although a school bus and several ambulances were rushed to the site, there was no indication that any cult members had been injured by the ramming or had surrendered.

Ricks said the federal agents never returned the cultists' fire.

The assault was by far the most aggressive action taken by the federal government since a gun battle on Feb. 28 that began the siege. Four federal agents died in the shootout, and cult leaders have said six of their members were killed.

Ricks said a non-lethal tear gas was being sprayed into the compound. He said the FBI believes there are enough gas masks inside for every adult member of the cult, but that the masks had a limited period of effectiveness.

The FBI had previously said it was reluctant to use tear gas because of the danger it might pose to children.

MORE

ap-kx-04-19-93 1120cdt

The next take was correctly designated.

BULLETIN PM-Armed Cult, 4th Ld-2nd

Add,0191

WACO, Texas: to children.

There are believed to be at least 17 children among the 95 followers holed up with Koresh, who has claimed to be Jesus Christ. Thirty-seven people, mostly children, have left the compound since the standoff began.

Ricks denied reports that the FBI intended to knock down the entire compound.

President Clinton said in Washington that he had advance notice of the assault, and that he believed Attorney General Janet Reno made the decision to begin the operation.

Before the operation began, Ricks said, federal agents telephoned the cult compound and warned one of its leaders that the cultists would be gassed if they didn't surrender. In response, he said, the person on the other end threw the telephone out the door.

Although the news media have been kept at least two miles away from the site, telescopic camera lenses captured the dawn assault in which the armored vehicle, with a battering ram attached, reached into a second-story window, tore down a portion of the outside wall and punched a hole in the roof.
Reporters had been, 13th graf
ap-kx-04-19-93 1128cdt

The pickup line told editors they could retain parts of the two previous leads. Then, just 50 minutes later, a fifth lead revealed a dramatic turn of events that required wire editors to scramble to revise their stories.

BULLETIN PM-Armed Cult, 5th Ld,0045
WACO, Texas (AP)—A huge fire erupted today at a religious cult compound after FBI agents in an armored vehicle smashed the buildings and pumped tear gas into them in an attempt to end a 51-day standoff.
MORE
ap-kx-04-19-93 1218cdt

Takes were kept short as developments unfolded. Deadlines had already arrived or were about to arrive at papers in the Midwest.

BULLETIN PM-Armed Cult, 5th Ld-1st Add,0039
WACO, Texas:
Flames engulfed much of the complex, sending huge clouds of smoke into the air.
None of the nearly 100 people believed to be inside the compound was seen leaving immediately.
MORE
ap-kx-04-19-93 1226cdt

BULLETIN PM-Armed Cult, 5th Ld-2nd Add,0116
WACO, Texas:
The fire began moments after an armored vehicle rammed one of the buildings. There appeared to be no immediate effort to put the fire out.
The fire broke about six hours after FBI agents in an armored vehicle began ripping holes in the walls of the compound where Branch Davidian leader David Koresh and his followers were barricaded. Agents were met by heavy gunfire but no injuries were reported.
"At this point we're not negotiating," FBI spokesman Bob Ricks said at a news briefing about a half hour before the fire began. "We're saying come out. Come out with your hands up. This matter is over."
MORE
ap-kx-04-19-93 1228cdt

BULLETIN PM-Armed Cult, 5th Ld-3rd Add,0078
WACO, Texas: is over.
Ricks had said agents were shielded from the gunfire and didn't return it. Before the fire, there were no reports of injuries to Koresh or any of his 95 followers.

Ricks had said non-lethal, "non-pyrotechnic" tear gas was being pumped throughout the compound, including through its compound's front door, into the room believed to be Koresh's, and into a buried bus and underground tunnel network, Ricks said.

MORE
ap-kx-04-19-93 1232cdt

BULLETIN PM-Armed Cult, 5th Ld-4th
Add,0213
WACO, Texas:

All of the nearly 80 adults inside were believed to have gas masks, though they likely would be effective only for up to eight hours, Ricks said.

"We will continue to gas them and make their lives as uncomfortable as possible until they do exit the compound," he said before the fire broke out.

The assault was by far the most aggressive action taken by the federal government since a gun battle on Feb. 28 that began the siege. Four federal agents died and 16 were injured in the shootout, and cult leaders have said six of their members were killed.

Asked why the agents took the action now, Ricks said, "Today's action was not a sign that our patience has run out. . . . This was, we believe, the next logical step in a series of actions to bring this to a conclusion."

The FBI had previously said it was reluctant to use tear gas because of the danger it might pose to children.

There are believed to be at least 17 children among the 95 followers holed up with Koresh, who has claimed to be Jesus Christ. Thirty-seven people, mostly children, have left the compound since the standoff began.

MORE
ap-kx-04-19-93 1240cdt

BULLETIN PM-Armed Cult, 5th Ld-5th
Add,0208
WACO, Texas: standoff began.

Agents had hoped "the motherly instinct would take place" and the children would be allowed to go free, Ricks said. "Apparently they don't care about their children, and that is unfortunate," he said.

Ricks said authorities believed the tear-gassing is the best way to avert a possible mass suicide.

President Clinton said in Washington that he had advance notice of the assault, and that Attorney General Janet Reno and the FBI made the decision to begin the operation.

Before the operation began, Ricks said, federal agents telephoned the cult compound and warned one of its leaders that the cultists would be gassed if they didn't surrender. In response, he said, the person on the other end threw the telephone out the door.

At midmorning, cultists hung a banner from one of the second-floor windows saying: "We want our phones fixed."

Koresh is the leader of the Branch Davidian cult. A Bureau of Alcohol, Tobacco and Firearms raid on the compound led to the gun battle in February. More than 100 agents tried to arrest Koresh and search for illegal weapons at the fortress-like cluster of light peach-colored buildings east of Waco.

No pickup
ap-kx-04-19-93 1243cdt

More new leads followed as the story kept changing for later editions. Then the AM cycle began with a whole new "writethru" for the following morning's editions. The wire watch never ends.

THE EXCITING JOB OF EDITING THE NEWS

The Branch Davidian story is just one example of the kind of fast-changing, challenging raw material a news editor deals with daily. Assembling a complete, coherent report and designing its display for readers are jobs that can be accomplished in many different ways, all of which may get the job done but only one of which can bear the individual stamp of its creator. The Associated Press is just one of many news sources available in most newsrooms. Others include United Press International, Reuter, supplemental wire services such as The New York Times and the Los Angeles Times/Washington Post, and the fact-gathering staff of one's own news organization. In addition, library files can be rich sources of background information and illustration ideas. The editor's creative opportunities are limited only by time and energy.

Public recognition has long been a missing element in the copy editor's rich bag of tangible and intangible rewards, but many publications have begun to supply "bylines" for editors on news or feature layouts, section fronts and even entire sections. An additional comfort for copy editors is the knowledge that the demand for their skills with words and images is likely to remain strong even if the method of delivering news shifts away from the printed page toward computers or other electronic media. There will always be consumers eager for reliable, well organized and edited information.

BIBLIOGRAPHY AND ADDITIONAL READINGS

Brooks, Brian S., George Kennedy, Daryl R. Moen, and Don Ranly. *News Reporting and Writing.* 3rd ed. St. Martin's Press. 1988.

Clark, Roy Peter, and Don Fry. *Coaching Writers: The Essential Guide for Editors and Reporters.* St. Martin's Press. 1992.

Clark, Roy Peter, Don Fry, Karen F. Brown, and Christopher Scanlan, editors. *Best Newspaper Writing 1979–1994.* The Poynter Institute for Media Studies and Bonus Books, Inc.

Mencher, Melvin. *News Reporting and Writing.* 4th ed. William C. Brown Publishers. 1987.

Metz, William. *Newswriting from Lead to "30."* Prentice Hall. 1991.

Murray, Donald M. *Read to Write: A Writing Process Reader.* Holt, Rinehart and Winston. 1992.

Rich, Carole. *Writing and Reporting News: A Coaching Method.* Wadsworth. 1993.

Chapter 6

THE INFORMATION PRESENTER

WORKING WITH WORDS

The job of presenting the news, putting it into a package that readers will find both interesting and attractive, challenges the editor's creativity. Some of the essential tools—typography, photography, graphic illustration and design techniques—are discussed in Part III. The focus of this chapter is the fundamental skill of working with words.

Words are the writer's indispensable tool. As information presenters, editors are writers and should see themselves as artists who use images on paper as their medium. Even within rigid formats determined by tradition, such as the front pages of many newspapers, artistry is practiced in the choices and arrangements of words.

THE ART OF THE HEADLINE

Foremost among the skills of the information presenter is headline writing. Headlines in themselves are works of art. A headline is any type larger than the text, used to demand the attention of readers and inform them of what the text contains. A title identifies a written work; a headline both identifies and describes it. Headlines can be blunt or subtle, dark or light, grim or beguiling. They can bludgeon, tickle, intrigue, mystify, shock or startle. In their worst forms, they can also lull or bore, like a series of z's across the page.

There is no universal definition of a good headline. Different publications have different standards. A headline that would be admired in a tabloid like the *New York Daily News* might not even be acceptable in *The New York Times,* and vice versa. Nevertheless, headline writing is a universal skill. Once learned, it can be transferred from place to place. That may seem contradictory, but good headline writers know how to adapt to the rules in any given setting.

PURPOSES OF HEADLINES

Headlines serve the same purposes everywhere:

1. Sales talk for stories. A writer's work goes for naught if no one reads. The most carefully crafted piece of prose is no more effective than a single leaf on an autumn day unless attention is drawn to it. That is the reason books have colorful jackets or paper covers emblazoned with enthusiastic comments from reviewers.

The headline writer's job is to grab readers' attention and draw them into the text. In a sense, it is a form of selling. By describing the attributes of the product, the news story, the headline writer reaches out to potential buyers.

2. Guideposts and decorations for pages. Imagine a newspaper or magazine page without headlines or any other form of display type, just text and illustrations. Where would a reader's eye go? Headlines guide the reader into the page and direct the reader from story to story.

They also dress up the page with the finishing touches necessary for completeness. A page without headlines is an uninteresting mass of gray type. As decorations, headlines have symmetry, contrast, balance and other artistic attributes.

3. Nuggets of information. Today's readers are in a hurry, perhaps more so than readers of the past because of competing, proliferating forms of communication. Everybody has just so much time to devote daily to gathering information unrelated to job, business or special interest.

As speedy sources of general information, newspapers excel because they offer a selected menu of news, arranged by category and priority. For readers who merely skim the surface of the news, headlines are the substance of the newspaper. To some extent, more demanding readers also depend on headlines exclusively for information. For this reason, the trend is for headlines to explain and inform, not just tease or entertain.

THE PARTS OF HEADLINES

A headline may consist of just one part, standing alone, or may contain multiple levels, or decks, called the main, the readout, the summary, the kicker and the label (Box 6.1).

A single-deck headline may consist of one or more lines of type. A "line" is a word or group of words arranged side by side on the same level.

Parts of Headlines

A line:

Panel urges

A deck:

Panel urges
courtroom
cameras

A spread:

Panel urges courtroom cameras

A readout:

Says experiment
worked so well it
should be a law

Another type of readout:

Clinton hit by harassment suit

Complaint alleges sexual advances as governor

A summary:

Jet crash in China
kills all 160 aboard

- ***2 Americans die; rapid expansion of air traffic causes a rise in mishaps***

A kicker:

Experiment works

Panel urges courtroom cameras

A label:

THE JUDICIARY

Panel urges courtroom cameras

A slammer:

CHOKE

Team blows 20-point lead in final seconds

Box 6.1

Several lines may be stacked to form a "deck."

A line that extends across multiple columns is often called a "spread."

In a headline that contains more than one deck, the section with the largest and usually the boldest type is called the "main." Like a single-deck headline, the main contains the essential facts and is complete within itself, relying on no other part of the headline for its meaning.

The "readout" is a secondary line or lines below the main, often in a contrasting font or in italics. The readout amplifies or explains the main and often uses the same subject. It is smaller than the main, often half as large, and may be lighter in weight.

One form of readout is the "summary," in which the headline writer condenses the most important facts into a summary sentence. Summary readouts are sometimes punctuated like body text.

A line that appears just above the main is called a "kicker" or "label." The kicker is usually half the size of the main. The principal function of the kicker is to add emphasis to the main.

The label identifies the category of news represented by the story. It is usually just one or two words.

A special form of the kicker is the "slammer" or "hammer," which consists of a single word in large type. In this case the kicker carries the greatest impact, and the main is the smaller and lighter section of the headline.

STYLES OF HEADLINES

CAPITALIZATION

The most commonly used form is called "down style," or more correctly, "modified down style." This means that the first letter of the first line and all proper nouns are capitalized. An example is the heads of the *Detroit Free Press.* A pure down style would create an e. e. cummings-style head: all lowercase, proper nouns included.

"Modified up style" headlines capitalize the first letter of each word, unless the word is a preposition or an article. The *Washington Post* uses this style. "All caps" or a pure "up style" capitalizes everything. *The New York Times* uses this style for some of its heads.

THE MAIN

The simplest main headlines consist of one line across one or more columns. Common but more difficult are one-column heads of two or three lines. Editors who design pages use a form of shorthand to describe the headlines they want. They give the headline writer a "headline order," which is a bit like a physician's prescription and uses standard abbreviations. For example, 1-18-3 (one column, 18-point type, three lines) or 3-36-2 (three columns, 36-point type, two lines). Unless further instructions are given, it is understood that the headline order refers to the main.

Almost without exception the main is set flush with the left side of the column, although some will be centered. The headline order notes only the exception, as in 1-18-3 ital centered or]1-18-3 ital[.

The New York Times, almost alone among American newspapers, uses indented main headlines on its front page, in which the top line is flush left, the second is indented and the third is indented more. It creates a very stylized, staggered look for the *Times,* but it is a quaintly dated style. The *Times* also uses an inverted-pyramid head that is centered and tapers down from a long first line to a narrower second line and much narrower third line.

The workhorse of most publications is the two- and three-column main, consisting of two or three lines (2-36-2 or 3-36-2 or 2-48-3).

BANNER

A spread headline that stretches across the width of the paper is called a "banner." It is used less frequently today than 20 years ago when the banner was a staple of every newspaper. Today the banner is but one more tool available to the editor for use as needed to trumpet major news, just like a healthy dose of hot pepper in a stew.

Tabloid newspapers use a modification of this style because of their format, and the result is a very brief headline, often no more than five or six words that pretty much fill the page. The *New York Post* is a master of this style. Rarely do editors use huge type for banners except for major stories. In newspaper circles huge type (generally 288 points) is referred to as second-coming type.

KICKER

Kickers seem to be returning to popularity in some design circles. The heyday of the kicker was the 1950s through the 1970s, but some publications used that style before and after that time. Occasionally the kicker has a thin line under it to further set it off from the main, but this practice is not popular. Some editors and designers complain that the line tends to separate too much the two parts of the headline.

SLAMMER

A slammer creates extra white space around the top line, which can be effective on a tight page. The general rule calls for the slammer to be twice the type size and about half the length of the main. While not used too often in today's design, it nonetheless is one more tool available for the designer. *The Milwaukee Journal Sentinel* uses a variation of the slammer effect, placing a bold phrase followed by a colon next to the main head. The visual effect is that of a slammer—good visual punch before leading the reader to the main.

JUMP HEADS

While research shows that the majority of readers do not follow stories to other pages, the necessity to jump stories remains. The line at the bottom of a story telling the reader where the article is continued is the "jump line." It should tell the reader which column to go to and should include one or two words to look for. Some editors think it only polite to say "Please turn to . . ." Others will merely say, "See House Budget on page 7A, column 2." The type for the jump line usually will be the same size or larger than body text. Occasionally jump lines will appear in italics or bold, so that they will stand out from the body type.

The headline on the continuation of the story is the "jump head." The usual practice is to repeat the words of the front-page headline or say something similar. This helps the reader turning to the page identify the correct jump quickly and continue reading. However, some newspapers prefer that the jump head reflect the content of the part of the story that appears beneath it. Others use no headline at all but simply a word or words of identification, followed by a thick line, or rule.

SOME GENERAL GUIDELINES FOR HEADLINE WRITERS

The attributes of a good headline vary with the requirements and policies of different publications, but there are some universal goals:

1. Say something. Headline writing is more than just picking up some words from a news story and putting them in larger type. The words selected for enlargement must mean something, both in the context of the article and on their own merits. The headline writer must step back, view the headline from the reader's perspective and ask himself or herself, "Does it really say something?" Anyone who fails to take this precaution may be guilty of shouting silently, or saying nothing in a big way.

Economy slips
Economists discuss
some of the reasons

The top part of this headline, "Economy slips," sends a message about the economy. Although vague, it does tell the reader things are not going well. The second part, known as the readout or deck, should amplify or explain the top. Instead, it expresses knowledge most readers already have: economists discuss the economy. Of course they do. One would be surprised if they didn't. What the reader wants to know is: What are they saying?

Database accesses
multiple categories

Jargon is even more objectionable in headlines than in general news stories. The computer world, like every other discipline, has its own argot. Using such words in headlines is like telling the reader: If you don't understand, go away. This story is only for insiders.

Often a barking dog is way beyond yelp

Puns have their place in some publications and are banned in others. The major reason for banning them is that bad puns, or groaners, which wring exclamations of affront from readers, tend to outnumber the clever ones. Better no puns than bad puns, the opponents say. Another objection to puns is that they usually send no message other than a tone of good humor. The reader of the example headline is "beyond yelp" in discovering that a scientific study has determined that dogs often bark without good reason.

What about the deficit?

Well, what about it? Question headlines, like this one, often have no answer. They are simply devices to introduce topics. They have an air of desperation about them, as if the headline writer has been stumped. When one is starved for a headline idea, the source of the poverty is likely to be the story, which probably lacks focus and facts.

Local woman switches to
life as traveling food vendor

A headline should be a little story, complete within itself. It should not require the reader to look to the article for the meaning of the headline. When this local woman switched to life, what did she switch from? Not death, surely. But what else? Some form of non-life? Perhaps she has just switched jobs? Or switched from local to traveling? Part of the obligation to "say something" is completeness and coherence within the framework of the headline.

2. Be conversational. Headlines should be written in conversational English, which means they should use words and phrases that might actually be spoken, either casually or formally. This does not mean headline writers should use slang, clichés or trite sayings, such as "you know." It does mean that headline writers should chat with their readers.

Weather pattern holds in area

This headline is not conversational. More likely, the same message, spoken between acquaintances, would be put this way:

Warm weather to stick around

A common form of the non-conversational headline is the large-type version of alphabet soup. Unfamiliar abbreviations are either not understood or, worse, are ignored by many readers.

County divided on
RWMC exemptions

3. Obey the grammar rules. It may seem that headline writers have their own set of rules and enjoy license to twist and distort the language to suit space limitations. The impression stems from bad headlines, written hurriedly and with regret by headline writers who know better.

Ruling could be
worse than it was

Headlines are normally in present tense, but in some situations other tenses are appropriate. In any case, proper sequence of tenses is necessary. "Ruling could be worse" clashes with "than it was," creating a non-statement. To be grammatical (if not informative), the headline would have to say, "Ruling could have been worse than it was." This won't fit and says nothing, so the headline writer must begin again with a new idea.

Four in family dead,
pressure is blamed

A comma splice, or run-on, is no more acceptable in a headline than anywhere else. The required punctuation is a semicolon.

4. Be accurate. The worst offense a headline writer can commit is to "kill" someone in the headline who is not dead in the story (Box 6.2). This can be a

Oops! He's Alive

Texas postmaster slain

A gunman walked into the Deweyville, Texas, Post Office on Monday and shot the postmaster three times during an apparent robbery, authorities said. The victim, 42, was listed as stable and undergoing surgery at a hospital. About four and a half hours after the shooting, a suspect surrendered to the Huntsville Police Department 120 miles away.

Box 6.2

capital crime in terms of one's career. A slightly less grievous offense is to report anything in the headline that is not true in the story.

JOBLESS
RATE
SORES

Misspelled words look bad anywhere, but they are even worse in large type. A headline like this one can do immeasurable damage to a newspaper's image of reliability and wisdom.

Kite crash mistaken
for ultralight plane

The rules of sentence structure also apply to headlines. Because a crash cannot be mistaken for a plane, the sentence is absurd unless key words are inserted: "Kite that crashed was mistaken for ultralight plane," or "Kite crash mistaken for that of ultralight plane."

5. Prefer active verbs. Passive voice is acceptable and may be a desirable choice depending on the circumstances, but headline writers should always opt for active verbs when they can. Active verbs, as their name implies, impart action to a headline that might otherwise be inert. Subject-verb-object is the best sentence form for newswriting; it is also best for headlines.

Version 1:

Schools burdened
by big enrollment

Version 2:

Huge enrollment
clogs classrooms

Notice how an adequate headline (version 1) is enlivened by the switch to active voice and a more vivid choice of verb (version 2).

To the preference for active verbs must be added an even more vehement preference for verbs, any verbs, over none at all. Verbless headlines are incomplete statements, like sentence fragments. They are more akin to book or essay titles than to headlines that tell a story. Verbless heads have a place on feature pages and even on news pages, but only when the focus of the story is on a topic rather than an event.

A head without verbs:

**Boomers'
retirement
prospects**

**Education, two
incomes keys to
future comfort**

6. Use standard English. Headline writers have developed their own language, known as "headlinese." It consists of short words that can be used in place of longer words even though they are not exact synonyms (Box 6.3). At best, headlinese words are clichés, but they do have the virtue of comprehensibility to readers who have learned the code. At its worst, headlinese is a graceless pseudolanguage used nowhere but in newspapers. All headline writers try to avoid headlinese, but most are forced to resort to it when no other choice seems possible. Regrettably, gobbledygook sometimes gets published.

A headline written entirely in headlinese:

**Jobless aid
said nixed
by prexy**

The "said head" is one of the worst forms of headlinese. "Said" is used as a qualifier, to express non-endorsement of something that was said by someone. It is the equivalent of "is said by someone to have been." Of course, dropping "to have been" is unacceptable, but such constructions are frequently seen nonetheless. The reason is the requirement that headlines state verifiable facts, not hearsay. Any information that relies on the source for credibility must be attributed within the headline, and "said," however clumsy, is a form of attribution. The unverified information is worth reporting because it may be correct, and it must be qualified because it may be wrong. Any newspaper that reports it without attribution risks an embarrassing inaccuracy.

Another form of headlinese is the "shorthand statement." "Jobless aid," for example, does not mean "aid that lacks a job." It means "assistance to the jobless" or unemployment compensation. Regular readers are presumed to understand such shorthand, and others are left to seek clarification in the story.

Commonly Used Headlinese Words

Accepted words	Headlinese
appoint, nominate, hire	tap
appointment, nomination	nod
consider	eye
criticize, assail	blast, flay, hit, rap, score, slap
deny, reject	nix
increase	boost, hike
mention, point out	cite
propose	urge
reported, declared	held, said
scheduled, planned	set, slated

Box 6.3

"Prexy" is shorthand for president and is as good as Greek for most American readers.

7. Tell what's new. Headline writers face a danger of sounding stale or stating the obvious. Readers expect to find only the latest, freshest information in headlines. Yesterday's or last week's disclosure is today's history. Information can become stale even between editions, so copy editors must keep up with events, even those outside their special areas of responsibility. This means, for example, that a copy editor who works only with local stories must also be aware of what is happening in the nation and abroad.

Even a fresh headline can state the obvious.

Moon is eclipsed by earth's shadow

If the moon were eclipsed by anything but the Earth's shadow, it would be major news.

Court to hear case

Of course it will. Hearing cases is what courts do.

8. Check for double meanings. It has been said that copy editors must have dirty minds, and it is certainly true that headline writers must be aware of the unintentional meanings of the words they use.

Warhawk girls should do it one more time

The Warhawk girls were a swimming team that needed one more victory. To some readers of this headline, another meaning was the first to come to mind.

**FBI wanted
man killed**

The FBI headline demonstrates the danger of two verbs in one headline. The first verb tends to be read as the main verb, and if it is not the main verb, confusion results. The FBI did not want anyone killed. The man killed was wanted by the FBI. A better way: "Fugitive is killed."

Large hog farmers are more efficient

Of course, the size of the hogs and the farmers is irrelevant. The scale of the operation creates the efficiency. A better way: "Large-scale hog farms more efficient"

Troopers log extra hours to beat drunk drivers

No doubt they are not actually beating anyone. The headline writer should look for a synonym.

Ugly or not, Osceola's girls will take victory

Danglers, like misspelled words, are even more objectionable and embarrassing in large type than in body text. A whole new approach is necessary here.

9. Be concise. Large type loses its impact when too many words are crowded together. In some publications, headline writers are not allowed to use articles (a, an, the), "and" or some forms of the verb "to be" (is, are, was, were). These are considered "padding," words added just to fill space. Other forms of padding are unnecessary adjectives and adverbs and redundancies.

**The American press has this
awful occupational affliction:
a terribly short attention span**

This headline, which appeared on an opinion page, could clearly be told in one line without loss of information: "Press has short attention span."

Publishing three lines of large type—or any size type, for that matter—where one would do is wasteful. It creates an impression of undisciplined squandering of time and news space. The shorter headline, by using space more economically, achieves greater impact. It is easier to read and understand than the bigger, wordier mass of type.

Trade Center bomb trial proceedings begin

Empty, redundant words like "proceedings" just fill space. In this example, like many others, the biggest word carries the smallest meaning. The padding is obvious.

10. Be appealing. Appealing does not necessarily mean dazzlingly brilliant or witty. One does not have to be a punster or jokester to write appealing headlines. A straightforward telling of a story is often the most appealing approach. Many ordinary, yet appealing headlines appear daily in the American press.

Nigeria's dream of global influence looking bleak

"Appealing" means a headline is attractive to readers. It draws their attention by becoming the focus of their curiosity or emotion. Sometimes headline writers accomplish this without "telling a story" in the conventional sense. When the space shuttle *Challenger* blew up, killing all aboard, most newspapers printed photographs that told the story. Henry Joseph of *The Bakersfield Californian* created this appealing headline, which complemented the photographs:

World looks up and cries

SOME HEADLINE PRACTICES TO AVOID

1. Editorializing. News sources usually have points of view, which they express in direct quotation and paraphrase in news stories. Headline writers can easily fall into the trap of appearing to embrace these opinions.

Adopting the speaker's point of view:

Citizens 'mad as hell' over complacent, inept Congress

Congress may well be complacent and inept, but it is not the headline writer's place to say so in news pages, where readers are accustomed to statements of fact. Such a headline places the newspaper's imprimatur on someone's pronouncement and makes it appear that the editors believe it is fact. This erodes the newspaper's reputation for taking stands only on opinion pages.

To avoid editorializing, headline writers must work in attribution or qualify the pronouncement in some way: "Many reported 'mad as hell' at a Congress they call inept."

A headline that adopts the speaker's point of view will appear one-sided and alarmist (Box 6.4). Attribution is essential no matter how tight the space: "Farm leader attacks environmentalists."

2. Assigning guilt. A headline writer can accurately reflect the content of a story and still distort the facts. Under U.S. law a person accused of a crime is presumed not to be guilty until convicted in court, yet police news usually makes innocence seem unlikely. Headlines must maintain doubt. When they do not, the distortion is unfair to the accused.

A janitor was accused of using radio equipment in his car to pose as an air traffic controller and give instructions to pilots. The "phantom" operated for six

An Example of Editorializing

Environmentalists threaten food supply

Environmentalists could be a great threat to agriculture, a spokesman for a leading farm organization said Tuesday.

People who advocate organic farming don't know what they are talking about, and most were not raised on farms, John L. Runyon of the State Federation of Farmers told the annual convention of the Cattlemen's Association.

He said production would fall to levels of 100 years ago without chemical fertilizers and warned of food shortages, malnutrition and starvation.

"They just don't understand their demands are impossible," he said.

Runyon said farmers would continue to feed more people with less farmland by using the tools "environmentalists are trying to destroy."

"The big job for American agriculture is to make sure we don't overreact, to make sure we don't do some silly, asinine things because of the attacks on farming," he said.

Box 6.4

weeks before authorities traced the signals and made the arrest. The headline left no doubt that the "phantom" and the janitor were the same person. It was a case of trial by headline.

Air control
"phantom"
is arrested

Fairness requires the headline writer to use words like "accused," "charged" and "suspect" to clarify that the trial is yet to come.

Man accused
as "phantom"
air controller

After the accused is convicted, headline writers have more freedom to characterize the criminal, but editors don't always agree on the appropriateness of judgmental words in heads.

For example, when a former county commission chairman in Florida was released from prison after serving only 817 days for the murder of his wife, the *St. Petersburg Times* published a headline that simply stated the facts. The *Miami Herald,* in contrast, decided to describe the case as "notorious" and the outcome as "lenient" (Box 6.5).

Editors might debate whether the *Herald* went too far or the *Times* didn't go far enough to enlighten the reader. The art of headline writing leaves room for both points of view.

Headline Writing: A Comparison

Ex-politician convicted in wife's murder leaves jail

This *St. Petersburg Times* headline tells the story straight, without drawing conclusions about the appropriateness of the ex-politician's punishment. It would be unacceptable in some newspapers because it splits a prepositional phrase and delays the news to the last two words.

Notorious case of murder has a lenient conclusion

This *Miami Herald* headline contains some opinion but would be regarded by many as a good way to inform the reader of the outcome of a well-known murder case.

Box 6.5

PUNCTUATING HEADLINES

In general, the same rules of punctuation apply to headlines as to any other use of the language. However, some special conditions are imposed on headline writers:

1. **The comma replaces "and."** "And" has long been regarded as a space-wasting word that has no place in headlines.

Senator, speaker support
North Korean sanctions

This headline is written "modified down style," with only the first word and the proper noun capitalized.

2. **The semicolon divides clauses that have different subjects.** Where a comma plus "and" would be used in body text (two independent clauses), the semicolon is used exclusively in headlines.

South Africa Bomb Kills 9;
Voters Growing Anxious

This headline is written "up style," with every word capitalized (prepositions and articles would be "down").

3. **The period is not used, except in some abbreviations.** The most common use of the period is in "U.S." and "U.N."
4. **The colon is used sparingly.** It typically introduces a list, a direct quotation or a topic.

Some hair-raising news:
'I'm rid of the cancer'

Sometimes the colon is a substitute for "say" or "says," but this use is frowned on by some editors and banned at some publications.

Analysts: Rate hike
appears imminent

5. **The dash is seldom used.**
6. **The hyphen is used to clarify the relationships of words. It is never used to break a word from line to line or to end a line.**

Cops looking for sex assault suspect

A hyphen between "sex" and "assault" would help remedy the ambiguity in this headline.

7. **Where double quotation marks are used in body text, single quotes are used in headlines.**
8. **A headline that requires no punctuation is usually best.**

THE RULES OF HEADLINE WRITING

Headline styles vary widely from newspaper to newspaper. So do the rules governing headline writers. The examples here represent different schools of headline writing.

THE TRADITIONAL STYLE

The rigidly formal appearance characteristic of this style has given way in many newspapers to trendier designs. The most prominent exception is *The New York Times.* News headlines in the *Times* are written according to time-honored rules that emphasize discipline in typography and language. The fit must be precise, and the appearance is intended to project steadiness, conservatism and reliability. Indeed, the headlines in the main news sections of the *Times* resemble the multiple decks of type used 130 years ago, when each character was hand-set. Tradition is paramount at the *Times.* Each edition speaks to its readers as the solemn voice of stability amid the sweep of change.

Traditional Rules

1. Each word begins with a capital letter (up style). The only exceptions are the articles (a, an, the) and short prepositions, such as "of" and "to," which are capitalized only as the first word.

Splits in the Traditional, Up Style

Used-Car
Glut May
Be Looming

This is an unacceptable split because the noun (glut) is separated from its modifier (used-car) and the parts of the verb (may be looming) fall on separate lines.

Glut of
Used Cars
May Loom

This split separates the preposition (of) from its object (used cars).

Sellers Face
Coming Glut
of Used Cars

This is an acceptable traditional headline. Notice that it not only avoids splits but also balances line lengths to eliminate the ragged look.

Box 6.6

2. Splits (also known as bad breaks and runarounds) are forbidden. A split is a division from line to line of the parts of a compound verb, a prepositional phrase or a modifier-noun combination. This means a line may not end with a preposition, a part of a verb or a modifier. The rule is based on the belief that each line is read as a unit and must stand by itself (Box 6.6).

3. Abbreviations, headlinese, puns and slang are not allowed. Some proper nouns, such as Eisenhower and Massachusetts, present insurmountable problems where space is tight. In the years when Dwight D. Eisenhower was in the news, many newspapers referred to him by his nickname, Ike. Other presidents were known by their initials (JFK, LBJ). Traditional headline writers are allowed no such shortcuts. In addition, they may not use state abbreviations.

Newsmakers who are "hit" or "rapped" in other papers are "assailed" in traditional headlines. Robberies are not "heists" or "rip-offs." Woe to the headline writer who yields to the punning impulse.

THE FREE STYLE

This modern style, in which forms are only minimally prescribed, treats a headline as a sentence, to be read all at once, not line by line. The emphasis is on readability and a chatty, informal tone. The main rule is that the rules are off.

Capitalization is limited to the first word in the sentence and proper nouns.

Splits are allowed, in the belief that sentences flow around corners, not just in straight lines. Abbreviations, puns, slang and even hyphenation from line to line are tolerated in the interest of easy reading (Box 6.7).

Free-style Headlines

These examples are from *The News* of Boca Raton, Fla.

Forecasters predict Andrew will change first name to Hurricane

It's too soon to tell, but South Florida could be hit

Mayor salvages bit of beauty pageant that ran out of funds

Moon jellyfish spreading out in S. County

Yanking trees gets to root of problem

Olympic Heights battling for bucks

RU 486 is effective morning-after pill

Box 6.7

THE IN-BETWEEN STYLE

Most newspapers have established their own variations of the traditional style and adopted elements of the freewheeling. The rules vary from newsroom to newsroom.

WRITING HEADLINES: THE METHOD

The headline writer's art is a mixture of inspiration and method. Inspiration is born in natural talent but thrives only with practice. Experienced headline writers develop the ability to compose a headline as they read. They don't always come up with the best headline on first try, but the essential elements are selected out, ready to be fine-tuned, during the initial examination of the story. Drawing a blank is unusual for experienced headline writers, and it signals potential problems with the organization and content of the story.

Less experienced editors and students of headline writing may use a step-by-step method.

The starting point is the headline order, which is the description of the size and shape of the headline the layout editor requests. It is likely to be expressed as a set of numbers, such as 2-36-2. The key to the code is:

column width-type size-lines of type

How much can be said in a 2-36-2 depends on the typeface, which may be bold and fat or light and slim. Familiarity with the standard type sizes and the

Headline Counting System	
Lowercase letters	1 unit
Uppercase letters	1 1/2 units
Exceptions	
Lowercase i, l	1/2 unit
Lowercase m, w	1 1/2 units
Uppercase I	1/2 unit
Uppercase M and W	2 units
Spaces	1/2 unit
Numerals	1 1/2 units
Period, comma, quotation mark, hyphen	1/2 unit
Dollar sign, percentage symbol, dash, question mark	1 1/2 units

Box 6.8

characteristics of typefaces, described in Chapter 7, helps the writer visualize the headline.

Computer programs in use at many newspapers allow precise fitting of headlines with key strokes. This eliminates the need for the less exact headline count system, a method of estimating the fit (Box 6.8). The count system assigns a value to each character and a maximum total for the space assigned. For example, a 2-36-2 might have a maximum count of 18, which means the characters in each line may add up to 18, or less than 18, but never more.

THE STEPS

1. Read the story. Some headlines can be written without benefit of a close examination of the story because the facts are well known. Examples are:

MEN WALK ON MOON

President resigns

Most heads are not that easy. Accurate headline writing requires intimate knowledge of as many facts as possible. Working with only a handful of facts skimmed from the top of the barrel is risky. It sharply increases the probability of error.

When the editor reads the story through to the end with a high level of concentration, the elements of a headline should present themselves (Box 6.9).

2. List the key terms. After reading the story, the editor should reduce it to essential terms, which are words and combinations of words that would have

Read the Story

By JAMES HANNAH
Associated Press Writer

DAYTON, Ohio (AP)——There may be "yes, yes" in her eyes, but unless her lips say the same thing—over and over—sex is a no-no at Antioch College.

The small liberal arts school in nearby Yellow Springs requires students to give and get verbal consent before any type of romantic contact.

And one "yes" won't do. Consent must be given for each specific act, from kissing to intercourse.

The policy—adopted in January 1993 at the school known for innovation and social activism—is aimed at date rape.

"What this establishes is, 'I did say no,' " college spokesman Jim Mann said. "It also establishes that if someone is drunk or passed out, they do not have the ability to consent."

Other schools are trying to define more clearly their policies on sexual harassment and other offenses. But Caryn McTighe Musild, a senior research associate for the Washington-based Association of American Colleges, said she knows of no other college with a policy like Antioch's.

"I think what it's suggesting is that students talk to each other and communicate to each other about the relationship they want," she said.

Violators can be expelled from Antioch, which has 700 students, 70 percent of them women. But Mann said he knows of no reported violations.

"On one level it has been widely supported," he said. "On another level it has been greeted with some humor."

Jonathan Platt, a 24-year-old sophomore, told the Dayton Daily News the policy is "well-cushioned in common sense."

"The policy is not radical," Platt said. "It's not asking too much from somebody."

Antioch developed a "relatively harsh" policy to deal with sexual assaults after an alleged date rape in 1990, Mann said. Under the policy, students can be removed from campus within 24 hours if accused of sexual offenses, and the alleged victims are assigned advocates to represent them.

The expanded policy reads: "Verbal consent should be obtained with each new level of physical and-or sexual contact or conduct in any given interaction, regardless of who initiates it. Asking, 'Do you want to have sex with me?' is not enough. The request for consent must be specific for each act."

"What this policy says is you better be sure she's giving consent," Bernice Sandler, a senior associate with the Washington-based Center for Women's Studies, said Wednesday. "Although it does put a burden on the person who is initiating the act, it protects them."

Antioch has a history of innovation. It opened in 1853 with a pledge of equal rights for women. It was the first liberal-arts college to offer a work-study program.

In 1971 it opened a law school in Washington to train lawyers in social activism. In 1987, it banned Peace Corps recruiters because, it said, the agency did not ban sexual discrimination.

Box 6.9

to be used in any effort to summarize the facts. These terms should be listed mentally or, if necessary, on paper, roughly in order of importance. Be selective. The list should not be long (Box 6.10).

3. Write the summary sentence. The key terms should now be used to compose a summary sentence (Box 6.11).

List of Key Words From the Story in Box 6.9

love	kiss
Antioch	date rape
College	policy
repeated	sex
consent	

Box 6.10

4. Compose the headline, using the key terms and the summary sentence as guides. Mindful that the first effort may not be the best, the headline writer now begins to experiment with the key terms, adding or substituting others as needed to make the head more appealing to readers. There may be occasion to engage in a little wordplay (Box 6.12).

SOME HINTS FOR BETTER HEADLINES

1. Be a designer, not a carpenter. Using the newswriter's exact words in the headline may sometimes be necessary because the words in the story are the best way to tell the story. However, good headline writers strive for originality. They are not technicians who, like carpenters, pick up a board from the story and nail it into the headline space. They create their own lumber. To excel at headline writing, one must never steal someone else's turn of phrase; instead, one tries to create a turn of phrase that is worth stealing.

2. Be a storyteller. The reader has not yet read the lead or the first three paragraphs or any of the text and relies on the headline writer for a clear, understandable introduction or summary statement. Assuming too much about the reader's knowledge can result in a headline that leads nowhere and, worse, means nothing to the reader.

3. Make every word count. Eliminate needless words, which add no information and contribute little meaning. Adjectives and adverbs are usually dispensable.

4. Check the headline by reviewing the information in the story. One can get so close to a story that one loses sight of it, and the memory plays tricks, turning non-facts into facts and vice versa. The best method of self-protection is to go back to the story after the headline has been written and check the head for accuracy.

THE ART OF THE NEWS BRIEF

Briefs and *shorts* as newspaper terms don't refer to underwear or any other kind of attire. They mean tightly written, concise news items.

The Summary Sentence for the Story in Box 6.9

Antioch College's date rape policy requires repeated consent for sex, for a kiss and for every other stage of lovemaking.

Box 6.11

In the past shorts were used strictly as fillers, items that plugged the holes left when longer stories failed to fill the space. Copy editors would often begin their workdays by preparing a variety of news shorts that might or might not be used later, depending on how much space became available. In some newsrooms this practice continues, but in many others pages are carefully designed down to the last line of type, leaving no space for unplanned shorts.

Editors have recognized the value of news briefs in the design of news pages that reflect new attention to the needs of readers in a hurry:

1. The news must be easy to grasp. In the past, the absence of competing media meant that newspapers could challenge readers to sift out the essential facts from long, gray columns of type without fear that the text might go unread. Readers had nowhere else to go. Today, however, the competition for the reader's time is fierce, and editors have realized that success depends on a format that places few if any unrewarded demands on consumers. This does not mean that the news must be oversimplified or written for the elementary school level. It does mean that news items must make their points concisely, in unadorned, informative, conversational prose devoid of redundancies. Newswriters for radio and television have long practiced this art. Newspapers are adopting many of the same techniques.

2. The news must be well organized. A news publication that presents items that are easy to find as well as easy to grasp will attract readers. News can be categorized by location, such as world, national, regional and local, or by subject, such as government, politics, science and medicine. Within each category, briefs and longer stories can be packaged together on the same page or in the same section. Readers also expect guidance by priority. In essence, this means more important events get more space and larger headlines.

As information presenters, copy editors manage and often write news briefs, a task equal in importance to headline writing. They are the creators and organizers of roundups, digests, breakouts, summaries and promotion boxes.

THE ROUNDUP

A roundup is a collection of short items under a heading, such as "World" or "People." The items are often tightly edited wire stories, each with a small

Attempts at Headlines for the Story in Box 6.9

The first effort:

College's policy requires repeated consent for sex

The second effort:

At Antioch, kiss and tell becomes ask, then kiss

New headline order, 1/24/3

The third effort:

Students get sexual code of conduct

Yet another effort:

No yesses, no kisses, code says

Box 6.12

headline. The typographical style usually matches that of other news stories (Box 6.13).

THE DIGEST

The digest is similar to a roundup but features shorter items, often in a typeface that contrasts with regular body type. The type may be unjustified, or "ragged," and each item is limited to a single paragraph. To achieve impact and improve the reader appeal of each item, many copy editors rewrite them in a conversational style similar to broadcast writing (Box 6.14).

THE BREAKOUT

Any story can be told concisely, but not all can be brief. Editors should not attempt to achieve less where more is clearly needed or desired. Some stories demand to be long because of the sheer forcefulness of the writing. Others are too intricate or contain too many diverse facts to be reduced to briefs. Sometimes extensive background is necessary to apprise readers of a story's full significance. Knowing how to tell the difference between a story that can be a brief and one that cannot is one of the editor's essential skills.

Long stories need not be endlessly gray. Devices such as subheads and pull quotes (discussed in Part III) can dress up a long text. In many cases parts of the story lend themselves to breakouts, which are short side items that highlight special information (Box 6.15). For example, a story about a fatal house fire could be accompanied by several breakouts:

- A list of the fire department's recommendations for safety in the home
- A chronology of the sequence of events
- A report on the history of fatal fires in the city, county or region
- A list of the conditions of the injured or vital information about the dead

A Roundup Item

A brief, or roundup item, runs two or more paragraphs.

Israeli planes hit Lebanon

JERUSALEM (AP)——Israeli warplanes and howitzers pounded guerrilla bases in Lebanon Tuesday for the second straight day.

Radio reports said the army moved tanks into the Israeli-occupied buffer zone inside southern Lebanon.

Arab guerrillas, who recently have stepped up attacks on Israeli forces in an attempt to wreck the Middle East peace talks, fought back with rockets. One salvo slammed into a northern Israeli town before dawn, killing a 14-year-old boy and wounding five other people, the Israeli army said.

Box 6.13

A Digest Item

A digest item consists of one compact paragraph.

Israeli planes raid Lebanon

JERUSALEM (AP)——Israeli planes and artillery pounded guerrilla bases in Lebanon Tuesday for the second straight day. Arab guerrillas, who have been trying to wreck the Middle East peace talks, fought back with rockets. One salvo killed a 14-year-old boy and wounded five other people in a northern Israeli town.

Box 6.14

Copy editors may or may not themselves do the research and writing associated with breakouts, but they are always the source of ideas.

SUMMARIES

Some newspapers carry daily summaries of the top events of the day, with page references for readers who want the complete stories. Each copy editor writes a summary of each story he or she edits and sends it to the summary editor, who compiles the summary package.

PROMOTION BOXES

Copy editors are key participants in the selection, design and writing of front-page promotion boxes that seek to lure readers to inside features. Some newspapers devote as much as 15 percent of front-page space to these promotion

A Breakout

Findings

- Social Security Trust Fund could go bankrupt by 2029.
- The Medicare Trust Fund might go bankrupt in 2001.
- Spending on federal health programs has risen 10 percent annually, even during the past five weak economic years.
- Spending on social entitlements, especially health-benefit programs, and interest due on the national debt together could consume all federal tax revenues by 2012.

—*Corpus Christi Caller Times*

Box 6.15

devices, which have grown in popularity as editors seek a wider and more diverse readership.

BIBLIOGRAPHY AND ADDITIONAL READINGS

Baskette, Floyd K., Jack Z. Sissors, and Brian S. Brooks. *The Art of Editing,* 5th ed. Macmillan. 1992.

Berner, R. Thomas. *Editing.* Holt, Rinehart & Winston. 1982.

Copperud, Roy, and Roy Paul Nelson. *Editing the News.* William C. Brown Publishers. 1983.

Gilmore, Gene. *Modern Newspaper Editing,* 4th ed. Iowa State University Press. 1994.

Highton, Jake. *Editing: Newspaper Editing, Headlines and Layout.* University Press, Roanoke, Va. 1983.

Riblet, Carl, Jr. *The Solid Gold Copy Editor.* Falcon Press. 1972.

Stonecipher, Harry W., Edward C. Nicholls, and Douglas A. Anderson. *Electronic Age News Editing.* Nelson Hall. 1983.

Westley, Bruce H. *News Editing,* 3rd ed. Houghton Mifflin. 1980.

DESIGN EDITING

PART THREE

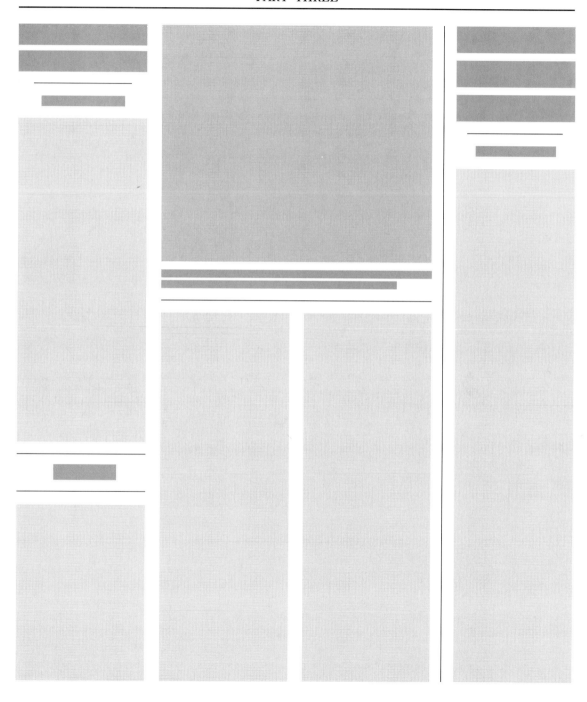

Chapter 7

A MANUAL OF TYPOGRAPHY

COMMUNICATING VISUALLY

Definitions of typography are as varied as those who practice it. During the days of hot-metal type, typography generally meant the setting of type in a pleasing manner. In today's computer era, the complexity of typography means an emphasis on type as produced on and, to a certain extent, controlled by computers in design and pagination.

For the purposes of this book, let's define typography as the art and craft of visually communicating a message to an audience. A glossary of typographical terms is given in Box 7.1.

Within this broad definition of typography, one can expect to be involved with the design and layout of the page, selection of type for headlines and body text and selection and proper display of illustrations. A person working for a small publication will probably do all of this. Someone working for a larger one might do just one part of it.

Typography, or graphic design as some will call it, is critically important in today's world if one works on any publication, and especially newspapers. Newspaper readership has fallen to critical levels in some markets, and other papers have folded entirely. The competition for the reader's time and money is fierce.

Glossary of Typography

body type The size and font in which the text of stories is set. It is usually a roman typeface with serifs, between 9 and 10 points in size.

box A rectangular space bordered by rules.

cold type Type produced photographically on sensitized paper.

cutline Type that identifies a picture and explains its contents. Pictures published in newspapers were once called "cuts" because the images were engraved, or cut, on metal for reproduction.

display type Any type, including headlines, that is larger than body type.

flag A nameplate or header.

folio A line of type on every page that identifies the periodical and gives the date of publication.

header Label at the top of a page that identifies the category of contents, such as "World" or "Lifestyle."

hot-metal type Type that is cast from molten metal in a mold called a matrix on a Linotype machine. In modern publications it has been replaced by cold type.

index A list that directs readers to standard features such as comics, editorials and classified ads. The index usually appears on the front page.

justified type Each line is set flush with both sides of the column. To achieve this effect, the letter spacing and word spacing are varied automatically by the computer, which also hyphenates words where necessary.

jump The continuation of a story from one page to another. When a story jumps from the front to an inside page, the part of the story that appears inside is "the jump." The headline on that part of the story is the "jump head."

Television viewing rates are going up and up, and newspapers are finding that they are less important to some readers than they would like to admit.

In short, a publication has to be relevant, not only in content, but also in design. But just as good design will not save a poorly written publication, neither will bad design sink a publication with strong content.

The short-lived *Sun* newspaper in St. Louis was a good example of a publication that featured strong design yet never connected with the readers. *The Wall Street Journal* is, to be charitable, archaic in design, but the content can't be beat.

Design is necessary to assist in communication. Design should never drive content, even though at times it seems as if it does.

GRAPHIC DESIGN GUIDELINES

Most design begins with, or is affected by, the establishment of certain rules or guidelines. These may be precisely written out in the form of a stylebook for design, or they may be shouted out by an editor who is particularly annoyed by another editor's "egregious deviation" from a publication's unwritten style.

kerning The space between letters. To kern type is to vary the letter spacing, causing the letters to nestle close together.

lowercase letters Letters that are not capitals.

nameplate The front-page block of type that identifies the newspaper.

pica A unit of measurement used in printing. Six picas equal 1 inch.

point A unit of measurement used in printing. Twelve points equal 1 pica.

ragged right Type that is set flush with the left side of the column but not with the right. This creates lines of differing lengths and makes the right edge of the column appear ragged.

readout The second deck, or layer, of a two-part headline. Sometimes called the deck, it reads out of the main head.

refer (pronounced reefer) A line that notifies a reader about a related story elsewhere in the newspaper. Refers are usually placed at the beginning of a story and sometimes are set in display type.

reverse type White or a light color printed on a dark or black background.

rule Any printed line. Rules come in many thicknesses, measured in points, and may include decorative elements.

pagination The placing of type and illustrations on a computerized page layout on a video screen.

sans serif A typeface that lacks the small finishing stroke at the base or top of letters.

sig A graphic that identifies a standing feature or continuing series.

skyline or skybox Promotion boxes above the nameplate.

typeface A family of printed letters that share the same design. Typefaces are often named for their designers.

Box 7.1

Some rules that are presented as gospel by editors are there for very good reasons, such as the rule that all body type must have a 1-pica margin between it and a box surrounding it. Other rules might be holdovers from a previous era or design director and will be less relevant than they were a few years ago, such as a rule that certain fonts can never be used in the paper.

Every rule has its exception. It's much better to think in terms of guidelines, which are flexible, but one must be careful not to reject all rules automatically. Most publications find that deadlines and staff turnover necessitate the implementation of some rules merely for the sake of design continuity from issue to issue.

With that in mind, the NUMBER ONE RULE of typography and design is: There ain't no rules.

THE SELECTION OF TYPEFACES

Type is the very foundation of printed communication, yet it is often the most misunderstood and misused component. Type is a very subtle communication tool that requires careful study and application to be effective.

The first stage of producing a publication is the writing. This is the act of transcribing mental coverage of, for example, a city council meeting onto paper or into a computer. In the first stage the story is the most important cog in the publication wheel.

In the next stage, the story will be edited and typeset onto a page. Setting a story into type may be as simple as selecting a typeface from a personal computer and cranking the story out on a laser printer. At the most complex, typesetting requires a *typographer,* one who is skilled in the selection and setting of type. The type can be set in-house, as on a laser printer or a high-speed typesetter, or out-of-house by a service bureau that does commercial typesetting for a variety of publications.

In either case, someone has to make decisions about what typefaces to use, the size, the weight, the leading and so forth. And since more and more publications are using copy editors to make these decisions, an editor needs to have some background in type so that his or her decisions will be informed ones, not guesses or erroneous assumptions.

Let's begin with the fundamentals.

PARTS OF TYPE

To talk intelligently about type one needs to know its nomenclature. The parts of type can be referred to in much the same way as human parts: the eye, the arm, the ear. Or plant parts: the stem. Even some furniture parts: the bowl, the counter. Still other parts sound like nothing else: ascender, descender, x-height.

The terms one needs to know are:

x-height the body of the letter. Actually the height of the lowercase x.

baseline the line on which thc body or base of the letter rests.

ascender the part of the letter that rises above the x-height.

descender the part of the letter that goes below the baseline.

stem the vertical or diagonal stroke of letters.

ear the small protuberance on the right of a lowercase g.

eye the closed portion of a lowercase e.

counter the enclosed portion of the lowercase a and the lowercase and capital O.

crossbar the part that crosses the stem of the lowercase t and forms the top part of the capital T.

arm a short, generally horizontal stroke that begins at the stem on the capital F, E and L.

loop the bottom part of the lowercase g. It is usually rounded and closed.

beard the small, generally downward stroke on the capital G.

bowl the outer, curved stroke on circular parts of letters such as the lowercase b, d, p and q.

serif the small finishing stroke at the base or top of letters.

finial the decorative, bulbous ending stroke on a lowercase r or f.

link the short stroke that connects the upper and lower parts of the lowercase g.

bracket The curved stroke that blends the stem with the serif.

curve an open, curved stroke on the C and G.

stress the axis of circular letters. The axis of some faces is vertical, while in others it can be slanted either to the right or to the left.

leg the downward diagonal stroke on the capital R and K.

CATEGORIES OF TYPEFACES

To the untrained, all typefaces can look alike, much as all trees, insects, cars and people can look the same, at least until one gets a chance to know them. Even then it can be hard to distinguish some faces, both of humans and of type varieties.

Typefaces can be split into categories or races, which makes for some ease in identification. There are several type classification systems, each with its own advantages, but only one will be introduced here.

The simple, but less precise, method divides type into the following races:

I. **Serif**—those typefaces with serifs. *Roman* is another term for the serif race.
   A. **Old Style**—generally characterized by having small x-height, little thick/thin contrast, heavy brackets and, occasionally, cupped feet. Examples are Garamond and Goudy.
   B. **Transitional**—typefaces with more contrast, larger x-height and thinner brackets than Old Style faces. Examples are Caslon and Times Roman.
   C. **Modern**—typefaces having the most contrast, little or no brackets and generally the largest x-height. Bodoni is the classic example.
   D. **Square**—typefaces with chunky, block-like serifs and little contrast, also called Slab or Egyptian faces. Cairo and Lubalin are good examples.

II. **Sans serif**—typefaces without serifs. Helvetica and Avant Garde are in this category.

III. **Script/cursive**—typefaces that look like handwriting. Examples are Commercial Bank Script and Zapf Chancery. Typefaces with letters that connect are called script. Those that do not are called cursive.

IV. **Decorative/novelty**—any typeface that does not fit into the above categories. Emigre's Remedy and Motion are examples.

Most copy editors will work with only a handful of faces, whereas senior editors and designers may be conversant with dozens. Some designers and typographers may be familiar with and use as many as 50 or 100 different faces. Being familiar with 20 or so faces will provide you with a very good background and make you much more valuable as an editor. Coupling some basic faces with a good type reference book or two, an editor can progress toward being an effective page designer.

One also should remember that type choices are every bit as important as word choices. Just as writers spend their careers searching for the right words to use in their stories, and just as editors spend their careers honing and polishing the writings of others, those who work seriously with type are constantly seeking to expand their understanding and practice with the subtleties of type.

TIDBITS OF TYPE

After discussing the races of type, one needs to look at variations within a typeface.

Each separate typeface is part of a *family,* such as the Caslon family or the Bodoni family. Each member of a type family, just like members of a human family, will exhibit certain distinctive features, coupled with variations in weight or height.

WEIGHT

Within a family, one variation, therefore, is *weight.* The weight of a typeface is generally given as extra light, light, medium (or book), bold or extra bold. Despite the variations in weight, a particular typeface will retain its distinctive features, much as Cousin Fred or Aunt Melba will still look like members of the Blanchard family regardless of how much or how little they weigh.

TYPE SIZES

Type sizes are measured in points, an archaic printer's measure that doesn't really correspond to much of anything today, other than type. One does, however, need to understand type size, since all publications use that measurement system.

There are 12 points per pica and 6 picas per inch. This means there are 72 points per inch. As a rule, body type is considered to be 12 points or smaller and headline or display faces are 14 points and larger. While that leaves the sizes between 12 and 14 points in never-never land, we won't worry about that.

When type was hand set (generally between 1455 and the early 1900s, although some print shops used hand-set type as late as the 1960s), type size was the base on which the type was made. Typographers merely measured the metal base of the type to determine the size.

Type sizes are generally measured from the top of the ascender to the bottom of the descender. Some type designs, however, include a smidgen of space above and below the type for aesthetic purposes. In those cases, our measurement system would indicate a smaller size than would the designer.

Type size specifications, however, are changing in usage because of computers. During the hot-metal era, display type was set in 6-point increments, specifically 18, 24, 30, 36, 42, 48, 54, 60. In today's computer era, type size is infinitely variable, including 18, 18.3, 18.127 and 37.61. In most typesetting situations the decimal point would be replaced with a p, meaning point, for instance, 18p3 or 48p6 or 25p53.

Most newspapers and desktop publishers will still begin with the traditional type sizes, even though certain copy-fitting operations will vary the size to fit a headline, for example, into a specific width. One may have begun with a 3-36-2 head (three columns, 36-point type, two lines), but the word choice leaves the head a bit short. A headfit operation on the computer may actually increase the size a bit to 37p3 to get the head to fit.

POSTURE

Another type variation is *posture.* Type will be either *roman,* meaning a vertical alignment, or *italic,* which is slanted to the right. Some faces will use the term *oblique* to mean an italic posture. (Please remember that in typography *roman* has two meanings: roman as a face and roman as a posture.) As if to confuse editors further, italic types frequently do not look much like their roman namesakes. One needs to look carefully to see that the italic version of Times Roman has some of the same distinguishing characteristics as the non-italicized version.

SET

The *set* of type refers to whether the type is *extended* (or expanded), meaning the type is elongated horizontally, or *condensed,* meaning the type is compressed horizontally. A normal set, therefore, means the type is neither extended nor condensed.

Set also can refer to the relative width of the alphabet. One can say, for example, that 9-point Avant Garde has a wider set than 9-point Futura, or that 11-point Century Old Style has a narrower set than 11-point Bookman. All typefaces, therefore, do not take up the same amount of space. This can be particularly important when selecting a headline face or a body face for a publication.

It's possible to select a face with a very narrow set, but ease of reading can be seriously compromised. Editors do the reader no service if a headline face is selected that allows 20 words to be fitted into a two-column head, yet be totally unreadable.

In summary, a family of type can have multiple variations, including posture, weight, size and set. One can expect to find Helvetica Bold Extended and Helvetica Light Condensed or Palatino Bold Italic and Palatino Light. Note that without an indication to the contrary, a typeface is presumed to be in the roman posture.

SPACING

Let's next take a look at the spacing of type. Spacing really takes three forms: letter spacing, word spacing and line spacing. Each is important if type usage is to be effective.

Letter spacing, also called *kerning,* controls how closely the letters are brought together. Some typefaces, like Times Roman, allow for closer-than-normal spacing and others, such as Franklin Gothic Condensed, do not. In most instances, designers will kern headlines so they're quite tight. In a headline size this does not adversely affect readability, whereas it would in body type.

Word spacing, obviously, is the spacing between words. Occasionally one can very slightly increase or decrease the spacing to fit a line into a given space, but care needs to be taken doing this. If the word spacing is too loose, then the words don't hang together as a sentence. Too tight and it might be difficult to differentiate where one word ends and another begins. It's a balancing act that requires a certain amount of experimentation.

Line spacing, also called *leading* (pronounced ledding), is usually accomplished in one of three ways. The first is with no leading, meaning there is no additional space between lines. In that case the type is said to have been set solid.

Second, line spacing can be increased. Lines of 9- and 11-point type with 1 point of additional leading can be written as 9/10 and 11/12. The first number is the type size, the second is the distance from baseline to baseline. With one and a half points of additional leading, 9- and 11-point typefaces would be indicated as 9/10.5 and 11/12.5 (or in some systems 9/10p5 and 11/12p5).

If it is necessary to increase leading, a very rough guideline is to take the type size times 5 to 30 percent. For example, if one wants more leading for 10-point type, one could increase it 5 percent, meaning an extra one-half point of leading would be added, or 10 percent, meaning an extra 1 point of leading. A 30 percent increase would add an extra 3 points of leading. This works pretty well throughout both body and headline sizes.

Third, line spacing also can be reduced. This is called negative leading and can be easily accomplished with the computer, whereas it would be almost impossible using hot-metal type. If one wanted less space between lines of type, and this would be done most often with headlines and rarely with body type, one would indicate it 36/34 or 48/45. This would mean 36-point type set 34 points from baseline to baseline and 48-point type set 45 points from baseline to baseline.

In most instances, headlines will benefit from both kerning and negative leading.

READABILITY AND LEGIBILITY

All type is not created equal, especially when it comes to reading. Some typefaces are much easier to read than others. Two important terms all designers and editors should know deal with how easy it is to read certain types. The terms *readability* and *legibility* are often used interchangeably, although they are not quite the same. Readability is how easy the type is to read. Legibility is the ability to distinguish type from a background.

Look at a sentence written in Helvetica and one written in Zapf Chancery. They are very different.

Typography is the process of communicating a message visually.

Typography is the process of communicating a message visually.

Which one is easier to read? The top one, obviously. That's readability. One could say, therefore, that the Helvetica sample is more readable or more easily read than Zapf Chancery. One could even say that Helvetica has high readability and Zapf Chancery has low readability, at least in this pairing.

The issue becomes clouded when one compares Franklin Gothic with Helvetica, both sans serif faces.

Typography is the process of communicating a message visually.

Typography is the process of communicating a message visually.

For most people, these two faces are virtually identical and therefore equal in readability.

Now, let's try Times Roman and Franklin Gothic.

Typography is the process of communicating a message visually.

Typography is the process of communicating a message visually.

Remember that both faces are the same size, even though Franklin appears larger. Some of the differences are the set of the two faces and the difference between serif and sans serif. In this sample, Franklin probably is easier to read.

Now look at Figure 7.1. Which line is easier to distinguish from the background?

In this pairing, the bottom sample of black on black is impossible to read, whereas black on white for the top sample is quite easy to read. This means the top one is more legible.

OPTIMUM LINE LENGTH

One of the most frequently abused guidelines is the one pertaining to optimum line length, or the best length to set a line of type. Two guidelines will help you immeasurably.

Figure 7.1 Legibility Notice how readability/legibility decrease as the contrast between foreground and background changes. Black type on a white background is quite legible; however, black type on a black background is impossible to read just as is white type on a white background. The darkness of the screens increases by increments of 10 percent, except for 60, 80 and black.

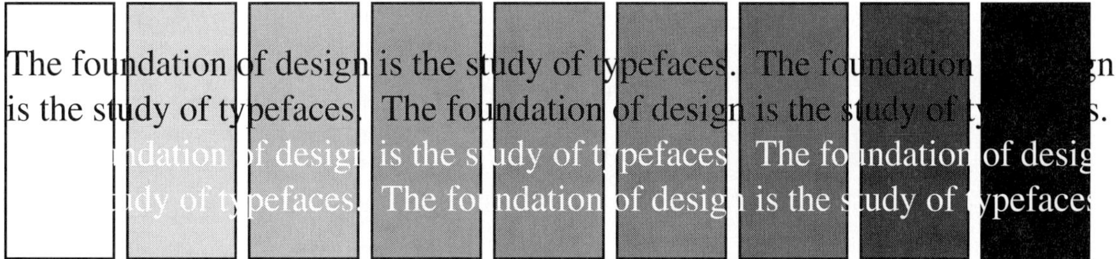

The first says optimum line length is one and a half times the type size. For example, you're using 10-point body type for a story. The optimum line length is $1.5 \times 10 = 15$ picas long. For 12-point type, the optimum line length would be $12 \times 1.5 = 18$ picas long. The maximum length one should set the type is two times the type size. For 10-point type, the maximum would be $2 \times 10 = 20$ picas and for 12-point type it would be $12 \times 2 = 24$ picas long.

This formula is quick and dirty.

The second formula says: Optimum line length is one and a half times the length of the lowercase alphabet. To determine this you would set the lowercase alphabet from *a* through *z* and measure it. Take that length times 1.5 and the optimum line length (in picas) will be determined. Maximum line length would be twice the length of the lowercase alphabet.

The second formula is the more accurate because it takes into consideration typefaces that are condensed or extended, whereas the first formula doesn't. For

Figure 7.2 Letterforms tend to look much the same, at least on the surface. Notice the subtle differences among these letters. Examine closely the thick-thin variations, the shapes of the letters themselves, the posture, and so on. Because each face is designed to stand alone rather than be intermixed, as in this sample, spacing between letters is not uniform.

example, 12-point Avant Garde is a rather extended face. If one used the quick and dirty formula, one would take 1.5 times 12 and come up with an optimum line length of 18 picas. Using the second, and better, formula, one would set the lowercase alphabet, measure that and take the answer by 1.5. The latter method would show a considerably different answer.

Note that each of the typefaces that follow is set in 12 point and that each has a different length. This should give editors some idea of why measuring the length of the lowercase alphabet will result in a much more accurate optimum line length.

Avant Garde: abcdefghijklmnopqrstuvwxyz

Franklin Gothic Extra Condensed: **abcdefghijklmnopqrstuvwxyz**

Broadway: **abcdefghijklmnopqrstuvwxyz**

Zapf Chancery: *abcdefghijklmnopqrstuvwxyz*

Text can be typeset to run beyond the maximum line length, provided line spacing is increased. For example, if one increases the line length of 10-point type to 30 picas, or considerably longer than the 20-pica maximum length the rule suggests, then line spacing should increase about 20 percent. That would mean type would be set 10/12. If leading is increased too much, readability suffers because the lines seem to be neither separate sentences nor one coherent one.

Figure 7.3 The top sample uses Times Roman in two different postures. Some typefaces are found in only one posture, but virtually all the serif faces are available in both. Computer-generated type often can be slanted (or set oblique), which can make the face look italicized. The bottom pairing, set in Futura, shows the results of this operation.

Posture

This is an example of roman posture.
This is an example of italic posture.

This is an example of a sans serif face.
This is an example of a sans serif face which is set oblique.

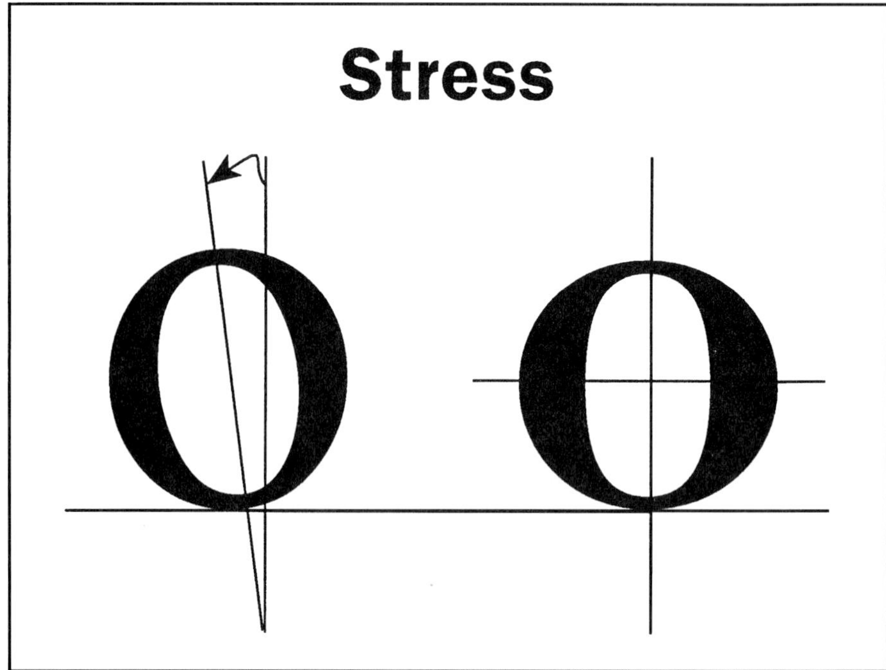

Figure 7.4 The stress of a letter indicates its orientation or rotation. Most letters have a vertical orientation, but some letters—particularly the circular ones, such as o, b, c, d, p and q—can have a stress that causes the letter to rotate off perpendicular. The stress of the letter is one of the identifying characteristics you should notice.

Figure 7.5 Some faces by their very nature have a wide set while others have a narrow set. Note the differences between Franklin Gothic in regular set versus the condensed and extra condensed versions. Then notice the rather wide natural set of Avant Garde. All these faces are set in the same point size.

Set

Franklin Gothic Demi.

Franklin Gothic Condensed.

Franklin Gothic Extra Condensed.

Avant Garde has a wide set.

Weight

This is Franklin Gothic set in Book weight.
This is Franklin Gothic set in No. 2 Roman weight.
This is Franklin Gothic set in Demi weight.
This is Franklin Gothic set in Heavy weight.

THIS IS LITHOS EXTRA LIGHT.
THIS IS LITHOS LIGHT.
THIS IS LITHOS REGULAR.
THIS IS LITHOS BOLD.
THIS IS LITHOS BLACK.

Figure 7.6 The weight of type can be determined, for the most part, by the names indicated. Book weight is about the same as regular weight. Keep in mind that bold for one typeface might be book or extra bold for another.

CHOOSING TYPE

At this point one has just enough information to begin making some type choices. In most instances, the editor's type choices on a publication will be severely limited and might consist of a half dozen faces available for headlines. Even that choice may be reduced to pressing some keys on the computer to get headline styles already in the system, such as Form 5 to get a 1-column 14-point Helvetica Bold headline, or Head 36B for a three-column 36-point Times Bold Italic. In situations like these, type choices are, shall we say, limited.

Type choices on most publications are limited to maintain a uniform appearance throughout. Some publications, however, such as *Texas Monthly,* have a well-deserved reputation for using headline type and display in an inventive and exciting fashion. Throughout most of the magazine, *TM* editors restrict their body and headline choices to very carefully chosen faces that are consistent from issue to issue. Their feature headlines are a different matter, varying wildly in race and style from article to article. It's no wonder *Texas Monthly* consistently wins awards for design and type usage. It's also a great magazine for ideas.

Let's assume, however that one is not working for a major publication, but rather starting a small local one. What typefaces does one choose and why?

One problem that most beginners and some professionals face is not knowing where to begin. Why choose one face rather than another? Several questions will help guide the editor through this process:

A Type Family

Garamond Book
Garamond Book Italic
Garamond Ultra
Garamond Ultra Italic
Garamond Light Condensed
Garamond Light Italic Condensed
Garamond Book Condensed
Garamond Book Italic Condensed
Garamond Bold Condensed
Garamond Bold Italic Condensed
Garamond Ultra Condensed
Garamond Ultra Italic Condensed

Figure 7.7 Type families include all the weights, postures and sets of a particular typeface. Note all type families contain the same number of variations, just as human families do not all have the same variations in height or weight. Most typefaces do have roman and italic posture and book and bold weights. Some faces will have only a normal set, rather than having normal, condensed and extended.

1. **Who is the audience?** Type choices should depend largely on the publication's target audience. Elderly people or the visually handicapped will require large type sizes and relatively plain faces. A very young audience might best be served with a sans serif face. Good research will pay for itself many times over in helping editors design a publication that will connect with its audience.

2. **How does the publication see itself?** Publications of insurance companies and banks probably will see themselves as conservative protectors of wealth, whereas a rock 'n' roll club's monthly magazine might be geared to the New Orleans philosophy of "let the good times roll." Each will choose a typeface for very different reasons.

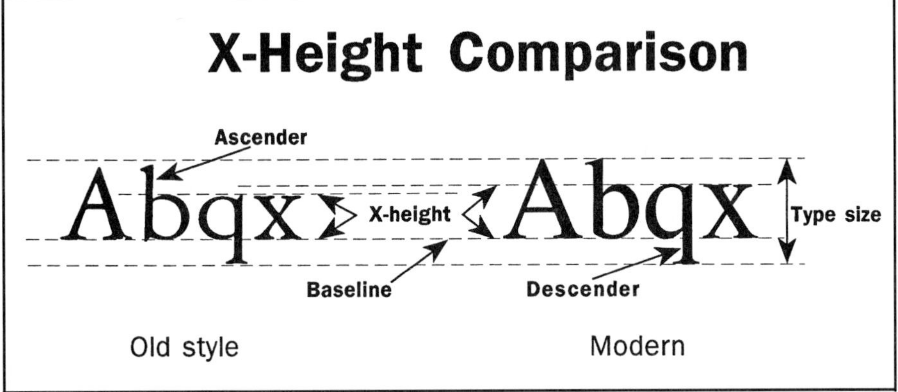

Figure 7.8 When comparing old style and modern faces, you need to remember that old styles will have smaller x-heights than modern faces. The result is that old style faces will look smaller than moderns, although the size is the same. In this example, the old style is represented by Garamond 3, while the other face is Times Roman. Note also that Garamond does not go all the way to the top alignment mark. This is another characteristic of some faces in which extra space is added to the design for aesthetic reasons.

Figure 7.9 Learning the parts of type will help you intelligently discuss typefaces and convey your typesetting or design instructions to anyone with whom you are working.

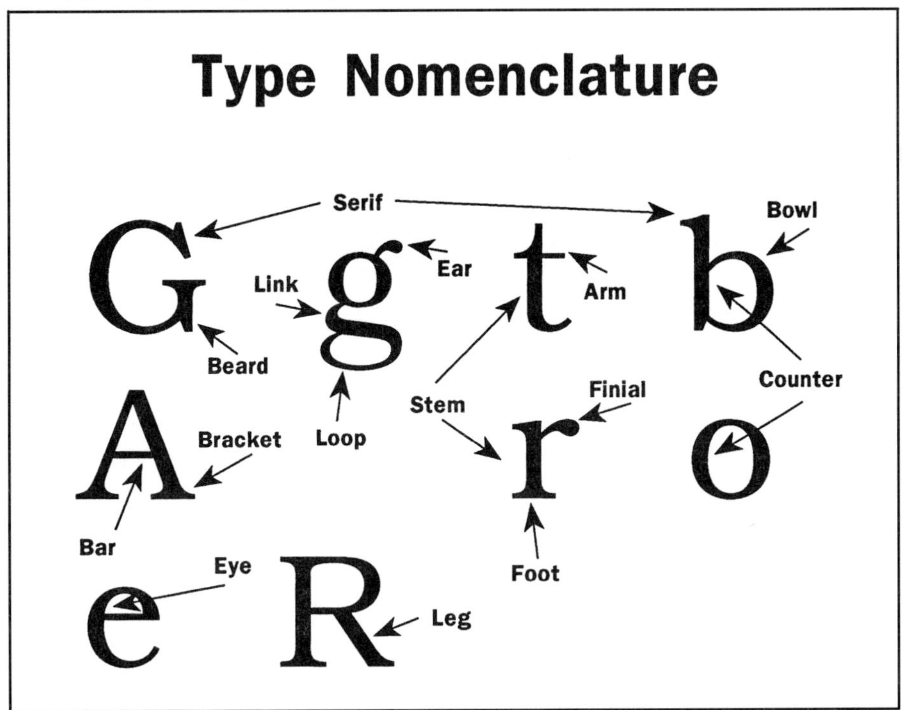

Kerning

WORLD NEWS ROUNDUP

Automatic letterspacing.

WORLD NEWS ROUNDUP

Operator-controlled kerning.

Rangers Raid
Wrong Place

Automatic letterspacing.

-.04 0 -.04 0 -.02 -.02 -.04 -.04 0 -.04

Rangers Raid

-.14 -.02 -.04 -.04 -.04 -.07 -.02 0 -.06

Wrong Place

Kerning (in ems) selected by the operator for each pair of letters.

Rangers Raid
Wrong Place

The kerned product.

Figure 7.10 Kerning is the processing of moving letters closer together. In most instances, headlines can be kerned rather tightly. Most typesetting operations will allow for manual or automatic kerning. Kerning pairs (pairs of letters that appear together on a regular basis, such as tt, mo, ee, re, and so forth) allow for tighter letter spacing than would be done by a typesetter on a regular basis. Kerning pairs are established by a type design company or by a typesetter manufacturer. Most newspapers will adjust kerning pairs to suit their own purposes. Popular computer programs, such as Aldus PageMaker, Aldus Freehand and QuarkXPress, allow the individual operator to kern type at will.

3. What does the competition use? Obviously one doesn't want to use the same face the publication down the street uses. If the first choice is taken, one might have a problem. At the same time, one shouldn't automatically assume that the competition has selected the correct face.

Imitation is flattering, but in the marketplace it can be deadly. *USA Today* has been immensely successful, and it's normal that some newspapers would try to wrap themselves in its design fabric. Unfortunately, too many papers have chosen to redesign their looks by using Times Roman, the same headline face as used in *USA Today.* The result is a certain sameness of appearance that becomes noticeable as one travels across the country.

The *Omaha* (Neb.) *World-Herald* uses an archaic face, Cheltenham, that has limited thick/thin variation. This means the paper has a less effective headline face, in terms of contrast, than do newspapers that use Times Roman. The advantage goes to the *World-Herald,* however, since virtually no other paper uses "Chelt." This means the *World-Herald* will stand out from a pile of competitors because it looks so different.

Note the term *different.* Not *better.* Typefaces can help support good content, which is not so readily apparent visually, but they cannot become good content.

4. What typefaces are available? If you're on a limited budget and working on a small "mom and pop" operation, budget considerations will drive your choices, and may succeed in driving you nuts in the process. Find out all the typefaces available, not just those that are in use in a particular computer. Maybe they are on diskettes that can be loaded into the computer. With luck, one will find a face that will work well.

5. What faces, among the available choices, are the most readable? Determining readability of typefaces ranks right up there with reading tea leaves, according to some editors. Showing samples to various test audiences is one way to check this out. Keep the test honest by setting the same stories or types of stories in the test faces.

TYPE FOR EVERY PURPOSE

No typeface is ideally designed for body text *and* pull quotes *and* headlines, just as no vehicle is designed for hauling 10,000 gallons of gasoline and 50 sheets of plywood and a dozen kids all at the same time. Some headlines can work for several applications, but generally speaking, one is better off using several different faces, such as one headline face, an accent face, one body face and maybe another for cutlines or quotes.

For those on a very tight budget, it is possible to use one face, say Palatino, for everything. Variety can be achieved by varying the posture and/or the weight. Headlines could be Palatino Bold, body text could be Palatino, cutlines could be Italic and credit line and byline could be Bold Italic.

Part of the reason for using different faces or posture/weight is to achieve a recognizable difference between the various parts of the layout. In other words, one wants the reader to note the difference between the headline and the body copy and the byline/credit line. While we, the editors, fully understand those differences, the reader often does not.

Some designers like a "seamless" appearance, in which one typeface is used throughout, with variations in size, posture and weight being used to achieve visual separation between elements.

Regardless of which way an editor chooses to go, here are some type suggestions to consider:

Headlines One will generally want faces that have strong contrast, that can be kerned tightly (to allow for more letters in the head) and that tend to be bold.

Examples: Bodoni, Bookman, Caslon, Helvetica, Franklin Gothic, Garamond, Goudy, Lubalin, Palatino, Times Roman, Univers.

Readouts Some publications use different faces for main heads and readouts. For example, a Times Roman main might be used with a Franklin Gothic second deck. It is possible to use the same face for both and merely vary the posture: For example, roman for the main head and italic for the readout. This latter combination would mean that all main heads would have to be roman, rather than some being roman and some being italic, and that all readouts would have to be italic.

Kickers and slammers Kickers most often are italic versions of the roman headline face, set half the size. Slammers, or hammer heads, are also called "reverse kickers." The larger line of type goes on top and consists of one to four words. Slammers are used for visual impact. They are usually 48- to 96-point bold, while the main headline is 36- to 72-point.

Body text Body text must be easily read in rather small sizes, and it should have a larger than normal x-height. Most readers prefer serif faces, although sans serif faces are just about as readable.

Examples: Caslon, Palatino, Times Roman, Century Old Style.

Cutlines Most cutlines will be set in a bold or contrasting face to the body text.

Examples: Franklin Gothic, Helvetica, Palatino, Times Roman.

Credit lines Credits for the photographer or artist usually are set in the same face, posture and size as the cutline, or they can be in a contrasting posture or weight. Occasionally credit lines are set 1 or 2 points smaller than the cutline.

Bylines Most bylines are set in the same face as the body text, but in a bold version. Some publications will use a larger size than the body type and even the same face as for the cutlines.

Quotes These tend to be set larger than body text, usually in 14 or 18 point and often in italic. The face can be the same as the body type or even the same as the headline.

Interesting Type Pairs

Goudy and Helvetica
Goudy and Franklin Gothic
Times Roman and Franklin Gothic
Caslon and Franklin Gothic
Bookman and Franklin Gothic
Bookman and Helvetica
Bodoni and Goudy
Garamond and Franklin Gothic
Palatino and Franklin Gothic
Lubalin and Goudy
Baskerville and Univers

Box 7.2

Special treatments Here's where designers break loose and have fun. Special treatments can include everything from the front of the lifestyle section to a special layout or logo for the upcoming city election. The general rule is: Achieve a strong, recognizable look without getting yourself called on the carpet by the publisher.

Box 7.2 lists some interesting pairings of type.

Remember that this is not a complete or necessarily a workable list. It's designed, as much as anything else, to show how types can be "married" in a design. One probably will find that some types should remain "single," rather than being combined with a different face. At the very least, one should experiment to achieve pairings that work for a particular publication. Don't be afraid to combine obscure faces with known faces, or even to combine obscure fonts if the result will give a publication either market recognition or results that are pleasing to both editors and readers.

WORKING WITHIN A GRAPHIC DESIGN

Editors who lay out pages for any publication will have a variety of options within the overall graphic design.

DISPLAY TYPE

The type palette one has to work with for headlines will be limited. Most publications achieve a uniformity of headline faces throughout all sections by using one face only in a variation of sizes and maybe postures. The exception is newspaper feature sections and magazines, which are allowed greater latitude in type choices.

The majority of editors therefore will select perhaps an italic posture over a roman one and decide whether 24-, 36- or 48-point type is better for a particular headline.

Given a chance to use a different face, the editor should choose one that complements or sets off a story. It should further underscore the content or seek to differentiate the story and layout from others on the page. For example, one could use a Franklin Gothic Heavy or maybe Ultra Bodoni to contrast with the publication's usual Times Roman headlines. A stencil-style face could be used for a feature about a local import-export firm or an Art Deco-style face might be considered for an article about old Paris.

BODY TYPE

Just as with headline faces, most editors do not have much choice about body type, except for features or projects. With the latter it may be possible to set the story in a different face or a larger size or in a ragged right form. At deadline, the fewer choices one has to make, the better.

Almost any change made from the usual body type will produce a noticeable change. One can vary, for example, the look of paragraphs by using block paragraphs (no indents) and an extra line of space between paragraphs. Or a visual difference can quickly be obtained by using flush left, ragged right rather than justified measure. And an increase of 1 point in the type size can be startling.

For a real change, one may use a sans serif face, set ragged right and in block paragraphs.

Most body type will run from 8 point to 11 point. Around the turn of the century newspapers used about 8-point type. Current design trends call for type in the range of 9 to 11 points, with larger being better for readability. Since the advent of computer typesetting and its infinitely variable size capacity, fractional sizes are quite common.

Young editors need to remember that the eyesight of many older readers, who make up the bulk of a newspaper's readership, requires a larger type size for comfortable reading. While 7- and 8-point type might look good on a computer screen up close, it does not look nearly as good on newsprint. Editors should therefore resist the temptation to use body type smaller than 10 point.

The general rule for line spacing calls for leading to be 10 to 30 percent more than the type size. For example, the leading for 10-point type should be 1 to 3 points more than the type size. For 8-point type the leading should be an additional 0.8 to 2.4 points.

ACCENT TYPE

After reading page after page of type in a constant face, one will find accent type quite noticeable. Accent faces should be used sparingly because heavy use may detract from the rather serious tone of a newspaper or magazine.

A bold sans serif face, such as Franklin Gothic or Helvetica or even Futura, works quite well as an accent to a modern serif; however, the opposite seems not to be used very often. Accents can be used as labels for helping provide a quicker read or as contrasting heads for stories that need a bit more punch.

DECORATION

Small typographical devices can help finish out a page. Just as some cakes do not need decoration, some layouts do not either. Decorations can help attract the reader's attention to an article but should not be expected to make up for the deficiencies of poor writing. The most that decoration can hope to accomplish is to provide closure to a layout.

Some devices that can be used include rules or borders, dingbats or decorative marks, screens or shadings and color for backgrounds or screens.

PARTS OF A PUBLICATION

TITLE/NAMEPLATE/FLAG

The name of the publication is one of its most important identifiers. It can represent the publication's lineage and history. In most instances the use of compound names in the flag indicates a series of publications that have been merged into one unit. Each of those names might represent hundreds of issues produced by dedicated journalists and craftsmen over a period of many years.

An examination of journalism history reveals proud traditional newspaper names such as Times, News, Telegram, Reporter, Chronicle, Post, Record, Tribune and Star, along with political names like Democrat, Independent and Republican. There are also whimsical names such as Clipper, Breeze, Boomerang, Headlight, Rustler, Locomotive and Tiller & Toiler. Each of these can be said to have served its community, for better or worse, for a long period and to have influenced thousands of readers over the years. The mere mention in a community that "The Herald said . . ." or "I read in the Globe . . ." was enough to establish an instant association with that publication. And with that name recognition came a visual image of the nameplate, of the look and "feel" of that paper.

In advertising this would be referred to as "name recognition." And for a newspaper, name recognition is incredibly important. It is therefore incumbent on editors and designers to remember that to even consider changing the name or design of a nameplate is to open an incredibly complex can of worms.

Granted, some nameplates are outdated in terms of design or were overly designed in the 1960s and 1970s and therefore are festooned with too many "doo-dads," but changes should be undertaken with the greatest of caution. When changes are introduced, the readership should be properly prepared with articles by the senior editor or publisher discussing the changes.

The change in typeface on a nameplate can be very subtle—from a complex Old English face to a similar one having a cleaner design, for example—or it can be an extreme change from a serif to a sans serif.

A change in the name of a publication should be considered only as a very extreme measure. The last thing a reader wants to do is grab a paper off the porch in the morning and be confused over the name. It makes for a rough beginning to the day.

Nameplates obviously should contain the name of the publication and, if appropriate, a line explaining the lineage of the name. And since current designs are taking advantage of historical elements, there is nothing wrong with using the same or similar typeface as was used by the publication when it was originated. Most people have a tendency to trust institutions, including newspapers, that have been in operation for a long time, so it does not hurt to use the historic type style of the original nameplate in a cleaner version for today's consumer. It is also recommended to display the year of the paper's founding prominently and maybe even to tell how many issues have been produced.

FOLIO

The combination of the name of the publication, the date and the page number is referred to as a "folio" and appears on inside pages. Folios are very important in large publications since they serve to help the reader find information, especially when many stories are teased on the front or referenced in the index. Can you imagine quickly finding the movie listing on page 39 if it's buried inside an 84-page paper?

Folios need to be large enough to be easily read, but not so large that they overpower the top of the page. While newspapers almost without fail place the folio at the top of the page, magazines and some tabloids place them at the bottom. One trend is to use page numbers and section indicators in a larger size, such as 14-point bold, while using 10-point type for the rest of the information.

MASTHEAD

The masthead is an important and legal part of a newspaper. It contains not only the name of the publication, but the publication's legal place of operation. This bit of information is required by the post office to be placed within the first three pages of a newspaper for the paper to receive a special mailing permit. Without the masthead, the newspaper would be mailed at a much more expensive rate.

The masthead can also list the publication's major staff members, such as the publisher, editor, managing editor and others. User-friendly publications also will list their readers' advocate (or ombudsperson) and the phone numbers of the news desk, circulation, sports and editorial editors. Found increasingly in major metro publications is an e-mail address and fax number.

The masthead can provide emotional assistance to the reader who feels that a matter must be discussed with an editor immediately. Journalists need to keep in mind that most readers will have their names in the paper just a few times during their lives, perhaps a birth announcement, a graduation or wedding announcement, and an obituary. Any other contact with a journalist has the potential to be the very best or the very worst experience of the subject's life. The masthead can provide a sense of comfort for those instances.

HEADLINES

As discussed in Chapter 6, headlines are the bread and butter of a newspaper and provide one of the major points of attraction. The type style, word choice, size of the letters and placement on a page all help a reader to determine if a particular story or event is of sufficient interest to warrant further examination. Editors who have a full palette of choices available to them will be able to create attractive, flexible designs guaranteed to attract attention. For guidelines on headline styles, see Chapter 6.

BYLINES

To most reporters the byline is one of the most important parts of the story, and it is also important to regular readers. It helps establish a connection between the publication and its reader, allowing for a nearly instantaneous judgment about the veracity of the story. Regular readers know which reporters they trust the most.

Bylines further allow a publication a very subtle way of showing readers that professionals they know are on the job, covering the events of the day. Some publications do not use a byline on every story, but many editors believe readers have a right to know the source of information and who is presenting it to them.

Most bylines contain not only the writer's name but also a second line indicating the writer's affiliation, such as "staff writer," "staff reporter," "Associated Press," "Reuter." The byline can be set flush left or centered, but is almost never set flush right.

In most instances the name is set in bold and all caps, but caps and lowercase also work well. Type size is most often 11 or 12 point, or at least it is larger than the body type size. The affiliation is usually set in light face and smaller than the name, often even smaller than the body type.

CUTLINES

One of the best-read parts of any publication is the cutline. As such it has a special obligation to be easily read in its placement and typography. Most cutlines consist of two or three sentences; they rarely run more than three or four lines under a photograph or piece of artwork. There is considerable discussion as to whether the type should run the width of the photo or, in the case of photos wider than four columns, be set in two legs of type. The optimum line length rule should prevail, although good judgment on the part of the editor may decide that type can run longer than that.

The optimum placement for a cutline is directly below the photo, but on photo spreads cutlines can be grouped together as a space-saving/design-look concept. While cutlines are traditionally set justified, there is little reason they cannot be set ragged or even centered. It all depends on the look desired. If a cutline is placed to the side of the photo, it makes sense that it be set flush left for placement on the right side and flush right for placement on the left side.

If cutlines for several photos are grouped together in one block of type, care must be taken to avoid confusing the reader. Be sure to include boldface words such as "ABOVE" or "CLOCKWISE FROM TOP RIGHT" to direct the reader. Avoid directing the reader counterclockwise, since that is contrary to the way people read. The editor could also use deltas (◀ ▶) to direct the reader to the proper photo. The major point is to avoid confusing the reader. If it's not clear, redo it.

Most publications will use sans serif type for cutlines as a way of contrasting with the serif body type. In no instance is it recommended that cutline type be the same face, size, weight and posture as body type. If the same face must be used, increase the size and use a bold version for the cutline.

CREDIT LINES

Just as bylines are important for reporters and readers, credit lines are important for photographers and readers. The credit will consist of the photographer's name and affiliation, as in "Terry Perez/Staff photographer" or "Terry Perez/*Daily News* photographer" or "John G. Gaps III/Associated Press" or "Associated Press/John G. Gaps III." Listing the affiliation is important since it helps the reader determine the validity of the image.

Credit lines tend to be found in two locations: at the end of the cutline or below the photo on the right. Some magazines will rotate the credit line 90 degrees to the left so it can be placed vertically next to the right side of the photo or 90 degrees to the right so it will fit on the left side of the photo. In those side placements the credit lines tend to be tiny, about 5- or 6-point type, and practically unreadable. Side placement is fine; unreadable type is not.

Editors should be cautioned against the very subtle discrimination caused by using larger type for writers' bylines than for photographers' credit lines. It's best to use equal-size type for both.

Credit lines, like cutlines, often use a face that contrasts with body type. The posture may be italic.

INITIAL LETTERS

The use of initial letters is usually restricted to features or special packages. These giant letters are an effective way to establish quickly that the story is special. They also produce a textural contrast with the mass of copy. Sans serif caps work quite well, usually in 36- or 48-point size, for indented initials; 256 point or larger are good for hanging initials.

Do some experiments to see what visual differences can be achieved by using italic, sans serif and script faces in different sizes and weights. Then observe the different visual effects of shadings and colors. The effects can be startling.

When running a multi-part series, be sure to use the same style of initial letters so that visual consistency is maintained. Remember also that initial letters should be used sparingly—about one every 15 inches or so. Used more often than that, initials lose their effectiveness.

QUOTES

Almost every story contains at least one good comment or quote. If it doesn't it probably isn't worth publishing. One way to maximize the flow of information to the reader is to incorporate quotes set in large type as one more design element in the layout. Quotes can be set in 14- or 18-point italic with a 12-point roman bold name afterward. The quote marks themselves take on added punch when they are the same height as the capital letters. Quotes can be set flush left, justified or centered. The last works well with feature or special packages.

It is recommended that quotes not be set in the same face as body type, but rather in the headline face used for the story. Occasionally the quote can be set large, say in 36-point type, if it is to be used as one of the main design elements, rather than a subordinate one as is usually the case.

SUMMARY READ-INS

Treated somewhat the same as quotes, summary read-ins are brief one- to four-sentence introductions to a story. They can be used in place of readouts or in addition to them. The read-ins usually are set in type ranging from 12 to 18 points, although they might appear in 24-point type for a special package. Flush left is the norm. Centered read-ins can be found, but not justified ones.

The type choice for the read-ins is the same as for the headline, although the *Des Moines Register* uses a mixture of Franklin Gothic for the first few words and Caslon for the remainder, to produce a visually interesting result.

HEADERS

As publications become more sophisticated about categorizing information for the benefit of the reader, section and page headers become quite important. The front page needs no heading other than the nameplate, but other sections are best identified by their major content: sports, living, opinion, business, national news, local news, fashion, arts. Pages devoted to a category of news or features, such as world news or book reviews, may also carry headers.

Headers are usually found at the top of the page, but some publications, such as *The News* of Boca Raton, Fla., use the outside edges and tilt the type on its side.

Type choices for section or page headers should be different from the headline face and need to be in a bold weight. Sizes generally will range from 36 to 48 points. Italic section headers are rare because they appear to have less authority than roman versions.

STANDING HEADS, SIGS, LOGOS AND BUGS

A term from the days of hot-metal printing, a *standing head* is one that is used several times. Today that term is often linked with graphical devices known as *sigs, logos* or *bugs,* such as an abstract drawing of a stethoscope for use with a health column or a graphic of a racehorse for use on a racing-results column or a very small mug shot of a columnist. The combination of the artwork or photo and the name of the column and the columnist is referred to by any of the foregoing names.

These devices are used for multiple reasons:

1. Standing heads are quick and convenient and eliminate the need for a different headline each time they are used.

2. Standing heads help the reader quickly locate a favorite columnist, like Ann Landers or Dear Abby or Click and Clack.
3. Standing heads, sigs, logos and bugs provide some visual contrast to gray body type.

The style for standing heads should be consistent throughout the publication, or at least consistent within a section. Photos and artwork should have the same style, employing the same techniques, such as dropped-out backgrounds for the photos or line shots instead of halftones. All the mug shots and artwork should be the same size to help achieve standardization throughout the publication. However, any time there is repetition of a style throughout, visual boredom can set in. The preference, nonetheless, is for a consistent look.

Standing heads most often are set off from the surrounding body type by thin hairline or 1- or 2-point rules. Occasionally the rules will be mixed in different weights, such as hairline across the top of the standing head and 2 point at the bottom or vice versa. The combinations of photo style and placement and type and rule treatment allow for a nearly endless variety. Again, consistency throughout the publication is foremost.

A sig or logo used as an identifying symbol for a series must be displayed large enough to attract attention at the start of the series, but be concise enough that it can be played rather small as the series continues, either on multiple pages or multiple days. On one-page projects the constraints are less onerous. The design of the logo can be tailor-made for the space available and need not be reduced.

Most logos will contain a graphic element, a few words of type, a box and some shading. The general rule for logos is to establish maximum impact that is in keeping with the tone of the story. In other words, avoid heavy, blocky black and white type and graphics if the article is about a childhood romance, unless the romance has a tragic ending. Use instead lighter screens, pastel colors and perhaps script or a classical serif type. Ultimately logos should help provide a ready visual reference for the reader but should not overpower the content.

RULES, BORDERS, BOXES AND SCREENS

Editors frequently overlook the tremendous range of visual effects that can be created from rules, borders, boxes and screens, relying instead on the traditions of the publication. While a visual consistency is of course desirable in a publication, a re-examination of different approaches should be undertaken from time to time.

Beginning designers often use rules that are too heavy, such as 2 or 3 point, when hairline would be much more effective. The coupling of hairline rules with a classical serif face, such as Caslon 540, can produce a sophisticated appearance that is missing with a 2-point rule and Bodoni.

While borders and boxes are really the same thing—a device that surrounds a story or layout—a difference will be drawn between the two so that no confusion will exist. For this discussion a box will be defined as a thin line that surrounds a story, while a border will be a thicker, more decorative line that goes around a layout.

First, editors need to remember that a border or box *excludes* as well as *includes.* Readers can be subtly encouraged to see relationships between stories and pictures and headlines when those elements are within a box. At the same time, it may be difficult for the reader to see relationships between boxed elements and other related elements right next to it.

Second, editors often tend to use boxes as a way of avoiding bumping heads or tombstones, which is not altogether bad. But since boxes do attract attention to themselves, it is incumbent that the story or elements within a box be worthy of additional scrutiny. To use the box merely as a way of separating competing elements is not enough. The box should be used because of what it is capable of doing: attracting attention, excluding competing elements and making relationships. That said, the press of deadlines forces editors to use boxes for different purposes, including simply separating elements.

Borders can be very simple one-line devices or complex and elaborate, incorporating lines of multiple thicknesses or shadings, such as Art Deco style. Almost without exception, borders of reindeer, firecrackers, balloons, flowers and the like should be avoided, unless there is an overwhelming design reason for doing so. Likewise, borders and boxes of wavy, hatched, striped or dotted lines also should be discarded in favor of the simple hairline or half-point rule.

Screens or shadings are another textural element that bears examining. In this area, more than most, the quality of presswork determines what can be used. With letterpress reproduction on coarse newsprint, the use of a very fine screen is almost impossible; the dot gain of the press would block up the screen, creating an unattractive gray blob, and probably a dark gray blob at that. Good quality offset reproduction on higher quality newsprint will result in finer tonal gradations and a greater tonal design palette.

Editors should periodically run, with the assistance of the production department, a series of press tests to see how various screens will reproduce. For most screened boxes, screen ranges from 5 to 20 percent are usable. A 30 percent screen can be used as a contrasting element or shading, but body type reproduction on it likely will be severely limited. It is best, therefore, to use screens of 5 to 10 percent behind type. The visual result will be a nice but subtle separation from the usual white of the newsprint, but still light enough that the readability of the type does not suffer.

Never—this is about as absolute as design rules get—use a textured screen (brick pattern, waves, hatched, etc.) behind type. It confuses readability to the point that while it can attract attention, the reader will likely give up rather than read the type. One way around this, provided the editor determines the effect is worth it, is to cut out the screen behind the type and one pica on either side of it so the screen surrounds the type block, yet the white of the newsprint is behind the type. This would allow the creation of a somewhat avant-garde appearance while not sacrificing readability.

REFERS AND TEASES

The front-page design of most publications takes so much of an editor's attention that the inside pages are given short shrift. Editors need to realize that the reader needs an incentive to turn to page 23 or to C11 or to the business section. Readers obviously depend on editors to choose appropriate stories, but readers also want editors to help them see and make connections among related pieces of information. This is one of the most important functions of an editor: To see and point out relationships, pointing out, for example, how rising soybean prices in the Midwest will affect Japanese tofu prices and how the latter will ultimately affect American consumers.

For this reason, among others, attention needs to be given to *refers* (pronounced reefers), or *teases,* informational devices designed to get the reader to look at specific stories or sections inside. It's one thing to group related stories together inside a box, and it's quite another to refer readers to such stories on the business, lifestyle or regional page.

Refers are placed next to a story and direct the reader to a related story or stories. Teases can be placed anywhere on a page, such as the top of the front page, where they might be called a *skybox* or *skyline.*

Teases can be boxed with or without a photo or graphic logo, the information set in a narrow-measure sans serif face or even set off with bullets under a "Related Stories" label. The choice depends on the location of the tease on the page and the vision of the designer.

The use of a photo or logo with a tease box is a good idea, but care must be taken to select visual elements that will stand up in the small sizes common to teases. For example, avoid selecting a photo that has 14 people in it or a very complex pattern in pastels, since the people would show up as ant-like and the complex pattern probably would look like a blob. Select, instead, photos and graphics with large faces or strong patterns that would look good in a 1-inch square (realizing that some teasers will use artwork that is 14 × 18 picas).

Ultimately a tease must grab the reader, provide succinct information about the content of the story and where it can be found, and wrap it up with perhaps a visual element or bit of color. Then, if the tease is successful, the reader will turn to that story and get one more piece of information that will satisfy and educate.

INDEXES

Readers are creatures of habit. They demand that specific items, such as television listings, movie schedules, crossword puzzles and Dear Abby, be easily found. Considering that newspapers regularly increase and decrease the number of pages because of advertising and news considerations, locating these desired items can be a bit of a chore. That is why the index is so important.

An *index,* which can also be labeled *Inside,* can be placed anywhere on the front page, or front of a section, so long as the location is consistent from day to day. Depending on the philosophy and coverage style of the publication, the index might include the following categories: state or regional news, international news, editorials, lifestyle or features, sports, business, obituaries, horoscope, comics, television listings, movies, classifieds and even the latest in lotteries.

Frequently paired with the index is the weather summary. For many morning readers, the weather summary helps them plan their day, including whether to take a raincoat or a snow shovel or whether to plan for a picnic or a day in the museum. Graphics are very appropriate in weather summaries for giving the reader visual cues on what to expect. At the bottom of the summary will often be a refer to get the reader to an inside page for an extensive compilation of weather maps, facts and predictions.

NEWS SUMMARIES

Useful devices for giving readers one more piece of quick-read information, news summaries are one- to three-sentence synopses of articles found elsewhere in the paper. They are usually compiled in an anchored location, often on page 2.

This device is one more tool in the designer's arsenal to convey information. It serves readers who do not want to wade through 36 inches of text to understand what's going on and also those who want a quick way to select the stories they wish to read. Summary design styles can mix a variety of sizes, weights and colors to create visual impact.

SOME TYPE GUIDELINES

1. Avoid using headlines that are all capital letters, except when they consist of just a few words. Caps are harder to read than caps and lowercase.
2. Roman posture is more readable than italic. Use italic sparingly and then only for accent.
3. Black type on a white background is easier to read than white on black. Reverse heads (white on black) do attract attention, but only if used sparingly and in large enough size.
4. Optimum line length should be followed religiously.
5. Use large x-height for body type. The type appears larger to readers, who like it.
6. Kern headlines for better appearance.
7. While justified type is the norm for body text, use flush left, ragged right for special features.
8. Fewer typefaces used well is better than lots of typefaces used poorly.
9. Keep it simple.

BIBLIOGRAPHY AND ADDITIONAL READINGS

Arntson, Amy E. *Graphic Design Basics,* 2nd ed. Harcourt Brace Jovanovich. 1993.

Carter, Rob, Ben Day, and Philip Meggs. *Typographic Design: Form and Communication.* Van Nostrand Reinhold. 1985.

Crow, Wendell C. *Communication Graphics.* Prentice Hall. 1986.

Denton, Craig. *Graphics for Visual Communication.* William C. Brown. 1992.

Garcia, Mario R. *Contemporary Newspaper Design.* Prentice Hall. 1981.

Gaur, Albertine. *A History of Writing.* Rev. ed. Cross River Press. 1992.

Lawson, Alexander. *Anatomy of a Typeface.* David R. Godine. 1990.

Morgan, John, and Peter Welton. *See What I Mean?* 2nd ed. Edward Arnold. 1992.

Perfect, Christopher, and Gordon Rookledge. *Rookledge's International Typefinder.* Sarema Press. 1983.

Pipes, Alan. *Production for Graphic Designers.* Prentice Hall. 1993.

Rehe, Rolf F. *Typography and Design for Newspapers.* Design Research International. 1985.

Typography: How to Make It Most Legible. Design Research International. 1974.

Smith, Robert Charles. *Basic Graphic Design.* 2nd ed. Prentice Hall. 1993.

The Society of Newspaper Design. *The Best of Newspaper Design.* Rockport. 1992.

Spencer, Herbert. *Pioneers of Modern Typography.* Rev. ed. The MIT Press. 1982.

White, Jan V. *Graphic Idea Notebook.* 2nd ed. Rockport. 1991.

Chapter 8

PHOTO EDITING

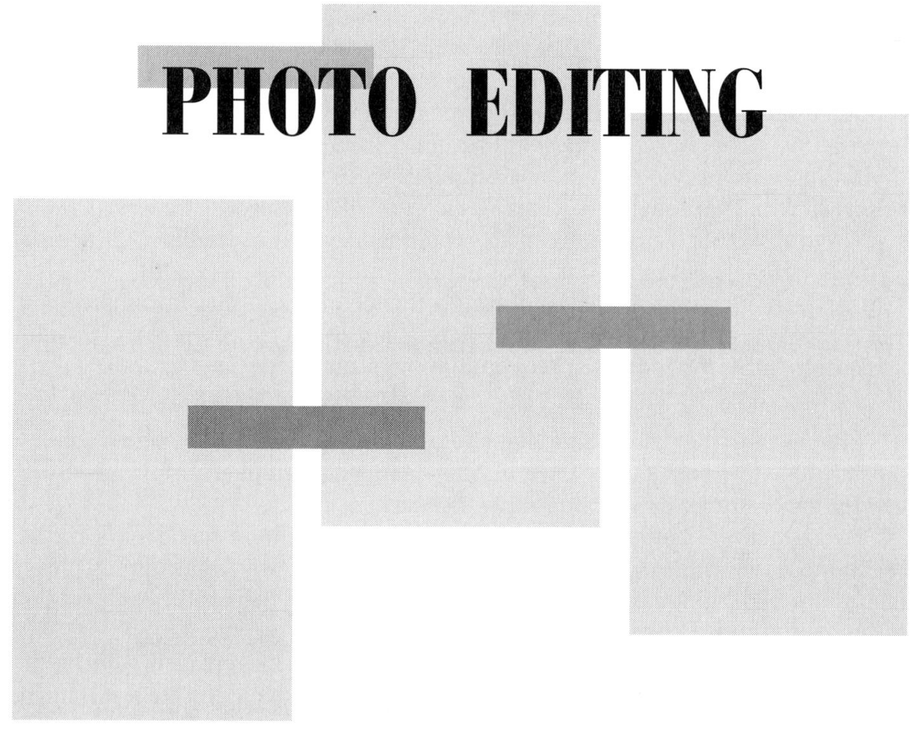

THE PHOTOGRAPHER'S ALLY

Picture editing, which today is often part of a copy editor's responsibilities, requires hard work, patience, news judgment and a tricky balancing act between the editor's and photographer's wishes, the availability of space and the reader's demands.

Some crusty, veteran editors may seem jealous of the space allocated to photographs, saying that a three-column picture is taking up good space that could and should be given to stories. However, the day has passed when a page could be built on gray type alone. Today's editors must be acutely attuned to the impact of both words and visual images.

Consider the following:

- A Consumer Photographic Survey found that almost 92 percent of American households in 1988 owned still cameras, up from 85 percent in 1985. Nearly 80 percent of households with under $10,000 in income had cameras, as did more than 80 percent of households with some high school education or less. Ninety-six percent of high-income households had cameras. This means that cameras—and photographs—are part and parcel of American life.

- Four in five women say that their photographs are very important to them, according to a study done for Fuji Photo Film U.S.A., Inc.
- The average American family uses an average of 15 rolls of film per year, the Fuji study found. This amounts to more than 33 BILLION photos per year, just for American families. Consider what that would be worldwide.
- The *Omaha World-Herald,* with a Sunday circulation of more than 300,000, printed an estimated 32,811 photographs in 1993, an increase of 6.3 percent over 1992. The *World-Herald* is not known as a picture-oriented newspaper, yet it uses more photos than one might expect.
- Research shows that more than 75 percent of newspaper readers notice a photograph or artwork, more than 50 percent notice a headline, 29 percent notice cutlines, but only 25 percent notice the text. This means the BEST way to get a reader into a story is through the photograph that accompanies it. EYE-TRAC® research by Dr. Mario Garcia and Dr. Pegie Stark of the Poynter Institute in St. Petersburg, Fla., came up with these startling figures.

Simply put, the photo and the photographer are not the editor's enemy. Indeed, just the opposite is true. Editors and photographers are partners in getting good stories the attention they deserve.

Ever since the beginning of photography in 1839, there has been a rift between those who consider photography an art and those who consider it a purely mechanical skill that can be mastered by anyone. The battle still continues on some publications between "word people" and "picture people."

Such divisions are counterproductive and need to be replaced with an understanding that photography/photojournalism/visual communication is a major player in the business of publications. Editors who treat photography as an integral part of journalism and become skilled in its use are likely to be more successful than those who do not.

WHY USE PICTURES ANYWAY?

Words, as powerful and rich as they are, can seldom explain or describe an event as eloquently as can a photograph. Chinese parables about pictures and ten thousand tellings aside, photographs do convey a three-dimensional sense of emotion, background information, subtle facial expressions, body language and a sense of time all at once.

Our world, and the readers in our world, are educated, titillated, frightened, cajoled and challenged by visual images. These images tell us about a devastating flood in Bangladesh and the weeping family in the foreground, about the rescue of a child from a near-certain death in a Midland, Texas, well, and about the ecstasy of winning the Super Bowl.

Pictures allow us to confront our own emotions and observe the emotions of others. Some photos cause our eyes to mist, while others cause them to crinkle in amusement. Photos can document the humdrum everyday life in an inner-city slum or the slow, bored social dance of the wealthy at a private club.

One simple exercise will point out the pervasive influence of photojournalism. Quickly recall the photographs that have made an impact on you. Next, quickly recall some examples of good writing that have made a similar impact.

Interesting, isn't it? If you're like most people, it's easier to remember pictures with impact than words.

Photographs, like words, should not be boring. If they are, journalists lose their ability to explain the world to others.

PICTURE SOURCES

Photographs for a publication can come from a number of sources, each with its own advantages and/or disadvantages. The sources include:

- Staff
  - —Photographers
  - —Reporter-photographers
  - —File photos
- Free-lance photographers
- Contract photographers
- Wire services
- Picture agencies

On the Fence (George Tuck) The composition of this photo, made in Beijing's Forbidden City, allows for a long, shallow cropping, which can be an advantage in the layout of the page. If necessary, it could be cropped into much smaller units, but the result would be much less effective.

- Stock agencies
- Public relations agencies

Most publications subscribe to one or more *wire services,* such as the Associated Press, from which they receive photos and/or news stories. The AP, for example, provides a stream of photos to publications that have contracts for the service. Today those photos are delivered by satellite feed, usually into a computer in the photo or picture editor's area. From the hundreds of pictures that arrive daily, publications (usually newspapers) will use but a few, mostly of national and international news and sports. Occasionally a good feature or fashion shot will be used too.

The Associated Press is a cooperative owned by member publications, again, mostly newspapers. Each member publication is entitled to use the pictures provided over the satellite feed, for a fee, and in turn is obliged to provide pictures requested by AP for use by member publications.

Occasionally a member will be asked to provide a picture that the member does not want to be used by a competing publication. The member will indicate on the transmission that certain cities or states or publications are "out," meaning they cannot use the photo. In virtually every instance, the members affected abide by the "out."

Members can request a "special" from AP, such as an action shot from a high school volleyball tournament or a special travel photo from Tahiti showing a resort being built there by a local contractor. In such instances the requesting publication is billed supplemental fees for that service, including transmission costs, photographer costs and, even on occasion, travel costs and other charges.

THE PICTURE EDITOR

The picture editor is a specialist in selecting images and determining their size and shape for publication. He or she usually comes from a strong photographic background, frequently having worked as a staff photographer for one or more publications. In addition, the best picture editors have good writing and editing skills, plus an ability to inspire good photographic work by the photo staff.

Most picture editors work under a director of photography or an assistant managing editor for photography and graphics. On some publications the picture editor is attached to the copy desk or is on a separate desk reporting directly to the managing editor.

Senior picture editors are ultimately responsible for the appearance of their publications, but they cannot succeed unless the publication's top editors make a commitment to use good photos well. On major newspapers and magazines, one or more picture editors are in charge of the day-to-day job of selecting photographs for the publication. Those photographs can come from wire services, staff photographers and other sources.

Major newspapers may have both news picture editors and feature picture editors. Occasionally a picture editor may be assigned to work for extended periods on special projects, leaving the daily assignments to others.

Picture editing, even on a small publication where it may be done by an editor who also works with words, is a multi-faceted job requiring one to do all or most of the following:

- Act as a liaison between the photo and news departments.
- Attend news budget meetings and present ideas for photo coverage.
- Make photo assignments.
- Work with various agencies and the public to gain access to certain news and feature events.
- Work with wire services, free-lancers and photo agencies to get special assignments covered.
- Deal with the public's photo suggestions or complaints about coverage (or lack thereof).
- Maintain a file of coming events, free-lance photographers and special suppliers (such as airplanes and pilots for aerial photos).
- Screen and edit assignments made by other departments.
- Edit film and prints (regardless of the source) to determine which photos best document an event and serve the needs of the publication and the reader. (The photographer should do the first edit, indicating which image or images should be considered. The picture editor will then look at the photographer's selects and choose the image to be presented to the copy/layout desk.)
- Determine the best cropping of the image.
- Write and/or edit cutlines.
- Work with the copy desk and layout editor to determine the best size for the photo to run.
- Act as the photographic conscience of the publication.

Obviously, the selection and cropping of photos, what most people consider to be picture editing, constitute a very small part of what a picture editor does.

THE PHOTO/CUTLINE PACKAGE

A photograph and its cutline, contrary to what some editors and photographers think, are viewed by most readers as a unit. Newspaper readers have been trained, seemingly since birth, to look to the cutline for explanation and clarification of the visual information contained in the photo. The story next to the photo obviously will provide additional information, but often the photo can act like another paragraph or even as a sidebar of the story.

Research by Mario Garcia and Pegie Stark of the Poynter Institute shows that newspaper readers enter the page through the photograph and that the direction of the photo controls where the reader's eyes go next.

The research also shows that the headline/photo/cutline combination attracts and holds the reader. If this research were carried to the extreme, daily newspapers would be filled with lots of headlines, photos and cutlines and very, very short stories.

The photo/cutline package should NOT have to repeat everything that is in the story. For example, if the story says the mayor is speaking to the chamber of commerce, it's not necessary to show a picture of the mayor speaking to the chamber of commerce. A better use of the space would be to show the reaction of the audience or the mayor working the crowd either before or after the speech.

It is imperative, therefore, that photos and cutlines complement and not repeat the story. This will help provide the reader with the best package possible.

The photo/cutline pairing provides an entry point into the newspaper that the story alone rarely provides. Large objects, such as photos and headlines, attract readers and allow for one more bit of information to grab the "scanner," or quick, superficial reader.

CREATING THE CUTLINE

Cutlines, or captions as they may be called, are very brief summaries or explanations of a photo's content. While each publication will have its own cutline style, ideally a cutline should answer the usual who, what, where, when, why and how.

Associated Press style, which provides a good cutline model to follow, says the first sentence will be in the present tense and tell what's happening, who's in the picture, when it's happening and where. The second sentence, in past

Uhh oh (Joel Sartore) A Wichita, Kan., police officer waits for a tow truck to clear away a car that broadsided him at a downtown intersection. Most fender bender photos will never make the paper, unless they involve something humorous, like a police car in an accident.

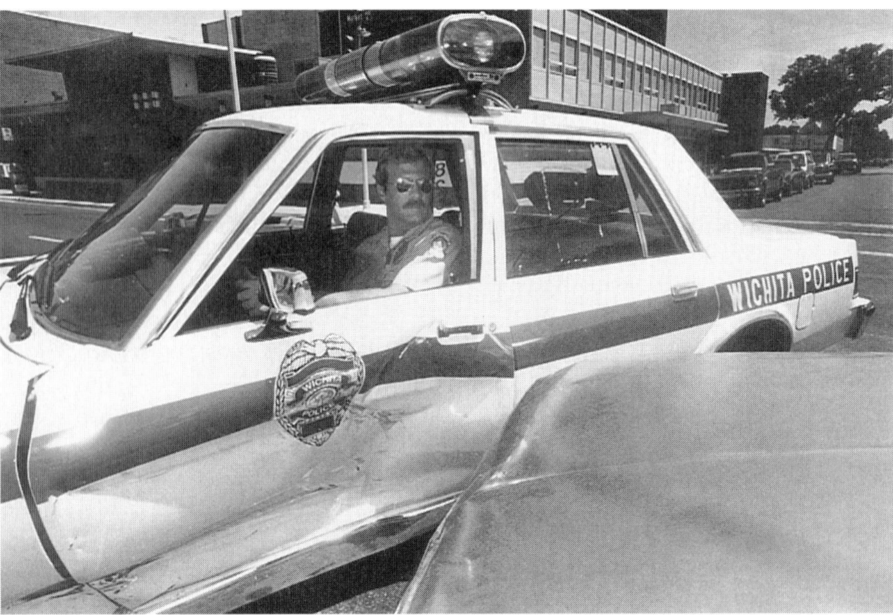

tense, sums up the action and provides the how and why. Occasionally a third sentence will be required to provide elaboration.

Now comes a hard and fast rule:

Each photojournalist must routinely provide accurate cutline information, including identification of all the pertinent subjects in the photo.

There are two reasons for this: One, most publications refuse to run photos in which dominant subjects are not identified or cutline information is inaccurate or missing. Two, every journalist is expected to cover and report accurately on every assigned event.

Please note the term *photojournalist* as opposed to *photographer.* Richard Wright, a hard-charging photojournalist, has said, somewhat facetiously, "A photojournalist without a notebook is just a photographer. A photojournalist without a camera is just a reporter. And a photojournalist without either a camera or a notebook is just a bystander."

Photojournalists can easily be made to feel a part of the news-gathering operation by being required to write complete cutlines, rather than just to hand

It Looks Different From Here (George Tuck) An aerial photo provides a dramatic view of the south face of the Nebraska Capitol. Aerials provide a welcome break from street-level photos and frequently are the best way to show large buildings, proposed construction sites, disaster areas and interesting visual patterns. Editors need to help orient readers to interpret aerials by including in the cutline compass directions and/or landmarks in the scene.

over "idents" to the desk. In fact it is our strongly held belief that all photojournalists must write the first version of the cutline. To do otherwise would be the same as having reporters turn over their notes to the desk for writing the story.

Obviously there are exceptions to requiring photojournalists to get names. It is difficult or downright dangerous, for example, for a photojournalist to ask rioters to put down their bricks and spell their names for cutline information. The same goes for large demonstrations or celebrating fans after a particularly rowdy football game. Even under those difficult circumstances, however, a resourceful photojournalist will get good cutline information.

Box 8.1 lists informal cutline "rules." A first one is that cutlines should not repeat the obvious. If a picture shows a child eating an ice cream cone, the caption shouldn't say, "Terry Smith eats an ice cream cone." That would waste space. It would be better to say, "Terry Smith beats the heat Friday . . . ," or "Terry Smith has a licking good time Friday. . . ."

The best cutlines use active, not passive, verbs and grab the reader's attention. Boring cutlines do not improve a good picture, and vice versa. At the same time, a caption writer shouldn't race to the thesaurus to find a complex, multisyllabic word when a simpler one will work.

FROM LEFT

Identification of two or more people in a photo can be handled easily by saying, "From left are Jennifer Johnson, Ernesto Gonzales and Kim Bond." Saying "from left to right" is redundant. If you begin at the left, where else can you go but to the right?

People who are not in neat rows can be identified by saying, "Clockwise from top right are. . . ." It's best not to identify counterclockwise, since that goes against American culture and training. Subjects who can't be identified this way might be identified on the basis of gender or clothing color or style.

"Margaret Smith (wearing red jacket) gathers her posters after. . . ."

"Margaret Smith (third woman from the left) appears at a rally. . . ."

READ THE PHOTO AND THE CUTLINE

Cutline writers or editors should always have the photo in front of them as they work. Many cutline errors can be attributed to editors or photographers disobeying this simple rule. It's beneficial to try to view the photograph through the reader's eyes and then check to see if the cutline answers all the pertinent questions.

When checking cutlines, the editor must be sure that the number of people in the cutline matches the number of people in the photo. Even major publications are not exempt from this mistake, which seems to happen on page remakes. Editors must be particularly vigilant on page revisions or when photos are recropped.

Cutline Dos and Don'ts

- Don't state the obvious.
- Don't bore the reader.
- Do have the photo in front of you when writing the cutline.
- Do keep the cutline to two or three sentences.
- Don't ever say "from left to right." "From left" is sufficient.
- Do use active verbs.
- Don't ascribe human characteristics to inanimate objects. Trees can't be lonely, windmills can't be forlorn and mountains can't ponder the magnitude of the universe.
- Do check the spelling and content.
- Do recheck the cutline whenever the photo is cropped.
- Do make sure the number of people in the photo jibes with the number identified in the picture.
- Do check the accuracy of the identification of any objects such as musical instruments or species of birds and flowers.
- Do make sure the tone of the cutline matches the mood of the picture. Avoid happy cutlines with sad photos, for example.
- Do remember that libel laws apply to captions as well as to news stories.
- Don't take a chance with "joke" captions not intended to reach the public. They may make it into print.
- Do remember that the caption and the photo are perceived by readers as being a single unit. Weakness in one hurts the other.

Box 8.1

CHECK THE GUT REACTION

If something about a photo or the cutline causes an uneasy feeling in the editor's gut, then something is likely to be wrong: The accuracy of the cutline, the identification of people in the photo, the location of the photo or maybe even the veracity of the photo itself.

When one edits a cutline, just as when one edits a story, one must retain a healthy skepticism. Check, check and check again.

As old-timers like to say, "If your momma says she loves you, check it out."

Problems with cutlines are most likely to happen if the photo comes from a free-lancer or stringer who does not know the publication's cutline requirements. Problems can be minimized by having the copy desk and photo desk come up with a joint memo about requirements for cutlines. A brief workshop on this topic can be quite beneficial as well.

At the extreme, photographers will lose their jobs when they cannot or will not get good cutline information.

PICTURE CATEGORIES

The categories of publishable photographs indicate the style or content of the photo, and, to a lesser extent, problems that might arise:

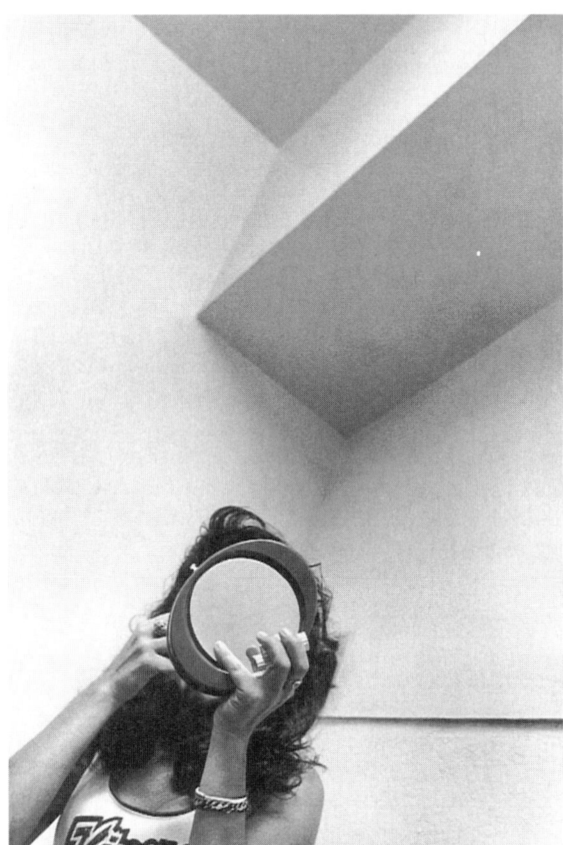

Fast Break (Cindy Schatz) The very dramatic composition of a Fast Break cheerleader applying her makeup would make some editors very uneasy. Notice the paralleling of the lines of the woman and the angles of the ceiling. The composition and the fact that the woman's face is obscured means this photo is atypical of most show-the-subject-looking-at-the-camera newspaper shots. Don't be afraid to use a shot such as this. It's very strong, and visually alert readers will respond well to it.

MUG SHOTS AND THUMBNAILS

The term *mug shot* is slang for a police photo, one in which a person is lined up against a wall marked with heights. Most mug shots used in newspapers, even of corporate executives or members of the president's Cabinet, look very little better than police photos of criminals.

In newspaper parlance, a mug shot is a front-on, head-and-shoulders photo used to identify someone in a story. The photo is usually one column wide by 3 inches deep (written 1 × 3) and can either come from the publication's files (called a file photo) or be a photo shot on assignment specifically for the story.

Mug shots are most useful in identifying lesser-known personalities, such as the high school band director, the head of the city street department or the undersecretary of agriculture. Mug shots of the president, the mayor or the state's senior senator are generally nothing more than space fillers and therefore probably should be eliminated. It is worth remembering that the research of Garcia and Stark has determined that only 45 percent of the mug shots are processed or seen by readers, compared with 92 percent of the three-column photos (*Eyes on the News,* p. 50).

Check, Check and Double Check Take a look at the captions under these five thumbnails. Only one is correct. In addition, mug shots, and especially thumbnails, are not very useful. Readers simply do not treat them seriously. As an editor you will be required to proof the accuracy of your work and the work of others. In this example, the editor who proofed this page fell down on the job. The identifications are, from left, Cranston, DeConcini, Glenn, McCain and Riegle.

Thumbnails are half-column mug shots and are pretty much useless, unless columns are 18 picas wide or more. For the usual 12-pica-wide newspaper columns, a thumbnail photo would be about three-quarters of an inch across, or just large enough to provide a little extra ink on the page, but not large enough to be visually useful. Editors who are tempted to use a thumbnail should sit down until the feeling goes away.

ENVIRONMENTAL PORTRAITS

Portraits that include some of the subject's surroundings, such as part of an office or factory equipment, are called environmental portraits. If these photos are little more than mug shots with some extra space thrown in, they are quite ineffective. Successful photos help explain more about the subject than can be divined from a usual mug shot.

Environmentals will give the reader a feeling for how the person's life is organized, what's important to him or her (such as family photos on the desk, framed commendations from the military hanging on the wall or even a prized dog or cat resting on a lap). These little vignettes help visually explain subtle things about the subject that could never be included in the cutline.

At their worst, environmental portraits are posed shots that depict the facade the subject chooses to show the world or, worse yet, what the photographer chooses to create. For the most part, a goofy *People*-magazine-style shot of someone prancing around on the beach dressed in a penguin suit is not realism. Most subjects are people who, for whatever reason, are about to receive their moment of glory by appearing in print. Editors do them a great disservice by asking them to appear other than as they really are.

Photojournalism, as practiced by the purists, does not allow for the posing of subjects, except for very specific purposes, such as portraits. Never is the subject asked to do anything that the subject would not normally do. Hence, environmental portraits that do not adhere strictly to a realistic portrait should be avoided.

FEATURES AND EVERGREEN FEATURES

Feature photos tend to be lighthearted or ironic looks at our world, such as the exaggerated expressions of junior high band members on their first day of marching practice, a wrecker being towed away, or even the old standby, a dog grabbing a child's ice cream cone.

The dreaded *weather feature* is often thrust on photographers whenever the managing editor breaks out in a sweat after getting out of an air-conditioned car or the first snowflake sticks to the publisher's glasses. This category of photos can produce some really interesting results, especially if the wind is turning umbrellas wrong side out. The best weather features are interesting and can produce laughs throughout the newsroom and living room both. The worst are predictable and stale.

Evergreen features are timeless and will hold for several days, or even weeks, before being published. Most layout desks love it when a supply of feature photos is on hand for those times when an anticipated story or photo falls through at the last minute. This is where evergreens can save the day. Obviously one must be careful not to run an evergreen made on a sunny day when it has been cloudy for two weeks running.

Taking the Plunge (Joel Sartore) A boy enjoys his last swimming class of the semester at a Wichita, Kan., high school. This strongly backlit subject is easily reproduced as a silhouette or line shot.

WILD ART

Also called "stand-alones," these photos are run without an accompanying story, something that is typical of feature photos. A mug shot, by contrast, rarely would be run by itself. In some instances, a story falls through or there might not be room for an accompanying story and thus a longer-than-normal cutline, called an extended cutline, is used. If the cutline runs much longer than five or six lines, a story might be called for.

GENERAL NEWS

Photos that can be scheduled, such as the mayor's speech or a news conference about an upcoming trial, are called general news. Photographers know where to go, roughly what equipment they will need and, most likely, what photos they will produce.

SPOT NEWS

These are unplanned, often difficult assignments to cover, and include fires, accidents, shootings, hostage situations, plane crashes. Spot news can also be called hard news, which readily distinguishes it from soft news, or feature-type assignments.

Spot news assignments can be unforgiving. If the photojournalist is not there when it happens, forget it. Most of these situations last just a few minutes, as far as the best photos are concerned, and can include a fireman carrying out an old woman from a burning apartment, rescue workers placing a wreck victim on a stretcher or police officers arresting a shooting suspect.

The image quality of spot news assignments can vary all over the field. Late-night shootings or accidents might result in rather flat, grainy images that nonetheless can be quite impressive in print.

Fires produce lots of smoke, which can seriously reduce the depth of field of the picture. Sprays of water can create real hazards for camera lenses, especially if the wind is blowing in the photographer's face.

Some spot news situations can require that the photographer shoot from an extremely long distance, which makes for smaller image size and a grainy print. Editors need to make allowances for less-than-desirable quality under such situations and judge the pictures more on content and much less on image quality.

PHOTO ILLUSTRATIONS

Found most often on feature pages, photo illustrations can be divided into food, fashion, feature and editorial categories. Illustrations are created, not found, with the images done under very tightly controlled situations, usually in a studio. Most illustrations use a series of lights, models and props to create a specific image required for a section front.

Food illustrations can be lots of fun, especially if there are leftovers. Often these photos can require someone to build props, someone to prepare thematic

Cobblestones (George Tuck) Houston police check an accident victim after he fell off a street-level fence surrounding a basement courtyard. It is rare that accident pictures have such graphic elements as patterned cobblestones and an interesting placement of people. Most accident scenes do not allow for an overhead view, but rather force the photographer to shoot around rescue workers and bystanders. The wide-angle lens causes distortion that is noticeable only in the top left figure.

dishes, such as for a Southwestern Fiesta, and maybe even someone to "style" the food by securing specific props, tableware and napkins, and even arranging food on the plates and the table. Good food illustrations are very time consuming to set up and shoot (from several hours to several days), but can produce images strong enough to make the reader want to eat the newsprint.

Some photographers, especially on small and medium-size publications, regularly create great food shots with little more than their imaginations and whatever they can find at the local grocery and in their basements at home. At the same time, editors should not request a food illustration if they are not willing to allocate the time and resources necessary to pull it off.

Fashion illustrations can be equally time consuming and complex, especially if location shooting is required. The photographer may have to carry additional lighting, props and equipment if the location is particularly remote, such as in the mountains or in the desert. Experience has shown that complex fashion shoots on large publications tend to require a small army of people, ranging from makeup artist to hair stylist to wardrobe person to fashion designer to drivers to caterers to assistants who move props and fetch things. Just as with food illustrations, a longer-than-usual lead time is necessary.

Editorial and feature illustrations tackle subjects that are difficult or impossible to photograph, such as car theft, stress, spouse abuse, retirement anxiety and grade inflation. Editorial illustrations are used on the news pages and must "illustrate" something like date rape without actually showing it or the actual people involved. When an editorial illustration is used, the cutline or credit line MUST state very specifically that the photo is an illustration using models to depict a specific situation.

Most editorial illustrations of serious subjects seem to use faces in silhouette, which can cause the photo to smack of sensationalism. Television's tabloid journalism programs tend to show "eyewitnesses" or "undercover informants" in silhouette. This technique can be effective, provided it is used sparingly and for the right reasons.

PICTORIALS

This is a special category of photographs that have strong graphic quality, tend to depict nature or landscape subjects and tend to be minimalist in composition. Pictorials rarely have humans as dominant subjects, but rather may use humans as a small part of the overall scene. These photos can provide a nice alternative to the publication's usual photographic fare, but care must be taken not to use pictorials in place of strong news shots.

SPORTS

In photo contests, and on the pages of the newspaper, sports photos can be divided into sports features and sports action. The action shots are very popular with the readers and provide a visual exclamation point to the coverage of virtually every kind of sporting event known to the human race.

The images of football players caught in mid-crunch, basketballers dunking a shot and gymnasts in mid-flip comprise a staple of sports pages around the world. A weekly paper depends on strong coverage of the hometown team to fill its pages and satisfy the photographic demand of its loyal readers. Daily and national publications do basically the same, except that their coverage area is a bit wider.

Sports action can be further divided into stopped-action and panned action photos. The former depends on fast shutter speeds or, in some instances, short flash exposures to "freeze" action. This frozen or stopped action allows the reader to analyze an extremely brief period or part of an event. The observant reader will be able to see other things going on around the main action, such as a missed tackle or another player's grimace, which will further increase that reader's understanding of the event.

This stopped action is what most amateur photographers seek to emulate but have difficulty achieving. The majority of truly outstanding stopped-action photos are currently being made with very long (and correspondingly expensive) telephoto lenses, mostly in the 400- to 600-mm range.

Successful action photos usually are tack sharp, with the background out of focus, with strong content and dramatic composition. Anything less is not worth considering, unless the content is of overriding importance.

Over Easy (Doug Carroll) Shooting into the sun allows the photographer to achieve a silhouette, an image that provides dramatic contrast to any page.

Sports features mostly appear on the sports pages, but some, such as action shots of plays that win the Super Bowl, might show up on the front page of a newspaper or the cover of a magazine.

These features can provide a lighthearted look at events the majority of Americans take far too seriously. Spectators, coaches and even the players themselves can become fodder for the sports feature.

Sports events seem to produce an inordinate number of cliché shots. Editors avoid:

- The hairy armpit basketball shot. (Look for action on the floor, rather than people jumping for the ball.)
- The gang's-all-here football shot. (Rarely do strong action shots have more than four or five people in them.)
- The somewhere-over-there action photo. (Sports shots made from too far away, or without a long enough lens, need to be cropped very tightly to eliminate the excess dead space.)

PICTURE ESSAY/PICTURE SEQUENCE/ PHOTO PROJECTS

Each of these types consists of a display of several photos, but the content can be dramatically different.

The picture essay is a collection of photos about one topic or event, generally with a feature orientation, such as a fall afternoon at the park or a classic car rally or a Little League practice. None of these topics is earthshaking, none requires a major outlay of time to shoot and none is difficult to lay out.

Essays most often arise either because a photographer has run across a good series of photos while "cruising" for features or because a story or project has fallen apart and something is needed to fill the space.

Not all essays are bad, but neither are all good. Occasionally a picture essay will touch the readers because of the pictures' quiet beauty or because they bring back pleasant memories. Rarely are picture essays insightful, mainly because not much time is invested in them.

At the same time, each story that *National Geographic* does is considered a photo essay. To the *Geographic,* a picture story has a definite beginning, middle and end, while an essay is a collection of images from a certain place or subject. *Geographic* typically spends a year or more on its essays.

Picture sequences are multiple photos of one event and usually require the least amount of time from the photographer. They most often arise out of sporting events, especially football, and show the progression of a play or player during a very few seconds. Sequences show a one-two-three occurrence, like catching a pass, dodging would-be tacklers and making a touchdown. In the case of controversial plays, the sequence can be quite informative, but taken as a whole, sequences tend to negate the power of a single image to command the reader's attention. Sequences most often lose their power if the page designer plays all the images the same size, rather than selecting one image and playing it larger.

While sequences are an excellent way of explaining complex actions to the reader, their use should be limited. Since high-speed motor drives on cameras are practically essential for sports photography, sequences are rather easy to come by. The trick is in knowing when to use a series and when to go with a single image.

If space is at a premium, the single image probably will work better. If the sequence is weak, three or four pictures will not add up to one good single image.

One should go with the best image. Always.

However, with proper editing, cropping and display, sequences can help explain complex events that most of us cannot see, short of instant replays.

A good time to use a sequence is when a building is being blown up. The rapid-fire change from a building to rubble is not often seen. It's worth capturing, and it does provide a historical record that will have good potential if the building site is reused.

At the same time, sequences can be overused. For example, an executive of one regional newspaper decreed that coverage of the home college football team would include a sequence made from a camera high in the press box. On some plays this can work, but as a standing rule, it doesn't. Readers lose interest quickly.

Photo projects, also called documentaries or picture stories, are highly desirable for photographers. Correctly done, they take a long time, generally months to more than a year, and focus in depth on one topic. Project ideas can originate with anyone: a photographer, an editor, a reporter, a reader. A successful project will blend the talents of a cadre of journalists, including the photographer and writer, plus copy editor, page designer and researcher, and the support of the project by a managing editor or other senior editor. Most important, a project requires a commitment from a publication for time, money and space. Without any one of those, the project will not succeed.

To a photojournalist, a picture story is akin to an in-depth story for a reporter. Both require extensive background research, multiple interviews or shooting sessions, extensive writing and editing and lab work before even getting to the production stage.

Some photographers, just like some reporters, will work on projects on their own time, including weekends and vacations, simply because their day-to-day assignments get in the way. Publications with well-developed staffs almost always allow photographers and reporters to pursue on company time stories that have been approved by supervising editors.

Occasionally an idea doesn't quite capture the fancy of the editors but is regarded as a winner by the photographer or the reporter. Hence the weekend and vacation work schedule.

One successful project was "Growing Up Gay," a 14-page special section published by the *Star Tribune* in Minneapolis. It consisted of 44 photos, only one of which was in color, and more than 20,000 words. The following information appeared on the back page of the special section:

> This project originated with Rita Reed, staff photographer, a lesbian who had the idea of documenting the lives and struggles of gay adolescents. Reed, 42, has been with the *Star Tribune* for six years and lives with her partner in Minneapolis.
>
> Kurt Chandler, metro reporter, was selected for his skills in personal reporting and also his viewpoints as a heterosexual man and parent. Chandler, 39, has been with the paper since 1986 and lives with his wife and two children in Minneapolis.
>
> Also contributing to the project were a photo editor, an assistant managing editor for graphics, an assistant managing editor for photography, a senior photo/graphics editor, an artist, two copy editors, a librarian and an assistant managing editor for special projects.

This editorial note about the project gives a lot of necessary information, including the backgrounds and possible biases of the photographer and the writer. It also says, very subtly, that the newspaper made a major commitment of staff and other resources to a topic that was of considerable social importance to its readership.

Most newspapers, unfortunately, have neither the staff, the resources nor the commitment for such projects.

Other projects begin with a news clipping or a journalist's desire to work through personal problems. A *Macon* (Ga.) *Telegraph* photographer, Maryann Bates, had photographed for years her father's declining health because of Alzheimer's disease. When an editor on the paper learned of this, the paper produced a special project about it.

The *Detroit Free Press* also did a project on Alzheimer's, which originated with photographer Al Schaben. Schaben pitched the idea to the paper's editors, who assigned a reporter. The resulting project, entitled "Ward of Lost Memories," details a man's regular visits to a hospital ward where his wife lives out her final years, no longer knowing that her regular visitor is her husband. The extremely powerful, poignant photos are supported with a moving text by a reporter.

PHOTO COMPOSITION

Content drives picture selection, although making a choice between two good pictures can be a pleasant task. For editors to be able to judge the visual merits of a photograph, knowledge of the elements of composition is necessary. These include:

- **Balance**—Images are either symmetrical (formal) or asymmetrical (informal) in balance. Most composition is informal, with the subject placed off center.
- **Rule of thirds**—A photo is divided into horizontal or vertical thirds (Figure 8.1). The optimum placement of the subject is at or near the intersection of those lines. This creates an asymmetrical balance, one in which there is an element of tension. Formal or centered compositions tend to be somewhat more static and generally not quite as interesting.
- **Leading lines**—Objects in the composition, such as arms pointing, roads leading off into the distance or signs leading in one direction or another are useful in guiding the reader to the most important part of the composition. Not every photo will have leading lines, although certain parts of the composition are useful in directing the reader to another part of the photo.
- **Contrast**—This can be a catch-all term, referring to, for example, big/little, light/dark, young/old, human/inhuman, male/female, smooth/rough, chromatic/monochromatic.
- **Repetition**—Occasionally the repetition of an object can establish a pattern that becomes much more interesting than does one object by itself. When a pattern is established and then broken (as in musical syncopation), the break in the pattern holds more attention for the viewer than does the pattern itself.
- **Color**—Although black and white are colors, let's talk about the basic colors of photography. Colors in print publications are composed of cyan (a blue-green), magenta (a reddish-blue) and yellow. These are known as subtractive colors. When blended together they form black. Television, for example, uses additive colors (red, blue and green) that form white when mixed together. A simple chart will help keep things sorted out:

  Red + **B**lue + **G**reen = White

  Cyan – **Y**ellow – **M**agenta = Black

  The colors above and below are complementary, meaning they are on opposite sides of the color wheel. Thus a green shape will balance a magenta shape and a blue shape balances a yellow one. To keep the colors straight,

Rule of Thirds

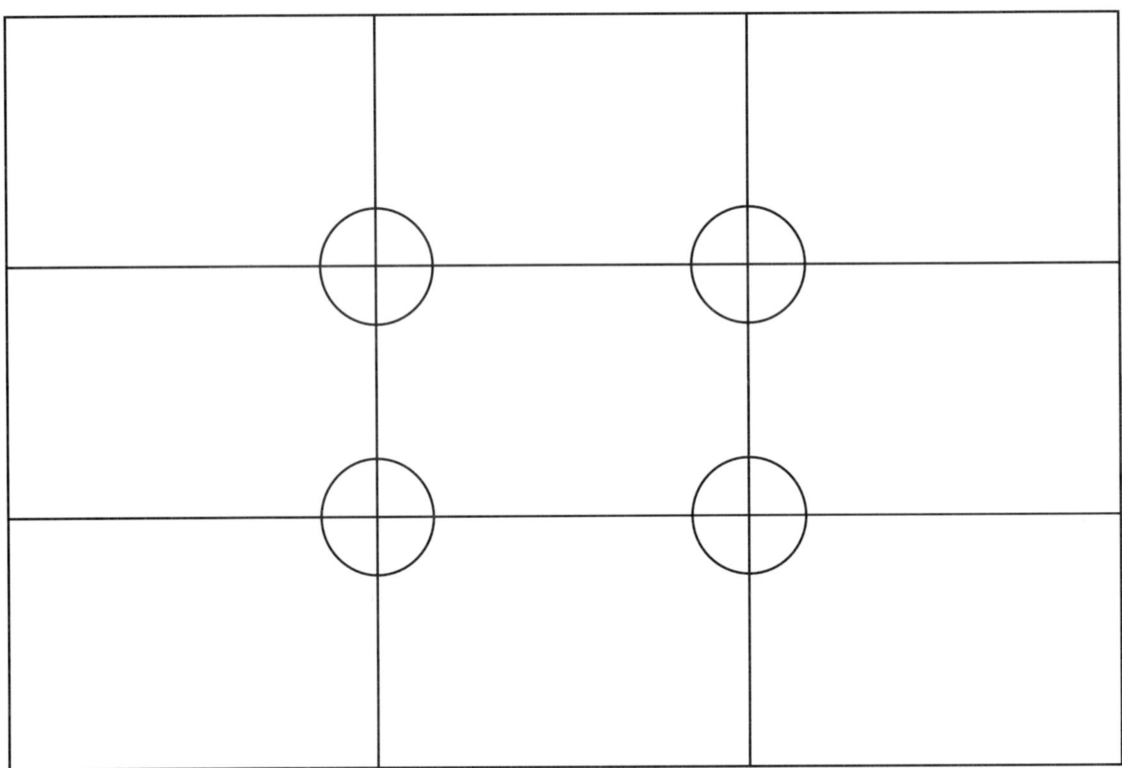

Figure 8.1 A very good compositional guide, the rule of thirds says a photo is divided into horizontal and vertical thirds with the strongest subject placement at or near the intersection of those lines. In some compositions the photographer will have one-third land and two-thirds sky, or vice versa. Frequently the rule is modified to a one-fourth/ three fourths rule, such as one-fourth land and three-fourths sky. The rule also works well for page layout.

remember them by this mnemonic: *R*ed *C*adillac *BY* *G*eneral *M*otors (*R*ed *C*yan *B*lue *Y*ellow *G*reen *M*agenta).

Frequently photographers will use a small patch of color to balance out a much larger piece of color on the opposite side of the spectrum. Look at photos coming out of Haiti and Africa for interesting colors and how those are balanced by the photographer.

While color pictures are the standard for most publications, black and white images should not be ignored. From a production standpoint, black and white photos are less expensive to print and frequently work better for certain

Interstate 80 and the Oregon Trail (George Tuck) Interstate truckers head east on Interstate 80 near Ogallala, Neb., just a few feet from wagon ruts left from the westward movement on the Oregon Trail. The rule of thirds works well for this photograph, which is divided into one-third land and two-thirds sky. The composition is actually closer to one-fourth and three-fourths, but the concept is the same; symmetrical composition is generally the least effective.

investigative or documentary projects than would color. Readers, and editors as well, often tend to respond to color pictures for the wrong reason, saying that the color is nice, which means they are effectively ignoring the content. Color can mask a lack of visual content. If you are in doubt as to an image's content, view the image in black and white. Does it still hold up? If so, then the content is probably there.

- **Action**—The mere shooting of a photo means that one particular piece of time has been frozen forever on a piece of film or a videodisc. The action can be stopped solid, as in the case of a soccer or field hockey shot, or panned, in which a slow shutter speed is used to create a blurring of the image.

  With the latter, the photographer is creating a Cubist-like image of the passage of time. Picasso, as one of the major Cubist painters, had images with two or more faces, which represented the subject at several points in time.

  A panned shot is sharply focused on the subject, and the camera is moved to follow that subject. The result is a blurred background that ceases to be recognizable, while the subject might show some blurring of the arms or legs. Panned action photos can be a very nice change of pace for sports pages.
- **Light**—By light, we mean the quality of it, not necessarily the presence or absence of it. Light helps define subjects, creating a mood that often helps sell the image to the reader. Lighting can be harsh, as in bright sun and strong

shadows, or soft, as in early morning or late afternoon. It can be romantic, coming from a candle or through a lace curtain. Light coming from beneath the subject can create "spook" lighting worthy of a Frankenstein or Dracula movie. Light coming from behind the subject can create a silhouette.

- **Depth of field**—Depth of field is a photographic term meaning the area of acceptable focus in front of and behind a subject. Most of the time there is twice as much in focus behind a subject as there is in front of it. Depth of field can be shallow, as produced by telephoto lenses in which the background is out of focus and the subject is therefore isolated. It can be great, as in the case of a wide-angle-lens shot that keeps almost everything in focus. This is a good technique for shooting environmental portraits in which the subject and his or her other surroundings are in focus. Depending on how it is used, depth of field allows us to concentrate only on the subject or to use background information to gain a better understanding of the subject's environment.

PHOTO CROPPING

The cropping of photos is an art. Actually it can be quite simple, much like creating a sculpture of an elephant. To do the latter, according to an old joke, you merely chip away everything that doesn't look like an elephant.

Now That's a Really Big Bug (George Tuck) Brett Ratcliffe, a University of Nebraska-Lincoln research entomologist, examines a rhinoceros beetle from UNL's collection. The photograph was made with a closeup lens that allows small objects to be shown close to normal size. Editors need to explain special photographic techniques so readers will be better able to interpret what they are seeing.

It's important to remember that pictures are cropped several times before they arrive at the copy desk. Photographers make the first crop in the camera when they're shooting an event, using a combination of lenses, distances, framing and exclusion/inclusion to arrive at a particular composition. The second crop takes place either in the enlarger when the print is made, or in the electronic darkroom when the photographer or picture editor does a further tightening of the composition.

A picture-savvy editor, just like a word-savvy editor, knows when not to edit further. A good tight composition is rarely improved when an editor shaves off another half inch just to prove the editor has the authority to do it.

One of the first rules of picture cropping is to crop for effect, not defect. Photos should always be treated with respect. This means that one should never subscribe to the Veg-a-matic school of picture cropping in which photos are attacked with a cookie cutter and hacked into funny looking stars or circles or tetrahedral rhomboids. Only under the remotest circumstances can such cropping be beneficial.

Photos begin as rectangles, specifically 24 by 36 millimeters, the size of a negative, and should remain that way. This does not mean that the proportions cannot be changed; they can. But the proportions should complement the image.

Headshots of people, for example, are oval or rectangular. People rarely have square faces. Hence mug shots should be rectangular, not square, unless there is a darn good reason for it. (Saying that one has to crop a mug shot into a square because that's all the room one has on the layout means the layout hasn't been done correctly. In purely correct terms, the artwork comes before the layout, not vice versa.)

One good technique to use when cropping a photo is to look at what's been left out. Lay a piece of paper over the photo (or the computer screen) and cover up the image, showing only what you want to crop out. Occasionally it will be nothing important, but in other cases it might be essential to the compositional integrity of the image.

In some instances, a photographer will use large amounts of open space to provide a visual tension in the image, something that editors may overlook. If excessive cropping is then undertaken, the result will be a radically weakened composition. In other cases, patches of color or light or dark will be used to balance a composition.

Remember also that most shooters, if they are good, bring to the newsroom tightly cropped or "finished" images. Photo-oriented publications, including the *Wichita* (Kan.) *Eagle* and *National Geographic,* expect this and don't tamper with well-cropped images.

Savage cropping was a term and technique used by Dick Sroda when he was director of photography at the now-defunct *The Paper* in Oshkosh, Wis. The term indicates that images are cropped into severe rectangles, often vertically right up to the edges of the eyes, or horizontally across the eyebrows and just below the lips. The results are dramatic, to say the least, and can be very disturbing to photographers and readers used to more traditional cropping. While this style of cropping is not used very often today, it nonetheless is a style to be studied and used when appropriate.

Just Waiting (Travis Heying/Gillette, Wyo., *News-Record*) High school rodeo cowboys check their equipment and mentally prepare themselves before a bull riding event in Gillette, Wyo. A good example of "tension cropping," the elimination of the face of the cowboy in the foreground forces attention to his hands and from there down his shadow to the cowboy in the background.

A variation on savage cropping is something we shall call *tension cropping.* With this approach, the photographer composes an image in which a large foreground object is reduced to minimal elements that force the reader's attention to the background. The foreground object is, however, necessary to provide a complete understanding of the whole image. Travis Heying's photo of high school rodeo competition is a vivid example of how effective this technique can be.

Creative editing is a collaborative effort between the editor and the reporter, requiring consultation and discussions before major editing is done. The same should take place when major cropping is done on a photo. The editor should discuss the proposed cropping with the photographer, who might agree or might offer an alternative. The photographer will appreciate being consulted. At the very least, the consultation will help maintain avenues of communication between the photography and editing areas. Box 8.2 sums up the guidelines for successful photo editing.

THE BIG TEN OF PHOTO CROPPING

No magic formula will guarantee perfect cropping of a photo. Remember also, please, that just as there is not one way only to edit a story, there is not one

Guidelines for Successful Photo Editing

- Select photos on the basis of news value and visual impact.
- Good photos have emotion, interesting lighting and clean backgrounds.
- Allow the photographer to make the first edit. (The photographer on the scene has an excellent idea of which images sum up the event. The picture editor should act as a quality control editor, double-checking the image quality and being sure that the most telling image is what goes into the publication.)
- Don't feel you have to crop a photo just to prove you're an editor.
- Check the cutline both for accuracy and to prevent libel.
- Avoid square mugshots.
- Avoid the Veg-a-matic school of cropping.
- Consult with the photographer when doing major cropping.
- Crop for effect, not defect.
- Select photos on the basis of content, not color.
- Play the dominant visual element 50 percent larger than any other element on the page.

Box 8.2

way only to crop a photo. With those caveats in mind, editors should use a step-by-step method to crop a photo:

1. **Read the photo.** Just as editing requires one to read the story before editing it, so picture editing requires the editor to "read" or study a photo before cropping it.
2. **Read the photographer's cutline.** There may be information in the cutline that requires the inclusion or even the emphasis of certain parts of the photo.
3. **Read the photo, cutline and story together.** After looking at each separately, look at all parts together. Make sure that each supports the other. Are parts in conflict? If so, what can be done to correct the differences? For stand-alone photos the cutline must carry the informational weight of the five w's and h.
4. **Decide what parts of the photo are essential or, conversely, what parts can be eliminated.** If an editor cannot determine what's important in a photo, then any attempts to do effective cropping will be unsuccessful. It's also an indication the photo probably should not be used. Just as some stories are too wordy and can be reduced to two or three effective paragraphs, some photos can be cropped radically.
5. **Can cropping emphasize the photo's impact?** Most photographers will present photos to the desk that are already printed rather tightly. Occasionally, however, the photo will allow for different cropping that will give the photo more impact. Look for ways to crop at a different point but do not arbitrarily crop off hands or feet. Another general rule is to avoid cropping at joints, such as at the elbow or knee or ankle.

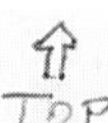

Amsterdam Reflections (George Tuck) The initial tendency is to turn the picture upside down, which would be the opposite of the way it was made. The orientation of photos such as this require the editor to clearly mark the top of the print, both on the front and the back, with the word TOP and an arrow pointed in the correct direction.

6. **Crop both from the outside in and from the inside out.** Mask parts of the print with your hands or pieces of paper and slide them from the outside of the print toward the center to see the effect this will have on the image. Now reverse the process and go from the center out, revealing a little bit of the print at a time. Often this will allow the editor to see necessary parts of the print that might have escaped attention before. Also, move the left mask separately from the right and vice versa. Do the same with the top and bottom masks. These approaches will help the editor to view the print in varying configurations.
7. **Tight is better and square isn't.** Nine times out of ten, cropping tight is better than cropping loose. This is because most photos are printed too loosely, leaving unnecessary space around the subject. At the same time, editors need to be alert to those photos that have additional space around the subject for a purpose. The resulting shape of a photo is important. Square photos are not the most effective shape because they are nondirectional. They neither are verticals nor horizontals. Tall, skinny verticals and long, thin horizontals are delightful images. They allow more variety in layout.
8. **Place crop marks on the top and one side only.** It is neither necessary nor desirable to place crop marks on all four sides of a photo. The odds of

What Not to Do Crop marks done in grease pencil are easily removed or altered as necessary. In this example, felt tip pens and grease pencils both were used, resulting in a mess when the photo was recropped. Notice the thin horizontal marks on the face of the print that align with the width crop marks. When a mask was laid over the print to achieve a drop out, the print was cut in the process. As a result of the cuts, the print can not be used for any other purpose. Editors need to work under the assumption that each print is one of a kind and cannot be duplicated.

an incorrect size and confusion in the back shop or paste-up room increase as more lines are added to a print.

9. **Crop, measure, proportion.** After cropping the photo, measure the cropped image and then calculate the reproduction proportions. Editors who want to live long do not arbitrarily draw a photo box on a layout and then try to force-crop a photo into it. It needs to be repeated again and again: Photos are not made of rubber; they do not stretch. Editors must remember to determine how wide and how deep the photo needs to be reproduced before drawing the photo box.
10. **Mask, read and recalculate.** Place pieces of paper (or use cropping L's or your hands) along the crop marks to mask the eliminated portions of the photo. Now, read the cutline again and make sure it has all the necessary information. Finally, recalculate the reproduction size and percentage just to make sure they are correct.

PICTURES TO AVOID

Photographers and editors alike have lists of photos they would rather never see. Some are universal, others are quite individual. Quite a few publications have an unspoken policy on what can and cannot be published. No list is sacrosanct; each is merely a guide.

Almost without exception, publications would be better off by half if they never published another photo of two people shaking hands while grinning stupidly at the camera. Photographers refer to these shots as "grip-and-grins." They are a staple in many papers, particularly those without strong picture editors, and are favored by politicians who view the photos as showing them "doing something."

In most instances the photo is either posed by the photographer or by the participants themselves. "G and Gs" are not candid. They do not reflect reality, other than the supposed reality of the poser. They rarely contribute to a reader's understanding of an event. And they consume valuable space that could be used for a really meaningful photo.

The largest set of no-no photos falls under a title we shall call "theme and variations."

The first no-no is "three people and a piece of paper." Most often these photos come about when an organization gives a check to a charitable fund or presents an award to a worthy citizen or city official. In almost every case there will be three people in the picture—the giver, the getter and a stander-by. Rounding out the content is a piece of paper, such as a check, a proclamation, a resolution or a contract, that often shows up in reproduction as a blank piece of paper. The worst offense is the photo showing two people with enough space between them for a third person.

Another variation is "two people and a piece of paper." Check presentations still appear in this category, but it seems handshakes substitute for the third person.

Finally, there is the "solo person with a piece of paper." Proclamation signings most often appear in this variation, although it's hard to keep out the "getters and bystanders." Currently there is a spate of solo-person-with-winning-lottery-ticket photos, but these likely will be replaced with another variation.

"Firing squad" shots are also despised by photographers and editors alike. These unimaginative pictures show a group of people lined up against a wall, most often brick, and staring back at the camera. Rather than having the group posed in a tight, triangular composition, the firing squad shot forces the image into a horizontal format, which many editors further hack at, cropping at the ankles, knees or other appendages, all to fit the photo into a too-small space.

One variation on the firing squad is the "fig leaf" shot, which has the subjects, usually men, standing with their hands clasped in front of their pants. The appearance is that the subjects are in urgent need of a bathroom or else are protecting their nether regions from imminent assault.

Also disliked is the "person-talking-on-phone" shot. Most often this is contrived to give the impression the subject is actually doing something worthwhile. A make-do photo such as this is rarely necessary for the publication. A photo of a money trader working seven phones at once is another matter. That image could be quite successful.

Some publications ban photos of accidents, unless several people are killed or maimed in an interesting fashion. The news business has an infinite capacity for publishing photos of strange accidents, until that kind of accident becomes commonplace. Murders, for example, are big news in most communities. Because of the number of homicides in Detroit, however, the *Free Press* doesn't do much more than a news brief unless three or more are killed, or unless the death is particularly gruesome or involves a child. When three people are killed in a single incident, the story and/or photo moves to the front page.

One curious category of photo editors tend to avoid is "person with large vegetable." Dick Smyser, the founding editor of the *Oak Ridger* in Oak Ridge, Tenn., actually likes this kind of photo so much that he has a large collection of them. He will even show them to professional organizations and journalism classes if asked. When viewed as a group, they're quite funny. However, when they run singly in a newspaper, the humor or news value is often hard to find.

Small newspapers frequently will show a person with a huge catfish or a small girl with a gigantic pumpkin or a woman with a rutabaga that looks like Woody Allen. Whether such photos are funny is a matter of personal taste.

Following close on the heels of people and vegetables are photos of "kids and dogs" (or cats or chickens or rabbits). For the most part, photographers feel these photos are easy to make and somewhat cheap, in that the news value is minimal. The readers tend to say, "Aww, that's precious," all the while ignoring or minimizing more serious, newsworthy photos.

Photos of children and animals can help adults regain their faith in the human race. Children and animals are relatively unspoiled and express awe and wonder at their surroundings. Perhaps that's why these photos are popular with the readers, but not necessarily with the photographers.

Obviously editors should avoid any photo about which they have serious legal or ethical questions. Pictures in which prominent subjects are not identified should also be shunned; most important, any questionable photo whose authenticity cannot be verified should not be published.

PICTURES THAT GRIP

Grabbers. That's a term photojournalists use to refer to photos with emotional appeal, those that grab the reader by the throat. Grabbers show people at the height of their joy and the depth of their sorrow, their smiles and tears telling the world what they're feeling more eloquently than can hundreds of words.

While the majority of assignments can produce good, usable images, few produce grabbers. The photographer, and the editor, must be alert to subtle expressions, such as a city councilwoman looking quizzically over her glasses, or excited contestants at a horseshoe-pitching contest.

Emotion is what attracts readers and draws them into the picture and related story and cutline. Without emotion, a photo has all the drawing power of a cold bowl of gruel. Joy, anger, excitement, frustration, fear, pain and love are all emotions each of us has felt. We identify with such emotions and plan our lives around them. Some of the time we avoid such emotions, other times we go in search of them. If the images in our publication trip those emotions in the reader, then we have succeeded.

The "gee whiz" element in photos is one that many publications ignore. It encompasses the element of surprise or wonder. It is a child seeing a frog or a rabbit for the first time, or, as Joel Sartore's photo shows so well, young cattle seeing fire for the first time. That's a gee-whizzer. Many of us have been around cattle all our lives and have never thought that most cattle never see fire in their brief lives.

Successful photos can help us retain a childlike curiosity about our world, despite our having seen everything at least once and some things more often than we would like.

Few journalists and even fewer readers would associate humor with newspaper photography. In reality, a lot of feature photography is loaded with humor, some of it obviously funny, and some of it more subtle. Joel Sartore's curious cattle can fit in both the gee whiz and humor categories. The picture of the man looking under the hood of a car while pipes on a building seem to point to the trouble spot is subtly humorous, but is not a gee-whizzer.

The Trouble Is Here (photo by George Tuck) A bystander peers at the engine of a disabled auto in Washington, D.C. The humor of the finger-pointing pipes coupled with the title creates a nice combination. If a photographer turns in a photo with a humorous caption and you don't get it, get the photographer. There might just be something in the photo you missed.

Some humorous photos are likely to play well in one geographic area and fall flat in another. For example, the humor in Sartore's photo might be lost on some city dwellers.

ETHICAL AND LEGAL CONSIDERATIONS

In the abstract, ethical dilemmas are easily seen and quickly dispatched. Reality, however, isn't quite that neat and tidy. Newspapers and other publications work under the sword of libel, invasion of privacy and other lawsuits. Ethical considerations are real, and the consequences of a mistake can be serious. Following are some potential problem areas editors should note carefully:

- **Libel.** The chance that a libel suit may stem from a photo is remote. The potential for libel really lies in the cutline. Check the cutline for accuracy and then check it again for the potential of libel. Cutlines, just like news stories, should have attributions, particularly when criminal charges or legal violations are noted. Be careful also of misidentifications, for obvious reasons.
- **False light.** Since everyone acts goofy from time to time and since cameras can indiscriminately cause even the sanest of people to look as crazy as a flock of loons, editors need to be very watchful for cutlines that make a linkage with questionable behavior. If a subject is stone cold sober, yet the image makes him appear otherwise and the cutline does nothing to dispel that thought, then the editor should consider selecting another image or clarifying the cutline.
- **Invasion of privacy.** This is a very tricky area. Subjects frequently will say a photographer has invaded their privacy, when in fact that is not the case. If a subject is visible in a public place, not inside a private business, then the photo can be safely published. If a photo shows a subject in a private swimming pool, not visible without climbing over a 12-foot fence, then there's a problem. If a red flag is raised here, the editor should be sure to check it out carefully with the photographer and, if necessary, with legal counsel.
- **Violation of copyright.** A copyrighted image may not be used without permission. Copyrighted photos that go over the wires generally can be used, provided the cutline notes the copyright and includes the holder's name.
- **Electronic alteration or created images.** If an image has been electronically manipulated, beyond the usual burning, dodging, cropping, enlargement and color correction that is typically done, this should be noted in the cutline. To do otherwise is to willfully mislead the reader. To a photographer, an editorial illustration indicates that certain liberties have been taken with the image, such as posing the subject to achieve a certain effect, the addition of certain props or the usage of "trick photography." To the reader, the term *editorial illustration* means virtually nothing. Make sure there is no question in the reader's mind as to what is real and what is fantasy (Box 8.3).

TOOLS FOR PICTURE EDITING

One can identify picture editors by the "loupes" worn around their necks. The loupes, which are special magnifying glasses used to look at photo negatives,

Statement on Manipulation of Photographs

As journalists, we believe the guiding principle of our profession is accuracy; therefore, we believe it is wrong to alter the content of a photograph in any way that deceives the public.

As photojournalists, we have the responsibility to document society and to preserve its images as a matter of historical record. It is clear that the emerging electronic technologies provide new challenges to the integrity of photographic images. This technology enables the manipulation of the content of an image in such a way that the change is virtually undetectable. In light of this, we, the National Press Photographers Association, reaffirm the basis of our ethics; accurate representation is the benchmark of our profession.

We believe photojournalistic guidelines for fair and accurate reporting should be the criteria for judging what may be done electronically to a photograph. Altering the editorial content of a photograph, in any degree, is a breach of the ethical standards recognized by the NPPA.

(Approved by the NPPA Executive Committee on Nov. 12, 1990, and revised by the NPPA Board of Directors on July 3, 1991)

Box 8.3

also come in fold-up pocket versions and can range from el-cheapo versions costing a few dollars to super deluxe models costing hundreds of dollars.

The differences between the two lie in the quality of the glass. For most users, the cheaper models will do nicely. Another solution is to use a camera lens. Merely take the lens off the camera body, open the lens to its largest aperture and look at the negative through the reverse end of the lens.

With the increasing use of electronic darkrooms, most copy editors do not need to "read" negatives, and when they do, a loupe can be borrowed from a photographer or picture editor.

Old-fashioned cropping L's are useful when working with prints if an editor needs to visualize the final cropping. These two pieces of L-shaped cardboard allow the editor to block out or crop the image to the needs at hand.

Most picture editors and/or layout editors tend to use proportion wheels or calculators to determine reproduction sizes and percentages for artwork. The proportion wheel is less accurate but is better than a calculator when determining cropping needs. If you choose to use a proportion wheel, be sure to get the largest one you can afford, since large wheels are easier to read than the small versions.

Grease pencils, also called china marking pencils, are the only instruments one should use to mark on photos. Felt tip pens, ball-point pens and pencils all leave marks that cannot be erased from the surface of a photo. Editors should keep a variety of grease pencil colors on hand, such as black, white, red and orange, for use on different images.

Good picture editors also have handy a dictionary and the *Associated Press Stylebook* for checking cutlines, plus local phone books, city directories, maps and phone numbers of photographers, including staffers, stringers and free-lancers.

CALCULATING REPRODUCTION SIZES

Depending on a publication's needs, measurements of photos are done in picas, inches or a combination of both. The first number in a photo proportion ALWAYS refers to the width and the second number to the depth. Sometimes newspapers will indicate a photo is going to run "two by five" or "one by three" or "four by six." In these examples, the first number refers to the number of columns the photo is going to cover and the second number to the depth in inches. Other publications will size photos strictly in inches, for example, 3 5/8 × 6 1/4. Still others will size photos in picas, such as 36 × 51 (that's 6 inches by 8.5 inches).

The basic rule for proportioning a photo is:

- **Crop** the photo first (only if cropping is necessary).
- **Measure** the cropped dimensions (width × depth).
- **Proportion** the photo to determine the reproduction size and percentage.

When cropping the photo, be sure to place the crop marks ONLY in the margins and ONLY use a grease pencil. If crop marks are placed on the image part of the photo using something other than a grease pencil, it's almost guaranteed that the image that reproduces in the publication will be the wrong size and will show the crop marks. It's happened before.

If cropping is critical, as in the case of needing a mug shot of an individual who's in a group of 20 people, put the crop marks on the border of the print, as usual, and then place a tissue over the photo showing the area needed. This bit of redundancy can help you make sure the right area shows up in the final reproduction. Remember to tape the tissue in place so it doesn't wander all over the place.

Proportion wheels are easy to use (the instructions are printed on the wheel), but some people don't realize that you can use the wheel to do proportioning when the figures are in picas. Although the wheel indicates the measurements are in inches, the wheel merely compares one number to another. The numbers can be camels per desert, fly balls per game, points to points or picas to picas.

Photos are not made of rubber. If one dimension increases 25 percent, the other dimension must also increase 25 percent. You cannot stretch a photo in one direction only.

Now for some basics:

- Photos are screened or halftoned to allow for reproduction in a publication.
- The original photo or artwork is referred to as a "continuous tone image," and the reproduction is called a "halftone" (especially appropriate since it only has about half the number of tones as the original).
- Continuous tone images are composed of shadows, midtones, highlights and lots of tones in between.
- The dot pattern used to make the halftone depends on the type of press and quality of paper used in the publication. Newsprint is a rather rough, porous paper and needs a relatively coarse screen to prevent an accumulation of ink

from filling in between the dots and ruining the image. Magazine presses usually run a slick paper called enamel or coated stock that will hold a much finer dot pattern.

- A photo reproduced without benefit of a halftone screen is called a "line shot." Line art refers most often to pen and ink drawings that reproduce as black and white images without any other tones being present. Occasionally one can achieve a very stark effect in a continuous tone photo by requesting a line shot.
- Special effects can be achieved by substituting a different screen for the usual halftone screen. Consider using concentric circle, wavy line, straight line, mezzotint or steel etching screens for special sections.
- If the original and reproduction are the same size, the percentage is 100 percent. If the reproduction is half as big as the original, the percentage is 50 percent. If the reproduction is twice as big, the percentage is 200 percent.

The percentage is very important if the photos are going to be screened or broken into halftone dots for printing. Without these halftone dots, the photo would be difficult to reproduce in the publication.

The percentage tells the engraver (the one doing the photo reproductions) the enlargement or reduction percentage, but not the size. In most cases, the engraver doesn't worry about the size until the halftone is ready to be trimmed. At that point mistakes in the percentage are likely to be noticed and, in extreme cases, one might get an angry call from the engraver asking why one's head is screwed on backward.

USE OF A PROPORTION WHEEL

To calculate reproduction sizes and percentages using a proportion wheel:

1. Measure the original width (after the picture has been cropped) and write it down. Do the same for the original depth (after the picture has been cropped). Depending on the publication, editors will work in inches or picas, although many editors prefer picas.
2. Determine either how wide the picture needs to be reproduced or how deep it needs to be.
3. Place the original width on the inner part of the wheel directly under the reproduction width on the outer wheel. "Marry" the two wheels together so the placement of the two numbers does not change.
4. Find the original depth on the inner wheel and look on the outer wheel directly opposite it to find the reproduction depth.
5. Look in the small window on the inner part of the wheel to find the percentage.
6. Roundings need to work like this: If the percentage is between two whole numbers, go for the larger number. If the size is between two units, go for the smaller size. This allows for a bit of a safety factor.

For example, an original photo is 4 inches wide by 7 inches deep. If it needs to be reproduced 2 inches wide, the reproduction formula would be:

4 × 7 Original width and depth

2 × ? Reproduction width and depth

The original width of 4 inches would be placed on the inner wheel and the reproduction width of 2 inches would be placed directly above it. Without changing the relationship of those two numbers, find 7 inches on the original (inner) wheel and look to see what is directly opposite it on the reproduction (outer) wheel. The answer, surprise, surprise, is 3.5 inches. Next look in the window on the inner wheel to find the reproduction percentage. The answer is 50 percent.

What this means is that if an original photo 4 by 7 inches is reproduced 2 inches wide, then it will go 3.5 inches deep. The reproduction percentage of 50 percent says that the reproduction is half as big as the original.

Let's look at another example, an original photo 43 by 39 picas. (Remember the first number is the width and the second is the depth. This means the photo is a horizontal. If it were 25 by 54 picas, it would be a vertical.)

If the photo has to be reproduced 28 picas wide, the calculation's relationship would be:

43 × 39 Original width and depth

28 × ? Reproduction width and depth

Another way to express it would be 43 is to 28 as 39 is to the unknown.

The answer is that a picture 43 picas wide by 39 picas deep reproduced 28 picas wide would go 25 picas deep (remember to round back). The percentage would be 65 percent (Figure 8.2).

USE OF A CALCULATOR

To calculate reproduction sizes and percentages using a calculator:

1. Measure the original (after it's been cropped).
2. Determine either the reproduction width OR the depth needed.
3. Divide the reproduction width, for example, by the original width to determine the percentage.
4. Multiply that percentage by the original depth to determine the reproduction depth.

For example, an original image measures 49 picas wide by 31 picas deep. If it's necessary to reproduce the image 35 picas wide, what are the reproduction depth and percentage?

35 ÷ 49 = .7142857 = 72%

.7142857 × 31 = 22.142 = 22 picas deep

Note that it's necessary to **round up the percentage** to the nearest percent, and to **round back the depth** to the nearest half pica, which allows for a little fudge factor.

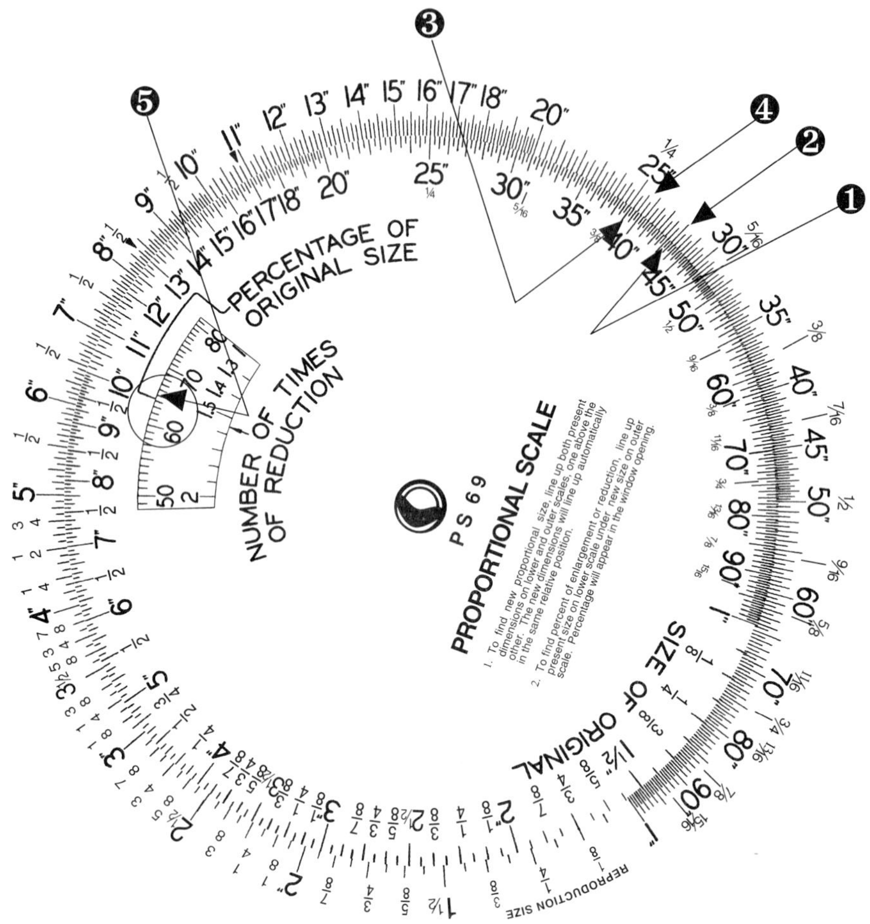

Picture proportioning is a five-step process. If, for example you want to reproduce a 43- x 39-pica photo 28 picas wide you would:

1. Locate 43 picas on the original (inside) wheel.
2. Place 43 so it is directly opposite 28 picas on the reproduction (outer) wheel.
3. Locate 39 picas on the original wheel.
4. Look directly opposite 39 to get the answer, which is 25.5 picas.
5. The reproduction percentage, which is 65 percent, is found in the window of the wheel.

Remember that the reproduction proportions and percentages can vary slightly from wheel to wheel.

Figure 8.2 Using the proportion wheel. The proportion scale is a product of the C-Thru Ruler Co., Bloomfield, Conn.

Flag/Teasers
Briefs/Index
Headline headline headline
Headline headlin headline line line
Headheadli line line Headline line
Headline head line headli headli headline headline he
Headline head line headli headli headline headline he

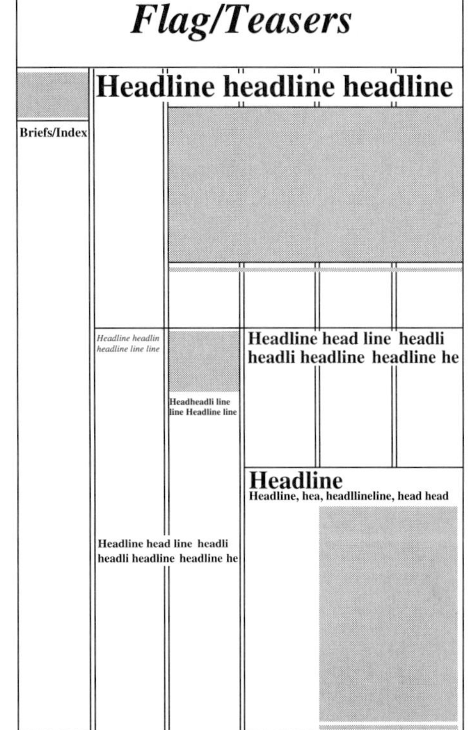

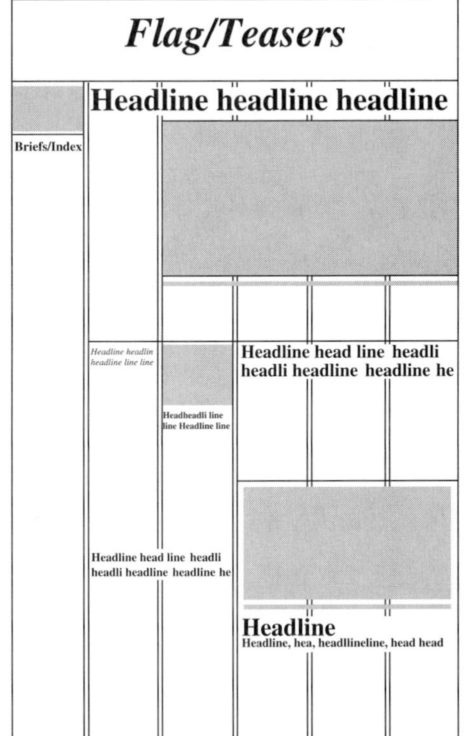

Figure 8.3 A block of space can be allocated in advance when a publication expects a photo and story to come in close to deadline. A horizontal or a vertical photo can be utilized within that space, provided the editor is flexible. As a result, an effective layout can be accomplished very quickly. Obviously the size and placement of the block on the page will be determined by the importance of the deadline event and other elements scheduled for the page.

The Associated Press, as the largest news cooperative in the world, transmits hundreds of photos and graphics each day, hoping to fill the news budgets of more than a thousand clients ranging from small town dailies to huge metropolitan dailies to magazines with circulations in the hundreds of thousands. It's a daunting task, but the AP does it well.

Every day the wire services provide a wide variety of mug shots of news makers and can, on request, provide mug shots of virtually everyone of importance taken from their libraries of more than a million negatives. They provide the latest in sports photos, business pictures from manufacturing companies, plus photos from breaking news from around the world. It's an ever-changing assortment of hard news, features and sports, all designed to act like a cafeteria of images for a ravenous mob with considerably varying tastes.

Other wire photo services are provided by Reuters and Agence France Presse (AFP). Major competition is now coming from AFP, particularly with its strong Caribbean and Central American coverage, and Reuters with its strong world-wide efforts.

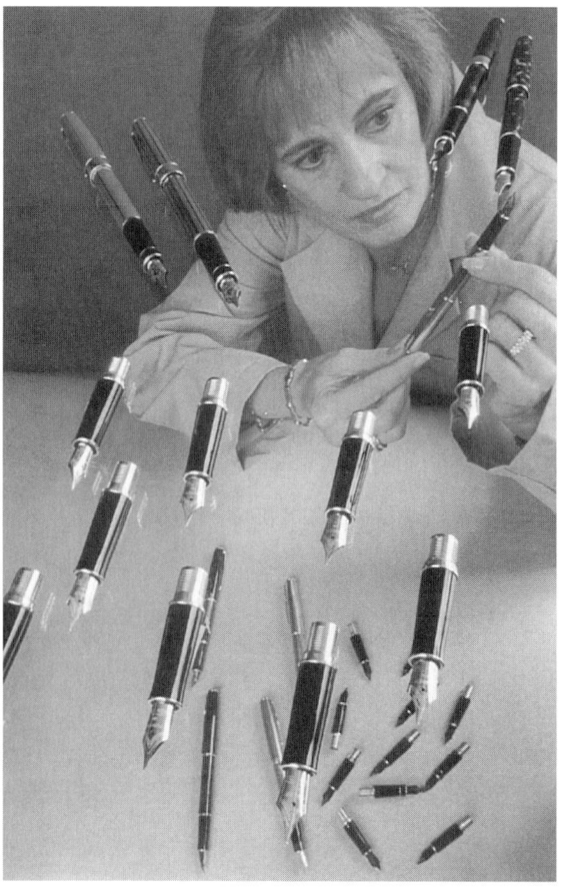

Fountain Pen Sales Gush (The Parker Pen Co.) Business photos are frequently provided by various manufacturing or sales companies. The Associated Press transmits several of these each week, including this one of a person inspecting pens at the Parker Pen Co., headquartered in Janesville, Wis. The cutline transmitted with the photo explains that the pens were displayed on a sheet of glass. This information is necessary to explain to the reader the highly three-dimensional nature of the picture.

Day in and day out, most publications use more than four AP pictures for every one provided by the other services. It's a ratio that is likely to continue, especially in view of the extremely high cost of providing wire photos.

To get the most out of the wire services editors need to know what each service offers, what its specialties are and what to look for regarding the photo caption.

First, the organization of the Associated Press wire photo network:

- Each member publication that wants to receive wire photos can subscribe to that service. Costs are based on the member's circulation.
- State bureau. This management group controls a series of members and acts as a sub-editor, assisting the member with requests and screening photos to determine who else should receive them.
- The next link is the regional district that controls a series of state bureaus.
- From the regional area, a request would move up to the control point, of which there are four: New York City, Washington, Chicago and Los Angeles.
- The overall national control is in New York City. The content of the wire is determined by photo editors working out of offices in Rockefeller Center, just to the north of the famous skating rink that is the scene of Christmas festivities, special television programs and movies.

Working at a computer showing the current photo possibilities, the *national editor*—the picture editor in charge of everything that goes on the national photo wire that shift—determines what sort of photo mix will serve the needs of the various members across the country. Since it's possible to transmit a black and white photo in about one minute (as opposed to eight minutes just a few years ago) and a color photo in three minutes (compared with nearly a half hour), lots of photos can be moved over telephone wire. In the early days of the Associated Press, all copy and photos moved over telephone wires, hence the name wire photo. Today, very little moves over so-called land lines, but rather via satellites.

Regional editors augment the national wire with photos that will be of interest to the states' members that are connected together in that region. Photos of regional college teams that aren't ranked probably will not be seen outside that region. A shot from the University of Rhode Island vs. University of New Hampshire football game, for example, probably won't be sent to California members unless someone there specifically requests. By contrast, a gymnastics photo from the Olympic tryouts at UCLA likely will be sent on the national wire.

Requests for "specials," a term applied to photos that are not part of the usual wire photo mix, should be sent to the state bureau, from where they will be sent directly to the specials desk in New York City. The specials desk editor will make arrangements to have a staff photographer or free-lancer shoot the photo, or, if the negative already exists, will get it printed and transmitted to the requesting member. While it is possible to have a two-hour turn-around on a special, it really can cause problems. You're better off to allow a minimum of four hours, but one day or more is even better.

Specials are appropriate if a high school band from a publication's circulation area has been asked to perform for a festival in Naples, Italy. If the publication cannot afford to send a photographer and reporter along, the authorizing editor should request that AP transmit a photo of the band in Italy. When the request gets to New York, the specials editor will arrange either for an AP staffer in Naples or a free-lancer to shoot the band and transmit the requested photos by the deadline needed. The publication will be billed for the photographer, the transmission charge from Italy and any other expenses that the photographer incurs, such as renting a helicopter for an aerial photo or rush processing at a commercial lab after hours.

USING THE ELECTRONIC PICTURE DESK

While newsrooms have been in the electronic era for nearly 20 years, led there by increasingly expensive human typesetters and the arrival of primitive reporting computers, darkrooms and picture desks were jolted into the electronic age with the 1990 introduction of the Associated Press Leafdesk, an electronic darkroom. AP, Leaf and other manufacturers had been experimenting with the electronic darkroom (ED) for several years.

The 1987 prototype ED was quite primitive, allowing only for the lightening, darkening, cropping, enlarging and captioning of black and white images. Although it also was used to transmit color images, color monitors were not available. Instead two black and white monitors were needed. One showed the typewritten codes used to accomplish the required process and the other monitor showed the visual result.

Today's variation of the ED, the AP Electronic Picture Desk (EPD), is just a highly specialized computer that is geared to working with pictures in a digital format. Most newsroom computers are "dumb" terminals without the ability to operate unless they are connected to a mainframe computer. By contrast, the ED and EPD usually are stand-alone micro- or mini-computers, such as high-powered Macintosh or IBM computers, other specialized computers made by AP's subsidiary Leaf or computers from other companies. Most EDs are connected to pagination terminals where selected photos are placed into the layout.

EDs are specialized computers that will allow the photographer or photo technician to scan photographic negatives or prints, both in black and white and color, and then to edit and even color correct the images. The EPD is not used for scanning and merely allows the editor to call up and edit wire photos or existing staff photos that already have been scanned. Since EDs and EPDs need massive amounts of computing power, most newsrooms have only a handful of them.

The publication's EPD probably will show a menu of all the pictures or visual images in the publication's computer system at that time, much like a copy-editing terminal will show the stories available when one opens the file. It is likely more images will be added to the menu while the editor works, particularly if the publication is receiving wire photos from the AP, Agence France Press, United Press International or others.

Depending on the menu or system being used, one will see the *slug* or name of the file, the date the photo was entered into the system, the time the photo was entered, the size of the file and, depending on the kind of computer or software being used, a visual directory of the images.

WHERE TO GET HELP

The National Press Photographers Association (NPPA) has several very useful items for those desiring to learn more about the ins and outs of photography and picture editing. The first one is membership in the organization. With membership comes *News Photographer,* a monthly magazine filled with photos, articles about photographers and various technical, philosophical and ethical situations. Worth the price of the membership is the yearly Best of Photojournalism, a collection of winning and outstanding images from the Pictures of the Year contest. The contest draws thousands of entries from newspaper and magazine photographers throughout the United States and from other countries as well.

Members and non-members alike race to attend NPPA's Flying Short Course, a day-long seminar featuring the top photographers and picture editors in the business. The seminar staff flies to four or five cities across the United States every fall and does a wonderful job of showing hundreds and hundreds of slides of assignments and picture editing and then, most important to young journalists, being available for questions or to review portfolios. It is the most reasonably priced photo seminar in the country and is well worth a 500-mile drive to attend.

NPPA also holds a yearly convention in the summer. It has a good list of speakers and exhibitions, plus a gathering of photographers and picture editors from around the country.

One event also worth attending is NPPA's Electronic Photojournalism Workshop, generally held in early fall. The hands-on workshop has the latest in electronic still video cameras, film scanners and pagination equipment. The workshop does a publication called *The Electronic Times,* which includes picture stories and layouts done by various methods, such as traditional black and white film versus black and white electronic still images, traditional color film versus color electronic images, and so on. This allows participants to see printed results and to report back to editors on their own publications about what is happening in the field.

The NPPA Foundation also holds the Stan Kalish Picture Editing Workshop during early summer at Marquette University in Milwaukee. Topics include working with photojournalists, meshing words and pictures, the visual content of newspapers, improving the writing in cutlines, assignment origination, and others.

The five-day workshop is limited to about 25 participants, which allows for good interaction between participants and staffers. For more information or to request a membership application, write to: National Press Photographers Association, 3200 Croasdaile Dr., Suite 306, Durham, NC 277054.

The Society of Newspaper Design has a membership consisting mainly of newspaper designers, graphic artists, photographers and picture editors, but with a good representation of copy and layout editors and managing and assistant managing editors.

The society grew out of a desire by graphic artists and editors to share information and to build a professional organization dedicated to improved publication design. In that, SND has been quite successful. In a very short time it organized an exciting contest and publication with such areas as informational graphics, front page design, breaking news, feature pages, illustrations and photographs.

Membership in the organization includes a monthly magazine and, best of all, *The Best of Newspaper Design,* a collection of the top entries in the yearly contest. Ideas for layout, design, picture usage and graphic organization abound in the book. SND's yearly gathering has speakers and workshops where designers ask and answer questions and ideas are virtually taped around the walls.

For more information, or to request a membership application, write to: Society of Newspaper Design, The Newspaper Center, Box 4075, Reston, VA 22090.

BIBLIOGRAPHY AND ADDITIONAL READINGS

Barnhurst, Kevin G. *Seeing the Newspaper.* St. Martin's Press. 1994.

Benson, Gigi, and Harry Benson. *Harry Benson on Photojournalism.* Harmony Books. 1982.

Consumer Photographic Survey, 1985 and 1988. Photo Marketing Association International, Jackson, MI. Table No. 389, Household Camera and Video Equipment Use, by Selected Characteristic: 1985 and 1988. Quoted in *Statistical Abstract of the United States.* U.S. Government Printing Office. 1992.

Finberg, Howard I., ed. *The Best of Photojournalism,* Vol. 18. Running Press. 1993.

Fuji Photo Film U.S.A., Inc. "Taking the Perfect Picture: A Study of the Amateur American Photographer." 1991, p. 7.

Ganzel, Bill. *Dust Bowl Descent.* University of Nebraska Press. 1984.

Garcia, Mario R., and Pegie Stark. *Eyes on the News.* The Poynter Institute for Media Studies. St. Petersburg, Fla., 1991, p. 70.

Gross, Larry, John Stuart Katz, and Jay Ruby, eds. *Image Ethics. The Moral Rights of Subjects in Photographs, Film, and Television.* Oxford University Press. 1988.

Hirsch, Robert. *Color Photography,* 2nd ed. William C. Brown. 1993.

Levey, Marc B., and James Lloyd. *Thinking in the Photographic Idiom. A Book of Perceptual Exercises.* Prentice Hall. 1984.

Roth, Dennis. *Rhythm Vision. A Guide to Visual Awareness.* Intaglio Press. 1990.

Curious Cattle (Photo by Joel Sartore)
Joel Sartore's subtly humorous photo of young cattle checking out a grass fire is a good example of "Hmmm-I've-never-thought-of-that-before." The rancher who owned them said that the cattle had never seen fire before.

Last of the Miners (Photo by Joel Sartore)
A lead and zinc miner points to an old picture of himself with a group of fellow miners in southwest Kansas. In the background to the right is the minehead where he used to work. This is an excellent photo, combining historical (the picture) and contemporary elements (the miner and the old mine) in a striking color composition. The placement of the subject along the left two-thirds of the scene balances the out-of-focus element at the right.

O.J.'s Last Run (Al Schaben/*Los Angeles Times*)
Al Cowlings, with friend O.J. Simpson in the back, pilots the now-famous Ford Bronco down a Los Angeles freeway as a horde of patrol cars follows him. Schaben's photo was used not only in the *Times*, but in magazines and newspapers around the world. In spot news events such as this, position and timing are everything.

▶ PAGE 4 • Friday, September 30, 1994 ▶ THE SIXTH ELECTRONIC TIMES • Chapel Hill, North Carolina

"We try to do in 90 days what should have been done over 18 years."

• Capt. Robert W. Webster, IMPACT Youth Center - East

At left, a drill instructor addresses trainee David Key shortly after his first-day haircut.

Trainee Doug Richards, right, dusts the top of the window in his two-man dorm room at 5 a.m. after reveille.

A new trainee, below, toes the line as he faces a drill instructor on his first day at IMPACT.

Sir, Yes Sir

PHOTOGRAPHER • STEVE JACOBS
EDITOR • KATHERINE FRIEDRICH

"The first word out of your mouth will be sir or ma'am and the last word out of your mouth will be sir or ma'am. Do you understand?" the drill instructor shouts. The new batch of youth offenders seems confused, bewildered – and afraid.

They have arrived at IMPACT-East, a state-run boot camp-style correctional facility located in southeastern North Carolina in an area known as the Sandhills.

A few moments earlier they had been in the custody of civilian probation officers, but now their minds and bodies are in the hands of 18 take-no-nonsense drill instructors. This will be their home for 90 days.

"You're gonna learn some authority here and you're going to learn some respect," a D.I. tells them in a voice set at parade-field volume. "Don't look at me! Eyes straight ahead!"

The youths, called trainees while in the IMPACT program, are told that "Sir, yes sir," is the only acceptable response to a drill instructor's query or command. "We're not running a girl scout camp here," shouts the D.I.

Staff Sgt. Wendell Armstrong gets face-to-face with trainee David Key, a 21-year-old from Sanford.

"What's your crime?" he barks.

"Sir, breaking and entering, sir," Key responds.

"So, you're a thief?" Armstong says, disgust in his voice. "Who did you rob?"

"My parents, sir."

Next comes a standard boot-camp gambit: the shame-and-humiliation speech. It is directed at one trainee, but is meant for all. It's the first of many tactics that state corrections officials hope will shock young criminals into constructive lives.

"I bet they're real proud of you," Armstrong says to Key with exaggerated sarcasm. "I'd be proud of a son like you, too. Sure would. I'd be so proud."

Then he shifts gears. "I tell you what," he says, his voice softer. "I got a little boy. I hope like heck he don't turn out to be like you, 'cause if that's what love is, I don't want no part of it. You say you love your folks; you got a funny way of showing it, son, you sure do."

Tears begin to form in Key's eyes.

"And don't let them eyes well up now 'cause, ya know, I don't care if you cry or not. It don't matter to me 'cause you don't love anybody but yourself," Armstrong continues. "Mom and Dad fed you and clothed you and done all that stuff for you and here's how you pay them back. You think about that for awhile."

On his second day at IMPACT, Key is asked by a visitor what got him sent here.

"Bein' a thief, ma'am," he responds, quietly, ashamedly.

The visitor asks him where he would like to be in five years.

Standing stiffly at attention, he replies, "I want to finish college, get married, have kids, get a good job. I just want to get my life straight."

For at least one trainee, the program already has had an impact.

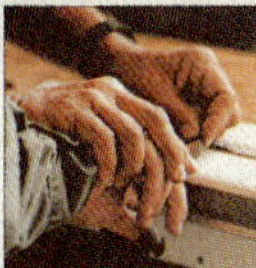

Above, a trainee is fingerprinted as part of the intake process to the program.

Alpha Company Third Platoon trainees, at right, line up for their first flag ceremony on the morning of their second day. The trainees will spend 90 days in the military-style youth offender program.

• INPUT: **AP NC2000 DIGITAL CAMERA** • PAGE PRODUCTION: **QUARKXPRESS 3.3.1** • IMAGE PRODUCTION/TRANSMISSION: **AP PHOTOLYNX, HSC SOFTWARE LIVE PICTURE 1.5, ADOBE PHOTOSHOP 3.0**
• COMPUTER PLATFORM: **APPLE POWER MACINTOSH 8100** • OUTPUT: **SCITEX DOLEV 400PS WITH V.I.P. PENTIUM RIP**

Digital Page (Steve Jacobs, photographer; Kathryn Fredrichs, writer/picture editor —*Albany Times Union*)

A product of Electronic Photojournalism Workshop 6, this picture story was shot using the Associated Press DC2000 digital camera. The story centered on a North Carolina prison boot camp for youthful offenders. The images were edited in a computer and transmitted over a phone line to the workshop site several hundred miles away. In other words, no film was used to produce this excellent picture story! Note the use of the large dominant photo, the initial letter and variety of sizes and shapes of the photos.

A Prayer for Bosnia (Al Schaben/*Los Angeles Times*)
The composition of this powerful image takes advantage of news value, proximity, a wide-angle lens used close to the subjects and dramatic cropping (we shall call this tension cropping). Editors should have the courage to play such images very large.

Surfers on the Beach (Al Schaben/*Los Angeles Times*)
A good example of an environmental portrait, the photograph shows these surfers in their element (the beach) and with the equipment of their jobs (the boards).

AN INTERNATIONAL DAILY NEWSPAPER TUESDAY, DECEMBER 6, 1994 75¢ ($1.00 CANADIAN)

THE CHRISTIAN SCIENCE MONITOR

VOL. 87, NO. 8

US Gets Its Space Plans In Shape for Next Century

By Peter N. Spotts

Staff writer of The Christian Science Monitor

BOSTON

AFTER years of meandering and blue-ribbon panels, the United States finally has a road map for space.

It is moving forward with a new national space policy – one that will guide US plans for space-flight in the 21st century and could determine if the US can compete with the rest of the world as a commercial launcher.

The goal: finding cheaper ways than the shuttle to spirit into the cosmos by developing a new generation of expendable and reusable rockets. While the policy doesn't push the country in a radical new direction, the mere existence of a blueprint is considered significant.

"Is the US in space to stay? If so, we need a new way of getting there," says John Logsdon, director of the Space Policy Institute at George Washington University in Washington.

White House action

The White House is expected to approve a pair of proposals this month that spell out approaches to developing a new generation of rockets. They illustrate the hedge-your-bets attitude embodied in the policy, which the White House unveiled in August.

The Defense Department is to focus on a new family of expendable rockets, evolving out of existing launchers. The National Aeronautics and Space Administration (NASA) intends to take a higher-risk approach: It will help the private sector develop technologies that could lead to a new generation of reusable vehicles, initially unmanned, with far lower operating costs than the shuttle's.

"This is our No. 1 priority," said NASA administrator Daniel Goldin in congressional testimony this fall. "If we have to eliminate tasks or cancel tasks, we are going to do it. Without a new launch vehicle, without low-cost access to space, without a high reliability system, I don't know that we'll be in the space business."

See **SPACE** page 4

NEWT GINGRICH

THE MAN BEHIND THE GAVEL

By Peter Grier

Staff writer of The Christian Science Monitor

WASHINGTON

NEWT GINGRICH was wearing a blue coat and pink pants when he walked into Eddie Mahe's office. It was 1974, and the young Georgian was looking for help in his first race for Congress. Mr. Mahe, then a top Republican Party official, pegged the situation in an instant: Mr. Gingrich was a college instructor and native Northerner who planned to run against a popular incumbent in the South while wearing weird clothes.

In other words, the man was doomed. "I couldn't even figure out how he got through my door in the first place," says Mahe, now a Washington GOP political consultant.

Mahe was right. Gingrich lost that year. But he ditched the double-knits, kept running hard, and in 1978 captured the seat when the longtime incumbent retired. Since then his political career has exploded forward with the force and subtlety of a fastball. Today Newt Gingrich is set to hold a position Republicans had despaired of ever again calling their own – Speaker of the House.

The man whose saber-tooth tactics won this prize for the GOP is arguably one of the most complex politicians of the post-cold-war era. A conservative revolutionary and ex-liberal, a champion of virtue with a troubled family past, a war-trivia buff who also loves zoos – Gingrich is utterly different from his predecessor, Speaker Tom Foley. He's not your father's leader of the House.

Even political opponents concede he has energy and intelligence.

"I have some hope for him," says Richard Dangle, who was dean at West Georgia College when Gingrich was a tenureless instructor. "Newt has a very strong sense of history. He

See **GINGRICH** page 4

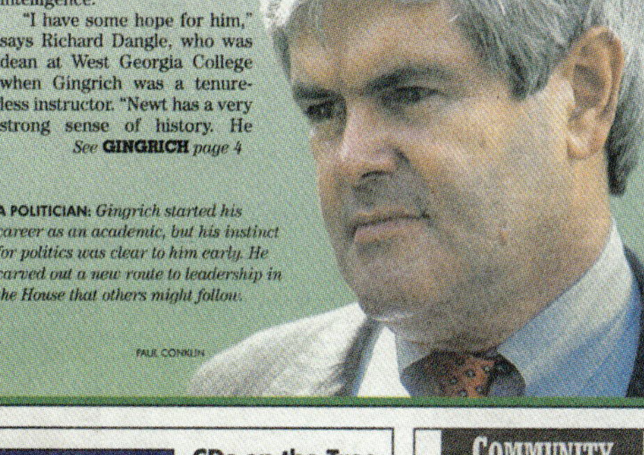

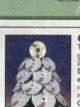

A POLITICIAN: *Gingrich started his career as an academic, but his instinct for politics was clear to him early. He carved out a new route to leadership in the House that others might follow.*

PAUL CONKLIN

After Bosnia, Balkans War Could Shift To Croatia

As Serbs take more land, Croats threaten attack

By David Rohde

Staff writer of The Christian Science Monitor

KNIN, CROATIA

THE "capital" of the self-declared "Serbian Republic of Krajina" inside Croatia could seem almost laughable, except that this corner of former Yugoslavia might become the next arena for war in the Balkans.

Inside the would-be "defense ministry" hang old maps, marked with fresh ink to outline parts of Croatia overrun by rebel Serbs in 1991. A spent artillery shell casing serves as a trash can.

But Knin's streets, filled with young and old men in fatigues carrying weapons, indicate that a widening of the war may soon begin or end here.

Diplomats fear Serbs, on a winning streak in Bosnia, may turn their sights back on Croatia. "We're at a very tense moment," says Peter Galbraith, United States ambassador to Croatia. And in Budapest yesterday, President Clinton told a European summit, "As we strive to end the war in Bosnia, we must work to prevent future Bosnias."

See **KNIN** *page 6*

Liberated Russian Women Doff Hard Hat, Don Apron

By Wendy Sloane

Special to The Christian Science Monitor

MOSCOW

ONCE she was an automobile engineer. Today many would call her a domestic engineer.

But elegant, mink-coated Lena, accompanying her son at Moscow's trendy McDonald's last week, prefers to be called a "society lady."

"I would never refer to myself as a housewife," says Lena, who quit her job when her husband became a prominent businessman – so prominent that she won't give her last name.

Lena may not call herself a housewife, but she spends her days cooking and cleaning, as well as making herself glamourous for her husband when he comes home from work. And in the New Russia, she's not alone.

See **WOMEN** *page 6*

CDs on the Tree

Today's CD-ROMs go beyond video-illustrated books. Entertainment, education, and reference titles would make great Christmas gifts.

10

COMMUNITY

Planned Rebirth For Black Cultural Area in Atlanta

City leaders hope for renovation of avenue where Martin Luther King Jr. was born.

12

Color usage by a publication depends upon several factors, such as the quality of the printing process, the education and social background of the audience and the background of the publication. *The Christian Science Monitor* has excellent reproduction which showcases its photojournalism. The newspaper serves an international audience that tends to be highly educated and well-traveled. Look at how the *Monitor* places its color and compare that with other publications. How would the differences be explained?

THE ORANGE COUNTY **Register**

Partly cloudy
Coast: **62/48** Inland: **68/44**
Details on Metro Page **12**.

Customer service (714) 972-9800

InfoLine (714) 550-INFO (550-4636)

ORANGE COUNTY, CALIFORNIA | WEDNESDAY, DECEMBER 7, 1994 | 23 CENTS

COMPLETE INDEX ON PAGE 2

O.C. seeks breathing room by filing BANKRUPTCY

COUNTDOWN TO FILING OF BANKRUPTCY

Orange County's bankruptcy filing in federal court capped frantic efforts by administrators over the past 10 days to keep its $8 billion investment pool from imploding. Key events Tuesday:

▶ 3 A.M.
County Administrative Officer Ernie Schneider calls supervisors at home and asks them to report to the Hall of Administration for emergency briefings. When he can't reach Harriett Wieder, a police car is dispatched to collect her.

WIEDER

▶ 5:30 A.M.
Wieder calls U.S. Sen. Dianne Feinstein, D-Calif., to ask if she will intercede on the county's behalf with the Securities and Exchange Commission.

Schneider calls James McConnell, Orange County's lobbyist in Washington, D.C., and instructs him to enlist the support of the county's congressmen.

▶ 8 A.M.
Rep. Jay Kim, R-Diamond Bar, gets through to SEC Chairman Arthur Leavitt and asks his help. Leavitt tells Kim that county officials should be calling state officials.

▶ 9 A.M.
McConnell's note is delivered to Rep. Chris Cox, R-Newport Beach, when he emerges from congressional leadership meetings. Cox tells reporters and word rapidly spreads.

COX

▶ 11:30 A.M.
The county investment pool defaults on a $1.2 billion loan.

▶ 5:30 P.M.
Board Chairman Thomas Riley announces the county has filed bankruptcy papers.

FINANCE: Record municipal filing means cities can't withdraw money, for now.

By CHRIS KNAP, JEAN O. PASCO and LIZ PULLIAM
The Orange County Register

Orange County defaulted on a $1.2 billion loan Tuesday, then became the largest municipality ever to file for bankruptcy.

The filing, under the little-known Chapter 9 section of federal bankruptcy law, stunned the international bond market and local taxpayers alike.

The county's bankruptcy attorney said the county would continue to operate and the fund now has protection from withdrawal and loan payoff demands. But 180 local governments, including every county school district and most cities, will not be able to withdraw operating funds.

"It really makes me angry that this situation developed," county Supervisor Roger Stanton said after the Board of Supervisors announced its decision about 5:30 p.m. "But the prudent advice given to us today was to stop the bleeding now."

Bruce Bennett, the county's bankruptcy counsel, made it clear that the Chapter 9 filing freezes all accounts of both the county and the investment pool. That means neither investment bankers nor schoolteachers can be paid.

But county officials were not sure, and Bennett would not say, how they planned to restructure the fund in the next few days. Whether city and county employees, contractors and other vendors will be paid was uncertain Tuesday night.

Orange County's losses on a series of complex bets on interest

Please see **BANKRUPTCY Page 20**

CHARLAINE BROWN/The Orange County Register

TURNING TO CHAPTER 9: Supervisor Thomas F. Riley speaks with county counsel Terry Andrus before a closed meeting Tuesday. Text of Riley's bankruptcy-filing speech is on **Page 19**.

PROJECTS ON THE LINE

CHAPTER 9 — The bankruptcy filing will affect the county's ability to finance large projects. Lenders and bond buyers will be more leery because of concern about the security of their investments. Here are four projects the county was hoping to finance in the next few months:

Eastern Transportation Corridor: Tollway officials say it is too early to tell how the bankruptcy filing would affect plans to sell bonds worth more than $1 billion to finance the Eastern toll road in the spring.

New for 'ball stadium: The filing makes it unlikely the county will be involved in building a stadium to help keep the Rams in Anaheim. "Right now the county's involvement with the new stadium for the Rams has dropped off the priority list," County Supervisor William Steiner said.

South-county courthouse: Financing construction of an $80 million courthouse in Aliso Viejo or Santa Margarita had been planned for the first quarter of next year. That is likely to be put on hold.

Santa Ana courthouse expansion: The county was on the verge of selling $40 million in bonds to finance this project. This also is likely to be delayed.

Source: Orange County, Transportation Corridor Agencies, municipal bond experts

GETTING ANSWERS

Do you have questions or comments?
▶ Call The Orange County Register's InfoLine at **(714) 550-4636**, category **7259**. We'll answer your questions and print a selection of comments in Thursday's paper.
▶ Call the Orange County NewsChannel's two live call-in specials today, from 12:30 to 2 p.m. and from 8 to 9 p.m. Call **(800) 225-5626** to reach OCN's panel of experts.

The Orange County Register

WHAT HAPPENED TUESDAY

Orange County filed for bankruptcy protection after an investment loss the size of the budget of South Dakota. Federal bailout rejected.

WAKE-UP CALL: Supervisors gathered before dawn. **Page 16**
BOND SHOCK: Local municipal bonds stop trading. **Page 17**
B.K. LAW: The chosen firm. **Page 21**

WHAT IT MEANS

The county gets protection from $12 billion of debt in its $20 billion investment portfolio — a fund once held up as exemplar to treasurers.

TARNISH: Taint will linger, Cathy Taylor writes. **Page 16**
QUESTIONS: Call the Register. **Page 16**
VENDORS: Suppliers worry they won't be paid. **Page 19**

HOW IT WILL AFFECT YOU

Schools, cities get locked out, blocking some operating funds. "The idea is to resolve this problem," Supervisor Thomas Riley said.

SCHOOLS: Officials welcome freeze of failing fund. **Page 19**
AGENCIES: Fire, sheriff, libraries, others watch, wait. **Page 18**
POLL: Supervisors responsible? **Metro, Page 3**

WHAT HAPPENS NEXT

Officials work to stabilize treasury and split money for investors. They must use shrinking assets to minimize losses of tax revenue.

RAABE: Citron's assistant and protege takes helm. **Page 16**
CITIES: List of what each invested. **Page 19**
RAMS: O.C. no longer can help pay for stadium. **Sports, Page 1**

Q & A: Why the bankruptcy filing? What will happen to public services?

By RICKY YOUNG
The Orange County Register

Q. Why has Orange County filed for bankruptcy?

A. As a shield from investment bankers and brokerage firms that loaned the county $12 billion to buy higher-return investments. Because bonds securing the loans lost value, creditors want cash for the difference.

Q. Will this affect schools, police and other public services?

A. County officials say no. But schools, the county and the Orange County Transportation Authority use the fund for day-to-day operations. They will be shut out and must use other accounts or incoming money. The OCTA, for instance, has $3 million with Sanwa Bank to help keep operations going.

Q. What money is in the fund?

A. The county and its school districts use the fund as their entire treasury. Many water districts and all cities except Garden Grove, San Juan Capistrano and Tustin also use the fund, but most use it for cash reserves.

Q. Can governments withdraw for something more stable?

A. Not anymore. After riding the crest of the county's high returns for years, they are now trapped as the wave breaks.

Q. Has anyone lost any money yet in the county fund?

A. The losses have been in the value of the securities purchased by the fund. If those are sold, investors lose money. With bankruptcy protection, officials hope to sell with a plan, not in a chaotic run on the fund.

Q. Wasn't the county fund successful?

A. The fund made higher returns than a more conservative state pool. The Orange County Transportation Authority made $80 million more in three years with the county pool than it would have with the state.

But if the OCTA's $1.1 billion investment in the pool has lost 20 percent of its value, that's a $220 million loss.

ALSO IN YOUR REGISTER TODAY

Joffrey, tripped up by financial woes, cancels O.C. run

Stumbling over a $1.6 million deficit, the Joffrey Ballet on Tuesday canceled its April 1995 Orange County performances. A Los Angeles presenter said the cancellation was a precursor to financial reorganization. New York representatives said the company will be on layoff, but would not confirm it was ceasing operation. The L.A. "Nutcracker" performance this month will go on.

Story in Show, Page 3

BELOVED BALLET: Joffrey dancers in 1993 performance.

FBI scrutinizing police behavior in July 4th brawl

After complaints that police mishandled a July 4th melee in Huntington Beach, the FBI has launched an inquiry into possible civil-rights violations, a federal agent said Tuesday. A rowdy crowd of more than 1,000 people jammed downtown streets that night, and the city defends officers' actions to contain violence. Police arrested 117 people on a range of charges before the night was through.

Story in Metro, Page 1

Building interest hurts home sales

November O.C. housing sales fell 6.1 percent, the first year-to-year drop since July 1993, as interest-rate increases hit homes. Story and list of sales by ZIP **in Business, Page 1**

On another Dec. 7, 3 sailors endured first waves of war

Jack Epperson thought bombers overhead were American – until his ship was strafed. Wilbur Salmon was lathering to shave, then a torpedo tore through the USS California. He dived into the flaming sea. Glen Gier said it felt like God picked up the USS Nevada and set it down again. All three think that, like on Dec. 7, 1941, when Japan attacked Hawaii, the United States is again vulnerable.

Story in Metro, Page 1

ANNOUNCEMENT: Rubin, Bentsen and Clinton.

Bentsen steps out, Rubin in

National Economic Council head Robert Rubin has been selected by President Clinton to replace Treasurer Lloyd Bentsen, whose resignation was accepted Tuesday. Rubin must be confirmed by the Senate. **Story on Page 3**

The *Orange County Register* has long been known for its graphics, photography and design excellence. In early December 1994, financial problems forced the county to file for bankruptcy protection.

Things to Note:
Dec. 7

- A huge read-in banner headline in two sizes telegraphs the seriousness of the situation.
- A heavy-rule box contains a time line of events.
- Icons help provide quick reads for county projects on the line.
- A question-answer format helps provide quick information.
- A series of information bars (What happened Tuesday, What it means, etc.) give summaries and keys to related stories inside.
- More teasers at the bottom deal with business, metro and national news.

Los Angeles Times

Sunday Final

CIRCULATION: 1,104,651 DAILY / 1,502,120 SUNDAY

SUNDAY, JUNE 19, 1994

COPYRIGHT 1994 / THE TIMES MIRROR COMPANY / CCY / 496 PAGES

$1.50 SUNDAY DESIGNATED AREAS HIGHER

COLUMN ONE

Teaching Patriarchs to Lead

■ Inspired by a football coach, Promise Keepers tells Christian men to take charge of their families. Critics fear politics may overshadow.

By LARRY B. STAMMER
TIMES RELIGION WRITER

Suppose 50,000 cheering, foot-stomping men show up at Anaheim Stadium not to watch the California Angels, but to confide in one another about sexual indiscretions, anger at their fathers, or being insensitive to their wives and children.

Suppose they laugh at their male habits—such as channel surfing with the remote control or refusing to ask for directions.

Then suppose they admit that they are self-absorbed, followed by penitential tears and promises to be better husbands, fathers and grandfathers.

This is Promise Keepers, a burgeoning men's movement rooted deeply in evangelical Christianity that is sweeping the nation.

In the three years since its founding by controversial University of Colorado football coach Bill McCartney, about 20,000 men have signed pledges committing themselves to improve as husbands and fathers. By the end of July, an estimated 225,000 men will have packed stadiums and sports arenas from the Hoosier Dome in Indianapolis to Folsom Stadium in Boulder, Colo. The conference last month in Anaheim was the first of six to be held this year.

The agenda? To strengthen the family and restore the nation by exhorting men to become "promise keepers instead of promise breakers."

Promise Keepers asserts that men, by walking away from their family duties, are responsible for much of America's societal dysfunction, which the group's leaders say includes high school dropouts, a soaring crime rate, racism, divorce, homosexuality and abortion. The women's movement, Promise Keepers says, is at least in part a reaction to the pain and abuse women suffer at the hands of men. This analysis worries critics, who say that such talk could move the group beyond the family to political activism.

Some observers see Promise Keepers as the latest turn in the search for male identity in a fast-changing and conflicted society. In American history through the 1950s, the family structure was

Please see PROMISE, A20

U.S. Ties Switzerland in Its World Cup Opener

U.S. forward Eric Wynalda scored on a free kick near the end of the first half, giving the American team a 1-1 tie with Switzerland in a World Cup soccer game at Pontiac, Mich. With the tie, the United States earned its first point in the World Cup finals since 1950. C1

More soccer coverage, A8-9, C8-11

Two Koreas Agree to First Summit Ever

By RONALD BROWNSTEIN
TIMES STAFF WRITER

WASHINGTON—The leaders of North and South Korea tentatively agreed Saturday to an unprecedented summit meeting, but the Clinton Administration cautioned that the United States will continue to maintain pressure on North Korea to freeze its nuclear program.

One senior Administration official hailed as a "positive development" the reports that South Korean President Kim Young Sam had accepted an offer from his North Korean counterpart, Kim Il Sung, to meet. Such a summit would be the first between the leaders of the two nations since

Please see KOREA, A25

World Cup's Passion, Pride Fill Rose Bowl

By SONIA NAZARIO and MARC LACEY
TIMES STAFF WRITERS

Throngs of giddy soccer fans turned the Rose Bowl on Saturday into a sea of curly blond wigs, flapping flags and World Cup-mania as the world's most popular sporting contest arrived in Southern California.

The game itself featured the Colombian and Romanian national teams—but much of the action was in the stands and on the streets: wig-wearing people paying tribute to the flowing locks of Colombia midfielder Carlos Valderrama; national colors painted on faces and flown on flags; drums pounding, horns blowing, celebrants hopping in pregame victory dances.

The Colombian fans greatly outnumbered the Romanians, but New York taxi driver Vladimir Moraru, who emigrated from Romania, remarked: "Don't forget that the ball is still round for both sides."

Moraru was proven correct as the Romanians defeated the favored Colombian team, 3-1. Throughout the hard-fought contest, fans tried to create an advantage with their cheers.

"Hagi! Hagi! Hagi!" the Romanians shouted, chanting the name of their star player, Gheorghe Hagi.

"Asprilla! Asprilla! Asprilla!" the Colombians shot back with the name of one of their stars, Faustino Asprilla.

The name of Gov. Pete Wilson, however, prompted a chorus of boos when he marched to the center of the field during opening ceremonies. From the moment Wilson was introduced, all the way through his three-minute speech, the mostly Latino audience jeered him for past comments blaming illegal immigrants for many of the state's problems. When Wilson left the field, he faced a sea of thumbs-down gestures.

"We booed Wilson because he is against all Latinos, not just the

Please see WORLD CUP, A9

Simpson Under Suicide Watch as D.A. Moves to Indict Him

AXEL KOESTER / For The Times

Curiosity-seekers gaze toward O. J. Simpson's Brentwood home. Simpson is being held in jail without bail.

■ **Crime:** But grand jury proceedings hit a snag as the first witness reportedly demands immunity. Arraignment of the football legend is expected Monday.

By GREG KRIKORIAN and RICH CONNELL
TIMES STAFF WRITERS

A day after being captured outside his 5,700-square-foot Brentwood estate, football legend O.J. Simpson spent Saturday under suicide watch in a 7-by-9-foot jail cell, where he is being held without bail as prosecutors prepare to seek murder indictments from the county grand jury.

The 46-year-old Hall of Fame running back, whose bizarre low-speed escapade through freeway traffic Friday capped a week of morbid melodrama, is expected to be arraigned Monday on charges that he fatally stabbed his ex-wife and her male friend in a bloody June 12 attack.

His attorney, Robert L. Shapiro, who failed earlier to surrender Simpson as promised, described his client as distraught and emotionally drained.

"He was morose. He was exceedingly depressed. And he was in tears," Shapiro said outside the Men's Central Jail, where a deputy is on guard to keep Simpson from harming himself. "And his words to me were that he apologized to me and to everyone else for what he put people through [Friday]."

Among the day's developments:

• Prosecutors have convened the Los Angeles County Grand Jury, according to sources, who said that the first witness was called Friday. Officials are using the closed-door proceedings to avoid the spectacle of a preliminary hearing, but they hit a snag after the unidentified witness reportedly refused to testify unless granted immunity.

• Although no decision has been made about seeking the death penalty, Dist. Atty. Gil Garcetti said that he may use Simpson's attempted escape as evidence of guilt in the brutal slayings of Nicole

Please see SIMPSON, A10

Simpson News Inside

■ IN CUSTODY—The special County Jail area, known as the "high power unit," where Simpson is being housed has held many famous—and infamous—defendants. A13

■ COMMUNITY—Once a sleepy enclave and "nice little secret," Brentwood squirms under the sudden media spotlight. A13

■ CHILDREN—Nicole and O.J.'s son and daughter are coping well with the past week's tragedies, the family says. A14

■ MIND-SET—Psychologists say Simpson appeared Friday to be out of control, suicidal and genuinely distraught over his ex-wife's death. A14

■ MORE COVERAGE—Additional stories, photos, graphics A11-A16

'I'm Sorry for Putting You Guys Out'

■ **Police:** Simpson collapsed in officers' arms. Details of bizarre day are revealed.

By JIM NEWTON
TIMES STAFF WRITER

When it was all over, O.J. Simpson turned to the Los Angeles police officers who had talked him into giving up, and he calmly, quietly apologized.

"I'm sorry for putting you guys out," said a drawn and haggard Simpson, whose flight from justice transfixed an anxious nation Friday night. "I'm sorry for making you do this."

According to Los Angeles Police Department Special Weapons and Tactics officers who brought the pursuit to its successful conclusion at Simpson's Brentwood [illegible], Simpson shook a few hands and [illegible] turned himself over to detectives.

"It was quite a moment," said Sgt. Charles L. Duke, a senior member of the SWAT team and former college football player for the University of Arizona who once met Simpson on the gridiron. "Quite an evening."

As he walked to the waiting police car, Simpson was escorted, at his request, by SWAT Officer Pete Weireter, a chiseled 17-year veteran who spent 50 tense minutes talking with Simpson over a cellular phone as helicopters buzzed overhead and the world-famous athlete sat alone in his best friend's car, cradling two pictures of his family, a rosary and a gun.

Simpson was confused and frightened in those conversations, officers said, but eventually agreed to come inside when he was promised that he could use the bathroom, have something to drink and call his mother.

He did, and less than an hour later, Simpson was booked on two counts of first-degree murder at Downtown police headquarters.

Here, based on interviews with key participants in the apprehension of Simpson, is an inside look at the most spectacular pursuit in Los Angeles police history.

The hunt began around noon, when LAPD officers made the shocking discovery that Simpson had fled the San Fernando Valley home where he was said to have been meeting with his doctors in advance of turning himself in on charges that he murdered his ex-wife and a male friend of hers.

News of Simpson's disappearance rocked the upper reaches of the LAPD, which had expected the Hall of Famer to surrender around 11 a.m. at police headquarters. Told that their suspect was, as police say, "in the wind," they scrambled to contain the damage and to recover their famous fugitive.

The first calls went to local law enforcement agencies—the Los Angeles County Sheriff's Department and neighboring police departments. The U.S. Border Patrol was alerted, a warning that had special significance because no one

Please see POLICE, A12

Simpson's Peculiar Behavior Could Aid in His Defense

By HENRY WEINSTEIN
TIMES LEGAL AFFAIRS WRITER

The thorny task of defending O.J. Simpson on charges that he murdered his former wife and her friend may have been aided by Simpson's peculiar behavior Friday, when he failed to surrender and led police on a two-hour journey from his ex-wife's Orange County grave site to his Brentwood home, according to legal experts.

"Somehow it seems to have generated a lot of sympathy for him," said Loyola University law professor Laurie Levenson. "I don't think the public will hold it against him that he took the police on this excursion, and the defense can use this bizarre behavior" to its advantage.

Other experts agreed. But they cautioned that it is likely to be at least several weeks before it becomes clear whether Simpson will maintain his innocence or decide to contend that he was mentally disturbed at the time of his ex-wife's slaying.

"Assuming that the prosecution's forensic evidence tying Mr.

Please see DEFENSE, A15

SUNNY SUNG / Los Angeles Times

In Pasadena, Carmo Sofio and other fans wear wigs in tribute to Colombian midfielder Carlos Valderrama.

INSIDE TODAY'S TIMES

ALLIES SALUTE BERLIN

Nearly 2,000 U.S., French and British soldiers marched for the last time down Berlin's main boulevard in a farewell parade. A24

MEXICO FANS KILLED

A plane chartered in Mexico and carrying World Cup fans crashed approaching Dulles International Airport, killing all 12 people aboard. A30

CHAPLAIN SLAIN

A volunteer L.A. County sheriff's chaplain was shot to death and a deputy critically wounded after giving a man a ride during a patrol. B1

WEATHER: Mostly clear and warm inland today and Monday. Civic Center low/high today: 62/86. Details: B2

■ TOP OF THE NEWS ON A2

The Old Man and the Boy: a Father-Son Bond Grows

■ **Parenting:** In Koreatown 13 years ago, a black man finds an abandoned baby. 'Roy is God's gift to me,' he says.

By K. CONNIE KANG
TIMES STAFF WRITER

In many corners of Los Angeles' Korean community, the old black man and the young Korean boy often cause heads to turn.

To be sure, they are an odd couple, but that's not the only reason they draw looks.

The love between them is so evident—the way it is between fathers and sons who are very close. They may not have the money to visit Disneyland or Universal Studios on a whim, but off they go to Kenneth Hahn Lake in Baldwin Hills to fish or to a church picnic in the South Bay, looking happy riding in the old man's gray 1985 Dodge Ram pickup. The car radio is tuned to a Christian station and the old man can be heard singing "Amazing Grace" as he negotiates the snarled traffic.

For nearly 13 years, Leon T. Graves, 68, has reared Roy Chung, whom he found crying and near death as an infant, abandoned by his mother.

"Roy is God's gift to me," said Graves, who despite his age and ailments, prepares Roy's meals, drives him to and from his school, music and martial arts classes and Korean church functions.

The African American and the Korean are inseparable, doing everything together. Roy has even taken to unconsciously emulating the posture of Graves, who walks

Please see FATHER, A35

The *Los Angeles Times* serves one of the most intensely competitive media markets in the world.

Things to Note:

- The use of modified up style headlines.
- Square bullets precede boldface label heads used under most headlines.
- Cutoff rules separate decks from bylines.
- Most stories are jumped.
- Refers for Simpson stories use a combination of bullets and boldface labels, plus short summary sentences.
- This page does not use skyboxes, which is unusual for most national Sunday newspapers.

■ FISHING REPORT: Herring still recovering / C-2 ■ MONEY MARKETS: Weekly wrap-up / C-4

BUSINESS

SUNDAY, December 25, 1994 ANCHORAGE DAILY NEWS SECTION C

DAVID REAUME

No need to maul the budget just yet

Last month's column closed with the statement that "Continued investment in the Alaska economy is not the bonehead play some Cassandras have been implying."

Two assumptions were spelled out that partially justified that conclusion, at least in my mind. First, anything that happens 10 or more years into the future should be heavily discounted when making today's decisions, and second, Gov. Tony Knowles is smart enough not to kill the golden goose prematurely by needlessly savaging the state government budget. The second assumption, of course, begs the BIG question. How can the governor avoid savaging the budget, given what "everybody knows" to be a gloomy outlook for state

Please see Page C-5, REAUME

OPEC dominating world oil production
In millions of barrels per day

World wide production

OPEC production

'85 '86 '87 '88 '89 '90 '91 '92 '93

U.S. oil production shrinking
In millions of barrels per day

U.S. production

Alaska production

'85 '86 '87 '88 '89 '90 '91 '92 '93

Fewer rigs drilling
Average number of rigs per month

Worldwide rigs

U.S. rigs

'85 '86 '87 '88 '89 '90 '91 '92

Sources: U.S. Department of Energy's "Annual Energy Review," Alaska Department of Revenue

RON ENGSTROM / Anchorage Daily News

In value-conscious 1990s, Consumer Reports almost hip

By CONNIE KOENENN
Los Angeles Times

YONKERS, N.Y. — It's Monday morning and Tara Casaregola and Ruth Greenberg are preparing hamburgers, shaping the meat into uniform patties and lining them up on a broiler rack precisely two inches apart.

"We're applying basic scientific methodology here," Casaregola says, closing the oven door. "They're the same thickness and they'll be on broil for exactly 11 minutes."

Beyond them in the immense kitchen 19 more ovens await. "We'll test each oven

Please see Page C-6, CONSUMER REPORTS

BOB HALLINEN / Anchorage Daily News

Roger and Donna Kimura, owners of World of Travel Ltd., with employees, from left: Carol Morgan, Gayle Brooks, Ruth Doolan-McNearney and Roxanne Fick

SOLDIERS IN THE FARE WAR

The dividend battle is hell.

Dec. 15 was nothing short of a battle zone for travel agents. Desks were stockpiled with chocolate, Diet Pepsi and other ammunition as customers, tickets and paperwork bombarded agents across the state.

By Danielle Stevens
Daily News business reporter

Travel agent Carol Morgan remembers the day vividly. The World of Travel Ltd. office was in a frenzy, she said. Phones ringing, customers swirling through the door and paperwork avalanching the desks. With her comrades, she sniffed on Kleenexes doused with aromatherapy oils to alleviate stress.

Agents played tag-team just to use the restroom. Others caught in the throngs skipped lunch, put in 12 hours and stayed late to clean up the mess.

"Everyone was in a panic," Morgan said. One way for her to cope was to take some work home over the weekend along with a "good stiff drink."

That day – Dec. 15 – was the first of a series of deadlines for Alaskans to

Please see Page C-3, TRAVEL

The *Anchorage* (Alaska) *Daily News* has a well-deserved reputation for being an innovative newspaper. Its relative isolation from traditional publication design centers, such as New York, Los Angeles, Amsterdam, Munich and Madrid, proves that distance has no bearing on good design. Note its use of color, type choices and layout formats in achieving visual impact. (Courtesy of the *Anchorage Daily News*)

Chapter 9

GRAPHICS

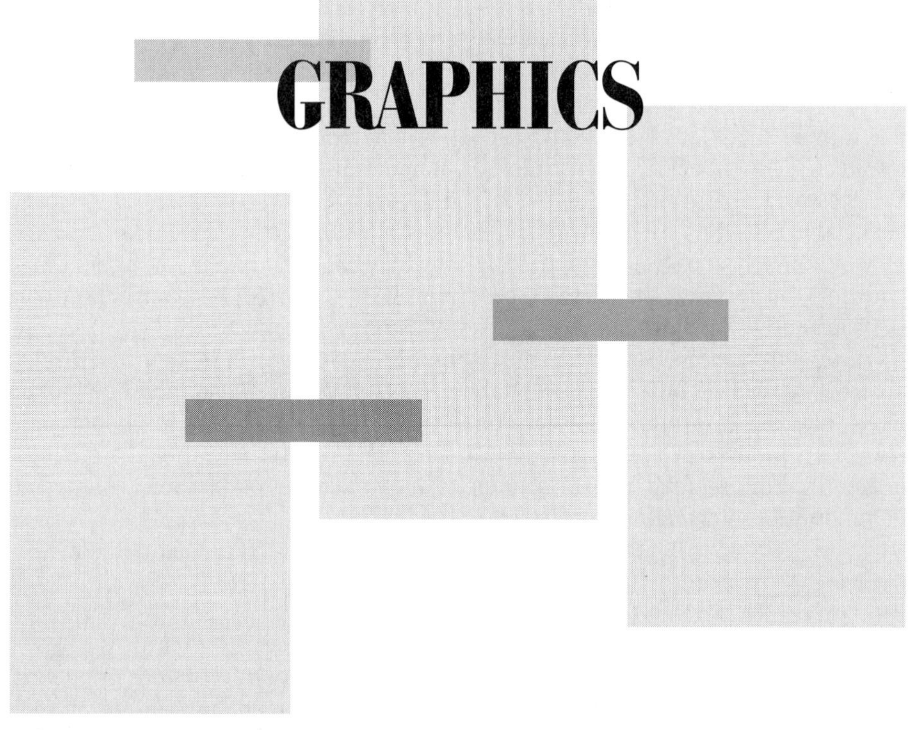

IT'S ALL *USA TODAY*'S FAULT

USA Today gets the credit, or blame, for popularizing a national revolution in the way publications present statistical and explanatory material: *infographics.* In reality, the *St. Petersburg Times* and a few others were doing many of the same experiments on a regular basis years before *USA Today* got off the ground. However, *USA Today*'s wide distribution gave it more influence in the development of a "national standard" of graphics. The end result has been that almost every publication in the country has since rushed to use increasingly elaborate charts, maps and graphics, even to the extent of running complex full-page color graphics about the weapons of war, dinosaurs, the solar system and the problems of overfishing.

Publications have jumped on the graphics bandwagon, in some instances despite themselves, because of the popularity of *USA Today* and the tremendous impact it has had on design in general. The paper was one of the first publications that made a really serious attempt at grabbing for a national audience. Specifically the paper was designed for business travelers and for those who have lived in numerous states. To that end the paper was designed to be a quick read, to have lots of sports and to have some news from each state on a daily basis.

To be read quickly, an essential element for business travelers, *USA Today* relies heavily on rather short articles (usually about 8 to 10 inches long), lots of color (used to help identify specific sections) and a heavy dose of infographics. The latter provides an ideal device to visually explain locations of countries, how a missile operates, where the bank robbery took place or even how many shoes are manufactured around the country.

Some curmudgeons criticize *USA Today* for its short stories and splashy color. They say it lacks depth and uses too many photos and way too many artsy graphics. The paper has been called "a monument to the short attention span."

However, infographics existed way before *USA Today,* perhaps as long ago as 30,000 B.C. when early Europeans painted a bison inside a cave near Lascaux, France. An arrow painted on a tree to show directions to hikers, an airport map showing the location of gate G-3 or a pie chart showing the distribution of a high school girl's allowance are all examples of infographics.

Our alphabet has evolved from somewhat concrete drawings into highly abstract symbols. The *A* of our alphabet means *aleph,* or oxen, and once looked like a stylized drawing of an ox. The *B* means *beth,* the word for house, and shows a window-like appearance. Both these letters, just like their 24 siblings, are nothing more than a form of infographic, a symbol or picture designed to communicate information quickly and effectively.

WHY USE GRAPHICS?

What if one produced an absolutely informative publication filled with great writing and only 25 percent of the people who picked it up spent any amount of time reading it? That would be pretty depressing, wouldn't it? Now what if one could take that same information and repackage it in a more visual format and have close to 75 percent of the people spend time with it? Would that be worth doing? What is the likelihood of one's doing that if one's salary and/or job depends on retaining readers? In all probability one's job and one's future do indeed rely on doing just that: producing a more visual product.

Infographics provide a quick read of information that sometimes is complex, confusing or just plain dull. Returning to a point made in Chapter 8, readers are not spending much time with newspapers, and the competition for the reader's time is growing more fierce as the so-called "information highway" becomes more crowded. It is simply incumbent upon editors to provide their audience with more information, not less, and in an easier-to-read format. That format must include informational graphics, especially since infographs, just like photographs, provide the largest amount of information in the least time.

Statistics from the Society of Newspaper Design and the American Press Institute show that use of infographics has skyrocketed from what we will call the infancy of contemporary graphic presentation in the early 1980s into rather commonplace acceptance of the art. At the same time, the bloom is off the computer, so to speak, and editors and readers alike have more sophistication about what graphics can and should do. The early crudely drawn black and white computer graphics have given way to very sophisticated multi-color presentations made possible by quantum leaps of both hardware and software.

Today's college-age reader cannot remember a day when television did not exist, when computers weren't commonplace in schools and homes and when video games and laser shows weren't staples of entertainment. It can be argued that because of the pervasive nature of television and its instant analysis and its 26-minute-from-crime-to-trial shows, today's readers have neither the training nor the patience to wade through vast amounts of information; hence the popularity of the infographic.

For whatever reason one cites, infographics can and do provide voluminous amounts of information quickly and effectively. An editor may be able to explain the city budget better with one graphic than with a lengthy story. Research shows that most readers spend time with less than 25 percent of the body text and that nearly 90 percent of the readers spend time with images.

This does not mean that a publication should devote itself entirely to photos and graphics; instead, photos and graphics must be recognized as integral parts of the information supply system.

CHOOSING GRAPHICS

Just as journalists have learned that each story can be written several different ways, including variations on leads, verb tenses, pacing and theming, graphics too can have different approaches. For the most part there is not one way only to do a graphic, but some situations do seem to lend themselves to a particular solution. Let's take a look at some of the choices available:

- **Charts**—Any time you have a story with a bunch of numbers in it, such as the city budget, inflation rates over the past few years, number of hamburgers consumed in the cafeteria or the costs of health insurance in five states, a chart is a likely way to present that information.

  Bar Bar charts use a series of rectangles along a common base to show the relationship of one number to another. For example, each separate column can represent one year or five years or a hundred years, while the height or length of that column can allow for a quick comparison of 1,000 units for one year with 1,250 units for the next year.

  Pie This kind of graphic is particularly useful for showing how any sort of unit, such as a budget or military unit or library, is divided or allocated. Pie charts require a known quantity, rather than an indefinite amount. Fever charts are much better suited to incomplete or indefinite amounts.

  Fever If you need to show a trend, then a fever chart is probably your best bet. Just as hospital charts of old show a patient's temperature over a period of days, so do fever charts show the rise and fall of stock or gasoline prices over days or weeks or years.

  Combination It is possible to use two or more different types of charts in one graphic, especially if one has to show different kinds of data. Pie and fever or bar chart combinations are not unusual.

- **Locator maps**—A staple of newspapers and magazines, locator maps are essential for showing readers where events are taking place. The rise in locator map use can be attributed partly to the fact that most readers have an abysmal understanding of geography, even on a local level. Locators show an event's location in relation to more easily recognizable landmarks, such as Pyongyang in relation to the Korean peninsula or Slovenia in relation to the former country of Yugoslavia.
- **How-to**—This special category of graphic is very useful for explaining how complex and not-so complex things work or take place. How-to graphics are frequently used to explain military and space hardware, and they crop up like mushrooms during wars, the Olympics and times of earthquakes, explosions, plane crashes and other disasters.
- **Info or stat boxes**—Less a graphic than a list, an info or stat box is an efficient way to show the highlights of a tax package, a person's very brief biography or even highlights of a sports figure's career. Usually the info box will use light screening to provide differentiation between alternate lines of type.
- **Time line**—A variation of how-to graphic, the time line works well for any story dealing with a sequence of events. A graphic showing the last hours of a murder victim, for example, can help the reader put the event in perspective. The time line might show the victim leaving a theater at 10:15 p.m., driving to a club and arriving at 10:45 p.m., leaving the club at 1:30 a.m., walking to a convenience store and arriving at 1:37 a.m., leaving the store at 1:50 a.m. and then getting shot at 1:52 a.m. in the parking lot. Time line graphics are usually combined with other explanatory graphics, such as info boxes or locator maps.

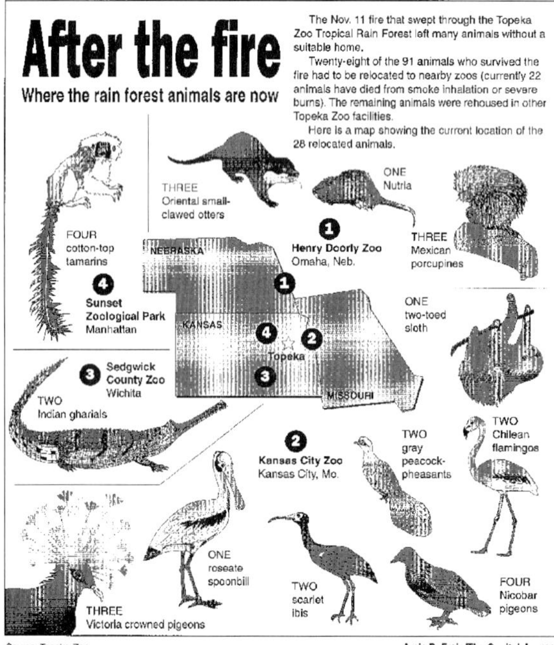

Figure 9.1 A combination locator map and detailed identifier by Amie DeFrain of the Topeka *Capital-Journal* shows how a follow-up graphic can be quite effective.

Things to note:

- The use of reversed numbers to match animals with their new homes
- Good copy provides a summary for readers
- Drawings of the birds and animals allow the linking of images with names

brain
Nervous system
spinal cord
nerve
Amyotrophic lateral sclerosis
(Lou Gehrig's disease)
What is it?
An incurable disease of the nerve cells in the brain and spinal cord that control your voluntary muscles.
Causing no pain or other signs of abnormailty, the affected nerve cells gradually shrink and disappear. Muscles then waste away since the nerves that stimulate them are gone.
What happens?
The person slowly loses strength and coordination in one or more limbs. Swallowing, speaking or breathing becomes difficult. As the disease worsens, a person can become completely paralized and need a mechanical ventilator for breathing.
Although people can live with ALS for several years, the disease is fatal. Most people die within 2 to 10 years after being diagnosed.
Who can get ALS?
People between 40 to 70 are most often affected. Men are three times more likely to be affected than women.
This disease is not contagious, but other family members are sometimes affected.
Sources: The Mayo Clinic Family Health Book (1990), The Marshall Cavendish Encyclopedia of Family Health (1991), Professional Guide to Disases (fourth edition, 1992), Diseases (1993) and World Book Encyclopedia (1987).
— The Capital-Journal

Figure 9.2 An explanatory graphic helps readers understand complex issues by using various summary and artistic devices to present stories in a concise, visual fashion. A deadly disease was explained in this fashion by the *Topeka Capital-Journal*'s Amie DeFrain.

Things to note:

- Numerous sources are listed for this graphic
- The use of a black figure allows the nervous system to stand out
- The information box is overlaid on the side of the figure, helping create a three-dimensional effect
- The neutral direction of the graphic would allow for placement on either side of the story, although the box probably would work better as an anchor on the right side of a layout

- **Complex**—Complex or blockbuster graphics use a bit of everything, such as a locator map to show where a plane crashed; an info box to list the specifications of the crashed plane (number of passengers, crew, engines, range, etc.); a fever chart to show the number of plane crashes over the last 10 years; a how-to graphic to show how the plane crashed, where the survivors exited the plane and the route the rescuers had to take to get to the plane. All this information can then be wrapped in a box and inserted into the layout as a self-contained element.

GRAPHIC ELEMENTS

The work of the graphics reporter or designer or editor often includes the origination of various graphics devices to help make a story stand out on a page or help create a specific "look" for a series or a special topic. Most of the devices that follow in this section can be used with any article; however, since most daily newspapers are quite conservative with their layouts, one finds that the devices tend to be used most often on feature sections and for series.

One of the most commonly used graphic devices is the *logo* or *bug* (so-called because this item can look like a bug when viewed from a distance). It is used

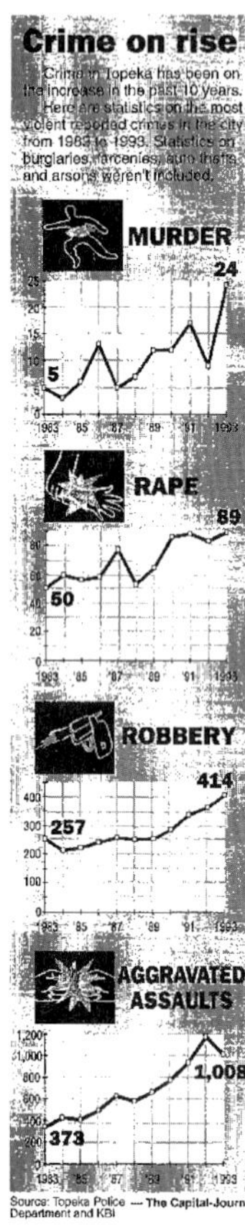

Figure 9.3 Statistics of any sort give editors instant graphics. The particular kind of graphic (pie, bar, fever, etc.) depends upon the statistics. For a series on crime, Amie DeFrain of the *Topeka Capital-Journal* used simple fever charts.

Things to note:

- The layout is in a deep one-column, which allows for good layout flexibility with copy, headlines and photographs
- Simple logos were used to help provide attention-getting artwork
- Bold beginning and ending numbers are used on the trend lines, which provides for a quick read on the graphic
- Vertical and horizontal lines on the graphics are shaded, which allows the darker trend lines to pop out

to create a visual symbol that can be easily recognized by the reader and is especially useful for multi-part articles that appear over several days. Most logos will vary in size from a half-column vertical to a multi-column horizontal, depending on the story.

Logos tend to be run larger when a series is kicked off and then in a reduced form for subsequent days. Logos can include a graphic symbol, such as a handgun, plus a few words of type, or just the words alone, usually set in more elaborate display type than is used for the publication's usual head face.

Pull quotes (also called drop quotes or quote-outs) and *pull-outs* (sometimes called readouts) are pulled from a story and inserted into the layout to provide a quick read of a salient fact or quote from someone mentioned in the text. Pull quotes are set larger than body type, perhaps 14 or 18 point, and frequently are set off from the text by rules (from hairline to 6 point) above and below the quote. Pull quotes are usually in italic type, and the attribution usually is in roman and may be in bold or a different size to separate it from the quote.

Pull quotes may be set flush left or centered. It is not recommended that pull quotes be set justified.

Pull-outs, which are not direct quotations from news sources but rather the writer's words repeated for emphasis, are usually set in roman type to differentiate them from pull quotes.

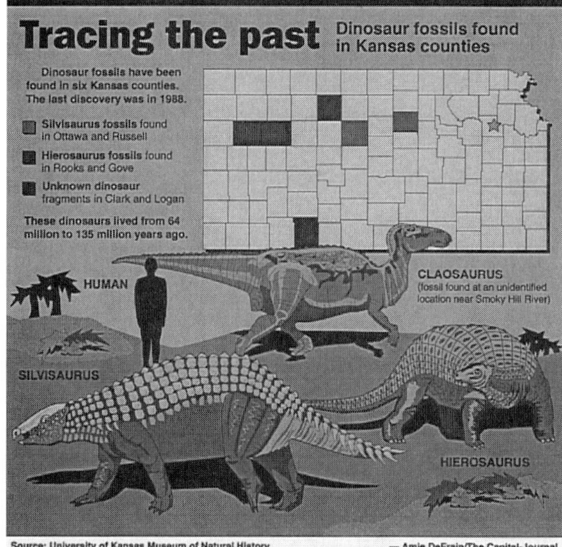

Figure 9.4 The use of a legend (originally in color) helps readers to quickly find which fossils have been found in which counties. A combination of scanning and drawing helped the *Topeka Capital-Journal*'s Amie DeFrain produce this complex graphic.

Things to note:

- Legends allow readers to quickly link geographic locations with the fossils found there
- The silhouette of a person is used to provide a scale to the size of the dinosaurs
- The use of a consistent light source results in shadows which generate a three-dimensional effect for the animals

Initial letters, which are set usually in 36- or 48-point type, help to kick off feature or project stories, but are not usually used on routine stories. Initials come in three forms, but only one form should be used per story. The forms are:

- Indented
- Stand-up
- Hanging

The *indented initial letter* has the text wrapped around it on the right and bottom and requires little additional space (just that taken by the letter itself). This makes it a favorite graphic device when space is tight.

The *stand-up initial letter* has the base of the letter aligned with the base of the body type, with the rest of the initial sticking up above the body text. An additional line of spacing is required above the initial for aesthetic reasons. One can use the stand-up initial in several ways, set flush left, indented some or even centered.

The *hanging initial letter* hangs out in space on the left side of the text and can be aligned with the base or top of the text. Bookman Bold with Swash is a good choice for this, particularly when the initial is a letter A. Generally one should have additional space on the left, such as an extra half-column or so, to take advantage of this kind of device.

Bullets are great devices for setting off a series of items in a story, such as the four major points of a new cat-licensing ordinance or the six issues in the mayor's re-election campaign. While bullets are large round dots, other devices that fall under this category can be triangles, called "deltas," or squares, either filled or open. Some of the time an open square can be combined with a check mark, much like a check mark on an old-style ballot. This form can be useful for enumerating election-oriented issues. Also, while most publications will continue to use traditional bullets, the delta is catching on, not because it's better but probably because it represents a change.

Another graphic device that can be used effectively is the *lead-in,* in which the top of the story is set in larger type and perhaps a contrasting face. Lead-ins are suited particularly for complex projects or lengthy articles, especially those that might be lacking strong visual elements. Either roman or italic posture

Figure 9.5 Spot news situations inevitably are confusing because of conflicting information. One way to help readers understand a situation is to use several graphics combined. A siege in a federal building in Topeka, Kan., was explained to *Capital-Journal* readers by Amie DeFrain with this graphic.

Things to note:

- An overview locator map puts the building in geographical perspective
- A north arrow and a distance scale are used to orient the scene and to provide a size comparison
- Pointer boxes are used to call attention to specific points in the graphic and to provide information
- Arrows are used to show general movements of the FBI and Topeka police

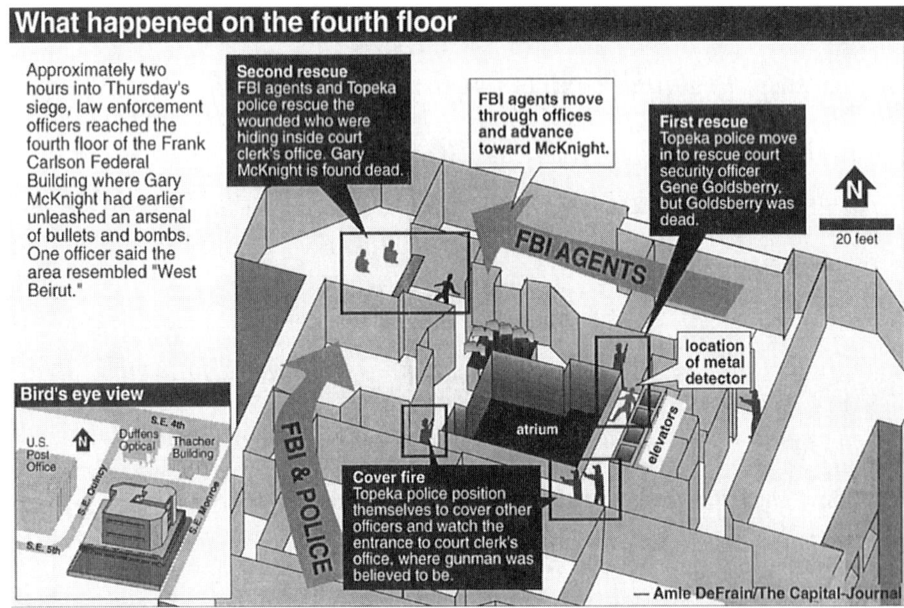

works well. Depending on the layout used, lead-ins can be set anywhere from 14 to 18 or even 24 points, if at least three columns of width are available. In some instances, lead-ins can taper down in size, with the first line using 24 point type, the second line 20, the third 16, the fourth 12 and the fifth line regular body type.

RESEARCHING A GRAPHIC

Producing a successful graphic requires more than just copying, in graphic form, what is in a story. A good graphic requires the use of visual, technical and statistical information to visually explain something. Some of that information might be explained in the text, but most often the graphic will require additional research.

While most large publications have good research facilities, including a small, specialized library and various on-line computer data bases, smaller publications might have to make do with a couple of dozen books and a library card for a local grade school, high school or college library.

Bill Pitzer of PITZOGraphics said one should begin the graphic process by making three lists:

- "What you know. Information already known and confirmed. The starting point when you go active.
- "What you would like to know. A visual and explanatory wish list of information you would want to acquire to help tell the story. This is a good list to share with reporters and photographers going to the scene.

Figure 9.6 The proofing of graphics is of critical importance. Editors need to avoid the urge to rush the graphic into print, taking time instead for a thorough examination of the location and accuracy of the information, not just the spelling. This correction by the Norfolk *Virginian-Pilot,* which has assumed legendary status among graphics editors, shows how important such proofing is to a newspaper.

CORRECTION

The map of Europe, Northern Africa and the Arab nations published in Monday's editions contained the following errors: Libya was labeled as the Ukraine; Bulgaria and Romania were transposed; Bosnia-Herzegovina was identified as Bosnia; Montenegro should have been identified as a separate state bordering Serbia; Cyprus and the West Bank were not labeled; Andorra, a country between France and Spain, was not labeled; the Crimean Peninsula appeared twice on the Black Sea; Kuwait was not identified by name, instead the initials of the Knight-Ridder News Service were in its place. The map was supplied by Knight-Ridder and labeled by a Virginian-Pilot staff artist.

- "What you don't want to know. Sometimes this can be the most difficult one to do. This list is constantly in flux as you shift through unfolding events. But once you have decided what to leave out, you can concentrate on the other two lists."

While this list was designed for those doing breaking-news graphics, it applies equally well to the non-breaking kind. In both situations the graphic artist and the copy editor have to ask basic questions designed to fill in holes, seek clarification and eliminate non-essential information.

GRAPHIC RESOURCES

PUBLICATIONS

Every publication involved in the production of infographics must have access to a variety of resource materials. Some of the resources are quite basic; others, depending on the complexity of the graphics involved, are rather exotic. Each graphics reporter will have certain favorite resource books that are used time after time, while others might be used once or twice a year. The list shown in Box 9.1 is by no means an inclusive one and the categories are somewhat arbitrary. Add to it or subtract from it as you need.

SOFTWARE

Virtually all infographics are done on computers, and most of those computers are from Apple. With the 1994 introduction of computer systems by Apple and IBM that run each other's software, graphics reporters can expect to see a boom in software available to them. For the most part, however, there will continue to be a handful of basic programs that all designers will be expected to use and another handful or two that might be used occasionally. One needs to keep in mind that the computer market is volatile and that the whims of the users mean that the popularity of various programs will come and go. With that proviso in mind, the non-inclusive list shown in Box 9.2 contains selected software programs you should learn about.

THE SUCCESSFUL GRAPHIC

Almost without exception, successful graphics will contain the following elements:

- **Headline**—You should never assume the reader will have read the story before looking at the graphic. Quite the contrary. Readers will almost always notice the graphic before the story or the headline. The graphic must therefore be self-contained.

Graphics Publications

Basic resource publications

- Dictionaries, both abridged and unabridged
- *Associated Press Stylebook*
- Encyclopedia
- Telephone books
- Almanac
- Atlas
- Maps (one can never have enough maps)
- Clip art (either books or on disks)
- *Statistical Abstracts of the United States*
- Specialty books (if your publication is close to a specialized industry or military base, get books about that industry or military unit)

Magazines

- *Aldus*
- *Publish*
- *U&lc*
- *MacUser*
- *Best of Newspaper Design*

Intermediate resource publications

- *The Way Things Work*
- *Pantone Matching System*
- *CIA World Factbook*

Magazines

- *Print*
- *Communication Arts*

Comprehensive resource publications

- *Jane's Fighting Ships*
- *Jane's Aircraft of the World*
- *Jane's Weapon Systems*
- *Jane's Artillery and Armor*

Box 9.1

- **Chatter**—A brief sentence or two is generally necessary to further explain the content of the graphic. Remember, the reader will almost never get through the story before reading the graphic.
- **Carefully researched information**—Facts appearing in the graphic must be every bit as valid and carefully reported as the story itself.
- **Compelling presentation**—The presentation of the information should be coupled with various graphic devices, such as artwork, screens and shading to underscore the data, plus help attract the reader.
- **Source**—The source is necessary to help validate the information. It helps the reader have faith in the data, just as a source helps the reader validate direct quotes. Sources must be used on every graphic, especially since data can come from various "authorities," each of which can present different and perhaps conflicting interpretations of the same material.
- **Credit line**—The inclusion of a credit line helps the reader validate the graphic in much the same way a byline allows a reader to determine the veracity of a story.

Graphics Software

Drawing programs

- Adobe Illustrator
- Aldus Freehand
- CorelDRAW

Page layout programs

- Aldus PageMaker
- Quark XPress

Photo scanning and retouching programs

- Ofoto
- Aldus PhotoStyler
- Adobe Photoshop

Flatbed scanners

- Apple One Scan
- Hewlett-Packard ScanJet II
- Microtek ScanMaker

Film scanners

- Microtek 35t and 45t
- Nikon Coolscan
- Polaroid SprintScan 35

Graphics tablets

- CalComp DrawingSlate and DrawingBoard
- Wacom UD Series tablets

Typefaces and modification programs

- Altsys Fontographer
- Image Club Graphics
- Emigre, Inc.
- Adobe Systems Inc., Adobe Type on Call (CD) and Adobe Type Library (individual fonts on disk)
- FontHaus Inc.

COLOR

A major component of design, both in infographics and in page layout, color can help establish the mood and visual impact so necessary in contemporary publications. Even though color surrounds each of us in nature, television and movies, it is rare that editors spend much time learning about the basics of color. As a result, many of the color decisions made by inexperienced editors are ill advised.

At the same time, good editors do not use color just to use color. A black and white graphic or photograph or page can be more effective than an item in which color is used badly. Use color if it adds something worthwhile to the flow of information to the reader. Avoid it if it doesn't.

Some basics are in order. A color may be discussed in terms of being a primary or a complementary color, a warm or cool color, advancing or receding, or maybe even as a calming or threatening color. Some of the terms are subjective, others are definitive.

Primary colors are definitive. According to the theory of light, the additive primaries are the "pure" colors of red, blue and green because they form white light when mixed together. Subtractive primaries are cyan (blue + green), yel-

Graphing packages

CA-Cricket Graph

DeltaPoint DeltaGraph

Type management tools

Adobe Type Manager

Adobe Type Reunion

Computer glitch solvers and virus protection

Norton Utilities

MicroMat Computer Systems MacEKG

Central Point MacTools

Datawatch Virex

Symantec Antivirus for Mac

Maps and clip art

Electronic Map Cabinet (CD)

Universal NFL Clip Art

Paragon Concepts, Inc., Nisus Complete Flag Edition

ClickArt (CD and disks)

Creativity stimulus and miscellaneous

Roger von Oech's Creative Whack Pack

Inspiration Software, Inc., Inspiration Attain, In Control

Box 9.2

low (red + green) and magenta (red + blue). When blended together these colors subtract or absorb light, therefore producing black or the absence of color.

Note that yellow is a subtractive color. Most people have learned in kindergarten, however, that the primary colors are red, blue and yellow. That is true for pigments, but not for light. And since light and not pigment is what the photographic process requires, red, blue and green are the additive primaries of photographic reproduction.

Red and cyan are on opposite sides of the color wheel, green and magenta are opposites, and so are blue and yellow. Each of these pairs is referred to as a "complementary," as in red is complementary to cyan, or yellow is complementary to blue.

The inks used to print color photographs in newspapers and magazines are subtractive color inks: cyan, magenta and yellow. These are frequently spoken of as "process colors," as in process red (which is magenta), process blue (which is cyan) and process yellow (which still is yellow). For four-color reproduction, a plate using black ink would be added to increase depth in the photo. Three-color reproduction would use only the three subtractive primary colors.

Cool colors such as blues and greens are called receding colors since they visually seem to go to the background, while warm colors such as reds and

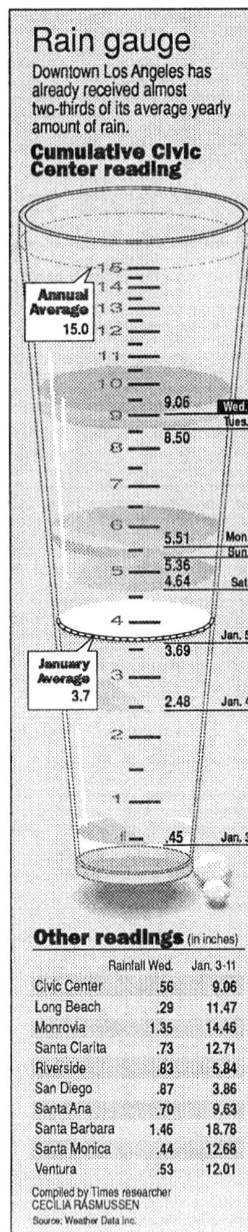

	Rainfall Wed.	Jan. 3-11
Civic Center	.56	9.06
Long Beach	.29	11.47
Monrovia	1.35	14.46
Santa Clarita	.73	12.71
Riverside	.83	5.84
San Diego	.87	3.86
Santa Ana	.70	9.63
Santa Barbara	1.46	18.78
Santa Monica	.44	12.68
Ventura	.53	12.01

Compiled by Times researcher CECILIA RASMUSSEN
Source: Weather Data Inc.

Lorena Iniguez / Los Angeles Times via AP

Figure 9.7 Graphing volumes can be quite difficult. Lorena Iniguez of the *Los Angeles Times* shows an excellent way of comparing that city's annual rainfall with that received during a few days one month. Note that when the volume of the glass increases, the increments come closer together. Many graphics err by increasing volume and maintaining the same measurement increments throughout.

Things to note:

- The use of dates and measurements in bold to show quickly how much rain had been received by what date
- The use of highlights and shading to help produce a three-dimensional shape
- The summaries at the bottom of other rainfall in the area
- The boxed pointer with white background indicating the January average and annual rain. The white contrasts very nicely with the screened background

yellows are referred to as advancing colors since they seem to come to the front of a scene. Knowledge about how a color "appears" to move to the foreground or background will help an editor in determining placement of color tints or borders.

Be sure to follow common sense on color placement: Advancing colors generally belong in the foreground and receding colors in the background. To intermix those colors or to use them inappropriately can result in an image that is flat or lacks depth. Remember also that in design there are no rules, only guidelines. It is therefore possible to totally mix the order of color placement and produce a winning combination, but the guidelines are good to follow.

If color selections are rather nebulous ("Let's make that headline a robin's egg blue," or a "pale red" or a "grass green"), then the printed results will likely

Editors: GRAPHIC IS A MEMBER or STRINGER CONTRIBUTION.

Some fonts used may not be AP standard of Helvetica or Times and may need to be converted. Some information may be of local interest and may need editing.

MANDATORY CREDIT.

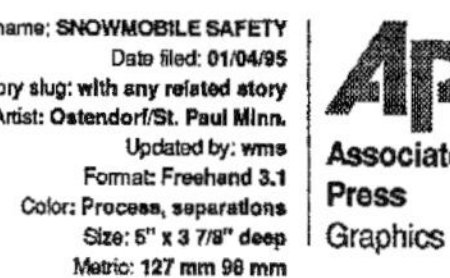

Filename: SNOWMOBILE SAFETY
Date filed: 01/04/95
Story slug: with any related story
Artist: Ostendorf/St. Paul Minn.
Updated by: wms
Format: Freehand 3.1
Color: Process, separations
Size: 5" x 3 7/8" deep
Metric: 127 mm 98 mm
Associated Press Graphics

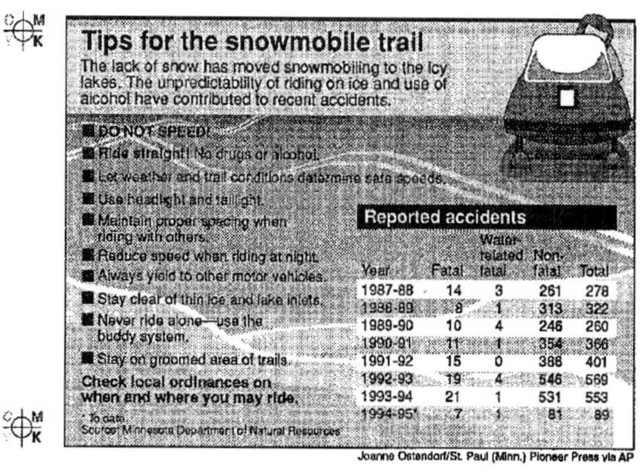

Year	Fatal	Water-related fatal	Non-fatal	Total
1987-88	14	3	261	278
1988-89	8	1	313	322
1989-90	10	4	246	260
1990-91	11	1	354	366
1991-92	15	0	386	401
1992-93	19	4	546	569
1993-94	21	1	531	553
1994-95*	7	1	81	89

Figure 9.8 A graphic that will assist readers is always appreciated, and this one about snowmobile safety is sure to be of interest throughout the snow belt. The graphic was intended for a local audience but was picked up and transmitted nationally over the Associated Press graphics network. (Source: Joanne Ostendorf/*St. Paul* [Minn.] *Pioneer Press*)

Things to note:

- Square bullets are used to list items
- Alternating white and background shades are used for the accident listing
- The box surrounding the graphic is broken by the helmet of the snowmobiler

vary considerably. What is needed is a method of indicating colors that are specific and reproducible at every printing plant across the country. Many such systems exist.

One color specification system, the Pantone Matching System, is used regularly in advertising to produce corporate colors, such as Coca-Cola red, IBM blue, United Parcel Service brown. These colors are a blend of some of the primaries and can be specified as Pantone 256 blue or Pantone red.

Pantone produces a series of swatch books that show thousands of very specific color combinations that are given unique numbers. A designer in Fargo, N.D., for example, could specify a precise color of red and be assured that the printer in Louisville, Ky., would know exactly which color of red was required.

This is all well and good, but the reality of the publication business is that each printing press, ink choice, paper stock and color separation produces its own variables in color reproduction. This is especially true with newsprint since it is a relatively low-quality product with somewhat inconsistent texture and color. For some newspapers, color reproduction is a hit-or-miss situation with rather low repeatability from day to day and even from section to section. What looks good on a computer monitor or proof might look rather bleak as copy number 30,134 rolls off the press.

Further compounding the problem is that humans do not see colors consistently the same way any more than they hear sound the same way or receive taste or smell sensations the same. Humans are individuals and their capabilities are quite different.

In other words, don't expect the designer and the editor and the customer to see a particular color in the same way. They won't.

Another problem lies with the lighting condition under which the publication is viewed. Colors do *not* look the same under various lighting conditions. A newspaper held under fluorescent lights will have a yellowish-green cast. That same page held next to a candle will have a reddish tinge, while it will appear somewhat blue in the shadow of a building. Most colors are calibrated to be seen under lighting called "noon daylight." As most journalists would agree, very few people read newspapers or magazines outdoors in bright sun. In reality, publications are most often read indoors, on buses, subways, or airlines and most often under artificial lighting, especially fluorescent.

The color monitors that are used by editors frequently vary all over the map on their color balance. The same image viewed on three different monitors might produce three different color balances. One image might be slightly redder on one monitor, while the balance is greener or bluer on the others. Calibrated production monitors, which are terribly expensive, usually are bang on in color balance, but the final product is left in the hands of the press operators, who might not give a hoot.

In spite of all these variables, some newspaper chains do demand and produce excellent color work issue after issue and from plants scattered across the continent. One secret is to standardize procedures, equipment and training as much as possible and to demand quality throughout.

Each newspaper should conduct a comprehensive series of tests several times per year, and especially when it has major changes in newsprint or equipment or personnel, to see how various colors reproduce. Blues, for example, might reproduce quite well, but reds show up as murky. The tests need to examine the reproduction of the primary colors (both additive and subtractive) in various percentages and blends. Once these tests are run, editors and designers will have a much more accurate understanding of what Pantone 173 will look like on this press with this kind of paper stock or how 10 percent yellow, 25 percent magenta and 10 percent black will work with a type overlay.

While it may seem as though color is one giant variable (and in a sense it is), editors, in consultation with designers and press operators, can select accent colors that reproduce consistently well. It is best to remember that the colors of borders and screens and type can vary all over the map and not be objectionable, whereas poor reproduction of a color photograph (in which subjects look greenish) can make readers nauseated.

Safe colors are cyan, magenta and yellow, since those inks come straight out of the can. Blended colors, such as 25 percent cyan and 10 percent yellow, become more problematic, but still possible. Experimentation will help determine the best possibilities for a given publication.

A final consideration is the disparity between the colors editors generally will use and what readers want. Editors tend to be considerably more conservative than their readers. As a result, editors choose softer, less garish colors than the readers themselves would use. Readers like bright, vivid colors: lots of turquoises, hot pinks, bright greens and vivid reds.

Color usage in graphics, as well as in design itself, should add to the flow of information to the reader, not hinder it in any manner. Research has shown that color attracts readers, but there seems to be no research that shows if color, such as a soft blue background, will actually help the reader retain more information.

Step-by-Step Graphics

1. Analyze the information at hand.
2. Research the information and gather additional data.
3. Summarize the information in two or three sentences.
4. Determine what kind of graphic will best present and clarify the information for the reader.
5. Do a preliminary design containing:
   a. Headline
   b. Chatter
   c. Graphic
   d. Artwork
   e. Source
   f. Credit
   g. Color (as necessary)
6. Consult with the originating writer and editor to be sure the graphic accurately reflects the content of the article.
7. Finish the design, adding or deleting items or information as necessary.
8. Proof the graphic one last time.

Box 9.3

It is quite important that editors and designers avoid using so many different colors on a page or graphic that the result looks like an explosion in a paint factory. A page or graphic with a rather pastel base will allow for the inclusion of very strong, vivid accent colors, whereas a base with a strong color will require an even stronger color to achieve a contrast. The result in the latter case would be multiple colors competing for the reader's attention.

In summary, editors should keep in mind that color reproduction is an inexact science, that people do not see colors the same, that multiple variables affect color reproduction, and that readers want bolder, more vivid colors than do the editors.

Box 9.3 summarizes all the steps needed to use graphics successfully.

BIBLIOGRAPHY AND ADDITIONAL READINGS

Baird, Russell N., Duncan McDonald, Ronald H. Pittman, and Arthur T. Turnbull. *The Graphics of Communication,* 6th ed. Harcourt Brace Jovanovich. 1993.

Barnhurst, Kevin G. *Seeing the Newspaper.* St. Martin's Press, 1994.

Chapter 10

PAGE DESIGN: PUTTING IT ALL TOGETHER

DESIGN AND CONTENT

Previous chapters have introduced numerous guidelines and techniques for effective use of written and visual material, including headlines, stories, photos and graphics. Although whole books have been devoted to publication design, this chapter is an introduction to the fundamentals.

Editors should realize that design is evolutionary and that design changes will take place throughout the life of a publication, just as fashions change from decade to decade. Beginners should expect to make mistakes as they learn how to do effective layouts, and experienced editors will admit they have never (or rarely) designed a page that was 100 percent perfect.

Daily newspaper editors have an excellent laboratory for learning design. Every day's mix of stories and photos stems from different events and allows for a variety of solutions to the design problem. If a mistake is made, the next day provides a clean slate. The editor may:

- Review what didn't work.
- Analyze why it didn't work.
- Try again.
- At the very least, have fun.

Some editors erroneously disparage the concept of design, placing their belief in the power of the written word. Packaging, however, is essential to today's journalism. It must be flashy enough to catch the attention of the casual reader, but not so overpowering as to deflect the conservative eye. Publication design is little different from the design on a box of cornflakes or a bottle of hand cream. Powerful design can be used to sell a weak product, but once burned, a consumer who feels that a product is bad will never buy it again. Editors can never afford to establish a flashy design and ignore the content.

Design attracts; content holds. Neither works without the other.

The guidelines in this chapter should be useful to all editors, whether they work on a newsletter or a tabloid daily or a broadsheet or a weekly. Keep in mind that the principles of design are the same. It's just the application that varies.

Box 10.1 presents a glossary of design terms.

THE BAUHAUS WAS RIGHT

One of the most influential design philosophies of all times arose from the Bauhaus, an art school in Germany during the 1920s and early 1930s. When the Nazi government forced the closure of the school and the scattering of its teachers, whose specialties included typography, painting, sculpture, photography and architecture, many of the leading practitioners emigrated to the United States.

The major philosophical tenet of the Bauhaus was "form follows function," a phrase that has been used recently by a variety of manufacturers, including Ford. That philosophy is particularly appropriate to publication design. The purpose of a newspaper or magazine or newsletter is to communicate; its form or design is secondary. There will always be discussions and even violent arguments at times about what constitutes *The Form.*

Form must allow for flexibility in the presentation of the content. It also must allow for the subtlety that knowledgeable designers bring to the editorial mix regarding the use of specific typefaces to underscore a special news or feature package, or the use of particular colors to guide a reader through a complex series.

THE FOUNDATION OF DESIGN

FORMAT

Publications are often discussed on the basis of their page sizes or *formats.* The majority of newspapers use broadsheet format, which is approximately 13.75 by 22.5 inches. Some will run their width or depth a bit either side of these numbers, but the approximate width to depth ratio remains about the same. Before the 1970s it was possible to find broadsheets that were extremely wide, often running 17 inches. These were called "horse blankets" because of their immen-

Glossary of Design Terms

art A photograph, graphic or any other type of picture used to illustrate a page.

broadsheet The standard page size for U.S. newspapers, 13.75 by 22.5 inches.

butt Lie side by side. Headlines butt if they are placed on the same level in adjoining columns.

clip art Drawings, cartoons and other illustrations available from syndicates in printed or computerized form.

dogleg Any shape, module or configuration of type that is other than a rectangle. Most doglegs are L-shaped.

double truck Two newspaper pages that are treated together as a single layout. The centerfold of an eight-page newspaper section, for example, may be treated as a double truck.

dummy A scale-model page on which a layout is drawn. A dummy may be a piece of paper with printed lines to represent columns or a computer simulation of an empty page.

ears Spaces at both ends of the nameplate, often used for promotion boxes or weather information.

file photos Pictures stored in newspaper or magazine library files for use as needed.

fold An imaginary line on a dummy representing the point where the newspaper will be folded in half for delivery.

free lance A writer or photographer who offers material for sale to a publication but is not employed on its staff.

graphic Any illustration that uses line drawing, perhaps along with type or photographs. A graphic that is not only decorative but also presents information is an informational graphic.

gutter The vertical space that divides columns.

horizontal layout A page in which most of the headlines extend horizontally across columns and the type is wrapped in legs under the heads.

horse blankets Very large newspaper pages, as wide as 17 inches, now rare.

illustration Any photograph or other art on a page.

infographics Informational graphics available from syndicates as clip art.

layout A scale model or "blueprint" of a page, drawn on a dummy.

sity. A few still exist, but the cost of newsprint has accomplished what style could not: a narrowing of page size to save money.

Tabloids are half the size of broadsheets, running about 11.5 by 13.5 inches. Notable tabloids include *Newsday,* the *New York Daily News,* the *Village Voice* and the *Chicago Sun-Times.* Other types of tabloids include alternative publications, suburban weeklies, shoppers (free circulation publications having lots of advertising) and supermarket scandal sheets.

Magazines, also called *quartos,* used to be half the size of tabloids and one-fourth the size of broadsheets. Now magazines are trimmed to approximately 8.5 by 11 inches, but larger sizes exist, mainly in the fashion genre.

Digest-sized magazines, like *Reader's Digest,* are known as *octavos,* or one-eighth of a broadsheet, which would be one-half of a quarto.

leg A block of text under a headline.

modular A type of layout in which the elements form rectangles.

mug shot A photograph of a human face.

newsprint The paper on which newspapers are printed. It is porous and non-durable, and photo reproduction on it is lower in quality than on glossy magazine paper.

octavo The page size of a digest-sized magazine, like *Reader's Digest,* one-half of a quarto.

package Any grouping of related stories and art.

photo illustration Any photograph that does not depict a spontaneous situation but is posed or otherwise manipulated to achieve an effect. Photo illustrations should be identified as such in cutlines.

picture page A layout consisting entirely of unrelated photographs and cutlines.

promotion boxes Front-page items that notify readers of features on inside pages or in other sections.

pull-outs Quotations or other segments of stories that are copied from the body text and reset in large type for emphasis.

pull quote A quotation pulled from the body text and reset in large type for emphasis. Also called a quote-out.

quarto The page size of most magazines. It used to be half the size of a tabloid page and one-fourth the size of a broadsheet. Now magazines are trimmed to about 8.5 by 11 inches.

raw wrap Any leg or legs of body type that do not fall under a headline or a related piece of art.

tabloid A publication with a page size about half as big as a broadsheet, 11.5 by 13.5 inches.

tease A refer or promotion box.

tombstone Two headlines of the same size and font placed side by side.

vertical layout A page in which most of the headlines are one column wide and the type is in single legs extending from top to bottom.

wire photos Photographs supplied by a wire service.

wrap The way legs of type are arranged under headlines and around art elements.

Box 10.1

WHITE SPACE

Every publication begins its existence on a blank piece of paper (or computer screen). That white can be thought of as the foundation or background on which all other items are placed and which shows through even when the design is completed.

Be careful not to fall into the trap of thinking that the white should be obliterated as soon as possible with headlines, photos and body type. Rather one should think of the white as an essential part of the whole design.

An editor/designer may be asked to design only one part of a page, rather than the whole thing. The concept remains the same: The beginning of the design is with the white space.

TOPEKA EDITION

THE TOPEKA CAPITAL-JOURNAL

WEDNESDAY

DECEMBER 28, 1994

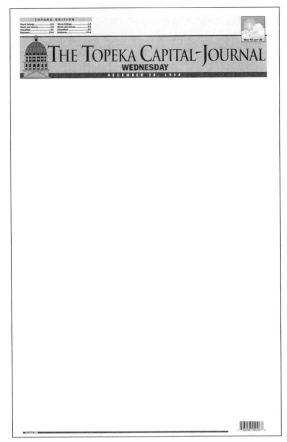

Figure 10.1 *The Topeka Capital-Journal* begins its day's layout with a blank page and some "must use" items, such as the flag, weather box, index and bar code. The rest of the page is wide open, unfettered by column restrictions. This open form of layout allows for more flexibility of design, but requires editors to make more decisions as to width of columns, artwork and headlines.

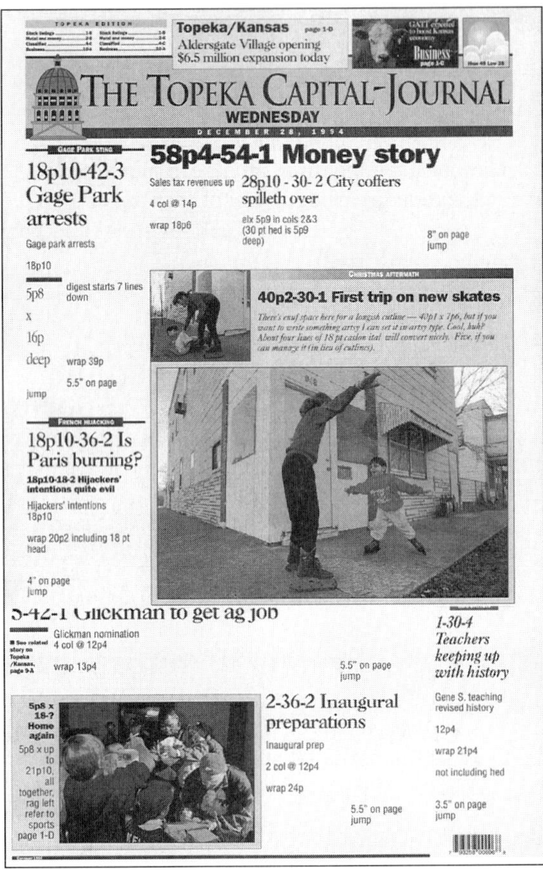

TOPEKA EDITION

Topeka/Kansas page 1-D

Aldersgate Village opening $6.5 million expansion today

Business page 1-E

THE TOPEKA CAPITAL-JOURNAL

WEDNESDAY

DECEMBER 28, 1994

GAGE PARK STING

18p10-42-3 Gage Park arrests

Gage park arrests

18p10

5p8 x 16p deep

digest starts 7 lines down

wrap 39p

5.5" on page jump

58p4-54-1 Money story

Sales tax revenues up

4 col @ 14p

wrap 18p6

28p10 - 30- 2 City coffers spilleth over

elx 5p9 in cols 2&3 (30 pt hed is 5p9 deep)

8" on page jump

CHRISTMAS AFTERMATH

40p2-30-1 First trip on new skates

FRENCH HIJACKING

18p10-36-2 Is Paris burning?

18p10-18-2 Hijackers' intentions quite evil

Hijackers' intentions 18p10

wrap 20p2 including 18 pt head

4" on page jump

5-42-1 Glickman to get ag job

Glickman nomination 4 col @ 12p4

wrap 13p4

5.5" on page jump

1-30-4 Teachers keeping up with history

Gene S. teaching revised history

12p4

wrap 21p4

not including hed

3.5" on page jump

5p8 x 18-? Home again

5p8 x up to 21p10, all together, rag left refer to sports page 1-D

2-36-2 Inaugural preparations

Inaugural prep

2 col @ 12p4

wrap 24p

5.5" on page jump

Figure 10.2 Hours later, after stories are written, artwork made available, and the news mix of the page determined, *The Topeka Capital-Journal* has a preliminary layout plan. Note the layout shorthand used by the editors to communicate with each other (upper left story) carries a designation of **18p10-42-3,** which means a bastard width headline running **18** picas and **10** points wide, using **42** point type, stacked **3** lines deep.

When beginning a design one is faced, in some instances, with a decision as to orientation. Is it to be horizontal or vertical? The components of the finished design might be somewhat similar in both cases, but the solution likely will be different.

Virtually all newspaper and magazine pages, save for double trucks (see glossary), are verticals. Some tabloids have a nearly square page format, which allows for some very interesting layout possibilities. Try this exercise: Use the same elements (photos and type) and produce designs in two different page orientations, horizontal and vertical, and two different page sizes, broadsheet and tabloid. Then analyze the results.

TOPEKA EDITION

Topeka/Kansas page 1-D

Aldersgate Village opening

$6.5 million expansion today

GATT expected to boost Kansas economy

Business page 1-C

THE TOPEKA CAPITAL-JOURNAL

WEDNESDAY

DECEMBER 28, 1994

GAGE PARK STING

Police arrest 19 men for gay activity

By PHIL ANDERSON
The Capital-Journal

■ Nineteen men have been arrested in Gage Park for alleged homosexual solicitation.

■ Police say they intend to keep Gage Park "a family park."

City tax money stacking up

Revenue report on sales tax joyful news for city officials

By MIKE HALL
The Capital-Journal

CHRISTMAS AFTERMATH

'You *did* it!'

Nicholas Hisey, 5, mastered the new in-line skates he received for Christmas but not before taking a spill. His sister, Brandy, 11, was there to give him a hand. The siblings were skating Tuesday at N.E. Thomas and Wabash.

FRENCH HIJACKING

Blast over Paris hijackers' goal

Commando raid may have averted catastrophic climax

By CLAIRE NULLIS
The Associated Press

Glickman to land agriculture post today

By ROBERT GREENE
The Associated Press

■ See related story on Topeka /Kansas, page 9-A

EDUCATION

Standards skew view of U.S., critics say

By GENE SMITH
The Capital-Journal

Coming home

Kansas State players Kirby Hocutt and Barrett Brooks signed autographs at Forbes Field upon their return Tuesday from the Aloha Bowl. About 100 fans greeted the team. See Sports, 1-D.

Finishing touches put on inaugural plans

By MATT TRUELL
The Capital-Journal

Figure 10.3 The finished layout of *The Topeka Capital-Journal* for Wednesday, December 28, 1994.

Beginning editors generally feel that magazines and tabloids are somewhat easier to work with, perhaps because the pages are smaller and accommodate fewer items.

FILLING THE WHITE SPACE

Facing the job of turning all that white space into an effective design, an editor should first ask two questions:

- What's the news?
- What's the art?

News judgment is one of the major bricks in the foundation of page design. Every news decision has as its genesis the question, "What is the news value of this story?" The more important the story is, the better the play it gets in the newspaper. More important stories get larger headlines and more art, and they compete with other important stories for the top of the front page.

Local stories about bus crashes and financial trouble in the school superintendent's office tend to be front-page news. It's important to remember that what makes the front page one day may not make it there another day. It all depends on the mix of news available at a given time. It also depends on circulation size. A homicide might be a banner story in a small community, but be buried on page 28 under a one-column head in a larger newspaper.

Editors and page designers must constantly sift through numerous stories and pictures, evaluating one against another in a delicate balancing game of grading the news. Typically, the editor will have too much or too little. News seems to happen in bunches. The same day the United States invades a country will be exactly the day there will be a particularly gruesome triple murder involving prominent citizens, the start of an important legislative session and the announcement of a major downtown renovation project. Another day will find no compelling candidates for the front page. Rarely is there difficulty finding enough material to fill the space, but finding the kind of stories that will appeal to readers is sometimes a problem.

Unless major news commands all the space, an editor may have a problem deciding the best mixture of stories. Ideally the mix should include, where appropriate, a heavy-hitting national or world piece, a human interest feature and some juicy local news.

Determining which stories will be used and where they will be played is the job of the news editor, whose judgment is made in partnership with the managing editor in most newsrooms. Good editors keep in mind that flexibility is important to allow for the proper placement of breaking stories that inevitably occur right on deadline. They know what stories can be placed inside, run the next day or sacrificed entirely if there is a major breaking story that must get into the page. Most of the time that flexibility will go unneeded, but when the need does come about, the inflexible editor will face insurmountable problems.

Good editors strive for coherence and organization in news coverage. They make sure related stories are placed close together or are linked by teases. They watch for quotes that will work well for pull-outs and elements that can go into graphics and other devices to enhance the reader's understanding of the story.

Just like football games and sales presentations, newspaper editions, too, are subject to postmortems. How did our publication play a story versus how the competition did it? Who had the best design? What stories did we miss? Why was this event given a two-column head on page 4 and another similar event given a three-column head on the front page?

The answers are always debatable.

PHOTOS, GRAPHICS AND ARTWORK

News editors select art as well as news for the front page. They need illustrations large and small to dress up the page and fill promotion boxes. Publications are often judged on the quality and display of photographs, informational graphics and illustrations. A visually oriented readership demands good art, yet too many publications use art as a secondary, rather than a primary component of design.

An editor's art choices may include wire photos, staff-produced photos, staff-produced illustrations, file photos, stock photos, clip art, infographics and even freelance work. The art may be available in black and white or in color. When no outstanding art is available, panic can set in, but the editor must make the best of what there is.

Daily Nebraskan

COVERING THE UNIVERSITY OF NEBRASKA SINCE 1901 VOL. 94 NO. 16

INSIDE TUESDAY

SPORTS

■ Osborne unsure of how good Huskers are, Page 5

ARTS & ENTERTAINMENT

■ "Charlotte's Web" weaves onto stage, Page 6

PAGE 2: Plane crashes on White House lawn

SEPTEMBER 13, 1994

Man arrested in shooting of UNL officer

Witnesses describe crime scene, arrest

By Jeffrey Robb
Senior Editor

Ryan Broussard was driving behind a University Police Chevy Blazer Monday night when he saw a man fire a semi-automatic weapon at the vehicle.

"He opened his door, got out and just started shooting," said Broussard, a UNL freshman, who had been traveling south on 16th Street behind the police vehicle.

Broussard was one of many witnesses who watched about 6:30 p.m. as a man fired nine shots at the Blazer.

University Police officer Robert Soflin, who was driving the Blazer, was taken later to Lincoln General Hospital with wounds to his hand and shoulder.

After the shots were fired, Broussard said, the officer walked to the back of the Blazer. Streaks of blood stained the rear panelling where Soflin leaned against it. Broussard said the police cruiser had been pursuing a faded black pickup truck.

Toshiyuki Taki was walking down 16th Street toward R Street when he saw the man step from the truck and start firing.

After the shots were fired, Taki saw the officer grab his hand. About the same time, Taki, an exchange student studying communication, said the shooter got back in his truck and drove away.

Police chased the suspect down 16th Street and then east on South street. The man then led police south on 27th street.

Nancy Reckewey was stopped in the left-turn lane on 27th Street, waiting to turn on Nebraska Highway 2 when she first heard sirens. She looked in her rear-view mirror and saw a faded black Chevy pickup truck being chased by police cars.

"When I turned around, they were out of their cars and their guns were pointed, and I didn't know where," Reckewey said.

She screamed at her son, Jon Klein, to get down on the floor of her Chevrolet Suburban. She put down her head but then lowered the passenger window to talk to a man in the next car.

"I said, 'What is the deal?' and he said, 'There is a gunman in the car behind you.'"

About 200 students drawn by guns shots and police sirens lined the crime scene at 16th and R streets to see what had happened.

Paul Vicary and Leyla Parra-Vicary, both UNL graduate students, stayed at the scene after they heard the rapid-fire gunshots. They had been heading west on R street when they were stopped by a red light.

"I thought it sounded strange," he said. "I've never seen or heard gunshots here in Lincoln. I saw smoke and I thought that had to be it."

Senior Editors Matt Woody and Jeff Zeleny contributed to this report.

Jay Calderon/DN

Robert Soflin, a University Police officer, receives medical treatment from members of the Lincoln Fire Department and Lincoln paramedics. Soflin, who later was taken to Lincoln General Hospital, was shot in the hand Monday evening near 16th and R streets.

Police chase former student

By Matt Woody and Jeff Zeleny
Senior Editors

A 31-year-old former UNL student was arrested Monday night for attempted murder after he allegedly fired nine shots at a University Police officer, authorities said.

Gerald Lee Schlondorf was taken into custody after a 20-minute standoff with police in south Lincoln. Schlondorf was arrested after he led police on a low-speed chase through rush-hour traffic from near State Fair Park to 27th Street and Nebraska Highway 2, where he was apprehended.

University Police officer Robert Soflin joined the pursuit when it reached the University of Nebraska-Lincoln City Campus. Soflin, who was wearing a bullet-proof vest, was shot twice in his police Blazer at 16th and R streets.

Soflin, a six-year University Police veteran, is the first UNL police officer ever to be shot, Sgt. Bill Manning said. Soflin underwent surgery at Lincoln General Hospital Monday evening. He was listed in fair condition early today.

Lincoln and University Police gave the following account of the incident:

About 6:15 p.m., Schlondorf, of 1331 N. Ninth St., drove past Lincoln Police officers, who were standing beside their cruiser near 14th Street and Military Road. As Schlondorf passed the officers in his faded black Chevrolet Custom Deluxe pickup truck, he brandished a gun and shouted threats at the officers:

The police officers pursued Schlondorf south on 14th Street, and then on 16th Street through the University of Nebraska-Lincoln campus.

At 16th and R streets, Schlondorf stopped in traffic. While stopped, he got out of his truck and shot nine rounds at Soflin. Soflin was struck in the hand and received minor injuries to his neck and shoulder.

Schlondorf then got back in his vehicle and left the scene, continuing south along 16th Street. Lincoln police continued the pursuit.

Schlondorf turned east on South Street. Between 20th and 21st streets he fired shots at a Lincoln Police cruiser. At least two rounds hit the car.

The suspect then turned south on 27th Street. Heavy traffic forced him to stop at the intersection of 27th Street and Nebraska Highway 2. After a 20-minute stand-off at the intersection, during which Schlondorf held his .45-caliber Thompson sub-machine gun replica in his truck, police apprehended him without incident.

Schlondorf was booked in Lancaster County Jail late Monday evening and will be ar-

See **SHOOTING** on 3

Search for former UNL student concludes in Seattle

By Matthew Waite
Senior Reporter

The week-long search for former UNL law student Kendra Marshall is finished.

Marshall was found near Seattle Monday about 6 p.m. central time, said Dennis Leonard, a criminal investigator in the Nebraska State Patrol on Monday.

"She was alone, she was safe, and she was sound," Leonard said. "There was no abduction. There was no foul play. There was no criminal activity."

Marshall was reported missing last Monday by her brother, Mitch, when she did not show up for work at Barnes & Noble bookstore in Lincoln.

Officials in the state patrol originally suspected foul play in Marshall's disappearance. The patrol described the incident as suspicious and out of character for Marshall.

Marshall

Marshall was identified from automated teller machine videotape taken in Chadron Thursday. The tape was the only confirmed sighting the state patrol had in Nebraska.

Another sighting of Marshall was reported in Kearney last Monday, but was not confirmed. Leonard said Sunday the patrol was confident, but not sure, about the Kearney sighting.

Marshall was found by an FBI agent in Seattle and has since contacted her family, he said.

"She was there because she wanted to be there," Leonard said from Holdrege. "Once it was determined that there was no criminal case, the case was closed.

"Any reasons she had for being there were personal and private."

Leonard and friends of Marshall said they were all elated by the outcome of the investigation.

Andrew Sigerson, a friend of Marshall who coordinated media relations for the Marshall family, said the news that they received Monday night was wonderful.

Her reappearance in Seattle, however, was a mystery to him, he said.

"I don't have any idea why she was out there," Sigerson said. "Sometimes people just need to get away."

It may seem like many hours were wasted by the media and the state patrol, Sigerson said, but the outcome of the investigation was worth the time.

Leonard agreed the time spent searching for the woman wasn't a waste.

"When we consider what some of the other alternatives and conclusions are to these things, I couldn't be happier," he said. "I'm not upset at all about the time I spent on it."

Michelle Snurr and Timarree Brown, Marshall's roommates, refused to comment Monday night, saying only that they were happy she was safe.

Tabloid newspapers provide space for a limited number of elements on the front page. A major story breaking just before deadline is always a challenge, yet the student-run *Daily Nebraskan* produced a commendable page on the shooting of a campus police officer by a university student.

Things to note:

- A boxed package for the main story
- Use of a large photo, main story and side bar
- A raw wrap used on the sidebar (another solution would have used a single line head stripped across all three columns)
- Teasers and the conclusion to ongoing coverage of a former student's apparent disappearance

Page designs are directly influenced by the size, shape and direction of the art. A one-column black and white mug shot will engender a different design than a four-column horizontal in dazzling color. Art that directs the reader's eyes to the right needs to be placed differently in a layout than does a photo that looks left.

Obviously the news value of the art, together with the quality of the image, determines how the art will be played. News judgment and photo editing go hand in hand. Does a somewhat interesting photo of a confrontation at a nearby school board meeting take precedence over a gut-wrenching wire photo of a starving child in a faraway country? That becomes part of the decision making, and this piece of advice needs to be repeated: There are no right or wrong answers in the layout business, only evaluations of effectiveness.

Every story has the potential for a visual element, provided the editor thinks about it in time. The assignment of artwork, like the story itself, requires some planning: assigning a photographer or graphic reporter or illustrator, understanding ahead of time the thrust of the story and artwork, integrating the story and artwork into a comprehensive layout. There is always the possibility of getting some sort of art from the files, but there is no substitute for planning.

A good editor makes a final art selection only after looking at everything available: what has been assigned, what is in hand, what is coming in or has fallen through and what is available through the wire services or picture agencies and can be obtained in time for a good design effort.

In deciding the best placement of art on the page, editors often arrange possible selections on the desk so the images can be compared and their directions are readily visible. When images are loaded into a computer and hard copies are not available, this obviously becomes difficult. An editor can make a rough sketch to accomplish a similar purpose.

Every page needs a "grabber" image that will become the focal point for readers. When one is found, it must be given the space it needs. Effective art display can help achieve what catchy leads and crisp headlines alone cannot always do: attract readers.

Flexibility in approaching the design is essential, as is a consideration of the amount of time available to complete the project. The result one achieves with a 30-minute lead time can be quite different from that achieved in four hours or five days.

THE BIG TEN GUIDELINES OF PAGE DESIGN

Like line editing, page design lends itself to a set of fundamental guidelines. The following list applies mainly to broadsheet layout, but the guidelines are similar for other types of pages.

1. **Make it modular.** A page consists of:

- Stories that stand alone with their headlines
- Stories that are packaged with other stories, with illustrations or with both

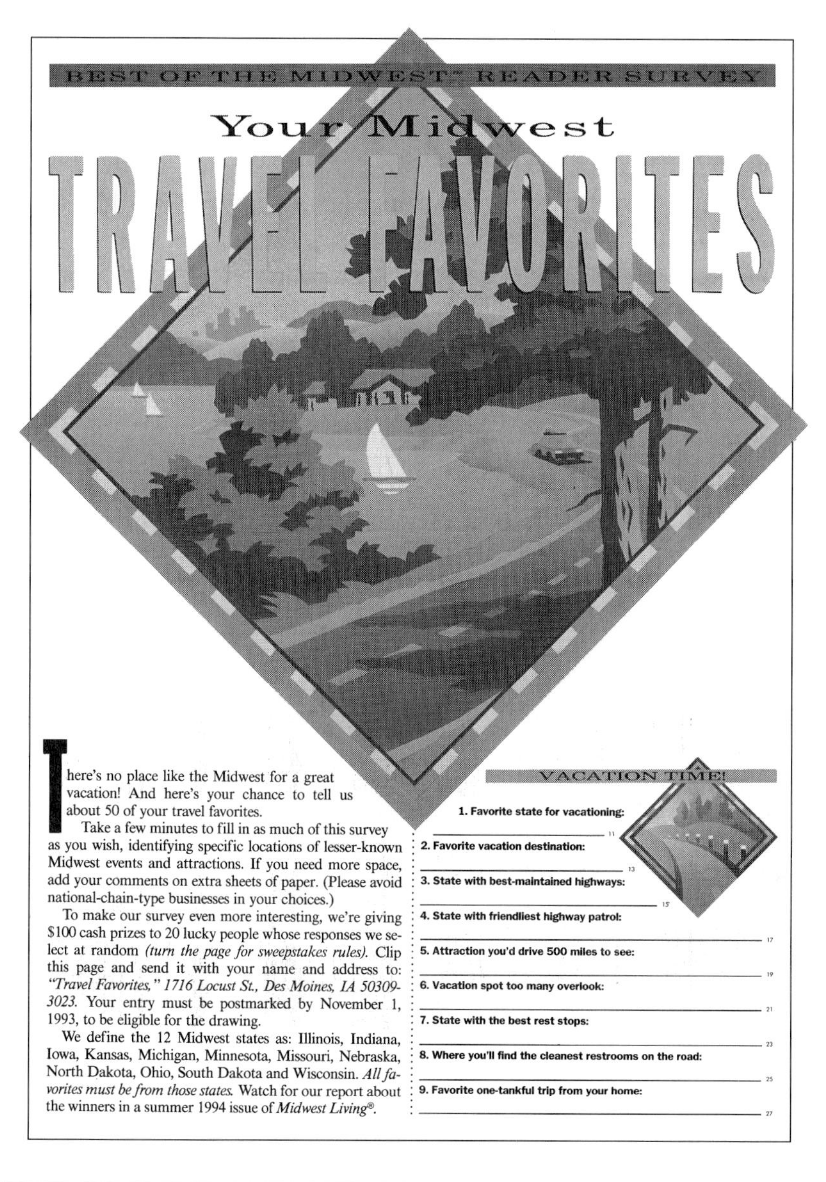

BEST OF THE MIDWEST™ READER SURVEY

Your Midwest

TRAVEL FAVORITES

There's no place like the Midwest for a great vacation! And here's your chance to tell us about 50 of your travel favorites.

Take a few minutes to fill in as much of this survey as you wish, identifying specific locations of lesser-known Midwest events and attractions. If you need more space, add your comments on extra sheets of paper. (Please avoid national-chain-type businesses in your choices.)

To make our survey even more interesting, we're giving $100 cash prizes to 20 lucky people whose responses we select at random *(turn the page for sweepstakes rules)*. Clip this page and send it with your name and address to: *"Travel Favorites," 1716 Locust St., Des Moines, IA 50309-3023.* Your entry must be postmarked by November 1, 1993, to be eligible for the drawing.

We define the 12 Midwest states as: Illinois, Indiana, Iowa, Kansas, Michigan, Minnesota, Missouri, Nebraska, North Dakota, Ohio, South Dakota and Wisconsin. *All favorites must be from those states.* Watch for our report about the winners in a summer 1994 issue of *Midwest Living®*.

VACATION TIME!

1. Favorite state for vacationing:
________________ 11

2. Favorite vacation destination:
________________ 13

3. State with best-maintained highways:
________________ 15

4. State with friendliest highway patrol:
________________ 17

5. Attraction you'd drive 500 miles to see:
________________ 19

6. Vacation spot too many overlook:
________________ 21

7. State with the best rest stops:
________________ 23

8. Where you'll find the cleanest restrooms on the road:
________________ 25

9. Favorite one-tankful trip from your home:
________________ 27

Any publication can provide ideas for editors. Just remember that not all the ideas are going to be suitable for every situation. Clip out the ideas that strike you as interesting, regardless of their immediate usefulness in your publication. *Midwest Living* has several ideas that are useful.

Things to note:

- Use of the points of a square artwork to break the boundary of the box
- A very condensed initial letter that is both indented and that stands above the copy block
- A small-point-size dotted column rule in the middle
- Use of a condensed all-cap title containing very thin shadows overlaid on the artwork

Each story or package should be regarded as a module that is rectangular and that interacts with other modules to form a page design.

Modular pages do not have:

- Doglegs
- Raw wraps

Squares, the least pleasing rectangular shape, should be avoided.

2. Observe the principle of dominance. This means one module clearly dominates the page. The dominant module is larger than any other element and is placed at or near the center and top of the page, where it becomes the focal point for readers. The dominant element may be:

- A picture with cutlines only
- A picture packaged with a story
- A boxed package containing stories and illustrations
- An informational graphic that stands alone

3. Break up the gutters. The design may be primarily vertical or horizontal, but in either case at least one module should cut across two or more columns. The goal is to avoid gutters that extend all the way from the top to the bottom of the page, unbroken by any headline, rule or illustration.

4. Avoid butting headlines, boxes or unrelated illustrations. Headlines that butt tend to be hard to read, even if they differ in size and font. Butting headlines in the same size and font are "tombstoned." Boxes that butt are redundant because a single box performs the function of setting off one module from the others around it. Illustrations that butt defeat the principle that pictures look best when framed by type. (The principle does not apply to picture pages, which once were popular but now are rare.)

5. Pay attention to the bottom of the page. Every page is divided horizontally at the middle by a fold. In a good design, the section below the fold is attractive even when viewed apart from the top. A weak design treats the bottom of the page as a place where the ends of stories accumulate.

6. Let the news determine the layout. The most beautiful and carefully planned layout becomes obsolete when major news breaks. The purpose of layout is to present information effectively and attractively, but the editor may be forced to compromise on attractiveness to make room for new information and more timely illustrations.

7. Respect the illustrations. When faced with tough competition among strong elements for limited space on a page, an editor may tend to think first of shrinking the illustrations. If the optimum size of an illustration has already been decided, shrinking it will damage not only the picture but also the layout. An editor who slights photographs and other illustrations is likely to become known for weak design skills. A good principle to remember is that the impact of a photograph is directly proportional to its size.

8. Avoid large, gray areas of body type. A guideline known as "the dollar bill rule" should be considered but not slavishly followed in every case. The

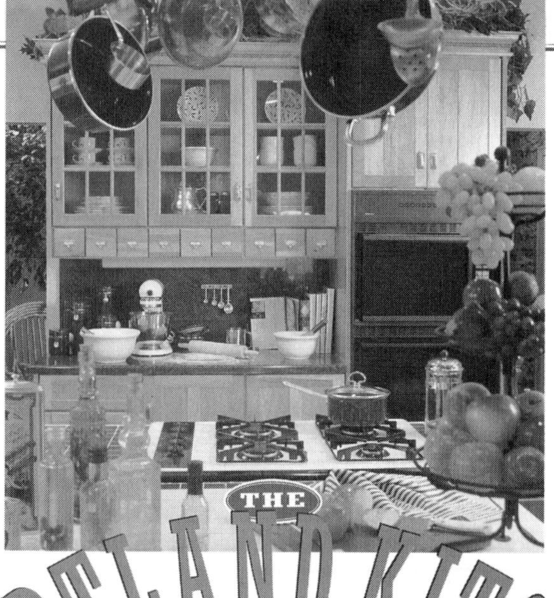

THE HEARTLAND KITCHEN

DESIGN IDEAS FOR YOUR HOME FROM MIDWEST LIVING®

Step inside the dream kitchen our editors and designers created just for you. Whether you're planning to build a new kitchen, remodel an old one or just add one small special something to the kitchen you have, you'll find inspiration in The Heartland Kitchen. It's a family-living center (sunroom, family room, informal and formal dining areas, deck, utility room and recycling center) with a hardworking kitchen at its heart.

In this brand-new home we built in Maple Grove, Minnesota (just northwest of Minneapolis), there's a just-right spot to bake a batch of bread, host a holiday dinner for a dozen, recycle yesterday's newspaper or dream by the fireplace.

We collected ideas from our readers, brainstormed a batch of our own, then took our wish list to our team of experts: builder Richard Kalow, architect Jack Bloodgood, Dayton's Interior Design Studio team—Barbara Blank, Marlene Lundgren and Teri Peterson—and KraftMaid Cabinetry designer Janice Pattee *(see Janice's kitchen-planning tips, page 78)*. The result: rooms packed with convenience and style that suit the way Midwest families live today.

MIDWEST LIVING OCTOBER 1993 67

Another page from *Midwest Living* with some useful ideas.

Things to note:

- The use of a photo to break the top boundary of the box
- A very tall shaded initial letter that begins in the center of the top line
- A deck that overlays the initial letter
- Copy that is set the same width as the photo
- A curved headline that overlays the photo and the box
- A ruled box with the thinner line out, which is opposite of the usual way it is used

rule says: If you can place a dollar bill anywhere on the page and it touches no headlines, display type or illustrations, you have a gray area that needs attention.

9. Use boxes and rules to clarify relationships. It should be easily apparent to readers which pictures and stories go together and which do not. Boxes and rules are best used to set off independent elements and define packages.

10. Don't neglect the details. No front-page design is complete or effective if it does not make use of promotion boxes and especially an index. Folios, nameplates, headers and standing devices such as sigs must not be forgotten.

EVERY ELEMENT IS A RECTANGLE

Virtually every element used in publication design is a rectangle. A headline is a long, skinny rectangle. A photo is either a horizontal or a vertical rectangle. A story can be a tall one-column rectangle or a shorter two-column rectangle or a shallow six-column rectangle.

When one is laying out a newspaper page, it is beneficial to think of every single component as a rectangle, rather than as a three-column cutline or a 300-word story or a three-line headline or an 18-point italic centered pull quote.

A page can be divided easily into rectangles or grids that are based on columns. A good approach is to place the must-use elements first. Next, place the dominant element, and finally, fill in the remaining space with the other elements in order of importance.

Remember that the dominant element must be at least 50 percent larger than any other. If you allocate smaller and smaller rectangles, using a good mix of horizontals and verticals, your page should go together well.

Modular layout can help solve one problem that can throw unprepared editors: the on-deadline event, such as a basketball game or city crisis. One trick is to dummy ahead of time a rectangle, probably a three- or four-column vertical space. If a three-column space has been allocated and the photographer brings in a two-column vertical, the photo can go at the top right of the space with the head running across the top and a one-column story on the left side. If the best photo is a horizontal, then place the photo at the top, head below that and copy below that. A hairline rule boxing the package makes for a neat display.

DESIGNING A PAGE STEP BY STEP

Every item the designer places on a page irretrievably alters the final product, and according to the Bauhaus philosophy, no more items than are minimally necessary to complete the design should be used.

1. **Make a list of "must-use" items.** These include the flag, weather box, index, news summaries and skyboxes. The sizes and placement of most of these will remain constant from issue to issue.
2. **List the available art.** Underline those images under consideration for dominant art. Try to have twice as many possibilities as needed. This will provide maximum flexibility. Some days there will be only one possible image to consider, but a dozen might be serious contenders the next.

Dos and Don'ts for Designers

1. Do build your layout around the art.
2. Do play the dominant element 50 percent larger than any other element.
3. Do use headline type in a dramatic fashion.
4. Do use white space as a design element.
5. Do favor hairline or 1-point rules.
6. Do select accent elements to enhance the layout.
7. Do use contrast to achieve visual impact.
8. Do use type as a design element in layouts that lack art.
9. Do keep art away from ads on inside pages.
10. Don't tombstone headlines.
11. Don't butt headlines if you can avoid it.
12. Don't place boxed elements next to each other.
13. Do use a mixture of vertical and horizontal elements.
14. Don't wrap a story out from under the headline.
15. Don't jump unless you have to.
16. Do use wrap-ups and summaries to help explain complex issues.
17. Do remember the KISS principle: keep it simple, stupid.

Some Things to Remember

1. There ain't no rules.
2. Design supports content.
3. Every design element, including body type, is a rectangle.
4. Color should complement or contrast but not clash.
5. Every page needs a dominant element.
6. The design should help the reader grade the news in importance and place it in perspective.
7. Shorter columns of type look better than longer ones.
8. Art should lead the reader toward the story, not away from it.

Box 10.2

3. **List the story possibilities in order of importance.** The first item on the list is your lead story.
4. **Sketch a layout showing placement of the "must-use" items.** What's left is the space you have for live news.
5. **Place the dominant art.** Play it the size it *should* be, not the size it *has* to be. Be sure to leave room for the cutline.
6. **Place the lead story above the fold.** Allow an additional 25 to 50 percent space for headline, decks, bylines, pull quotes and other typographical devices.
7. **Dummy in the second story.** Leave 10 to 25 percent more space for typographical treatment. Then do the same for the third story and so forth until the page is complete.
8. **Check your lists.** Has anything important been omitted?
9. **Turn the layout upside down and look at the overall effect.** (If the layout is done on a computer it will be necessary to print out a rough copy to see what has been done.) The editor needs to remember that the look and "feel" of a page will appear one way on the screen or dummy and quite another when the page is printed out. The editor should be looking for erratic positioning of stories and the overall balance of the page.
10. **Have another editor look at the page.** Another eye can help make sure that everything makes sense and that something is not being overlooked.

As soon as possible after completing a page, a beginning editor should make reference notes indicating how the page came about. (Were last-minute stories dropped in? What solutions were attempted? In retrospect, what solutions should have been attempted? What efforts should be undertaken to solve design or news problems?) After much experience editors will be able to find better solutions to design problems and in much less time. Initially, however, these lessons are hard won, and notes will facilitate learning.

Box 10.2 lists informal rules for designers.

DEVELOPING A DESIGN STYLE

Each publication should have a distinctive personality, just as should each person. The personality of a publication should reflect a complex mixture of readership interests, the publication's values, and the diverse abilities and individual personalities of the staff itself, plus the community in which the publication is circulated.

Unfortunately, some publications, just like some people, develop "copycat" personalities, adopting the look, language, color, typeface schedule and layout style of a favorite newspaper or magazine. This is easily seen in high schools where a group of students will style themselves from their leader—similar hairstyles, jewelry, word choices, musical preferences, and of course similar clothing.

Many publications have altered their design styles to be similar to *USA Today,* adopting, or at least attempting to adopt, the same headline choices, similar section headers, graphics approach and short, snappy writing style. Some have done so successfully, taking selected parts and incorporating those into an existing mix that ultimately produces a better product. Other newspapers have tried to copy almost everything, resulting in a publication that looks like a copy and failing in that.

It is particularly troubling to travel across the country and see newspaper after newspaper that looks like so many others: Times Roman headlines, Helvetica cutlines, a column of wrap-ups down the left side, a series of teaser boxes above the flag. Newspapers do not need to look like one another to be successful.

Of course newspapers have similarities, just as people do, but superficial similarities must not crowd out the deeper personalities, like the quirks, the warts, the core values.

Designers must learn about the community the publication is attempting to serve. They must find out what the community (or more likely the communities) holds dear to itself: what races predominate, what languages the people speak, what their political interests and religious beliefs are, on what they agree and disagree, how they view themselves, to what they aspire, what their fears are, what their triumphs are, what works within the community, what doesn't, how people view their local government and schools and institutions, what information they think they need to operate at a minimal level and as productive and informed citizens?

Finding answers to these questions is not an easy task, but one that is essential for every publication to do continuously. Since successful businesses continually sample their customers to find out how the product is being accepted and what can be done to improve service, so also must publications find out

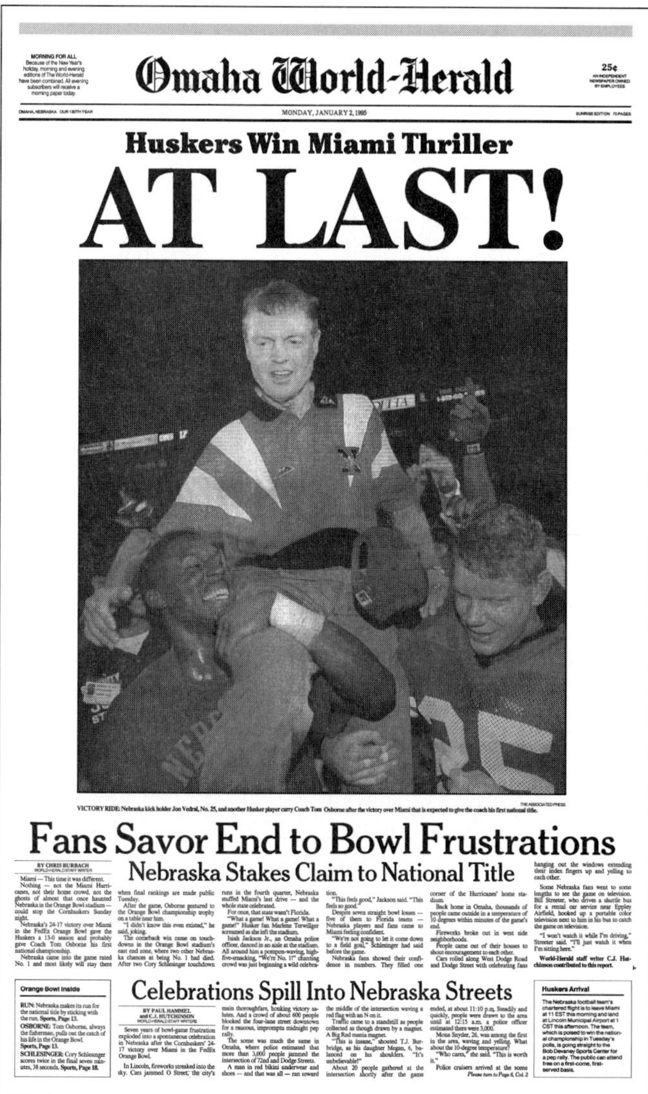

MORNING FOR ALL
Because of the New Year's holiday, morning and evening editions of The World-Herald have been combined. All evening subscribers will receive a morning paper today.

Omaha World-Herald

25¢
AN INDEPENDENT NEWSPAPER OWNED BY EMPLOYEES

OMAHA, NEBRASKA OUR 130TH YEAR — MONDAY, JANUARY 2, 1995 — SUNRISE EDITION 70 PAGES

Huskers Win Miami Thriller

AT LAST!

THE ASSOCIATED PRESS

VICTORY RIDE: Nebraska kick holder Jon Vedral, No. 25, and another Husker player carry Coach Tom Osborne after the victory over Miami that is expected to give the coach his first national title.

Fans Savor End to Bowl Frustrations

Nebraska Stakes Claim to National Title

BY CHRIS BURBACH
WORLD-HERALD STAFF WRITER

Miami — This time it was different.

Nothing — not the Miami Hurricanes, not their home crowd, not the ghosts of almost that once haunted Nebraska in the Orange Bowl stadium — could stop the Cornhuskers Sunday night.

Nebraska's 24-17 victory over Miami in the FedEx Orange Bowl gave the Huskers a 13-0 season and probably gave Coach Tom Osborne his first national championship.

Nebraska came into the game rated No. 1 and most likely will stay there when final rankings are made public Tuesday.

After the game, Osborne gestured to the Orange Bowl championship trophy on a table near him.

"I didn't know this even existed," he said, joking.

The comeback win came on touchdowns in the Orange Bowl stadium's east end zone, where two other Nebraska chances at being No. 1 had died. After two Cory Schlesinger touchdown runs in the fourth quarter, Nebraska stuffed Miami's last drive — and the whole state celebrated.

For once, that state wasn't Florida.

"What a game! What a game! What a game!" Husker fan Marlene Terwillger screamed as she left the stadium.

Isiah Jackson Jr., an Omaha police officer, danced in an aisle at the stadium. All around him a pompon-waving, high-five-smacking, "We're No. 1!" chanting crowd was just beginning a wild celebration.

"This feels good," Jackson said. "This feels so good."

Despite seven straight bowl losses — five of them to Florida teams — Nebraska players and fans came to Miami feeling confident.

"We're not going to let it come down to a field goal," Schlesinger had said before the game.

Nebraska fans showed their confidence in numbers. They filled one corner of the Hurricanes' home stadium.

Back home in Omaha, thousands of people came outside in a temperature of 10 degrees within minutes of the game's end.

Fireworks broke out in west side neighborhoods.

People came out of their houses to shout encouragement to each other.

Cars rolled along West Dodge Road and Dodge Street with celebrating fans hanging out the windows extending their index fingers up and yelling to each other.

Some Nebraska fans went to some lengths to see the game on television. Bill Streeter, who drives a shuttle bus for a rental car service near Eppley Airfield, hooked up a portable color television next to him in his bus to catch the game on television.

"I won't watch it while I'm driving," Streeter said. "I'll just watch it when I'm sitting here."

World-Herald staff writer C.J. Hutchinson contributed to this report.

Orange Bowl Inside

RUN: Nebraska makes its run for the national title by sticking with the run. **Sports, Page 13.**

OSBORNE: Tom Osborne, always the fisherman, pulls out the catch of his life in the Orange Bowl. **Sports, Page 13.**

SCHLESINGER: Cory Schlesinger scores twice in the final seven minutes, 38 seconds. **Sports, Page 18.**

Celebrations Spill Into Nebraska Streets

BY PAUL HAMMEL
and C.J. HUTCHINSON
WORLD-HERALD STAFF WRITERS

Seven years of bowl-game frustration exploded into a spontaneous celebration in Nebraska after the Cornhuskers' 24-17 victory over Miami in the FedEx Orange Bowl.

In Lincoln, fireworks streaked into the sky. Cars jammed O Street, the city's main thoroughfare, honking victory salutes. And a crowd of about 600 people blocked the four-lane street downtown for a raucous, impromptu midnight pep rally.

The scene was much the same in Omaha, where police estimated that more than 3,000 people jammed the intersection of 72nd and Dodge Streets.

A man in red bikini underwear and shoes — and that was all — ran toward the middle of the intersection waving a red flag with an N on it.

Traffic came to a standstill as people collected as though drawn by a magnet. A Big Red mania magnet.

"This is insane," shouted T.J. Burbridge, as his daughter Megan, 6, balanced on his shoulders. "It's unbelievable!"

About 20 people gathered at the intersection shortly after the game ended, at about 11:10 p.m. Steadily and quickly, people were drawn to the area until at 12:15 a.m. a police officer estimated there were 3,000.

Mona Snyder, 26, was among the first in the area, waving and yelling. What about the 10-degree temperature?

"Who cares," she said. "This is worth it."

Police cruisers arrived at the scene

Please turn to Page 6, Col. 2

Huskers Arrival

The Nebraska football team's chartered flight is to leave Miami at 11 EST this morning and land at Lincoln Municipal Airport at 1 CST this afternoon. The team, which is poised to win the national championship in Tuesday's polls, is going straight to the Bob Devaney Sports Center for a pep rally. The public can attend free on a first-come, first-served basis.

The *Omaha World-Herald* used a poster-style front page to celebrate a football victory by the University of Nebraska–Lincoln Cornhuskers over the Miami Hurricanes in the 1995 Orange Bowl. The coverage of events important to a newspaper's readership is difficult enough without having the event fall after the usual copy deadline. While it is unusual for metro newspapers to play sports on the front page, winning a national championship game requires desperate measures.

Things to note:

- A symmetrical balance was used, which parallels the paper's usual conservative approach to layout
- All headlines are centered
- A Times Roman all-cap second-coming size head contrasts with the paper's usual headline face of Cheltenham
- Twin boxes at the bottom of the page mirror the information ears at the top of the page
- The deck for the main story is nestled into the copy

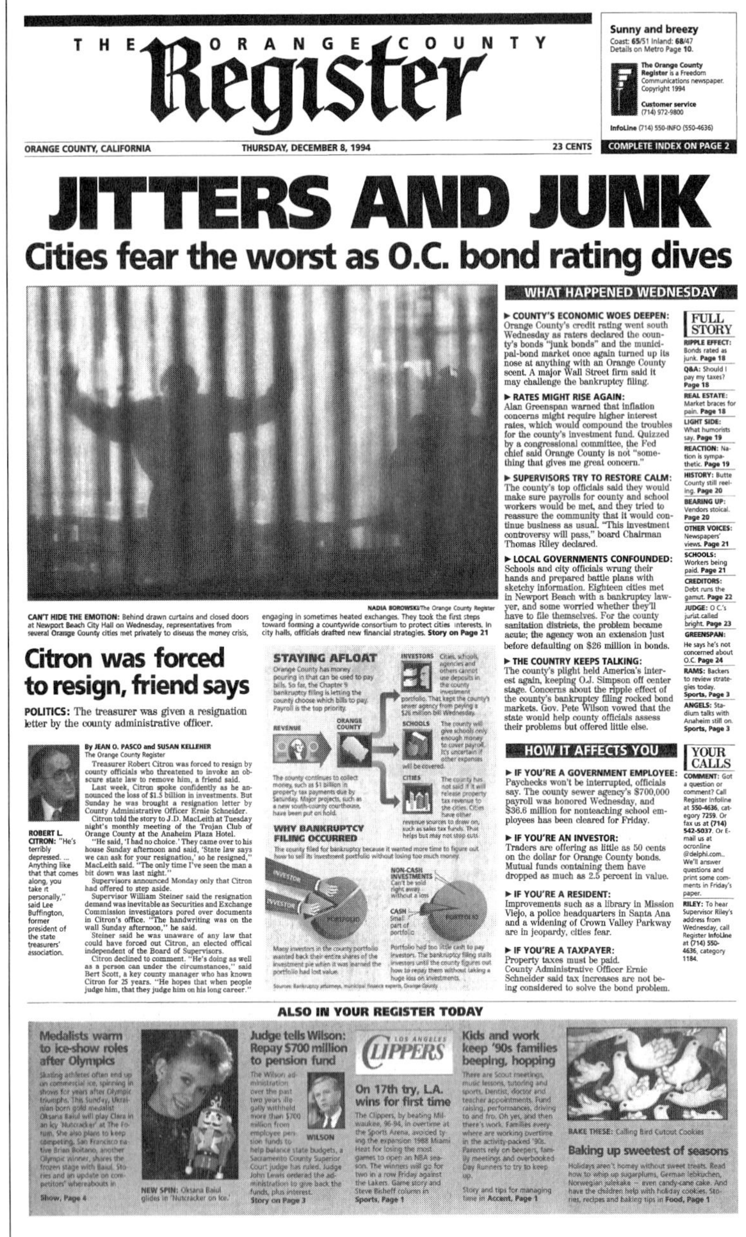

THE ORANGE COUNTY **Register**

ORANGE COUNTY, CALIFORNIA | THURSDAY, DECEMBER 8, 1994 | 23 CENTS

Sunny and breezy
Coast: **65**/51 Inland: **68**/47
Details on Metro Page **10**.

The Orange County Register is a Freedom Communications newspaper. Copyright 1994

Customer service
(714) 972-9800

InfoLine (714) 550-INFO (550-4636)

COMPLETE INDEX ON PAGE 2

JITTERS AND JUNK

Cities fear the worst as O.C. bond rating dives

CAN'T HIDE THE EMOTION: Behind drawn curtains and closed doors at Newport Beach City Hall on Wednesday, representatives from several Orange County cities met privately to discuss the money crisis, engaging in sometimes heated exchanges. They took the first steps toward forming a countywide consortium to protect cities interests. In city halls, officials drafted new financial strategies. **Story on Page 21**

NADIA BOROWSKI/The Orange County Register

WHAT HAPPENED WEDNESDAY

▶ **COUNTY'S ECONOMIC WOES DEEPEN:** Orange County's credit rating went south Wednesday as raters declared the county's bonds "junk bonds" and the municipal-bond market once again turned up its nose at anything with an Orange County scent. A major Wall Street firm said it may challenge the bankruptcy filing.

▶ **RATES MIGHT RISE AGAIN:** Alan Greenspan warned that inflation concerns might require higher interest rates, which would compound the troubles for the county's investment fund. Quizzed by a congressional committee, the Fed chief said Orange County is not "something that gives me great concern."

▶ **SUPERVISORS TRY TO RESTORE CALM:** The county's top officials said they would make sure payrolls for county and school workers would be met, and they tried to reassure the community that it would continue business as usual. "This investment controversy will pass," board Chairman Thomas Riley declared.

▶ **LOCAL GOVERNMENTS CONFOUNDED:** Schools and city officials wrung their hands and prepared battle plans with sketchy information. Eighteen cities met in Newport Beach with a bankruptcy lawyer, and some worried whether they'll have to file themselves. For the county sanitation districts, the problem became acute; the agency won an extension just before defaulting on $26 million in bonds.

▶ **THE COUNTRY KEEPS TALKING:** The county's plight held America's interest again, keeping O.J. Simpson off center stage. Concerns about the ripple effect of the county's bankruptcy filing rocked bond markets. Gov. Pete Wilson vowed that the state would help county officials assess their problems but offered little else.

FULL STORY

RIPPLE EFFECT: Bonds rated as junk. **Page 18**

Q&A: Should I pay my taxes? **Page 18**

REAL ESTATE: Market braces for pain. **Page 18**

LIGHT SIDE: What humorists say. **Page 19**

REACTION: Nation is sympathetic. **Page 19**

HISTORY: Butte County still reeling. **Page 20**

BEARING UP: Vendors stoical. **Page 20**

OTHER VOICES: Newspapers' views. **Page 21**

SCHOOLS: Workers being paid. **Page 21**

CREDITORS: Debt runs the gamut. **Page 22**

JUDGE: O.C.'s jurist called bright. **Page 23**

GREENSPAN: He says he's not concerned about O.C. **Page 24**

RAMS: Backers to review strategies today. **Sports, Page 3**

ANGELS: Stadium talks with Anaheim still on. **Sports, Page 3**

HOW IT AFFECTS YOU

▶ **IF YOU'RE A GOVERNMENT EMPLOYEE:** Paychecks won't be interrupted, officials say. The county sewer agency's $700,000 payroll was honored Wednesday, and $36.6 million for nonteaching school employees has been cleared for Friday.

▶ **IF YOU'RE AN INVESTOR:** Traders are offering as little as 50 cents on the dollar for Orange County bonds. Mutual funds containing them have dropped as much as 2.5 percent in value.

▶ **IF YOU'RE A RESIDENT:** Improvements such as a library in Mission Viejo, a police headquarters in Santa Ana and a widening of Crown Valley Parkway are in jeopardy, cities fear.

▶ **IF YOU'RE A TAXPAYER:** Property taxes must be paid. County Administrative Officer Ernie Schneider said tax increases are not being considered to solve the bond problem.

YOUR CALLS

COMMENT: Got a question or comment? Call Register Infoline at **550-4636**, category **7259**. Or fax us at **(714) 542-5037**. Or E-mail us at ocronline @delphi.com.. We'll answer questions and print some comments in Friday's paper.

RILEY: To hear Supervisor Riley's address from Wednesday, call Register **InfoLine** at **(714) 550-4636**, category **1184**.

Citron was forced to resign, friend says

POLITICS: The treasurer was given a resignation letter by the county administrative officer.

ROBERT L. CITRON: "He's terribly depressed. ... Anything like that that comes along, you take it personally," said Lee Buffington, former president of the state treasurers' association.

By JEAN O. PASCO and SUSAN KELLEHER
The Orange County Register

Treasurer Robert Citron was forced to resign by county officials who threatened to invoke an obscure state law to remove him, a friend said.

Last week, Citron spoke confidently as he announced the loss of $1.5 billion in investments. But Sunday he was brought a resignation letter by County Administrative Officer Ernie Schneider.

Citron told the story to J.D. MacLeith at Tuesday night's monthly meeting of the Trojan Club of Orange County at the Anaheim Plaza Hotel.

"He said, 'I had no choice.' They came over to his house Sunday afternoon and said, 'State law says we can ask for your resignation,' so he resigned," MacLeith said. "The only time I've seen the man a bit down was last night."

Supervisors announced Monday only that Citron had offered to step aside.

Supervisor William Steiner said the resignation demand was inevitable as Securities and Exchange Commission investigators pored over documents in Citron's office. "The handwriting was on the wall Sunday afternoon," he said.

Steiner said he was unaware of any law that could have forced out Citron, an elected offical independent of the Board of Supervisors.

Citron declined to comment. "He's doing as well as a person can under the circumstances," said Bert Scott, a key county manager who has known Citron for 25 years. "He hopes that when people judge him, that they judge him on his long career."

STAYING AFLOAT

Orange County has money pouring in that can be used to pay bills. So far, the Chapter 9 bankruptcy filing is letting the county choose which bills to pay. Payroll is the top priority.

REVENUE

ORANGE COUNTY

The county continues to collect money, such as $1 billion in property tax payments due by Saturday. Major projects, such as a new south-county courthouse, have been put on hold.

INVESTORS: Cities, schools, agencies and others cannot use deposits in the county investment portfolio. That kept the county's sewer agency from paying a $26 million bill Wednesday.

SCHOOLS: The county will give schools only enough money to cover payroll. It's uncertain if other expenses will be covered.

CITIES: The county has not said if it will release property tax revenue to the cities. Cities have other revenue sources to draw on, such as sales tax funds. That helps but may not stop cuts.

WHY BANKRUPTCY FILING OCCURRED

The county filed for bankruptcy because it wanted more time to figure out how to sell its investment portfolio without losing too much money.

INVESTOR

INVESTOR

PORTFOLIO

NON-CASH INVESTMENTS: Can't be sold right away without a loss

CASH: Small part of portfolio

PORTFOLIO

Many investors in the county portfolio wanted back their entire shares of the investment pie when it was learned the portfolio had lost value.

Portfolio had too little cash to pay investors. The bankruptcy filing stalls investors until the county figures out how to repay them without taking a huge loss on investments.

Sources: Bankruptcy attorneys, municipal finance experts, Orange County

ALSO IN YOUR REGISTER TODAY

Medalists warm to ice-show roles after Olympics

Skating athletes often end up on commercial ice, spinning in shows for years after Olympic triumphs. This Sunday, Ukrainian-born gold medalist Oksana Baiul will play Clara in an icy 'Nutcracker' at The Forum. She also plans to keep competing. San Francisco native Brian Boitano, another Olympic winner, shares the frozen stage with Baiul. Stories and an update on competitors' whereabouts in **Show, Page 4**

NEW SPIN: Oksana Baiul glides in 'Nutcracker on Ice.'

Judge tells Wilson: Repay $700 million to pension fund

The Wilson administration over the past two years illegally withheld more than $700 million from employee pension funds to help balance state budgets, a Sacramento County Superior Court judge has ruled. Judge John Lewis ordered the administration to give back the funds, plus interest. **Story on Page 3**

WILSON

LOS ANGELES CLIPPERS

On 17th try, L.A. wins for first time

The Clippers, by beating Milwaukee, 96-94, in overtime at the Sports Arena, avoided tying the expansion 1988 Miami Heat for losing the most games to open an NBA season. The winners will go for two in a row Friday against the Lakers. Game story and Steve Bisheff column in **Sports, Page 1**

Kids and work keep '90s families beeping, hopping

There are Scout meetings, music lessons, tutoring and sports. Dentist, doctor and teacher appointments. Fund raising, performances, driving to and fro. Oh yes, and then there's work. Families everywhere are working overtime in the activity-packed '90s. Parents rely on beepers, family meetings and overbooked Day Runners to try to keep up.

Story and tips for managing time in **Accent, Page 1**

BAKE THESE: Calling Bird Cutout Cookies

Baking up sweetest of seasons

Holidays aren't homey without sweet treats. Read how to whip up sugarplums, German lebkuchen, Norwegian julekake — even candy-cane cake. And have the children help with holiday cookies. Stories, recipes and baking tips in **Food, Page 1**

The second of a series of consecutive front pages from the *Orange County Register* (see color insert for Dec. 7 front page) shows how editors deal with an ongoing topic.

Things to note:

Dec. 8

- A hammer head kicks off the page
- Quick summaries explain "What Happened Wednesday" and "How It Affects You"
- Teasers down the right side provide additional information points
- Graphics provide a visual sense of how the county got into financial trouble

THE ORANGE COUNTY

Windy and cool
Coast: **67**/49 Inland: **73**/42
Details on Metro Page **12**.

The Orange County Register is a Freedom Communications newspaper. Copyright 1994

Customer service (714) 972-9800

InfoLine (714) 550-INFO (550-4636)

COMPLETE INDEX ON PAGE 2

ORANGE COUNTY, CALIFORNIA | FRIDAY, DECEMBER 9, 1994 | 23 CENTS

SELLING FRENZY

O.C. defaults on bond as lenders sell collateral

Photos by YGNACIO NANETTI/The Orange County Register

POINTING FINGERS: Orange County Supervisor Thomas Riley, above, listens Thursday as Tustin attorney Stephen Johnson, right, suggests he resign over the state of the county's investment fund. Confusion and anxiety reigned in meetings throughout the county as officials tried to assess the effect of the unloading of Orange County securities.

WHAT HAPPENED THURSDAY

▶ **WALL STREET ACTS:** Major Wall Street brokerage firms continued to seize and sell securities Orange County had pledged for loans, liquidating a total of $8 billion so far. Angry county officials authorized their attorneys to sue anyone who grabbed their collateral.

▶ **COUNTY REACTS:** Supervisors lined up former state Treasurer Tom Hayes and top Wall Street investment firm Salomon Brothers Inc. to join its financial-restructuring team, and created a second county treasury to keep incoming revenue separate from the crippled investment pool.

▶ **CONFUSION REIGNS:** Worried residents and vendors called city halls seeking elusive information. Anaheim froze hiring and put major projects on hold.

▶ **SHOPPERS WORRY:** Individual shoppers expressed queasiness and said they probably would spend less than they had originally planned on Christmas presents. Retailers expressed confidence and hope.

FULL STORY

EXPERTS: Crisis 'not a death blow.' **Page 18**

ECONOMY: O.C. workers worry. **Page 18**

SCHOOLS: Cash continues to flow. **Page 19**

VOICES: Readers give views. **Page 20**

MEDIA: Do they deserve some blame? **Page 20**

ANGER: Callers tell supervisors: Quit. **Page 21**

RESCUER: Ex-state treasurer hired. **Page 22**

LAW: It may be on the county's side. **Page 23**

TIMING: Debacle offsets recovery. **Page 24**

BUSES: Federal funds sought. **Page 28**

CALL US: Got a question or comment? Call Register InfoLine at (714) 550-4636 category **7259** We'll answer questions and print some comments.

HOW IT AFEECTS YOU

▶ **IF YOU ARE A COUNTY RESIDENT:** Property taxes are due Saturday and will go into the separate new treasury fund. Tom Hayes, brought in to manage the crisis, said it was too early to say if higher taxes or service cuts will occur.

▶ **IF YOU ARE A COUNTY VENDOR:** Ernie Schneider, the county's chief administrative officer, told city officials that some vendors probably will not be paid. He said the county does not know the full extent of the county's losses.

Dow drops 50; county hires crisis manager

FINANCE: A new fund is set up to safeguard property taxes. But cities are told some vendors won't be paid.

By LIZ PULLIAM, JEAN O. PASCO and MARILYN KALFUS
The Orange County Register

Orange County's financial mess deepened Thursday when the county defaulted on a $110 million pension bond and Wall Street rushed to escape the taint of the county's bankruptcy.

County supervisors ordered lawsuits to prevent further hemorrhaging caused by lenders seizing and selling off $8 billion in securities that backed Orange County loans.

They also sought to prop up public confidence by assuring taxpayers that money they owe on property taxes due Saturday will go into a new, separate treasury that will be invested solely in government-backed Treasury notes.

And former state Treasurer Thomas Hayes was brought in to take over management of the financial crisis, with the help of respected Wall Street investment firm Salomon Bros. Inc.

But the hopeful steps were offset by somber words from Hayes: "This is a problem for every citizen of Orange County who pays taxes and uses services."

He said it was too early to say if residents faced higher taxes or cuts in services, or even to give specific figures on the fund's status. Officials also couldn't say how much cash on hand the county has.

"Some vendors are probably not going to get paid," County Administrative Officer Ernie Schneider told a meeting of city managers.

It was unclear Thursday how much of the $1.5 billion paper loss Orange County officials announced last week in their investment fund would be turned into a real loss by the Wall Street sales.

For the day, the stock market dropped 50 points, which ana-

Please see **FUND Page 25**

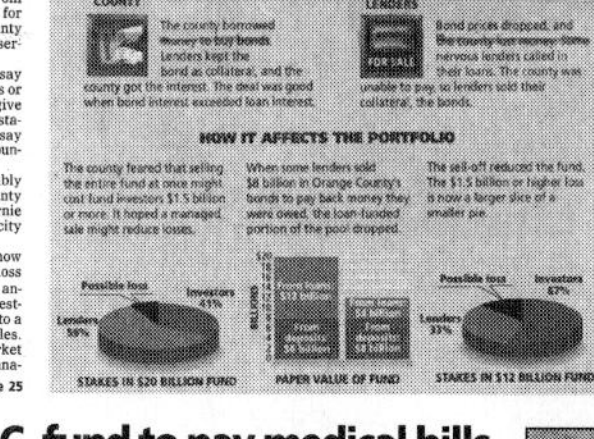

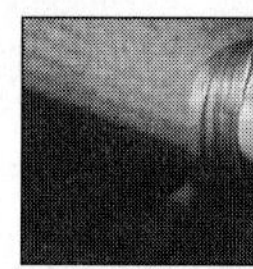

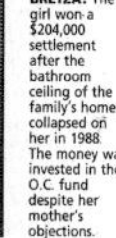

Girl was counting on O.C. fund to pay medical bills

PEOPLE: Mom worries because accident settlement money is frozen.

By CAROL MASCIOLA
The Orange County Register

Patricia Bretza has spent a tearful, anxious week wondering whether Orange County has gambled away her brain-damaged daughter's $204,000 medical fund.

Kristy Bretza, 17, won the money in a settlement after the bathroom ceiling of the family's Trabuco Canyon home collapsed on her in 1988.

Her lawyer and a judge ordered that the money be invested in the county bond fund, against the wishes of her mother.

Now her money and judgments belonging to about 400 other minors are frozen in the county bankruptcy. The county is releasing money only to pay school and county employees' salaries.

"This money was supposed to provide for her medical care for the rest of her life," said Patricia Bretza, a registered nurse. "She'll never get health insurance, and doctors predict a lot of problems in the future. It just scares me to death because she's already suffered so much and lost so much."

Bretza says she has repeatedly called the county seeking information about her daughter's money, but has been told "not to worry."

"Nobody's giving us an answer," she said.

For the rest of her life Kristy is expected to need medical care for seizures, soaring blood pressure and fainting spells.

She wasn't able to finish high school and won't ever be able to earn enough money for all the doctors bills ahead of her.

She was relying on the county

Please see **JUDGE Page 20**

MICHAEL KITADA/The Orange County Register

KRISTINA BRETZA: The girl won a $204,000 settlement after the bathroom ceiling of the family's home collapsed on her in 1988. The money was invested in the O.C. fund despite her mother's objections.

ALSO IN YOUR REGISTER TODAY

TRAINING: Marines board a helicopter on the USS Nassau in the Adriatic Sea on Thursday.

Clinton OKs sending in troops

The president has given preliminary approval to include U.S. forces in a NATO rapid-deployment force that may be called upon to evacuate U.N. peacekeepers in Bosnia. **Story on Page 3**

Post office drops atom bomb stamp after complaints

After calls from the White House, the Postal Service decided to drop a stamp design depicting a mushroom cloud over Japan. The atomic-bomb design caused a stir almost from the moment it was announced. Japanese officials were outraged and filed protests. **Story on Page 3**

TWIRL WITH TWANG: Michelle Howard steps lively.

Boots are made for toeing the line to a country beat

All across the county, seven nights a week, thousands are doing the Tush-Push, the two-step and the Western swing. Country-Western dancing is the rage on the dance floor and there are no signs of its letting up. **Story in Show, Page 18**

Also in Show:

▶ Poster of Demi Moore, star of 'Disclosure.' **Page 40**

▶ A day in the life of the creator of 'X-Files.' **Page 41**

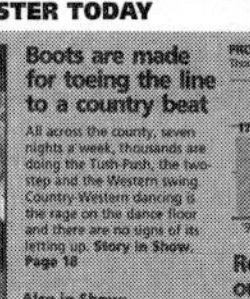

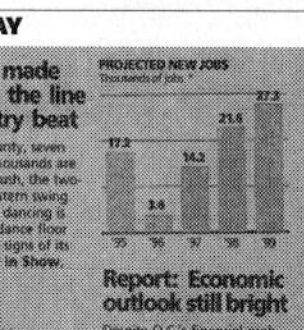

Report: Economic outlook still bright

Despite O.C.'s financial problems, Chapman University is forecasting 17,200 new jobs will be created next year. **Story in Business, Page 1**

Darryl Strawberry accused of hiding $500,000 from IRS

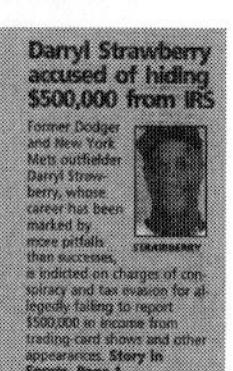

STRAWBERRY

Former Dodger and New York Mets outfielder Darryl Strawberry, whose career has been marked by more pitfalls than successes, is indicted on charges of conspiracy and tax evasion for allegedly failing to report $500,000 in income from trading-card shows and other appearances. **Story in Sports, Page 1**

The third of four front pages from the *Orange County Register,* this issue continues the style begun with the Dec. 7 issue.

Things to note:

Dec. 9

- Deltas are used along the right third of the paper to help point out what happened on Thursday.
- A centered hammer head.
- Because a single topic dominates the front page, a screened box at the bottom serves to highlight key inside stories.

THE ORANGE COUNTY **Register**

Mostly sunny
Coast: 65/45 Inland: 69/40
Details on Metro Page 8.

The Orange County Register is a Freedom Communications newspaper. Copyright 1994

Customer service (714) 972-9800

InfoLine (714) 550-INFO (550-4636)

ORANGE COUNTY, CALIFORNIA SATURDAY, DECEMBER 10, 1994 23 CENTS

COMPLETE INDEX ON PAGE 2

CRISIS DEEPENS

Citron painted rosy picture of shrinking fund

FUND: Interviews and documents show local officials often didn't ask questions. When they did, they weren't told of big paper loses.

By CHRIS KNAP, JIM MULVANEY and LIZ PULLIAM
The Orange County Register

At least 13 local governments eager for profits borrowed $1.2 billion last summer to invest in county Treasurer Robert L. Citron's fund at a time when it was suffering huge losses estimated at more than $500 million.

Interviews and reports show Citron gave rosy assessments of what were really high-risk investments, even as losses were occurring — losses some experts now say he must have known about. And government investors were willing to believe his promises of safety, even without proof.

"The temptation to get something for nothing became too overwhelming," California Treasurer Kathleen Brown said. "They lost sight of that in Orange County. It was greed overcoming common sense."

Now the 7.8 billion fund has collapsed, the county has declared bankruptcy and some of the agencies may not be able to repay the loans. They blame Citron for not warning them when he accepted their money. The Securities and Exchange Commission has launched an investigation into his activities and those of the underwriters who marketed the deals.

But Citron says he did nothing wrong and hadn't calculated the losses because his strategy was to hold his investments to maturity. Although he boosted county government's borrowing from $300 million to $700 million in June, he said it was to increase revenue, not to cover losses.

"We did not know at the time. We never made a calculation of market value. Our strategy was to hold until maturity. They were just paper losses," Citron said in an interview with the Register this week after the fund collapsed and he resigned.

But many experts say Citron had to have known the shaky condition of the fund — and should have been disclosing it.

"I would think Bob would know. If you looked at (your portfolio) and looked at the market, you would know your stuff was going down. This guy's had 20 years doing it," said George Jeffries, chief investment officer for Los Angeles County and a longtime Citron acquaintance.

"In retrospect, I think Citron knew everything that was going on," agreed Zane Mann, publisher of the California Municipal Bond Advisor.

"He was too sophisticated not to know exactly what was going on, in the market or in his fund," Mann said. "He just made a bad

Please see CITRON Page 22

OFF THE WALL: A nail marks where Robert Citron's photo once hung — at the Treasurer's Office beside past O.C. tax collectors. Officials yanked the photo and scraped Citron's name off his door after residents lined up Friday to pay taxes and heap abuse on the resigned tax collector. Story on Page 24

MICHAEL GOULDING
The Register

Experts say loss is bigger: $2.25 billion

BONDS: Trade paper's publisher calls the estimate conservative.

By RONALD CAMPBELL/The Orange County Register

Orange County has lost $2.25 billion and could lose much more from its bad bond-market gamble, an investment trade paper reported Friday.

The estimate by New York-based National Mortgage News exceeds the county's $1.5 billion loss projection. The weekly paper is widely read by lenders and tracks the market for mortgage bonds, key investments in the county's pool.

The paper's publisher, Stan Strachan, said he used experts at a major investment bank and another expert in complex bond strategies to price the portfolio. He called the $2.25 billion loss estimate conservative.

The paper said much of the losses the county suffered were tied to an exotic $5.4 billion bet that interest rates would fall. That's how much former county Treasurer Robert Citron spent on "inverse floater" bonds, federal securities that stop paying dividends when interest rates rise.

"This guy kept buying and buying like a guy at a blackjack table who's lost four straight hands and says, 'This can't happen to me again,' " Strachan said.

Total losses could reach $3 billion, or 43 percent, National Mortgage News estimated. Nine days ago, when the crisis became public, county officials pegged the loss at 20 percent.

Other experts agreed with the paper. "We call it the roach-motel scenario," said Laird Landmann of Irvine, a bond-fund manager at Hotchkis and Wiley Funds in Los Angeles. "When you see one problem, you know there are at least 10 others."

Register staff writer Jonathan Lansner contributed to this report.

HOW THE COUNTY LOST MONEY ON BONDS

Wall Street firms this week sold more than $11 billion in bonds that the Orange County Investment Pool had pledged as collateral to get loans, turning paper losses into real ones. The following transaction, repeated hundreds of times in the financial markets, explains how.

1 The county pool bought $20 million in bonds known as Fannie Mae, July 10, 1993. The bonds mature in five years and pay 5.2 percent interest.

2 The bonds were given as collateral to Nomura Securities Sept. 15 as part of a loan due Dec. 14 (at that time, the county could have bought back the bonds or renewed the agreement.) The county got about $18.6 million in cash, with an interest rate of 4.98 percent.

3 The county bought more bonds with loaned money.

4 Rising interest rates whittle the price of bonds. Just before the pool's problems were revealed Dec. 1, the collateral bonds were worth $18.32 million. The county filed for bankruptcy, an action Wall Street firms say amounts to a default on the loan agreement.

5 Nomura seized and sold the bonds for $18.30 million to Hotchkis and Wiley mutual-fund firm on Friday.

6 If the county had been able to hold the original bonds until their 1998 maturity date, it would have gotten its $20 million back. The county's loan is erased, but the pool now has at least a $1.4 million loss.

Source: Orange County Investment Pool records, bond traders. Graphics reporting: LIZ PULLIAM

WHAT HAPPENED FRIDAY

▶ **CITRON HIRES LAWYER:** Resigned county Treasurer Robert L. Citron hired a former federal prosecutor to represent him. Citron has denied doing anything wrong, but his dealings are under investigation.

▶ **AWAITING BAD NEWS:** County officials will find out next week how much money has been lost from Orange County's $7.8 billion investment fund. The county also had calculated $172 million in interest income from fund investments as part of the current year's budget.

▶ **TROUBLES GROW:** Two more lawsuits seeking class-action status were filed by bondholders who claim the county and brokerage firms hid the fund's problems from investors.

▶ **IN THE COURTS:** Orange County sued Nomura Securities, one of at least seven Wall Street firms that sold $11.4 billion in seized county securities this week. The Securities and Exchange Commission subpoenaed employees of two major brokerage houses that dealt in Orange County securities.

FULL STORY

CALL US: Got a question? Call Register InfoLine at (714) 550-4636, category 7259. We'll print answers in the Register.

HOW IT AFFECTS YOU

▶ **IF YOU BUY A HOME:** You could pay a few dollars more each month because of the investment losses suffered by Orange County, analysts say. The massive sale of county securities on Wall Street could result in a one-eighth-point increase in mortgage rates.

▶ **IF YOU ARE A SCHOOLTEACHER:** A local credit union offered emergency loans to teachers whose school districts might be unable to issue payroll checks.

LITTLE CITY OF MONTEBELLO HURTING WITH BIG BOYS

It's like a good marriage gone bad. People in Montebello find it hard to believe that their bedroom community in Los Angeles County may be forced to join Orange County in filing for bankruptcy in the wake of bond-fund losses. But there's this $25 million debt coming due at the end of this month. Story on Page 26

ALSO IN YOUR REGISTER TODAY

UNSAFE? ATR maker reveals dangers of icing.

FAA limits flights of turboprop

The FAA banned the use of ATR turboprop commuter airliners during conditions where ice may collect on the plane's surfaces. Icing is suspected as a cause of the crash Oct. 31 of an ATR in Indiana that killed 68 people. **Story on Page 3**

Turning the tables on holiday decor

There's no place like Southern California for traditional Christmas decorating. Well, maybe not. Residents just couldn't contain themselves designing holiday tables for a recent museum benefit, drawing on themes from Hawaii to rustic France.
Home & Garden, Page 1

JOYCELYN ELDERS: Clinton demands her resignation.

Clinton dismisses surgeon general over latest flap

Joycelyn Elders, who frequently had drawn fire from conservatives for her outspokenness on issues such as abortion and sex education, was fired a week after she said schoolchildren should be taught about masturbation. "There have been too many areas in which the president does not agree with her views," White House chief of staff Leon Panetta said. "This is just one too many."
Story on Page 3

MALL MOUNTIES: On patrol.

Malls add muscle to war on crime

Malls and police took steps to battle the increase in crime that holiday crowds bring.
Story in Metro, Page 1

Newport Harbor defeats Servite with 'the catch'

It was supposed to be a running play, but it was changed at the last minute and turned into a 38-yard touchdown pass with 2:37 to play. The touchdown lifted the Sailors to a 20-15 victory in Friday night's CIF Southern Section Division V title game.
Story in Sports, Page 1

MATER DEI: The Monarchs and their students prepare for another big game, vs. Bishop Amat **Sports Page 1 and Metro Page 1**

The final of four examples from the *Orange County Register,* the Dec. 10 page features most of the items noted on the other pages. How many can you identify?

Things to note:

Dec. 10

- A large graphic showing how the county lost money on bonds.
- Use of a boxed item on the lower right column with lots of white space around it so it stands out quickly.
- Continued usage of a centered hammer head with a banner-width deck below.

about their audiences and their communities. It is very sad to note that most publications will undertake such an analysis only when circulation figures start to drop. By then it can be very difficult to correct the problem.

Once an analysis of the audience and the community is completed, it will be necessary to analyze the publication and the staff itself. Newspapers for decades and decades have been run by editors and publishers who adopted a paternalistic approach to both content and design: "We know what is best for our readers. There's no point asking them about their core values because we know."

Perhaps in the early days of this country that was true. A publication's staff tended to come from the community. The staff, and therefore the editors and publisher, knew a tremendous amount about the audience because in a sense they were the mirror of the audience. That is no longer true. Today's society is very mobile, moving from apartment to apartment and from house to house at the drop of a hat. It is not uncommon for some adults to have lived in five or six different cities in almost as many states by the time they reach their mid-30s.

Listen to people in the community talk about how "their" town has changed over the past 20 years and you'll begin to get some idea of the audience analysis problem facing newspapers today. The days of a stable, non-mobile community are long past.

In summary, a publication must reflect its community, and its design must do the same. Designers will have to listen carefully to the audience and interpolate those comments with the selection of appropriate typefaces, colors, headline styles and so forth.

DESIGNING FOR ELECTRONIC PUBLICATIONS

Traditional publications are being slowly, or occasionally not so slowly, transformed because of the growing importance of electronic publications. The Internet, that loose affiliation of thousands of computers around the world on the information superhighway, provides users with access to overwhelmingly large amounts of information.

Access to those data is over fiber optic cables, traditional telephone lines, microwaves and satellites, and the data arrive on a computer screen. The superhighway is still so new that large media conglomerates are making available their wares, such as computer files, newspapers, magazines and just about everything else they can think of, to a fantastically large audience, already numbering in the tens of millions.

Information that arrives on a computer screen is handled differently by the viewer than would that same information arriving in a traditional newspaper or magazine. The latter is portable, the former is not quite so, yet. The flickering of the computer screen causes viewers to see type in a much lower resolution than that in print publications. That lower resolution means that small, delicately serifed type is more difficult to process than sans serif type. Until high-resolution computer screens make their way to the consumer market, that low resolution is likely to trouble viewers.

Another consideration is that most computer screens are limited to showing approximately 28 lines of type, seriously limiting designers in their layout possibilities. The mass of a typical six-column broadsheet containing a feature page or even an editorial page is lost on the computer screen.

While it is possible to design vertical layouts for a computer screen, most computers are not equipped with portrait screens, and the usual landscape screen accommodates the image by radically reducing the size of the image to fit it on the screen. Enterprising designers can produce all sorts of layout shapes on a broadsheet merely by changing the orientation of the page from a vertical to a horizontal. Eventually that might be possible for most computers, but the horizontal format of the screen must be viewed as a somewhat limiting characteristic.

A major problem facing designers of electronic publications is that of typeface choices. Current computer technology available to most users does not allow for fine resolution of thin serifs; in fact visually the problem is worse on computer screens than for type smeared with ink and pressed onto newsprint. While most readers still indicate a preference for serif faces, designers should take care to use those faces in a sufficiently large size to counteract the disadvantages of loss of detail on a screen.

Electronic publications, at least right now, are still very much in the experimental stage. Computer "techies" and many journalists are quite curious about these new electronic magazines and newspapers, but are not quite sure what to do with them. Several large publications are taking experimental plunges into the world of electronic publications, and it appears that some of those experiments are paying off, at least in an examination of the new medium. Financially, there will be several market adjustments as companies with deep pockets come and go, mergers are formulated and innovators rise to the occasion.

As the Internet matures and more standards are derived and rules made and enforced, electronic publications will become much more accepted, but in the meantime, most of the publications that are available over the "Net" are text, rather than visually based. The latter requires a tremendous amount of computer memory and processing to achieve a look even remotely resembling contemporary publications.

Some electronic publications, however, have achieved a remarkable blending of text, photos, video and sound. And, for young readers, this mix is going to be irresistible. It's a safe bet that the next generation of readers will grow up with computers connected to the "Net" and will develop a very early taste for receiving their information on a computer screen, rather than on a printed medium. Just remember that the generation that is now in its 40s and 50s is the last generation to have been born when television was a rarity. That same generation is the last one to have been reared when newspapers were THE dominant medium.

When designing for electronic publications it is important to remember that the publication will be, to a large extent, driven by menus. On startup, a menu listing parts of the publication appears, giving the reader a sense of what lies, in one sense, below the surface of the visible screen. Various "hot buttons" can be embedded within the copy itself, allowing the reader to access further levels of information. These in turn can contain other buttons, giving the designer, and the reader, virtually unlimited levels of information.

For those who want only a cursory look at the news, the general menus listing the headlines for top or "must read" stories might prove satisfactory.

AN INTERNATIONAL DAILY NEWSPAPER TUESDAY, DECEMBER 13, 1994 75¢ ($1.00 CANADIAN)

THE CHRISTIAN SCIENCE MONITOR

VOL. 87, NO. 13

R. NORMAN MATHENY – STAFF

Increase the retirement age to 70 for full Social Security and Medicare benefits and means-test all entitlements.

– Sen. John Danforth (R)

DAVE HERRING – STAFF

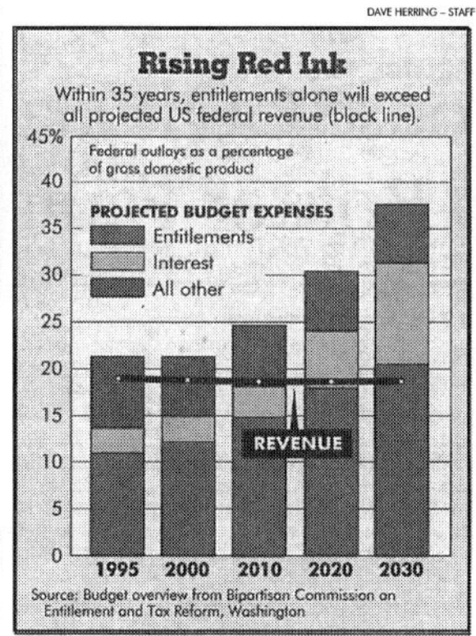

R. NORMAN MATHENY – STAFF

Entitlements and debt payments will eat up all revenues by 2012. They now consume 60 percent.

– Sen. Bob Kerrey (D)

Parties Trumpet Tax Cuts to Woo The Middle Class

GOP, Democrats fashion dueling proposals, but critics question if nation can afford them

By Amy Kaslow

Staff writer of The Christian Science Monitor

WASHINGTON

THE tax-cutting race is starting, with politicians from both parties lining up to offer Americans relief from their yearly payments to Uncle Sam.

Clutching their copies of "Contract With America," GOP lawmakers promise that easing the tax burden for businesses and families will top their agenda when they officially begin work next month. **(GOP plan to assist families, Page 2).**

Democrats, still smarting from a stinging loss on Capitol Hill and worried about wooing the electorate in 1996, are rushing to draft their own rebates for the middle class and credits for employers.

This week President Clinton gave his strongest hint yet that he intends to propose a tax cut for middle-income families – provided it can be paid for. He is also considering ways to compensate employers willing to train wage earners who have suffered long-term declines in skills and incomes.

But as partisans busily tweak their tax-rate plans, critics question just how realistic this all is. The federal government, saddled with a burgeoning deficit, can hardly afford to cut revenues. Or can it?

See **TAX CUTS** *page 2*

Should Nation's Young Be Restless? Social Security Funds May Run Out

By Jonathan S. Landay

Staff writer of The Christian Science Monitor

WASHINGTON

DEEPLY divided, a bipartisan commission enters its final deliberations tomorrow on a controversial plan to scale back Social Security and other entitlements for millions of Americans.

The panel chairman, Sen. Bob Kerrey (D) of Nebraska, insists that drastic action is needed now to avert the future bankruptcy of Social Security.

Among other steps, Senator Kerrey and his vice chairman, Sen. John Danforth (R) of Missouri, favor a gradual increase to age 70 in the retirement age for full Social Security and Medicare benefits. They would also means-test all entitlement programs.

Critics, including liberal Democrats and spokesmen for organized labor and the elderly, denounce the plan as a betrayal of America's workers and its neediest citizens. They say it relies too heavily on benefit cuts and not enough on health-care cost containment and tax hikes.

The plan represents "the most fundamental attack on Social Security and Medicare since their beginning," contends United Mine Workers President Richard Trumka, a commission member.

The panel's disagreements highlight one of the most politically charged issues in Washington.

Because of its internal differences, the Bipartisan Commission on Entitlements and Tax Reform tomorrow could end its last scheduled session without fulfilling its mandate. President Clinton charged the panel in November 1993 to recommend ways to hold

See **DEFICIT** *page 4*

Russia, Chechnya Talk Peace, Make War in Rebel Region

By Peter Ford

Staff writer of The Christian Science Monitor

MOSCOW

RUSSIA opened negotiations yesterday with the breakaway republic of Chechnya, as its invading troops there ran into trouble, and domestic opposition to Moscow's military intervention mounted.

But there seemed little chance that the talks would achieve much, given the strong demand for independence among leaders in this region in southern Russia.

Meanwhile, the Russian troops that were ordered Sunday to restore order in the rebellious republic ran into unexpected difficulties as they advanced on the capital, Grozny. Two of the three advancing columns were held up by local opposition, reports from the area said.

In Moscow, political leaders from across the spectrum voiced their opposition to military action in Chechnya. President Boris Yeltsin found support for his move only from two unlikely bedfellows who normally oppose the government as violently as they oppose each other – Vladimir Zhirinovsky and liberal Boris Fyodorov.

At a meeting yesterday, all faction leaders in the State Duma (lower house of parliament) agreed that there was still a chance for a political solution to the Chechnya crisis and appealed for a halt to military action.

"Even now we think that there is an opportunity for a peaceful

See **CHECHNYA** *page 4*

'Divorce School' Helps Kids Cope Better With the Difficulties of Breaking Homes

By David Holmstrom

Staff writer of The Christian Science Monitor

SAN FRANCISCO

'IF my mom and dad wanted to go back together again, would you let them?"

This was the heart-wrenching question put to Alameda County Superior Court Judge Roderic Duncan from a child of divorced parents.

The setting was a Kid's Turn workshop, casually called "divorce school" by some of the children in it. A pioneering program, Kid's Turn has helped hundreds of children aged 4 to 15 to adjust to the stormy upheavals that often come with divorces.

It has also helped parents to help their children.

Separated or divorced parents and professionals in the Bay Area laud the workshops as the greatest thing since Mr. Rogers.

"This is really an idea whose time has come," says Lynne Gold-Bikin, chair of the Family Law Section of the American Bar Association, "and these kinds of programs are sprouting like little mushrooms around the country. There are good divorces and bad divorces. The difference is to not make a divorce utterly miserable for your

See **CHILDREN** *page 4*

BOOKS

Reads to Wrap

This season's releases of children's books are bound to include a favorite for a child on your list.

10

The Christian Science Monitor has long been an excellent source of international news. Financial woes forced the newspaper to change many years ago from a broadsheet to a tabloid format. Although the paper is not nearly as influential as in years past, the paper is still a good journalistic and design model. The paper's 11 × 14-inch size is about 30 percent larger than a standard 8.5 × 11-inch letter, which makes it a relatively familiar size for design purposes. The Monitor also uses a rather flexible front page design that provides for a fresh appearance each day. Note how these four front pages (pages 303–305 and in the color insert) vary and how each uses different techniques to play the day's news.

AN INTERNATIONAL DAILY NEWSPAPER THURSDAY, DECEMBER 22, 1994 75¢ ($1.00 CANADIAN)

THE CHRISTIAN SCIENCE MONITOR

VOL. 87, NO. 20

How States Are Revamping Welfare

By David Holmstrom and Kurt Shillinger

Staff writers of The Christian Science Monitor

BOSTON

IN Massachusetts, Gov. William Weld (R) wants to wean people from the public dole by encouraging them to take at least minimum-wage jobs. His carrot: the state will provide child care and health care to any welfare recipient who works.

In Wisconsin, Gov. Tommy Thompson (R) is spearheading a program to put a two-year cap on welfare benefits and require most recipients to work 20 hours a week.

California offers cash bonuses to families on public assistance whose children receive good grades in school.

Across the country, states have become the laboratories for changing the way welfare works – one of the dominant issues of the 1990s.

> 'Work. You cannot get around work. And we have to stop demeaning low-wage jobs.'
> – *Eloise Anderson*

Increasingly encouraged to do so by Washington and a public more restive about government assistance, more than 40 states from Florida to California are experimenting with ways to get people off the public dole and into the workplace.

The ideas run the gamut: from barring additional benefits to mothers who have children while on public assistance to devising family investment schemes.

But some of the elements, such as the so-called family caps, are highly controversial. Thus, which directions the states go from here will be important. Already they are setting the agenda for much of the debate in Washington, where lawmakers from both parties are pining to revamp the welfare system. The only question is how much and in what ways.

At the heart of every effort across the country are two simple principles: work is the only road out of poverty, and states need flexibility.

See **WELFARE** *page 3*

MEDIATIONS: *Former US President Jimmy Carter (c.), Bosnian Serb leader Radovan Karadzic (l.), and army commander Ratko Mladic (r.) sign an agreement that could lead to for an immediate four-month cease-fire.*

A Bosnia Cease-Fire May Depend On Serb Intentions in Land Swap

By David Rohde

Staff writer of The Christian Science Monitor

SARAJEVO, BOSNIA-HERZEGOVINA

IT wasn't pretty, but former President Jimmy Carter's trip to Bosnia-Herzegovina this week allowed a tragically rare commodity to momentarily appear in this war-ripped land: compromise.

Mr. Carter, who earned points for his tireless shuttle diplomacy and lost points for appearing unfamiliar with the details of the conflict – mispronouncing leaders' names, and confusing the positions of various sides – may have been the right man at the right place at the right time.

Only the next few weeks will tell.

Carter's presence gave each side enough political cover to agree to a one-week cease-fire and to start talks tomorrow on ceasing hostilities for four months in Europe's worst conflict since World War II.

But neither side compromised on the crucial issue of how Bosnia might be divided in a final peace settlement. Dozens of other cease-fires have come and gone in Bosnia, and it remains clear that Bosnian Serb leader Radovan Karadzic, and not Carter's diplomatic skills, is driving the sudden peace talks.

See **BOSNIA** *page 6*

Tales of Holiday Generosity Around the World

While holiday giving to the poor is common, a few people in Brazil, Pakistan, France, and China have gone beyond the norm. Their examples have started a new tradition of philanthropy.

A Brazil activist rallies his nation to feed the hungry

IN the past two years, Brazil has won fame as a nation without a conscience, plagued by corrupt politicians, rogue police who murder street kids, and gold miners who massacre rain forest Indians.

Yet countering that image is a massive grass-roots campaign against hunger led by a sociologist who has turned into a tropical Santa Claus for Brazil's poor.

This month, Herbert de Souza, known as "Betinho," has cajoled his compatriots to donate food for needy Brazilians in a campaign called "Christmas Without Hunger."

In a nation with little traditional philanthrophy, this is no small feat. And most observers give credit to Mr. de Souza, who has become a national idol.

De Souza has used the media to convince major newspapers to include food sacks in Sunday editions, supermarket chains to provide collection bins, restaurants to give leftover food, prisoners to fast and donate their meals, advertising agencies to give free publicity, and the nation's leading entertainers to charge food in lieu of admission.

"It's like a Frank Capra movie, where the good citizens lend money to the honest banker so he can fight the dishonest banker," wrote a São Paulo newspaper columnist.

De Souza is a Socialist activist who spent 15 years in exile during the 1964-85 military dictatorship. In 1979, he returned to found a private think tank, the Brazilian Institute for Social and Economic Analysis.

See **GIVING** *page 4*

SPORTS

Master of Monday Night

Frank Gifford has called 'Monday Night Football' games for 24 years.

12

The Home Forum.

Memorable Christmases

Monitor writers recall their most unusual experiences on Christmas Day, including omelet dinners and trees made of coat hangers.

16

The Dec. 22, 1994, issue of *The Christian Science Monitor* uses several design elements that will work well individually or in groups for many publications.

Things to note:

- The box on the top left side uses heavy rules at the top and bottom.
- A shaded box containing a pull quote is inset into the copy on the top left story.
- A flush-left italic summary is placed to the side of the bottom story.
- Initial letters are used on all stories.
- The two lower right teaser boxes are not closed at the top.

AN INTERNATIONAL DAILY NEWSPAPER  FRIDAY, DECEMBER 23, 1994 75¢ ($1.00 CANADIAN)

THE CHRISTIAN SCIENCE MONITOR

VOL. 87, NO. 21

©PATRICK DE NOIRMONT/REUTERS

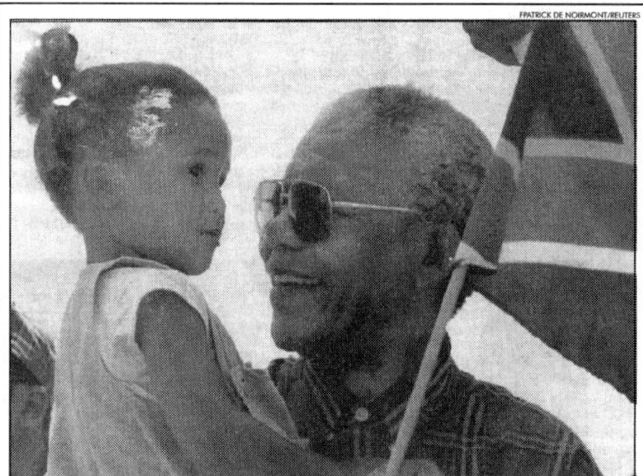

FATHER FIGURE? *Nelson Mandela greets an admirer last week in Orange Free State, with South Africa's new flag. Revered for his forgiveness, Mandela's leadership style is crucial to unify a fractured nation.*

After Seven Months as President, Mandela Loses Little of His Style

By Judith Matloff

Staff writer of The Christian Science Monitor

BLOEMFONTEIN, SOUTH AFRICA

THE hall resounded with songs of adulation as Nelson Mandela suddenly left his chair among the African National Congress leadership to sit among ordinary folk.

As he descended from the podium to join the 3,000 party faithful in the gallery at last week's ANC national conference, he paused to joke, shake hands, and dance with delegates. "Nelson Mandela, Nelson Mandela. There is no one else like him," they spontaneously cried out, a derivation from a spiritual chorus. **(ANC tries to follow, not lead, Page 6.)**

His leadership wins hearts, riles critics, and may set a precedent for future leaders of South Africa.

The scene spoke volumes about South Africa's first black president. Venerated by fans as a saint, criticized by detractors for being too conciliatory to former white oppressors, one thing about Nelson Mandela is clear: he has not lost his charismatic touch after seven months at the helm.

See **MANDELA** *page 7*

Tax Cuts Imperil Drive to Clean US Weapons Sites

Clinton would trim nuclear program to fund tax cuts, but binding deals make it hard to do

By Peter Grier

Staff writer of The Christian Science Monitor

WASHINGTON

DECAYING old nuclear-weapons plants are among the most difficult environmental problems facing the United States.

In recent years, the Department of Energy's cleanup fund for this old infrastructure has been one of the fastest growing parts of the federal budget, as scientists struggle to eliminate a legacy of pollution dating back to the early days of the cold war.

Now the Clinton administration wants to whack a large sum of money out of the nuclear cleanup program to help pay for a proposed middle class tax cut. The cleanup's efficiency has been questioned in the past; as a big budget item, it makes a tempting target for reduction.

But Energy Department officials admit that carrying out this budget cut won't be easy. Binding agreements with affected states will have to be reopened. Congress may well have to pass legislation allowing program change.

The whole thing is a case study in a Washington truism: raising spending (and cutting taxes) is as politically easy as falling off a table. Cutting budgets, on the other hand, can be a nightmare.

"These cuts may not come to pass. There's a strong possibility they will create a great deal of opposition from state and local

See **NUCLEAR SITES** *page 4*

Hollywood Wish: To Rewrite the Ending On Holiday Earnings

By David Holmstrom

Staff writer of The Christian Science Monitor

DON'T roll the credits yet, but the Christmas movie season is just about over and Hollywood may need a hanky for a good cry. Those hopes for blockbuster hits have nearly all fizzled big time at the box office.

Stung by last year's relatively weak Christmas showing, with the notable exception of "Mrs. Doubtfire," more producers released Christmas big-budget films in mid-November this year.

"Big films like 'Interview With the Vampire' might have waited until December to be released like a few years ago," says Peter Garbenya, film critic of the Columbus Dispatch in Columbus, Ohio. "But distributors want the Thanksgiving crowds, and all of December," he says.

Success remains a guessing game in Hollywood: Do big stars, big budgets, and brilliant scripts add up to big profits? Or do low-budget, sleeper films like "The Crying Game," or "Four Weddings and a Funeral" increase the odds against box-office success?

Put megastar Arnold Schwarzenegger with Danny DeVito and Emma Thompson in a comedy called "Junior," and watch the

See **MOVIES** *page 4*

US Country Music Takes Beating in Canada

By Mark Clayton

Staff writer of The Christian Science Monitor

TORONTO

EACH day 28 million Canadians watch as relentless waves of American culture – from Ms. magazine to Madonna, Mr. Rogers to the Mighty Morphin Power Rangers – crash on the shores of Canadian society.

As with all that is American, Canadians both love it and, in a measure, hate it, too.

Nine of 10 Canadian moviegoers are headed to a United States film. Canadian television viewers get NBC, ABC, CBS, FOX, and PBS and a slew of US-based speciality cable channels. On newsstands, about 3,000 US magazines occupy 90 percent of the space, squeezing out most of 1,400 Canadian periodicals.

Yet cultural anthropologists say Canadians dread waking up one day to find no Canadian TV programs, movies, or magazines – all of it instead made by the big US entertainment machine.

Now there are signs Canada isn't going to take it anymore, and a US-Canada trade battle over entertainment and culture is looming.

"Let us get one thing clear," Heritage Minister Michel Dupuy told Parliament recently. "We must bring back culture to the forefront of society's concerns, for it is essential to our identity ... and our independence."

See **CANADA** *page 4*

Compare this issue of *The Christian Science Monitor* with that on page 304 and note how different treatments are used in the display of news.

Things to note:

- Bold rules set off a summary of the Mandela story.
- Bold rules paired with thin twin rules are used to set off bylines and date lines.
- A screened box counter balances the dominant photo.

METRO EDITION

WEDNESDAY, JANUARY 4, 1995 / Leftover flurries today, 35; clear and cold tonight, teens / Details, Page 18

50¢

City mourns death of hero rookie fireman

Page 3

Furor over letters 'from' 1st Cat Socks

Page 3

BRAVE NEWT WORLD

Gingrich vows action on Day 1

Incoming House Speaker Newt Gingrich arrives on Capitol Hill to preside over the 104th Congress, which will be sworn in today.

Full story: Pages 4 & 5

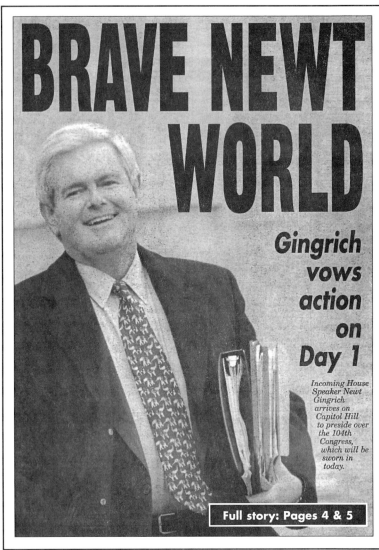

One of the last blue-collar, gutsy tabloids in America, the *New York Post* survives in the very competetive New York City market by being brash and irreverent. It also features some of the best headline writing around.

Things to note:

- Dominant head is overprinted on the photo
- The bottom deck is contoured along the subject's sleeve
- Narrow boxed teasers feature condensed centered type

STEVE SERBY

PACKERS: WE CAN BEAT THE COWBOYS

Page 53

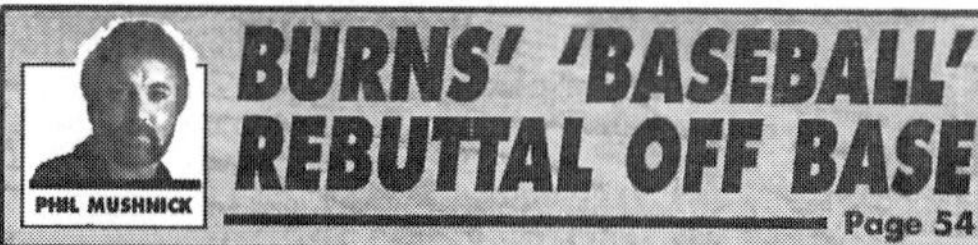

PHIL MUSHNICK

BURNS' 'BASEBALL' REBUTTAL OFF BASE

Page 54

NEW YORK POST

The Best Sports In Town

WEDNESDAY, JANUARY 4, 1995

JAY GREENBERG

Greenberg's message to Paterno:

STOP WHINING

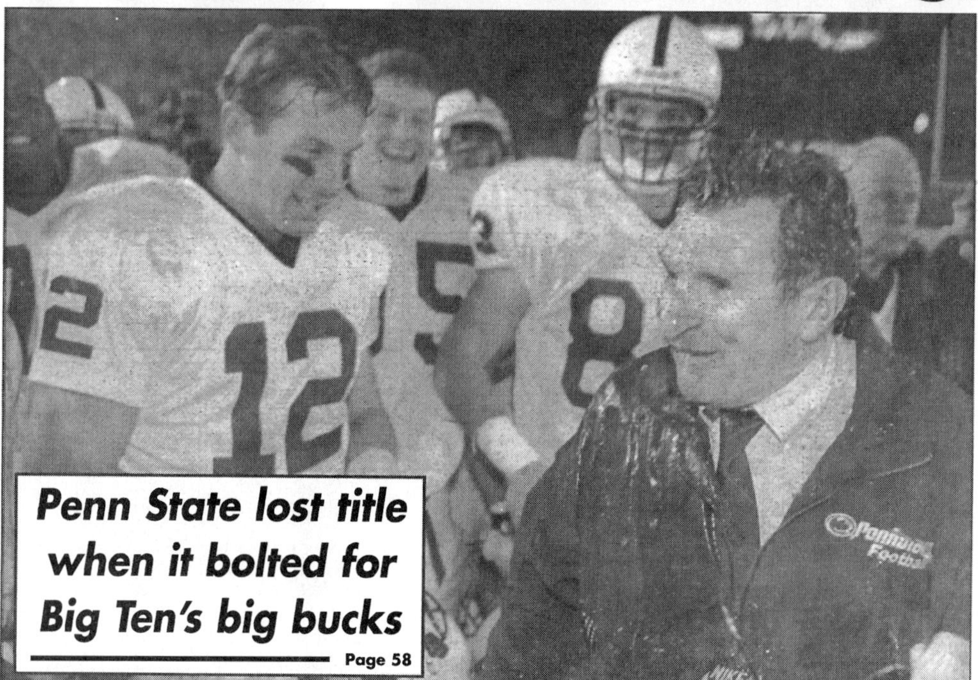

Penn State lost title when it bolted for Big Ten's big bucks

Page 58

Joe Paterno, celebrating Monday's victory with QB Kerry Collins, shouldn't complain about Nebraska's No. 1 ranking, Jay Greenberg says. That's because if Nittany Lions were still independent, they could have taken on 'Huskers in Orange Bowl instead of Oregon in Rose Bowl.

The back cover of the *New York Post* is always for sports.

Things to note:

- Teasers across the top feature columnists
- A dominant photo with a huge headline is also tied to a columnist

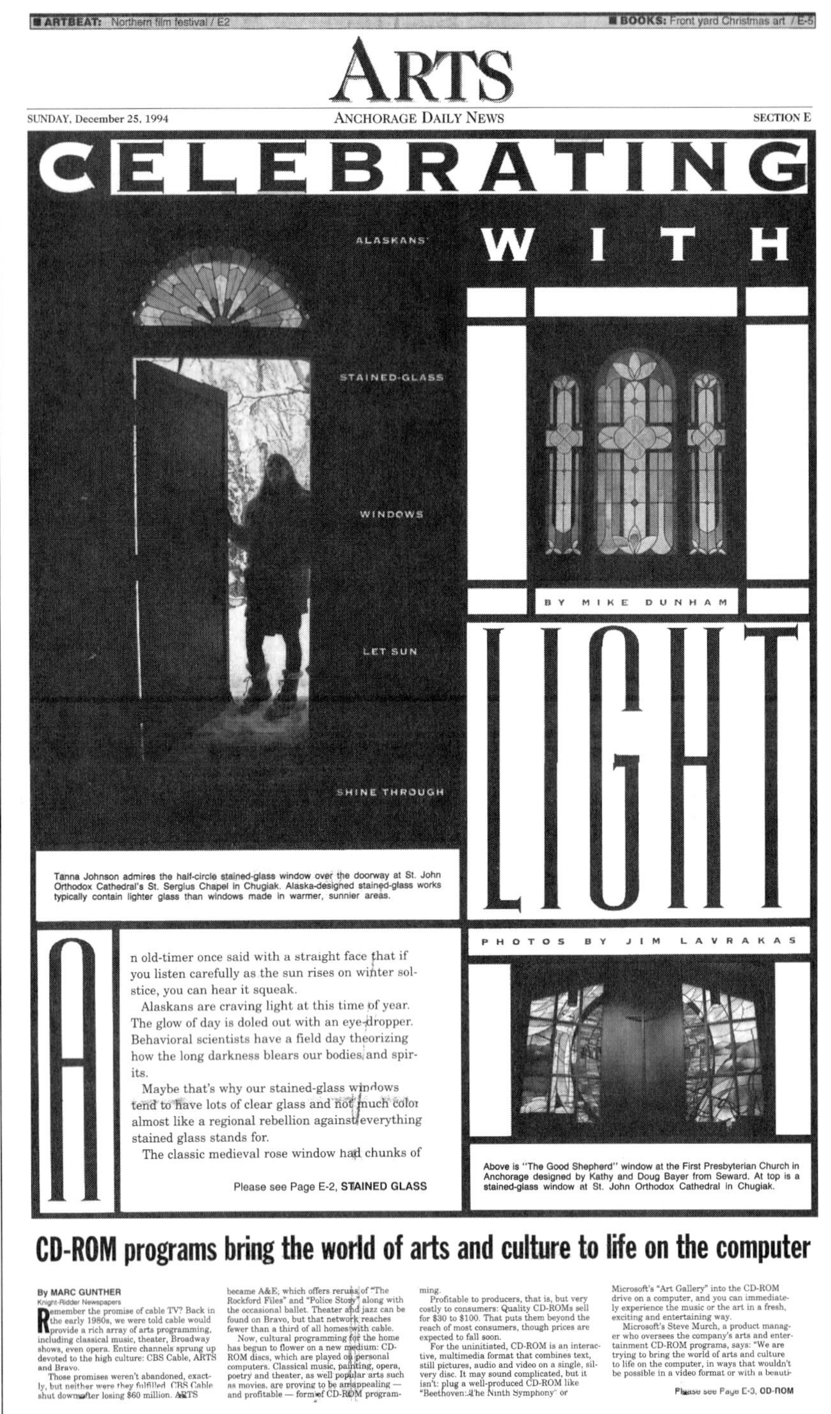

■ ARTBEAT: Northern film festival / E2 ■ BOOKS: Front yard Christmas art / E-5

ARTS

SUNDAY, December 25, 1994 | ANCHORAGE DAILY NEWS | SECTION E

CELEBRATING WITH LIGHT

ALASKANS' STAINED-GLASS WINDOWS LET SUN SHINE THROUGH

BY MIKE DUNHAM

PHOTOS BY JIM LAVRAKAS

Tanna Johnson admires the half-circle stained-glass window over the doorway at St. John Orthodox Cathedral's St. Sergius Chapel in Chugiak. Alaska-designed stained-glass works typically contain lighter glass than windows made in warmer, sunnier areas.

An old-timer once said with a straight face that if you listen carefully as the sun rises on winter solstice, you can hear it squeak.

Alaskans are craving light at this time of year. The glow of day is doled out with an eye-dropper. Behavioral scientists have a field day theorizing how the long darkness blears our bodies and spirits.

Maybe that's why our stained-glass windows tend to have lots of clear glass and not much color almost like a regional rebellion against everything stained glass stands for.

The classic medieval rose window had chunks of

Please see Page E-2, STAINED GLASS

Above is "The Good Shepherd" window at the First Presbyterian Church in Anchorage designed by Kathy and Doug Bayer from Seward. At top is a stained-glass window at St. John Orthodox Cathedral in Chugiak.

CD-ROM programs bring the world of arts and culture to life on the computer

By MARC GUNTHER
Knight-Ridder Newspapers

Remember the promise of cable TV? Back in the early 1980s, we were told cable would provide a rich array of arts programming, including classical music, theater, Broadway shows, even opera. Entire channels sprung up devoted to the high culture: CBS Cable, ARTS and Bravo.

Those promises weren't abandoned, exactly, but neither were they fulfilled. CBS Cable shut down after losing $60 million. ARTS became A&E, which offers reruns of "The Rockford Files" and "Police Story" along with the occasional ballet. Theater and jazz can be found on Bravo, but that network reaches fewer than a third of all homes with cable.

Now, cultural programming for the home has begun to flower on a new medium: CD-ROM discs, which are played on personal computers. Classical music, painting, opera, poetry and theater, as well popular arts such as movies, are proving to be an appealing — and profitable — form of CD-ROM programming.

Profitable to producers, that is, but very costly to consumers: Quality CD-ROMs sell for $30 to $100. That puts them beyond the reach of most consumers, though prices are expected to fall soon.

For the uninitiated, CD-ROM is an interactive, multimedia format that combines text, still pictures, audio and video on a single, silvery disc. It may sound complicated, but it isn't: plug a well-produced CD-ROM like "Beethoven: The Ninth Symphony" or Microsoft's "Art Gallery" into the CD-ROM drive on a computer, and you can immediately experience the music or the art in a fresh, exciting and entertaining way.

Microsoft's Steve Murch, a product manager who oversees the company's arts and entertainment CD-ROM programs, says: "We are trying to bring the world of arts and culture to life on the computer, in ways that wouldn't be possible in a video format or with a beauti-

Please see Page E-3, CD-ROM

The creation of interesting section front designs is the hallmark of the *Anchorage Daily News.* Notice the variation of typefaces and overall concepts on these pages which are from a single issue.

■ **CROSSWORD:** The New York Times puzzle / F-3 ■ **COMPUTERS:** Best of 1994 software / F-4

LIFESTYLES

SUNDAY, December 25, 1994 ANCHORAGE DAILY NEWS SECTION F

The Dunham family in front of the Quinhagak Church.

Kuyana Yesusak

By Mike Dunham
Daily News arts editor

CHRISTMAS IN QUINHAGAK, 1955. HUMBLE FOOD, ONE GIFT AND INDESCRIBABLY HAPPY CHILDREN

Quinhagak choristers in 1955, from left: Elizabeth Sharp, Emily Friendly, Julia Fullmoon, Annie Cleveland.

Photos courtesy Mike Dunham

In 1955, like this year, Christmas came on a Sunday. Not that it mattered in Quinhagak, where there was no "Christmas break" and only two village men had paying jobs during the winter.

Quinhagak held a population of 235 Yup'ik Eskimos, seven non-Natives and 211 dogs, including puppies. Sixteen villagers were out of town being treated for tuberculosis, another 55 were on medication for the disease. Polly Evon said she would have a happy Christmas because, after months of hearing nothing, she had received word that her sister was doing fine in the sanitarium.

Aside from the Bureau of Indian Affairs school and Moravian missionary's quarters, there were 46 wood houses that averaged 225 square feet. Half the homes had some form of electricity provided either

Please see Page F-2, **KUYANA**

KUYANA YESUSAK

(Yup'ik words to "Silent Night," with phonetic spelling used in Bethel-area churches in the 1950s and '60s. "Kuyana" is often spelled "Quyana.")

KUYANA, KUYANA,
UNUGME ENUME
YOGTSAN YESUS
ANEGTOGTA
WHONGKOGLUNTA
PITIKTLUTA.
KUYANA YESUSAK,
KUYANA YESUSAK.

To hear August and Bonnie Alexie sing "Kuyana Yesusak," call the Daily Newsline, 277-1200, and enter code 1298.

The author and sister Molli in front of the BIA school.

Know legal rights before donning bunny suit

DAVE BARRY

Like most people, you probably often ask yourself: "What, exactly, are my legal rights if I am wearing a bunny outfit?"

The answer, you will be relieved to learn, is: "It depends."

■ **NEXT SUNDAY:** Dave Barry's Year in Review.

To understand why this is, let us first consider a 22-page legal decision filed in October by U.S. District Judge David G. Larimer and sent to me by alert attorney James G. Vazzana of Rochester, N.Y. Here, according to Judge Larimer's decision, are the Facts of the Case (and I want to stress that I am not making ANY of this up):

On April 23, 1992, Timothy Wagner and John Payment were traveling on holiday through western New York state. They stopped their van in a Cattaraugus County town called

Please see Page F-2, **BARRY**

Test your yuletide savvy with a quiz

By JEFF LYON
Chicago Tribune

Something different for you on this toasty holiday morning. A Christmas trivia quiz, designed to test your yuletide savvy. Get 'em all right, and we'll toast your health. Get none right, and God rest ye, anyway, merry dudes.

1. When was Dec. 25 designated as the official date honoring the birth of Christ?

2. Has the celebration of Christmas ever been illegal, outside of certain Communist countries?

3. How did Charles Dickens come to write "A Christmas Carol"?

4. How many plums go into a traditional plum pudding?

a. 4
b. 3
c. 8
d. 0

Please see Page F-2, **QUIZ**

The *Anchorage Daily News* uses a photo album approach for the lead article on the Lifestyles page.

Things to note:

- A centered, condensed all-cap summary provides a nice lead-in to the copy.
- A shaded oval and circle accent the headline and the initial letter.
- Cursive beginning letters are paired with condensed sans serif type for the headlines.
- Bold sans serif type is reversed out in the box.
- White space is used well on the layout.
- Brief beginnings of a column and a feature article are jumped from the bottom of the page.

Summary of Electronic Publications

Advantages

- Can provide access to tremendous amounts of data that can be accessed through data bases held by the publication or others.
- Can combine sound, text and video into one package, which can provide a greater depth in information for the reader than is now attainable individually through newspapers, radio, magazines or television alone.
- Are accessible at the reader's schedule.
- Information can be revised quickly and output almost as rapidly.
- Can provide quick scans or in-depth information about almost any subject.
- Are likely to be the medium of choice for younger readers who have grown up with computers and electronic games.

Disadvantages

- Are not easily transportable.
- Require access to an electronic network, at least while downloading information.
- Require a reader to have a certain level of computer sophistication, or at least not to be intimidated by computers.
- Their products are considerably more expensive than traditional print publications.
- Require an expensive investment in personal computer equipment, unless access is through a public facility in a library, business or academic institution.

Box 10.3

Other readers acutely interested in specific topics might follow an electronic trail to get the desired level of information.

While traditional publications encourage the reader to browse or randomly flit from one section and article to another, browsing can be slower with computer publications simply because of the time it takes for a computer to access information from a distant file server (assuming, of course, that the information is not contained on the viewer's own CD or diskette).

What this means is that designers must take into consideration HOW the readers will use the medium: as a primary source of information, as a secondary source or simply as a novelty. WHERE will the reader use the electronic publication: at work in an office, at home in a computer room/office or on the road? Currently computers are still somewhat place-bound, meaning they usually are in a fixed, rather than a movable location. Access to a telephone still is a requirement for connection to the Internet, which means complete mobility still is a major consideration. As laptop computers become more powerful and have longer-lasting batteries, and as inexpensive cellular phones and virtually omnipresent cellular telephone service become more available, mobility will become much more the norm. Modern books, newspapers and magazines are totally portable, requiring neither telephone lines nor computers nor even electricity (during daylight hours) to be utilized.

Paperbacks are easily stuffed into pockets or bags and magazines can be rolled up or even folded, but electronic publications, again, are substantial and computers don't really take kindly to being folded.

Since electronic publications are sailing in uncharted waters, much that can be said about them is based on preliminary information. Newspapers, which have been around in one form or another for close to 500 years, have been dissected, analyzed, revised, discussed, designed and redesigned continually. There is little reason to expect that electronic publications will come to maturity overnight.

Once again, each medium has its own peculiarities and method of usage, requiring designers to be acutely aware of the many ways consumers think about and use each one. At the same time, good design is good design, regardless of the medium, although what might work well on one might not necessarily work on another.

Box 10.3 summarizes the advantages and disadvantages of electronic publications.

BIBLIOGRAPHY AND ADDITIONAL READING

Arntson, Amy E. *Graphic Design Basics,* 2nd ed. Harcourt Brace Jovanovich. 1993.

Bivins, Thomas, and William E. Ryan. *How to Produce Creative Publications.* NTC Business Books. 1991.

Denton, Craig. *Graphics for Visual Communication.* William C. Brown. 1992.

Donkin, Scott W. *Sitting on the Job.* Parallel Integration. 1987.

Goldberg, Howard. *Virtual Community.* St. Martin's Press. 1994.

Gracia, Mario R. *Contemporary Newspaper Design.* Prentice Hall. 1981.

Küpper, Norbert. "Information on the subject of newspaper design." Office for Newspaper Design, Düsseldorf, Germany. 1994.

Lichty, Tom. *Design Principles for Desktop Publishers,* 2nd ed. Wadsworth. 1994.

Lubar, Steven. *Infoculture.* Houghton Mifflin. 1993.

Pipes, Alan. *Production for Graphic Designers.* Prentice Hall. 1993.

Smith, Robert Charles. *Basic Graphic Design,* 2nd ed. Prentice Hall. 1985.

Spencer, Herbert. *Pioneers of Modern Typography.* Rev. ed. The MIT Press. 1983.

Toffler, Alvin, and Heidi. *War and Anti-War: Survival at the Dawn of the 21st Century.* Little, Brown. 1993.

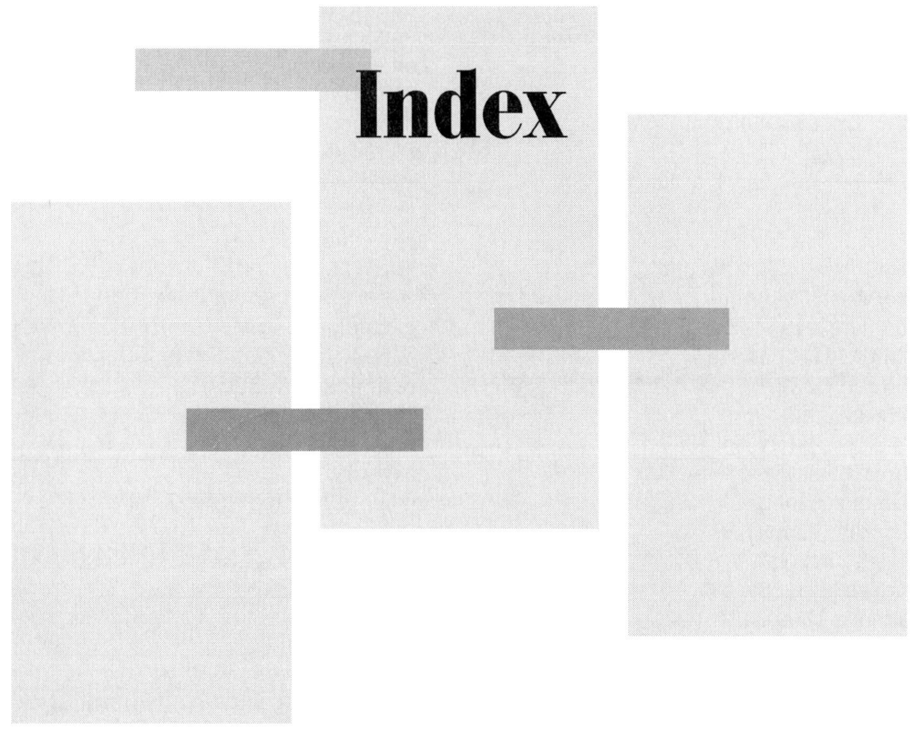

Index